TAKING THE LIBERAL CHALLENGE SERIOUSLY

The authors dedicate this book to their longtime colleague and friend, Professor Timo Airaksinen, University of Helsinki, on the occasion of his 50th birthday, for his extensive philosophical work dealing with the problems and prospects of modern liberal thought.

Taking the Liberal Challenge Seriously

Essays on Contemporary Liberalism at the Turn of the 21st Century

Edited by
SIRKKU HELLSTEN
MARJAANA KOPPERI
OLLI LOUKOLA

Routledge
Taylor & Francis Group
LONDON AND NEW YORK

First published 1997 by Ashgate Publishing

Reissued 2018 by Routledge
2 Park Square, Milton Park, Abingdon, Oxon OX14 4RN
52 Vanderbilt Avenue, New York, NY 10017

Routledge is an imprint of the Taylor & Francis Group, an informa business

A Library of Congress record exists under LC control number: 97074447

ISBN 13: 978-1-138-35047-2 (hbk)
ISBN 13: 978-1-138-35050-2 (pbk)
ISBN 13: 978-0-429-43585-0 (ebk)

Contents

List of contributors

Martin A. Bertman, Ph.D. from Syracuse University is Docent in Practical Philosophy at the University of Helsinki. He has been Visiting Professor in various universities in Germany, Ireland, Israel and the USA. As a Hobbes scholar he has published several books and articles on the subject and is also President of International Hobbes Association since 1985. Among his recent book publications are Hobbes: 1588 - 1988 (1990); Body and Cause in Hobbes (1991). His interests include also literature and art.

Ruth Chadwick, MA (BA), BPhil, DPhil (Oxon), LLB (London), Head of Centre and Professor of Moral Philosophy in the Centre for Professional Ethics at the University of Central Lancashire. Co-ordinator of two multidisciplinary and multinational research projects funded by the European Union; EUROSCREEN – genetic screening: ethical and philosophical perspectives, and BIOCULT: cultural and social objections to biotechnology – an analysis of the arguments, with special reference to the views of young people. Her publications include the four volume edited collection, Kant: Critical Assessments; Ethics, Reproduction and Genetic Control; and a large number of papers in learned journals. She is joint series editor of the Routledge series on Professional Ethics. She is secretary of the International Association of Bioethics and a member of the National Committee of Philosophy.

Bruno S. Frey is Professor of Economics at the University of Zurich and Director of Institute for Empirical and Economic Research. He has written over 250 articles in professional journals in economics (and a few in political science, sociology and psychology journals). Among his book publications are *Democratic Economic Policy* (1983); *International Political Economics* (1984); *Muses and Markets: Explorations in the Economics of Arts* (1989) and *Economics as a Science of Human Behaviour* (1992). Several of these books have been translated into nine different languages, among them Japanese and Chinese. His new book, *Not Just for the Money, An Economic Theory of Personal Motivation* was launched in April 1997.

Jay L. Garfield is Professor of Philosophy, Head of the Department of Philosophy and Director of the Tasmania-Tibet Partnership Program at the University of Tasmania. His books include *Belief in Psychology: A Study in the Ontology of Mind, The Fundamental Wisdom of the Middle Way: Nagarjuna'smulamadhyamakakarika*, and *Western Idealism and Its Critics*, as well as several textbooks and anthologies in applied ethics and cognitive science. Professor Garfield is currently working on a research project on the history and structure of Buddhist idealism as well as projects in the foundations of cognitive science and moral philosophy.

Wojciech W. Gasparski is Professor of Humanities at the Institute of Philosophy and Sociology in Polish Academy of Sciences. He is Vice Chairman of the Institute Scientific Board, a member of its Logic of Language and Action Department, and head of the Research Group of Ethics in the Economy and Business. He has published several books and over two hundred articles and conference papers, the latest of which are *Design and Systems: General Applications of Methodology* (1995), *Philosophy of Practicality* (1993), and *Practical Philosophy and Action Theory* (1993, with Timo Airaksinen).

Jonathan L. Gorman is Professor of Moral Philosophy and Head of the Department of Philosophy at the Queen's University of Belfast. He has recently published a second book on analytical philosophy of history and a number of articles in moral philosophy. He is currently researching on pluralism and pragmatism for a book on the foundations of political philosophy.

Heta Häyry is Docent and Head of the Department of Practical Philosophy at the University of Helsinki, Senior Research Fellow at the Academy of Finland and Docent of the Philosophy of Law at the University of Lapland. Her publications in English include *The Limits of Medical Paternalism* (London and New York: Routledge, 1991) and many articles on practical ethics and applied philosophy. She is currently preparing a critical book about the main strands of contemporary social and political philosophy.

Matti Häyry is Docent and Research Fellow in Practical Philosophy at the University of Helsinki, Director of the Project *Biotechnology, Liberty and Responsibility* at the Academy of Finland and Docent of Bioethics at the University of Tampere. His publications in English include *Liberal Utilitarianism and Applied Ethics* (London and New York: Routledge, 1994) and many articles on bioethics and general philosophy in academic journals. In January 1997 he started working with his research group on a book tentatively entitled 'Genetic engineering: facts and philosophies'.

Sirkku Hellsten is Research Fellow in the Department of Practical Philosophy at the University of Helsinki, Finland. She has published various articles on social and political philosophy, particularly on the subjects of justice, democracy and the liberal-communitarian debate. Her recent publications in English include *In Defense of Moral Individualism* (North-Holland, 1997). She is currently working on a research project on the ethics of biotechnology.

Manfred J. Holler is Professor of Economics at the University of Hamburg and currently Dean of the Faculty of Economics and Business Administration. Among his publications are the edited volumes *Power, Voting and Voting Power* (1982); *Coalitions and Collective Action* (1984); *The Logic of Multiparty Systems* (1987); "Political Entry", a special issue of the *Journal of Theoretical Politics* (1991); with J.-J. Thisse, "The Economics of Standardization", a special issue of the *European Journal of Political Economy* (1996). Currently he is preparing a collection of papers on "Power Indices and Coalition Formation" together with Guillermo Owen. He is founding editor of the *European Journal of Political Economy*, managing editor of The *EURAS Yearbook of Standardization*, and editor of the quarterly journal *Homo oeconomicus* which publishes in the English and German language.

Katri Kaalikoski is Lecturer in Practical Philosophy at the University of Helsinki. She has published several articles on ethics and moral philosophy. She is currently working on a book on Iris Murdoch's philosophy.

Shyli Karin-Frank, Israel, is the author of *Utopia Reconsidered* and the co-author of *Uri Givon - A Philosophy Book for Children*. Her papers concern moral issues of civil disobedience, revolution, war, terrorism, the right to privacy, medical ethics. At present, she is working on books on *Moral Resolution of Political Conflicts, The Morality of Doing the Best Possible, The Quest for Privacy and the Fear of Loneliness*. She is an associate editor of the Journal of Value Inquiry.

Jukka Kilpi works currently in investment banking and is an Associate of The Securities Institute of Australia. He holds undergraduate and postgraduate degrees in Philosophy from the University of Helsinki and completed his Ph.D. in 1996 at Monash University in Melbourne, Australia. Jukka Kilpi has contributed to a number of philosophical journals, including *The Journal of Business Ethics, Australasian Journal of Philosophy* and *Public Affairs Quarterly*. His book entitled *The Ethics of Bankruptcy* will be published by Routledge in 1997.

Marjaana Kopperi is a Junior Research Fellow at the University of Helsinki. Her recent publications include articles on liberalism and communitarianism, on normative foundations of the welfare state and on business ethics. She has also given lectures in business ethics at the Helsinki School of Economics and Business Administration. Currently she is working on the study of modern ethics, defending modern moral theory against various communitarian, postmodern and neo-Aristotelian criticisms. She is also writing a textbook on business ethics.

Olli Loukola is Lecturer of the Department of Practical Philosophy at the University of Helsinki. He has lectured and published articles on various topics in the field of political and moral philosophy. His interests vary from free market theories and the Post-Soviet situation to the problems of contemporary moral theory and the pedagogic of philosophy.

Jan Narveson is Professor of Philosophy at the University of Waterloo in Canada. His recent books include *Moral Matters* (1993), and (with J. T. Sanders, eds) *For and Against the State*. He is currently working on environmentalism and the theory of liberalism.

Ilkka Niiniluoto was born in 1946. After studies in mathematics, logic, and probability theory at the University of Helsinki, he wrote his doctoral dissertation in 1973 on scientific inference. Since 1977 he has been Professor of Theoretical Philosophy in Helsinki, working mainly in the philosophy of science, philosophical logic, and epistemology. His interests include the philosophy of culture, the philosophy of technology, and the foundations of science policy. Niiniluoto has been the Chairman of the Philosophical Society of Finland since 1975 and the Editor-in Chief of *Acta Philosophica Fennica* since 1980. His main works are *Is Science Progressive?* (1984) and *Truthlikeness* (1987).

Tapio Puolimatka is Research Associate in social and moral philosophy at the University of Notre Dame. He has recently published *Democracy and Education: The Critical Citizen as an Educational Aim* (Helsinki: The Finnish Academy for Science and Letters, 1995) and is currently working on a research project on the concept of indoctrination.

Nicholas Rescher is Professor of Philosophy at the University of Pittsburgh where he served for many years as Director of the Center for Philosophy of Science. A former president of the American Philosophical Association, he is a member of the Institut International de Philosophie and several other learned academies, as well as an honorary member of Corpus Christi College, Oxford. In 1984 he was awarded the Alexander von Humboldt Prize for Humanistic Scholarship. A visiting scholar at Oxford, Constance, and Salamanca, Professor Rescher has received four honorary degrees from universities in the USA and abroad. Author of more than seventy works ranging over many areas of philosophy, he is currently writing a book on the role of complexity in science and in everyday life.

Mikko Salmela is Junior Research Fellow at the University of Helsinki. His main research interests are ethics, value theory and the philosophy of culture. He is currently concluding his dissertation on the philosophy of culture in Finland in the 20th century.

John T. Sanders is currently Professor of Philosophy at the Rochester Institute of Technology. He is the author of *The Ethical Argument Against Government* (University Press of America: Washington, 1980) and *Contra Leviathan: On the Legitimacy and Propriety of the State* (Rodopi: Amsterdam and Atlanta, forthcoming 1998). He has recently co-edited (with Jan Narveson) *For and Against the State: New Philosophical Readings* (Rowman and Littlefield: Lanham, Maryland, 1996) and (with Jozef Niznik) *Debating the State of Philosophy: Habermas, Rorty, and Kolakowski* (Praeger: Westport, Conn. and London, 1996). He is the author of more than 30 published or forthcoming articles in a variety of areas of philosophy.

Arto Siitonen is Teacher of Philosophy at the University of Helsinki. He has recently published an article (in Finnish) on skepticism and values and written a textbook, with a co-author, on thinking and argumentation, due to appear soon (in Finnish). Is currently working on a research project on Hans Reichenbach's relation to Kantianism.

Arto Tukiainen is Junior Research Fellow at the Department of Philosophy of University of Helsinki. He has published articles on ethics and philosophy of mind. He is currently writing a book on post-modern ethics.

Introduction

The term 'liberalism' refers to the line of modern Western intellectual and political thought that supports a democratic regime based on a market economy and individual freedom. The idea of liberalism, however, covers such a wide range of philosophical and political viewpoints and diverse thinkers with different motivations that it can hardly any longer be defined as a particular philosophical theory or set political ideology. Instead the intellectual and political views defined as 'liberal' involve various socioeconomic, moral and political approaches to the modern Western world view at different times. This gradual change in the tradition has led contemporary theory into a state of confusion. In fact, it sometimes appears that the latest versions of liberal theory, such as the welfare liberal line of reasoning, have very little in common with the original ideas of classical liberal thought. Moreover, such liberal values as equality, autonomy, individual rights and tolerance can be, and sometimes are, turned against their original purpose and used to justify inequality, suppression and intolerance. It is not always clear whether contemporary liberal theory is mere political rhetoric used to maintain prevailing power structures and material values or whether it actually presents a comprehensive moral view that a liberal political order is meant to promote.

Part of the problem is that the liberal tradition appears to face challenges on two different levels. On one hand, the liberal attempt to justify market democracy by the fictive contractarian method is claimed to have estranged liberal theory from liberal political practice. On the other hand, the political practice adopted in the Western world is seen to produce just these isolated and egoist individuals described by abstract contractarian theory. The problem is that these critiques of contemporary liberalism contradict each other and thus cannot both be true at once. We are then forced to ask whether it is the liberal political theory that influences the political practice or vice versa. Has the adoption of the new contractarian justification method given the modern individual the ideal of rationality, egoism and competitiveness he or she is now after? Or have the Western social and economic changes as such really changed people gradually into selfish and isolated units with no shared values and no common will to virtue?

Because of this deep confusion in the liberal world view and liberal politics, it is important to find fresh viewpoints and new interpretations on both liberal theory and the practice of modern market democracies. In order to do just that this book brings together a combination of well-known philosophers as well as promising junior scholars from distinguished universities from different parts of the Western world. The purpose is to discuss the extensive challenges the liberal world view faces at the turn of the 21st century. As a whole this collection offers a critical view of modern liberal theory and attempts to present some signposts that could show a way towards a new form of liberal individualism.

The first part of this collection, **New Interpretations: Liberal Theory at the Crossroads,** takes a look at the theoretical aspects of contemporary liberalism. It analyses certain classics whose ideas have once again become central to the new formulation of liberal theory. This analysis begins with Jan Narveson's (University of Waterloo) article *Classical vs. modern liberalism: advantage, classical* which gives a straightforward analysis of the roots of classical liberalism. Narveson defends the classical view of liberalism which promotes negative freedom and a minimal state. He argues that contemporary welfare liberalism, which promotes more collectivist distributional politics and thus requires more extensive state involvement, can hardly be seen as representing original liberal viewpoints. Matti Häyry (University of Helsinki), for his part, also takes a look at Western political and philosophical history, but his approach to the problems of modern democracy is a consequentialist one. In his *Why not liberal utilitarianism?* Häyry claims that the prospects of liberal thought do not lie in the return to classical liberal economics but instead in liberal utilitarianism, which combines the liberal concept of rights with the utilitarian principle of harm.

Ruth Chadwick (Centre for Professional Ethics, University of Central Lancashire) moves from the libertarian and consequentialist viewpoints to liberal deontology. In her article *Kant and liberalism* Chadwick discusses the interesting but complex role that Immanuel Kant plays in the liberal tradition. She argues that while Kant's humanism and his political views are sometimes taken to support even socialist interpretations, the starting point of Kant's moral and political philosophy is still essentially liberal. This analysis of the history of liberal deontology is particularly important now, since John Rawls's controversial neo-Kantian liberal deontology has once again brought the moral and political works of Kant into the debate. Arto Siitonen (University of Helsinki) discusses David Hume's liberal concept of justice. His article *Hume on the laws of nations and the relaxation of rulers' morality* examines how the individual morality of the rulers is connected with the international relations between separate democratic regimes.

Arto Tukiainen's (University of Helsinki) article *Rorty on liberalism and postphilosophy* leaves behind the liberal classics and discusses the problems involved in Richard Rorty's disputed philosophical and political agenda. Tukiainen's main thesis is that Rorty's postphilosophical program, which questions the very process of liberal justification, cannot be compatible with

Rorty's personal liberal commitment. Mikko Salmela (University of Helsinki) takes a Nordic turn in the criticism of modern liberalism and writes on *G.H. von Wright's critique of liberal society.* Salmela discusses Georg Henrik von Wright's cultural criticism of modern democracy and his attempts to root the idea of value-rationality to be promoted in Western value-pluralistic culture in an Aristotelian notion of 'phronesis'.

Tapio Puolimatka's (University of Notre Dame) *In defense of a moral concept of democracy* also searches for liberal values, but this time in the humanistic liberal tradition of Kant and other theorists of continental idealism. Puolimatka shows that whereas Anglo-American empiristic, naturalistic and atomistic market rationality presents a value relativist view, continental liberal humanism actually presents a form of moral realism and value objectivism by regarding the individual worth as the moral ideal which also sets requirements for the political system. It is this moral concept of democracy that gives us the ideal of a critical citizen. Puolimatka therefore argues that the legitimacy of modern democracy depends on a moral framework which is independent of the social contracts made by citizens, and on citizens who take this moral framework seriously. In *Liberal identity and moral individualism* Sirkku Hellsten (University of Helsinki) continues the theme of moral democracy by attempting to integrate the contemporary liberal and communitarian viewpoints in the questions of value-pluralism and multiculturalism. She defends the teleological objectivity of the value of moral and political agency that is to be promoted within and by pluralist liberal democracy. What Hellsten defines as moral individualism presents then the normative agenda that can be found at the core of the humanistic formulation of the liberal justification for the requirement of of tolerance in liberal democracy.

An interesting view of liberal politics is also presented by Heta Häyry (Academy of Finland). Her article *Women vs. emotions, community and the moral law or why would any sensible woman want to uphold communitarian ideals* looks at communitarian thinking from a historical perspective in order to show that the new communitarianism cannot lead the way to a bright future for liberal democracy, particularly not from the viewpoint of women. On the contrary, communitarianism is a reactionary doctrine that aims at keeping women in or returning women to their traditional roles in social and political life.

The second part, **Facing the World: The Liberal State and Its Policies,** takes the discussion from theory to practice and to actual policies adopted in liberal Western welfare states. Its main interest is in the economic doctrines which have formed an essential part of classical liberal thought. Particularly today, in the world of the globalized market economy and transnational corporations, evaluation of the ethical aspects of the free market economy and the business world are even more important. Issues of central importance in the information age are also found in the analysis of science and technology.

This section begins with Jukka Kilpi's (Monash University) question 'What kind of moral entities are corporations?', in *Limits of corporate personhood: a new philosophy of the corporation.* Kilpi critically examines contemporary theories of corporate moral personhood and proposes a new philosophy of the corporation as a nexus of contracts. In *Insiders and outsiders – ethical theorising in concrete business life,* Marjaana Kopperi (University of Helsinki) discusses the role that different ethical theories have in the concrete business life of a liberal market society. Olli Loukola (University of Helsinki), for his part, discusses the structures that control behaviour in the *laissez faire* markets and the background principles that are to justify it. In *The background requirements of markets* Loukola drafts a framework for adjoining the guiding principles of free markets, those of fairness and efficiency, which are usually thought to antagonistically contradict one another in this setting.

Bruno S. Frey (University of Zurich) and Manfred J. Holler (University of Hamburg) stress the role of morale in the context of tax compliance. In *Moral and immoral views on paying taxes* they claim – on the basis of empirical findings and a game theoretical model – that instead of stern deterrence an efficient tax policy maker should try to appeal to citizens' moral considerations.

Ilkka Niiniluoto's (University of Helsinki) article *Technology policy in a democratic state* takes up the theme of technology policy. Niiniluoto discusses the question of the appropriate technology policy for the liberal democratic state. In his view it is a major political decision whether technology is allowed to develop in a deterministic or chaotic manner or whether it is assessed and controlled in democratic ways. Niiniluoto argues that the technology policy of a liberal democratic state should try to find methods and decision procedures that allow citizens to participate in the assessment and control of technological change. Nicholas Rescher (University of Pittsburgh) continues the theme of technological development. His article, *Technology, complexity, and social decision* notes that while technological progress makes particular tasks easier to perform, its overall effect is to make life-as-a-whole more complicated. He argues that in these circumstances, a practice of political horse-trading based on sustainable claims is more realistic and productive than a policy of rigid demands based on putative rights.

The third part, **Beyond Good and Evil: Neutrality, Tolerance and Individual Morality,** moves yet another step further in its analysis of contemporary liberal challenges. It concentrates on the problems of the liberal requirement of freedom, neutrality and tolerance. This part is set to show the central paradoxes involved in these conceptions and to demonstrate when and why there are social contexts in which these principles can be and sometimes have to be overridden.

This section begins with Jonathan Gorman's (The Queen's University of Belfast) analysis on *Truth and toleration*. Gorman discusses the issue of tolerance by calling attention to the variety of stories told about the same social reality. He maintains that no single, objective story can explain our social reality on the whole but understanding social reality requires understanding the points of view of the others involved and, consequently, tolerating their stories. The theme of toleration continues with Katri Kaalikoski's (University of Helsinki) question *When tolerance is too much to ask.* Kaalikoski claims that the requirements of tolerance can sometimes be justifiably overridden in the context of family, and particularly in the relationship between parents and children. A somewhat similar kind of argument is presented by Shyli Karin-Frank (Israel) in her *Taking friendship seriously.* Karin-Frank asks what should we do when we must choose between impartial moral obligations and personal loyalties. She discusses especially the kind of personal commitments involved in friendship and suggests that friendship can, under certain conditions, override obligations of impartial morality.

John T. Sanders (Rochester Institute of Technology) presents *Reflections on the value of freedom* within the liberal tradition. His central questions are, 'Is freedom an unquestionable good?' and 'Does it (or should it) always have priority over other values that could be sought?' Sanders notes that the underlying importance given to freedom within a society's scheme of values varies with historical circumstance and social context and attempts to determine whether this relativism endangers the liberal argument.

Wojciech W. Gasparski (Polish Academy of Sciences) further develops the theme of freedom in his article *In the prison of freedom: human action and its praxiological explanation.* Gasparski introduces the Polish, praxiological view – based originally on the ideas of the liberal Austrian economist, Ludwig von Mises – to the discussion of freedom (and responsibility) that is at the heart of liberal reasoning. Martin A. Bertman's (University of Helsinki) article *Evil: a shining in blackness* goes beyond liberal neutrality in its attempt to understand the psychological position of an individual who is consciously dedicated to maximizing evil instead of good. Finally, Jay L. Garfield's (University of Tasmania) *Choosing coercion and subordination: a preliminary moral study of academic life* discusses the power relationships that appear in the academic life of modern democracy. Garfield argues that what is in general, by definition, seen as a coercive relationship between people can sometimes be entered voluntarily, such as the relation between teachers and students. Garfield argues for the personal moral responsibility of those who are entrusted with the power to coerce others.

1. NEW INTERPRETATIONS: LIBERAL THEORY AT THE CROSSROADS

Classical vs. modern liberalism: advantage, classical

Jan Narveson

Introduction and summary

Over the 'past century' or so, the political outlook going by the name of 'liberalism' has undergone an evolution so drastic - the divergence between what the contemporary world thinks of under that title and what was imputed to it a century ago, which we may call 'classic' liberalism, is so great - that one may well wonder why the same name is used; nor would the reader be alone in wondering about this.[1] Despite that, this paper proposes a straightforward analysis of the root notion of liberalism: liberalism is the view that (1) government, or more generally, a set of fundamental social rules, is justified (if it is) exclusively on the basis of expected benefit to the ruled, and not at all on the basis of benefit to the rulers), where (2) it is the ruled who determine, ultimately, what constitutes 'benefit' in their case. Which is to say, that ruling must be justified only by its promotion, overall, of the realization of the preferences of the ruled. The question is whether this is to be understood on a basis of individualism, calling for Pareto restrictions on policy, or collectivism, in which case the good of some may be sacrificed in the interest of the greater good of others. Modern 'liberalism' is collectivist; classical liberalism is pareto-constrained, that is, libertarian. Classic liberalism is fundamentally anti-State; modern calls for heavy state involvement. I shall argue that the classical view has it right, and explain why.

We do well to approach the matter of liberalism by looking at its alternatives; it helps, too, to do so in a historical way, thus keeping track of the development of the idea, and, at some distance, also of reality, to a reasonable degree. Liberalism, in fully fledged form, came on the scene in roughly the 17th century. We should first consider what it was objecting to, what it took itself to be a departure from.

Political theory: the options

Like so much in philosophy, and perhaps even more so in political philosophy, the main basic options are discernible in Plato's Republic. There are, in my reading of it, three of these, associated with three characters in that indispensable book: Thrasymachus, Glaucon, and Socrates. The first says, famously, that 'justice is the interest of the stronger party'. The second sees justice as a noble ideal of life, an ideal at once for the individual and therefore - so Plato thinks - a program for the State. And the third suggests that justice is a sort of contract among sensible people. To supply tags for the three, we may call them respectively 'realism' (with many qualms), conservatism (or, in a sense, 'idealism'), and liberalism. Let's give each a brief look, by way of leading us into the central idea of liberalism, the subject of this essay.

Thrasymachean 'realism'

Thrasymachus misleadingly presents his view[2] as a 'definition' of justice. But in saying that justice is the 'interest of the stronger party', he presents a view so dissonant with what everybody thinks of as justice that Thrasymachus, notoriously, has very heavy weather of it in his exchanges with the wily Socrates, and in the end comes out as an advocate of injustice rather than as the proponent of a new and different theory of it. Responding to a proposed analogy by Socrates between the good ruler and the good shepherd, Thrasymachus insists that the smart ruler will spend his time figuring out how he can best fleece his 'flock' for his own benefit. That, he says, is the way it really is.

The thesis that this is how things **really are** earns Thrasymachus' view the title of 'realism' - later to be picked up and expanded by Machiavelli.[3] A better way to put his proposal is to say that we should forget about trying to decide what rulers **should** do, and have a look at what they, simply, **do**. And what they do is, like everybody else, pursue their own interests - except that, being in a position of much greater power than the rest of us, they can pursue it on a much grander scale - and, generally speaking, at the expense of the rest of us. Rulers exploit.

But Thrasymachus presumably intended to be offering a normative theory as well. It has two components: (1) always do whatever maximizes your own satisfaction; and (2) do this, if you are in a position to do so, **by** exercising power over others, against their interests and in favor of your own. Thrasymachus thinks that any sensible person will, if he should be so fortunate as to get into a position of power, do what he claims (with uncomfortably high plausibility) that rulers in general actually do. Reason tells us to exploit, if we can; and if we have power, then we indeed can. For that's what power is, after all: the means to achieve one's will, whatever others may like. And if you aren't in such a position? Well... expect a tough time of it. And duck, hoping that the lash will descend on the other fellow's back, not yours.

For reasons that we'll go into shortly, Thrasymachus scarcely can be said to have a political philosophy at all. His own proposal is manifestly absurd, if it is addressed to the people who would be exploited and robbed under his regime.

Plato and conservatism

We turn next to Plato, whose view is a kind of antithesis of that of Thrasymachus. Plato, familiarly, constructs an analogy between the soul and the state, the idea being that justice will really be the same thing in each. Justice is identified with whatever promotes the good of the personage being 'ruled,' or with that good itself. In the case of the individual, this is that person's own soul, which is analyzed as having three 'parts' - Reason, Spirit, and Appetite, justice being, as it turns out, the 'harmony' among these three - though a harmony that really consists in the domination of the entire soul by one of them, Reason, which tells the appetites what to do in no uncertain terms, and enlists the emotions as ally to get them to do it.

Aristotle later defined the subject of moral virtue as the rational control of the emotions, the principle being observance of the 'mean'. In either Plato's or Aristotle's version, ethics for the individual is a sort of science, aimed at producing the happiness of the whole person via an insight into the nature of the soul. And so - not surprisingly - the ideal of the harmony of the whole will likewise be the appropriate theory of justice for the state. Its ruling element will likewise be Reason; but since only individual people actually have faculties of reason, the ruling element in a community, will have to be those people who are possessed of the best faculties of Reason - rather than, say, those with the most courage ('timocracy') or the most money ('oligarchy'), or simply the most people on their side ('democracy'). In fact, the good state will be one in which everyone else is subordinate to the wise, who - somehow - know what is best for them and, since hoi polloi can't really be expected to know that for themselves, to bring about the happiness of the whole, by force when necessary. As it often will be, since the irrational parts of the soul are notoriously unruly in themselves.

It is central to the Platonic idea, then, that there should be a discernible answer to the question of how we ought to live, that this answer can be and at least to some reasonable approximation actually has been discerned by the most intelligent members of the community, and thus - Plato's 'thus,' not ours - that the right way to run a community is by making those most intelligent people the rulers - the king, if there's just one, or (what we are led to expect, generally speaking, by Plato's exposition) an aristocratic committee. Rule by the Central Committee is the upshot.

The common good

Before turning to the idea of the 'social contract' so tantalizingly but evanescently suggested by Glaucon, it will be useful to make a short excursion, in order to emphasize the common element between Platonic conservatism and liberalism: the idea that the ruler ought to aim at the good of his community. For the classic exposition of this as the central idea of political philosophy, we turn to the work of St. Thomas Aquinas, writing a millennium and a half later. It is found in his analysis of the idea of Law. Law, says St. Thomas, is 'an ordination of reason for the common good, promulgated (and enforced) by the one who is in charge of the community'.[4] The point of my bracketed insertion is that Aquinas has already made it clear at this point that laws are not just pieces of advice, but are **enforced**. That's what politics is about, then: what order may be imposed on a community, by force if necessary.

What is distinctive about Aquinas' idea, however, is the reference, not simply to 'the good' of the community, but to it as a 'common' good. Is the idea of a 'common good' interesting? What makes it so, if it is, is due to an important point about communities that distinguishes - or at least possibly distinguishes - them from, say, flocks of sheep, or for that matter from groups of slaves: namely, that they are composed of individuals with minds of their own: 'The proper end of a group of free men is different from that of a group of slaves, for a free man determines his own actions, whereas a slave, *qua* slave, belongs to another'.[5] A society is an interacting group of organisms each of whom has a capacity for **self**-direction, and some likelihood of using it in such a way as to direct himself in a different way from what the others do. This being so, we will be able to distinguish 'individual' goods, which vary from one person to another, from 'common' goods, which are the same for all. Aquinas, probably following Plato and Aristotle in this, says that individual goods tend toward community discord, whereas common goods tend toward community unity - or, as might as well say, toward *community*, which contains the word 'unity'. One of the more important questions in political theory, I think, is whether and in what sense he is right about this.

Writers have tended to talk, loosely, about something called 'individualism' in social theory. To use this term as a descriptive one is to suggest that there is some alternative - 'socialism', or 'organicism', perhaps. But the idea that there is an alternative to individualism needs careful analysis, for after all, society consists of individual people; it is, as Aquinas saw, **essentially** a group rather than, say, a single large organism. If individualism in this sense is to be called a 'view', then we have to be aware that there is no alternative to that 'view' - indeed, it hardly deserves the title of 'view'. But what are these individual people like, of which the community consists? After all, flocks of sheep also consist of individual sheep, and in any sense in which it is undeniable that individual people have minds of their own, so too it is undeniable that individual sheep have minds of their own. If we are to say that sheep are nonindividualistic in a sense in which people are not, this is going to have to be an observation about the way those individual minds work, or what is in them, and not an observation that sheep, or sheepish people for that matter, don't have minds whereas people do.

That is why I have put the matter in terms of there being some **likelihood** of using that individual mind in such a way as to direct himself in some different way from that in which others do. The feature of having interests different in kind from, and quite possibly such as to conflict with those of other individuals is the characteristic of humans in social settings that creates the background for political philosophy, this being a normative theory intended for the direction of individuals in light of their social situations. That theory addresses the question, What should one do, taking into account the fact that there are other people around, potentially and perhaps actually quite different from oneself? So characterized, the theory in question includes both moral and, in a more specific sense, political philosophy.

Before leaving Aquinas, we should take note of the fact that he does not think that legislated law is the only kind of law is. He supposes that his dictum on the nature of law comprehends not only the kinds that are issued by human rulers of human communities, but also every sort of law there is, including the laws that physicists and chemists are trying to discover. All, he thinks, are laws in *the same sense of the word 'law'*. The most notable implication of this, to the modern reader, is that what we call morality is likewise a system of 'law' - law discerned or at least discernible by natural reason, based on the nature of things rather than on any ruler's pronouncements. Of course, in his view as a Roman Catholic monk in good standing, those things, in turn, are the way they are because God makes them that way, and so in a very general sense all law is ultimately going to be God's. It is that theological view that saves Aquinas' theory of law from sheer equivocation, assimilating laws in the scientific sense to laws in the familiar legal sense. But it also plunges it into an unacceptable metaphysic.

Aquinas takes it to be a consequence of his view that 'human' law - that is, legal-type law, the ordinances of human rulers of communities - ought to be founded entirely on 'natural' law, that is, on morality. But although it ought to be, it won't always in fact be so, for various reasons, among the most important being that human rulers sometimes go wrong, turning into tyrants rather than true kings. In the terminology adopted here, those are the rulers that go Thrasymachean, ruling in the interests of themselves rather than of their subjects. Or, to be fairer to Plato's intentions, they rule in the interests of the 'baser' parts of their own souls at the expense of the nobler elements. Had they done the latter, they would have been good Platonic rulers, ruling in the interests of all even as they promoted their own interests, namely by catering to the best parts of their own souls rather than the worst. When rulers behave in the Thrasymachean way, on the other hand, natural law will clash with legislated or proclaimed law, and then we'll have a problem. For natural law is inherently superior to any legislated law, and so when there is such a clash, there is a real question what individual people subject to legislative rule are to do - to the point that it could even justify rebellion by otherwise patient citizens.

With these points in mind, let us now turn to the subject of liberalism.

Glaucon and liberalism

After this lengthy excursion into the Platonic idea and Aquinas' formulation of the idea of law, we are ready to identify liberalism, again leaning, a bit, on contributions to the early discussions in the *Republic*, this time by the character Glaucon, who presents an embryonic version of the idea of the 'social contract' in the context of trying to extend Thrasymachus' ideas in a more reasonable direction, and in hopes of eliciting Socrates' best efforts. According to Glaucon,

> What most people say is that what's bad about injustice is to suffer from it - when Thrasymachus' wicked rulers rob or enslave me, that's bad - bad for me. But what about the fellow who does the wronging - he isn't suffering, is he? No way! He may be laughing all the way to the bank where he deposits his ill-gotten gains. However, ordinary people, seeing the danger of people like that, band together and make a sort of compact, the purpose of which is to commit them all against injustice, so that nobody will suffer from it. Still, they only make such deals because they know they are weak.[6]

There are two notable points in this. First, it represents justice as essentially a means rather than something good 'in itself'; moreover, as something in a sense 'artificial' rather than 'natural': as a kind of human construct or institution rather than a preexisting rule of life or something of that sort. And second, it represents **individual people**, rather than a king or other leader, as the agents of peace. Each person, seeing his own weakness and consequent liability to the depredations of his fellows, is motivated to 'band together' with his fellows, which banding together really consists of a set of mutual, conditional commitments to refrain from engaging in such depredations.

From this we may glean the essence of liberalism. If individual people can make the rules, then they will do so on the basis of their *own*, possibly divergent, values - not on the basis of the uniform values for all that would be authoritatively imposed by the King, but rather of the quite possibly different ones actually held by the citizens.

Liberalism may be expounded either in political or in moral terms - as one would expect, given the pioneering work of Plato. In political terms, liberalism consists in a rejection of *fundamental authority* in the person of the king. What makes the rules of society click is not something imposed from without, but our own interests as individual persons, divergent though they may in some respects be. Glaucon, in short, is accepting one part of Thrasymachus' philosophical program: that the individual is basically his own boss, his own sense of what is good and bad is what counts, and this is just as true of the tradesman or farmer as of the philosopher.

But Glaucon rejects another part of Thrasymachean theory, namely egoism *as a rule for social life*. This rejection, as we will be seeing in greater detail later, is based on an important insight: that egoism, though necessarily right as a theory about individual rationality in itself, is something like necessarily wrong as a theory about social rules: a kind of nonsense or madness, *because wildly contrary to the interests of each individual person*. Instead of the lawless and frankly mindless social condition in which each knows no limits to his behavior, the Glauconian liberal will impose restrictions, based on our respective interests and on our admitted 'weakness', that is, our obvious inability to simply get our way regardless of what others may do.

There is a close moral analogue of this political idea, however. As we have seen, Glaucon rejects the king as the basic source of authority, insisting that each person is competent to do such directing, at that level, as needs to be done. The underlying moral theory is also strikingly at odds with Plato's. In Plato's view, 'Reason' can discern how the soul should organize itself, and when it does, will come up with a blueprint, the same for every man.

Perhaps I have here crossed the line from Plato to Hobbes. If Glaucon *probably* rejects that idea as unreal, Hobbes *certainly* does. People are different, and there is no rationale for supposing that the right rule for one individual life is going to be the same for others: you, me, sumo wrestlers, used car salesmen, violin virtuosos, mothers, and all the rest. Morality, therefore, has to be *distinguished from* what we may call Ethics - the study of 'the good for Man', the subject of Aristotle's book of that name. Morality is a set of rules for action that relates to our fellows - rules meant to be imposed on all of us by all of us. Such rules may nevertheless be grounded in the interests of each separate person, despite their disparity. What grounds the unity is our **common** interests.

Those interests include in particular, in the view of the liberal, our interest in not being subject to exploitation and depredation at the hands of our fellows. This is a truly *common* good: absolutely all of us, short of the marginally human, are capable of inflicting major or even fatal damage on others, and they on us. It is safe to say that no normally expectable damage at the hands of one's natural environment, including the animate part of that environment, offers anything like the prospect of loss that the intentional activities of our fellow persons can manage. Protection from this common source of evils is therefore a top priority for anyone.

Morals, as Aquinas later saw, is prior to politics, grounded in the facts about our own natures, our environments, and our relations to each other and to nature. Politics, in turn, is subordinate to morals. The rules of social life - rules for the *common* good - will likewise guide whatever political activity there is. Those who 'rule the community' must rule not only for the Common Good - in which respect, the liberal is arguably at one with Plato; but they also must accept that that good is the good of each individual person, *as seen by that person*, rather than as seen by the supposedly wise ruler himself - a ruler who, however wise he may be, is certain to get it wrong when it comes to telling each one of us what is good for us. Indeed, we might as well say that rulers have no business being separate from us anyway: laws are fundamentally made *by us*, by the ruled, rather than by independently operating self-styled superpersons. For indeed, the whole idea of the State as superman, as being the agency of some person or some few persons superior to the rest of us, is just out to lunch, silly, once one exposes the idea to a moment's critical thought.

Liberalism defined

That, then, is Liberalism. Its definition has just two components: it holds (a) that the **sole** justifying purpose of government - if it is justified at all - is the common good *of the ruled* and *only* the ruled - or more generally, the sole justifying purpose of social rules is our interests qua ruled, rather than any interest we might have qua ruler; and (b) that that good is basically interpreted and ultimately assessed *by us*, the people whose good is to be promoted, and not by anybody else, however well-intentioned.

Liberalism thus differs from the views both of Thrasymachus and of Plato. It differs from the former in that it sees the need for genuine laws, that is, interpersonally authoritative rules, calling on us sometimes to do what we really would have preferred not to do on that occasion, but which we must do anyway in view of our natures and situation, that of organisms with the vulnerabilities and limited powers inherent in the human frame. Yet it differs from Plato in making each individual basically his own appraiser and assessor of what is good and bad for that individual, and that enormous set of individual values is all there is to be the basis of the social rules of morality and politics.

To thicken out this plot, we shall need to look much more carefully at the idea of common good as it emerges in liberalism. Once we take seriously the idea - though let us call it the fact, for that is what it is - that different people have seriously differing interests, different points of view, different ways of evaluating things, and in short, *different* values, then the idea of 'common good' gets complicated. Indeed, the question arises whether there can even be any such thing as a 'common good'.

And in turn, we must be on our guard not to let liberalism degenerate, on the one hand into Thrasymachean egoism, or on the other into some subtle version of Plato after all. The latter, I think, is the course to which contemporary erstwhile liberal writers have succumbed. It is a fundamental mistake.

We shall have to be particularly careful about political power, for in contrast to Plato, we understand that rulers are not to be trusted. This is obviously true when those rulers are outright Thrasymacheans, but it is equally, though more subtly, true when they are noble Platonic types - trying to promote *our* good, indeed, but in *their* view of what is good for us. To have a good society or community, the powers of rulers are going to have to be strictly limited and controlled, so that they will do what they are supposed to do - namely, to promote *only* the *common* good of us citizens, the ruled, rather than that of the ruler or his friends *or*, as we now realize, those designated as preferred by his favorite philosophical theory.

Whether any political power at all can survive this set of strictures is, as we shall see, a pretty interesting question, and definitely a very live issue. In this respect, those professing 'liberalism' in the present day have virtually thrown in the towel. Contemporary 'liberals' are dyed-in-the-wool Statists: they don't even consider the possibility that perhaps the State isn't a good idea. Democracy is their favored form of government, and its necessity is unquestioned and, as far as they are concerned, unquestionable. Plato, as we know, had the gravest of misgivings about it, and we shall find reason, perhaps surprisingly to many readers, to share those misgivings. What to do about them is an interesting question. But one thing is immediately clear. Anyone who thinks that the State is literally necessary, at the most fundamental level, is under suspicion of not being a liberal at all. For if it is necessary that must mean that the individual cannot rule himself, and that individuals in groups cannot rule themselves, on the basis of their own values, their own perceptions about what is good, their own interests. Something has gone very wrong in any theory that can say that, and yet claims to be liberal.

The social contract: liberty as the common good

I have represented Glaucon to be the first to formulate and suggest the idea of 'social contract,' though it no doubt predates Plato. Ideas of such a 'contract' crop up frequently in the later history of philosophy - notably in three of the greatest philosophers of the early modern era (Hobbes, Locke, and Kant). This is no accident. There is a commanding rightness about the idea that gives it pride of place among those thinkers who actually try to supply fundamental reasons for political principles.

Of course it may be claimed that the very notion of a 'reason' in matters moral and political is one of those 'essentially contested ideas' of which recent philosophers have become enamoured. I am not among them. While it is admittedly unclear what an 'idea' is, it is extremely puzzling what it is for an idea to have the supposed status of 'essential' contestability. Ideas, one would think, are the sort of things that you should be able to clarify and define, rather than be reduced to forever 'contesting'. Principles can be contested, certainly: but not **ideas**. That this or that is indeed the idea that matters in a certain context is, to be sure, a subject about which dispute can be expected. But whether those disputes can be settled is surely not something we should expect to be able to see in the light of pure reason. Whether we should at least be *trying* to settle them perhaps is, on the other hand.

In the case of morals and politics, however, there is a notion of reason and reasoning whose relevance one disputes at one's peril; considering it will also show why there is not much point in invoking other conceptions for these purposes. Which is to say, I think, that the social contract idea is indeed, when it comes to moral theory, the only game in town.

When people reason about action - and let's admit that they often do not - they apply their practical ideas to their actions. Or, as the case may be, to other people's. But one applies either one's own or someone else's practical ideas to others' actions in a quite different way from that in which one applies them to one's own. When I deliberate and reason about what to do, and finally make up my mind, I then, simply, do it. But when I deliberate for **others**, all I can do is present to those others my results, for their consideration. There is no sense to the idea that having decided for them, I can then 'do' it, nor that they will do it simply as a result of **my** having 'decided' so. In that obvious sense, we **cannot** reason for others, and can only reason for ourselves. We can, of course, try to coerce those others and people often do this. When they do that, they appeal, in a sense, to those other people's reasons. That important possibility will be discussed a bit further below.

Practical reason issues in actions, in other words, and only the actions of the person who does the reasoning are under the direct control of the reasoner. So if we are concerned about other people's actions, it might be a good idea to pay some attention to the actor's reasoning.

Reason and force

That's especially true if you can't just order him around or, as they say these days, 'kick butt'. The procedure of getting others to do as we wish by doing the latter is, to be sure, frequently enough resorted to, and is enshrined officially in the institution known as The State. Thrasymachus obviously envisages it as the typical procedure for promoting one's interests, should one be fortunate enough to be in the position of the Ruler. Clearly, force cannot be ignored in this area.

The place of (interpersonally wielded) force in the moral and political scheme of things needs to be carefully considered. We can have reason to use or refrain from using force. Now, most of us are **not** The Ruler - though in a democracy, to be sure, we are all rulers 'a little bit'; the democratic option will be duly considered a bit later. Meanwhile, almost all of us are also in a position, now and then, to wield some amount of force, small or large, against some of our fellows, whether or not we are in any sort of official capacity. Obviously we can think about whether to use or not use what little we may have. Thinking about such matters is precisely what we are trying to do in undertaking an essay such as this; how and in what way the output of this may be effective in changing actual behavior is an important question, of course, and must form a central part of the inquiry.

We can now present the reason why we would do well to take reason into account - why, in fact, we should do political thinking at all. The reason, in brief, is that the actions of others make a difference to us, and yet those actions are under the control of those very others. And since those actions are very often affected by, and always susceptible to some influence by, reasons, the practical reasoning of others makes a difference to us, this being so no matter who we are or what we want. Finally, practical reasoning is the sort of thing that is intrinsically amenable to input from other reasoning beings. If it is of the right kind, it can be of inestimable value; if wrong, it can lead to tragedy, or at the least confusion and loss. That's why we want to find out what that 'right kind' is, and why it's worth going to considerable trouble to do so.

Liberalism and liberty

The challenge for liberal foundations is to find a true Common Good among the welter of disparate ways of life and bundles of preferences that must expect actually to find in any large group of people. But as hinted above, it is a challenge that can be met. Persons able to make things difficult or impossible for each other, yet all having ends of some kind that they are concerned to achieve, clearly do have a special interest in each other's behavior: namely, the interest that those others not exercise those fatal powers. In all sorts of ways, various pairs, trios, and n-tuplets of persons can also cooperate in common endeavours. But you can't do that unless you have a common endeavour, and even then, you can't succeed in your cooperation without the forbearance of yet others, of whom there are always plenty - in the billions, these days.

The term 'cooperation' is most at home in those common endeavours just mentioned: think of Mennonites building a barn, or eight people rowing a racing skiff. We may call this, to be very general about it, 'positive' cooperation. But we needn't stretch the word to any appreciable degree if we allow that in addition to such cooperation, there is what we may reasonably call 'negative' cooperation as well. This is where one person *refrains* from doing something, provided that another likewise refrains. Given that we are often in a position to descend on some of our fellows with weapons or spanners to throw in the works, and they in ours, the idea of negative cooperation soon emerges as a perfectly reasonable and, in fact, extremely important idea. Any set of people who could make things difficult for each other, but don't, in recognition of the fact that each has much to lose if the power to make things difficult is actually exercised, are cooperating. Their mutual behavior is mutually advantageous: namely, in avoiding what would otherwise be severe disadvantage.

What makes this rational? The formula for rationality is always the same. Each of us chooses what, on the whole, is most highly preferred, on consideration, in light of such information as we can glean concerning the effects of our various options. Thus the reasoning behind refraining from using force, or more generally our power to meddle and disrupt, must be this: that the cost to ourselves from the exercise of those powers by the others is greater than the gain we might make by exercising our own powers to do that. The tenability of the Social Contract lies in the hypothesis that this calculation will always, all things considered, favor confining our behavior to nonviolent, noncoercive behavior, so long as the behavior of the others with whom we interact is itself similarly noncoercive.

Well, is it tenable? That depends on how widely we cast our net. Dealing with an isolated other person, it is easy to believe that 'invading and despoiling', as Hobbes calls it, will pay off - at least if that other person is small enough, and a few other modest conditions, all of them satisfiable.

But then, we all know that. And so we will be inclined to enlist the help of others in similar plight. Soon our hypothetical agent will not be encountering a single other, of modest strength, but an angry mob with clubs - or an army with M-16s. Quite another story! But the point is that the road from the one to the other is paved with the ill intentions of people like our hypothetical invader.

And when we reach these extreme situations, what shall we say? Viewed from the abstract perspective of history, there is ample reason to proposing that in biggish armed confrontations, *both sides lose.* It isn't just that the 'winning' side has plenty of casualties, along with the losers. It's also that the victorious soldier has himself expended a great deal of time and effort that almost anyone can think of better ways to spend: he acts, generally, under necessity, not like one who goes forth to play tennis or see the sunset. And in contemporary cases, one has but to have attained rudimentary competence at arithmetic to see that the cost of war is immense, far outweighing anything that could possibly be gained by it *except* peace itself. That is, war to defend oneself, despite its immense expense, is worth it; war to aggress, on the other hand, is not.

It is this reasoning, so nearly universally true, that enables us to close the case in favor of a certain set of social rules, with potential for enforcement. We do not care whether there are some few who so love to fight that they will consider any war, win or lose, worth its price, just for the adventure, glory, or whatever, of it. We don't care, because if such persons want war, they shall have it, and they shall *lose*. Against the united efforts of almost all of one's fellows, no one can stand. Proposing to do so is near enough to insanity; whatever is left will moulder in the grave with its short-lived exponent.

When we seek social rules, in other words, things are very different from what they are when we look at a handful of small-scale cases. But why should we seek social rules? Here too the answer is simple. We seek social rules because we want, need, the company of our fellows - not merely for social purposes, though that is no small point in almost anyone's scheme of life; but for the potential for more robust cooperation of the 'positive' type. And there can be no positive cooperation without negative - as Plato observed early on in *The Republic*, with his beautiful point about the need for trust among the members of a band of thieves.

The basic terms of cooperation for any society, then, are a general pact for the enormous mutual advantage of the *absence of mutual disadvantage.* This is Hobbes' first Law of nature: 'Seek Peace and Follow it'; and only if not attainable, use 'all the helps and advantages of war'. Hobbes' second law, following close on its heels, says that we are to insist on no more liberty in relation to our fellows than we are willing to grant them in relation to us. But how much is that? The answer is deducible from his First Law, just as Hobbes says. It is, namely, as much as mutually possible. David Gauthier has admirably summed this up in a generalization of the Law of Nature in Locke's version: We are not to seek advantage *by* disadvantaging our fellows; only in the case where the alternatives are even worse may we do what imposes costs on our fellows, making their situations worse than they would be in the absence of interaction with us.[7] Immanuel Kant and John Stuart Mill both join this distinguished group of thinkers as well, Kant with his 'Supreme Principle of Right', and Mill with his famed Principle of Liberty. All these come, I believe, to the same thing, and I make no attempt to improve on Gauthier's elegant formula.

Positive rules?

The benefit of the liberal No-Harm principle is obvious to all. But 'modern' liberals want more. Most of them think to impose some kind of 'equality' condition, especially to limit our 'acquisition' of the sort of goods that can be traded, bought and sold. And all of them want to impose a requirement that the community take care of its most helpless members. It is plainly of first importance whether they are right about either of these. I conclude with the briefest of complaints that they are in the wrong about both.

Let us remember that what we are asking here is *not* whether it is *all right* for people to help other people in need, or for that matter give away half their fortunes to those they perceive as being less fortunate. The issue here is solely whether we will *amend the No-Harm Principle* in the pursuit of these ends. Will we, that is, impose taxes, costs, on people in order to bring about either equality or, at least, the care of the needy, the indigent, the lame, and so on?

There is one consideration, which might be termed a 'practical' one, that would decisively resolve this issue without further ado. For those who think that such amendments are in order invariably are thinking only of their own communities - at most their own nation-states. Britons do not envisage equality's being enforced on all Britons with a view to equalizing their situations with the Somalians, the Chinese, the Bolivians, and so on and so on for the remaining many billions of the people there are today. But why not? We are entitled to ask that question, because the thesis was supposed to be that equality or the cure of total poverty or disease are rights. But the implication if that is taken seriously is, assuredly, general poverty for the whole world, at best, and certainly poverty by the standards to which Britons have become accustomed. Scarcely anyone will remain a friend of such proposals who has that much to lose from it. And that is strong testimony to their fundamental absurdity. It is not reasonable for all persons in the world to commit themselves to share their fortunes equally with everyone in the world, or even to rescue from dire need whatever of their fellows, in the entire world there may be thus to rescue or save. In so reasoning, we apply Plato's model: we look at the large picture and see what it implies for the individual, rather than confining our gaze to the possibly very atypical situations of some few of us in the 'advanced' countries of today's world.

There is a more abstract but more fundamental and decisive refutation of this idea - of what we might call 'Moral Positivism'. Each person wants to do as well as he can by his lights, whatever they may be. In almost all cases, these lights are personal and inegalitarian, calling for far more effort on behalf of some few persons - family, friends, and self, for instance - than for the myriad others there may be. Assuming a preference schedule of that very typical type, then, let us next recall something noted earlier: positive rights presuppose negative, not vice versa. The right to have one's wounds tended is subordinate to the right not to be shot in the first place. More generally, the right to be free to do x or not as one pleases is logically prior to the right to have x done to one.

What this means is that a schedule of positive rights is *necessarily* more costly than the general schedule of negative rights bundled in the no-harm rule.

That general rule of liberty, of course, leaves every individual free to make arrangements with any other individuals he pleases to take precaution against certain risks, and the like. We may form insurance groups, mutual aid societies in which the levels of aid extended to fellow members are much higher than those we are willing to commit ourselves to in relation to the miscellaneous billions around the world; and so on. Freedom is not coherently to be thought of as an 'intrinsic value': its value is whatever may get from what one would do with the unrestricted actions thus made available. So of course people will bind themselves in any number of ways. But different people will do so in different ways, and some scarcely at all. For the rest to propose to prevent their having those liberties in the first place is to invite the myriad of impositions of contemporary societies in their (futile) efforts at 'social security', health, education, and the like. But going into details on those matters lies very far beyond the limits of this modest essay. What I have done here is to throw down a kind of philosophical gauntlet to those who would defend a narrower slate of liberties in the name of liberalism.

Notes

1. See as a particularly instructive case in point, Jerzy Szacki, 1994, which devotes a chapter, 'Instead of a Definition of Liberalism', to giving up the search for such a thing.
2. Or rather, his translators do; I am no Greek scholar and must take their word for it. It is found in Book I of *The Republic.*

3. Or at least, in Machiavelli's *The Prince* - which has been plausibly argued to be a parody rather than to represent Machiavelli's real views.
4. For the text of this famous 'definition', see *Summa Theologica*, I-II, Q. 90, AA. 2. E.g., in William P. Baumgarth and Richard J. Regan, 1988, p. 13.
5. Aquinas, *On Kingship*, para. 2.
6. Glaucon's speech, in *Republic*, Bk. II. I have somewhat modified the translation.
7. Gauthier, 1986, Ch. 7.

References

Baumgarth, W. P. and Regan, R. J. (eds), (1988), Saint Thomas Aquinas on Law, Morality, and Politics, Hackett: Indianapolis, USA.

Gauthier, D. (1986), *Morals by Agreement*, Oxford University Press: Oxford and New York.

Szacki, J. (1994), *Liberalism after Communism*, Central European University Press: Budapest, distributed in English, translation by Oxford University Press, 1995.

Why not liberal utilitarianism?

Matti Häyry

The majority of today's moral philosophers in the West regard utilitarianism as an uninteresting and immoral doctrine, at least as far as the regulation of social and political life is concerned. Some moralists from the English-speaking parts of the world, notably J.J.C. Smart,[1] R.B. Brandt,[2] R.M. Hare[3] and Peter Singer,[4] defend utilitarianism as a theory of individual morality, but even these self-confessed utilitarians usually keep a low profile when it comes to defending classical utilitarian views on such legal and social issues as punishment, infanticide, or the redistribution of harms and benefits by state coercion.

Especially among liberal moralists the quasi-contractarian and libertarian theories of John Rawls[5] and Robert Nozick[6] are far more popular than their utilitarian counterparts, apparently for two main reasons. First, the deontological principles assumed by Rawls and Nozick seem to offer a firmer ground for morally sound policy decisions than the endless preference or welfare calculations that consequentialists are supposed to engage themselves in. And second, strict liberal and libertarian rules can be employed to defend many civil liberties which have traditionally prevailed in the West, and which are thought to be in danger if utilitarian thinking prevails.

My claim in this article is, however, that a carefully formulated *liberal utilitarian* view can avoid both problems attributed to standard consequentialist theorizing, and can thus successfully compete with the contractarian, libertarian and other deontological alternatives. The advantage of utilitarianism in the comparison is its basic commitment to equality, which is generally the weak point in deontological liberal theories such as Rawls's and Nozick's. A liberal utilitarian theory which is sensitive both to claims of individual liberty and to demands of equality can in fact offer a far firmer ground for morally acceptable legislative and social policy decisions than its current liberal competitors.[7]

Types of utilitarianism

Since the critics of utilitarianism often attack man of straw versions of the view, I shall first briefly outline and discuss what I take to be the most important types of utilitarianism. The main forms of the doctrine, as put forward by British clergymen, social reformers and philosophers during the last four centuries, are, first, *descriptive* utilitarianism, or psychological universal hedonism, second, *theological* utilitarianism, and, third, *classical* utilitarianism. Elements of a fourth alternative, for which I have coined the label 'liberal utilitarianism', can be found in the works of Jeremy Bentham and especially in the later work of John Stuart Mill.

The first traditional form of the doctrine, descriptive utilitarianism, states that human beings either inherently are, or can be educated to be, universally benevolent towards their fellow beings. Bishop Richard Cumberland[8] in his critique of Thomas Hobbes was one of the first to express this view, and the theory has been further developed by David Hume,[9] Francis Hutcheson,[10] James Mill,[11] and more recently by R.B. Brandt.[12]

The second version, theological utilitarianism, assumes that human beings are by nature egoistic, and can only be motivated into doing something by threats of punishment and promises of reward. It is the existence of a benevolent and all-mighty God, who by religious sanctions regulates our lives, that makes it in fact rational for every human being to act benevolently towards others. Bishop George Berkeley opted for this view in a sermon 'on passive obedience',[13] and it was held in one form or another by, for instance, Abraham Tucker,[14] William Paley,[15] and James Fitzjames Stephen.[16]

The third, classical type of utilitarianism is a curious mixture of psychological pessimism and social optimism. Like its theological counterpart, the view denies the innate benevolence of humankind, but, like descriptive universal hedonism, it states that even without divine interference the happiness of all is - or should be - the main regulative factor of our lives. William Godwin's uncompromising applications of the utilitarian calculus gave the view the bad name it still has in many quarters. The best known versions of classical utilitarianism, however, are the views of Jeremy Bentham[17] and John Stuart Mill.[18] Most 20th century utilitarians have assumed the Benthamite or Millian doctrines in some modernized form.

Utilitarianism has been criticised for the feature that it does not provide one with an adequate theory of moral motivation. Although we may well see that the good of all humankind would be the optimal goal for human action, we can nevertheless fail to be moved by the fact when we make our own decisions. It was because of this deficiency that, for instance, Henry Sidgwick refrained from stating that utilitarianism is the one and only universally valid 'method of ethics'.[19]

The division into the three types of utilitarianism I have mentioned helps to illustrate that this stock critique of the doctrine is misplaced. It is true that classical utilitarianism lacks the psychological explanations and theological justifications offered by the earlier versions of the theory. But the same observation also applies to all other secular theories of normative ethics. Why should I be morally motivated by the rights or liberties of other people, or by contracts which do not suit my own purposes, any more than I am motivated by the good of humankind? Unless ethical theories are chosen by people for their theoretical or practical appeal, people quite naturally fail to be moved by them. The acceptance of utilitarianism is a moral choice as it is a moral choice to believe in natural rights or in the sacredness of hereditary private property. My main point in what follows is, accordingly, to show that utilitarianism can in fact be presented in a form which is appealing to many of us both theoretically and practically.

The definition of utilitarianism

In its most general form modern (classical) utilitarianism simply states the following:

> Those and only those actions are right which among the alternatives open to the agent at the time of the choice produce, or can be expected to produce, the maximum of net good or the minimum of net evil to those influenced by the actions.

There are, however, at least four points in this straightforward formulation which have to be specified before the exact nature of the utilitarian theory in question is defined.

First, most utilitarians have assumed that the actions which are evaluated by the good and evil they produce can be extended to include negative actions, or omissions, as well as positive actions. I shall, later on, show that if this assumption is rejected, utilitarianism can with certain additional premises come very close to the ideals of libertarianism.

Second, the good aimed at can be defined in many ways. Bentham's solution was to define good as happiness and happiness as pleasure. This hedonistic view was then partly challenged by John Stuart Mill, who in his eudaemonistic axiology differentiated between higher and lower pleasures as constituents of happiness. James Fitzjames Stephen rejected the pleasure-related approach altogether, and stated that the goal of all human action should be the ideal set by the moral elite. G.E. Moore in his turn claimed that what is good can only be recognized by intuition - he then went on to proclaim that the best things 'we' know about are 'the pleasures of human intercourse and the enjoyment of beautiful objects'.[20] More recently, average material welfare,[21] the satisfaction of rational desires[22] and the satisfaction of preferences[23] have featured as cornerstones of the utilitarian theory of value. In my defence of liberal utilitarianism I have defended the view that the hierarchical satisfaction of needs or interests is the most tenable basis for a consequentialist axiology.[24]

Third, 'those influenced by given actions' can be interpreted either narrowly or broadly. Narrow interpretations usually restrict the attention to sane, competent human beings. Bentham - rightly, I think - assumed a broader view, and in his theory took into account all those human and nonhuman beings who have the ability to suffer. His points are relevant when objective needs and subjective needs, or interests, are compared as basic value entities within the utilitarian theory. In order to exist, interests have to be recognised by those who have them. Objective needs, on the other hand, can be possessed by beings who do not consciously recognize that they have them. The main difference between the views, in practical terms, is that the theory based on subjective needs allows one to restrict one's attention to present and future human or nonhuman beings who are capable of recognizing their own good, whereas the objective-need theory demands that one extends one's attention to all living beings (such as viruses and trees) which can be described as needing something (in order to survive, for instance).

Fourth, the ideal of maximizing net good or, in the phrase of earlier utilitarians, promoting 'the greatest happiness of the greatest number' is not always unproblematical. The utility calculus which is supposed to determine the status of actions is, after all, an imaginary rather than a concrete device: one cannot seriously expect utilitarians to estimate and count the value of all the consequences of the action alternatives open to an agent at a given time. Lack of knowledge very efficiently prevents us from predicting the future with the amount of accuracy that would be required for such exact moral calculations. Besides, as I shall show in the next section, the simple multiplication of people's pleasures can easily lead to the victimization of minorities in the name of the greatest good. It must be carefully considered, therefore, how the ideal of maximizing what is good should be applied to practical issues.

Simple hedonism and the problem of victimization

The combination of two features in the classical Benthamite doctrine makes it an easy target for one particular criticism. When unqualified hedonism is joined together with the idea of multiplying pleasures and pains by individuals, the results are often counterintuitive. Consider, for instance, the following situation in a Roman amphitheatre. Ten thousand spectators have gathered to see how one non-consenting human being faces a number of irritated lions in the arena. The probable outcome of the performance is that the human performer will suffer serious injuries, the disvalue of which will be 9999 units of pain. The spectators, on the other hand, will achieve one unit of sadistic pleasure each, making the gross positive value of the performance 10000 units of pleasure. Assuming that the comparative value of an afternoon without the performance is zero, and that long-term consequences do not tip the scales, the Benthamite utilitarian is forced to say that the performance should be held.[25] But surely reasonable people would wish to reject a moral theory whose application leads to such inhumane practical conclusions.

There are many other instances in which simple hedonistic utilitarianism states that it is one's duty to victimize one person in order to produce minor benefits to others. The defenders of the doctrine can react to these cases in three ways. They can follow William Godwin[26] and J.J.C. Smart,[27] and shrug their shoulders, saying, 'Well, you can't make an omelette without breaking eggs'. Another alternative is to challenge the crude hedonistic axiology assumed by Bentham and James Mill - I shall sketch this solution below. Finally, one can reject the multiplication of pleasures and pains by individuals - this alternative will be examined in the following sections.

The revision of classical utilitarianism can be set off by presenting three axiological responses to the problem of victimization. First, John Stuart Mill suggested that in the utility calculation one should prefer higher pleasures to lower ones, 'higher pleasures' being, by his definition, those which would be preferred by refined persons who are familiar with all kinds of pleasure. Mill's own actual application of the view had, however, some elitist implications which render it less than optimal in the more democratic spirit of the twentieth century.[28] Second, James Fitzjames Stephen added a moralistic dimension to utilitarianism, stating that the moral good, as defined by those in power, should guide individual behaviour as well as legislative work.[29] But moralism is seldom a good starting point for supposedly neutral axiological considerations. Third, my own suggestion is that utilitarians who are reasonably sensitive to the undesirability of victimization should in fact assume a hierarchically ordered system of values. The idea can be instantiated by constructing a hierarchy of needs, where the less basic needs may not be fulfilled unless the satisfaction of more basic needs is already guaranteed. For example, life, physical health, and the enjoyment of pleasurable experiences can be regarded as a set of hierarchically ordered needs, on the ground that pleasure cannot be experienced unless one is at least minimally healthy, and one cannot be healthy without being alive.

Hierarchical needs and the problem of paternalism

But although reference to hierarchical needs solves victimization problems such as the amphitheatre problem, the solution is not without its own difficulties. The most acute of these is the threat of illegitimately constraining paternalism.[30] Today's legislation and social policy already curtail individual liberty by regulations which are put forward by the authorities in the name of benefiting the individuals themselves. An axiology based on hierarchical needs would offer grounds for far more restrictive policies. If, for instance, epidemiological data unquestionably show that citizens shorten their lives by smoking, drinking, and keeping an unhealthy diet, the authorities following the need-utilitarian teaching would probably have to ban all these practices by legal restrictions. Prolongation of life would according to this view always take precedence over other types of need satisfaction. Yet most reasonable people would presumably shudder at the idea of such a totalitarian 'health state'.

The rigid paternalism implied by the need-utilitarian view can, in principle, be alleviated by an addition to the list of needs. Assuming that human beings need freedom and autonomy in order to flourish, an argument could be constructed to the effect that by restricting freedom in the name of furthering health the paternalistic authorities would in fact be setting two mutually dependent values against each other. This, according to the argument, would not be wise, since it is not, in the last analysis, possible to make people truly healthy against their own will.

The addition of autonomy to the list of needs does not, however, solve the problem. Whatever the relative statuses of health and freedom are, survival is without doubt the most basic need in the sense defined above. The risk of premature death always remains, therefore, a valid reason for restricting individual liberty.

In fact, the only way to amend the utilitarian theory seems to be through introducing the quasi-deontological considerations John Stuart Mill presented in *On Liberty*.[31] Mill divided human actions into the self-regarding and the other-regarding, claiming that only other-regarding actions can be justifiably restricted by law and public policy. Constraint which is intended to protect adult persons who are free, sane and knowledgeable from themselves is generally illegitimate, because it violates their right to self-determination. Following this lead, one could state that legislation and social policy should be aimed at maximizing need satisfaction, but only when the actions about to be regulated are other-regarding in some significant sense. This would remove from the classical utilitarian theory its inherent paternalism.

Anti-paternalism and the problem of just distribution

Mill's ideas concerning freedom mark the demarcation line between classical Benthamite teaching and what I call liberal utilitarianism. The utilitarians of the twentieth century have without exception developed their views in the 'classical' spirit, and quite understandably so, since respect for liberty for its own sake tends to undermine the basic utilitarian ideals. I am convinced, however, that the best alternative overall can in the end be found by assuming the liberal approach.

Mill presumably thought that individual freedom in the self-regarding sphere can be ultimately justified by an appeal to utility, or the maximization of happiness.[32] His argument was that liberty, self-assumed responsibility, freedom of thought and freedom of expression produce, in the long run, individuals who can form sound opinions and nations which have the ability to create effective economic systems. These factors then join to give rise to the greatest happiness of the greatest number.

Unfortunately, Mill's argument, which seems to rest on empirical claims and should therefore be open to factual verification and falsification, has never enjoyed the support of unequivocal statistical or historical data. As a matter of fact, the whole approach may be only quasi-empirical, in that Mill's seemingly factual statements may be based on ideology rather than concrete reality.

An alternative interpretation of Mill's liberalism rejects the burdensome empirical element, and states that individuals are entitled to autonomy and privacy regardless of the consequences of this entitlement and its applications. This approach, which centres upon the concept of a *right to liberty*, is deontological rather than consequentialist, but it is nonetheless deductible, with very few additional premises, from the basic principles of liberal utilitarianism. I have labelled this view *strict liberalism*.

Strict liberalism is certainly an anti-paternalistic doctrine which does not allow violations of individual liberty in the self-regarding sphere. Seen from the utilitarian viewpoint, however, the theory is problematical on another account. The difference between self-regarding actions and other-regarding actions is by no means clear, and the distinction must be defined separately within each competing view. In drawing this important line, strict liberals mostly employ traditional devices, such as the doctrine of acts and omissions, or the doctrine of the double effect. The practical corollary of applying these schemes is that strict liberals reject any notion of positive rights, or rights to be aided by others. Subsequently, they also reject legal and social duties to help people in distress, and scorn the idea of economic justice by the redistribution of wealth.

Although strict liberalism can be seen as a branch of liberal utilitarianism, the moral connection between the two theories is thin, and it would be a major mistake to suppose that the doctrines of Bentham and Mill can be best developed in this direction. The basic tenets of utilitarianism include the credo that all people (or all sentient beings) should be treated equally as regards their happiness (or pleasure or needs). This is certainly not the case within strict liberalism, which implies that property acquired in a 'fair' manner ought to remain in the control of those who presently possess it, regardless of the prevailing distribution of happiness and suffering. Besides, the traditional act-omission and direct-indirect distinctions are patently unsound. If one took them seriously, one should condemn only direct acts which inflict harm on other beings, condoning at the same time omissions and indirect acts which produce the same harmful consequences. Within the framework of consequentialism it is clear that such a view is both theoretically untenable and, if put into practice, dangerous.

Other-regarding behaviour hierarchically defined

Given that the Millian and strict liberal solutions have to be rejected either as counterintuitive or as counterproductive, the question of adequately defining self-regarding and other-regarding behaviour is left wide open. My own suggestion is that the idea of hierarchical needs should be employed once again. The definition would then state the following:

> Actions are other-regarding in the proper sense if they frustrate the need satisfaction of others at some level but are not aimed at the need satisfaction of the agent herself at a hierarchically more basic level.

Or, perhaps more illuminatingly, one could start from the other end by stating that:

> Actions are self-regarding in the proper sense if they do *not* frustrate the need satisfaction of others at any level or if they do, they are aimed at the need satisfaction of the agent herself at a hierarchically more basic level.

Assuming that self-regarding behaviour should always be condoned by law and social policy, as declared by Mill and other liberals, two things follow from the application of these definitions. First, in matters which concern only the happiness, welfare, pleasure or need satisfaction of the agents themselves, they should be left free to make their own decisions. Second, it would not be right to force or coerce people to sacrifice their own lives to save the lives of others, or to give up their own health to improve the health of others, or to forego pleasurable experiences to provide others with them.

As for other-regarding behaviour, it seems obvious that if no rectifying appeal to one's own more basic needs can be made, then the frustration of other people's needs at a relatively basic level clearly constitutes a harm which can be justifiably prevented by law. This formula applies both to 'normal' criminality[33] and to more exotic practices like civil disobedience, sabotage, terrorism, revolutionary action and warfare. It can also be employed to throw light on indirect and cumulative wrongdoing, such as obscene art and environmental crime. In the remainder of the article I shall say a few words about the application of liberal utilitarianism to some of these real-life legal, moral and socio-political issues.

Civil disobedience, sabotage, terrorism and warfare

Conflicts between social classes and between interest groups, as well as hostilities between nations, have generally been approached by deontological rather than consequentialist theoretical equipment in contemporary philosophy. No doubt those interested in the moral aspects of war and conflict have thought that the all-embracing solutions of classical utilitarianism are too insensitive or too crude to be employed. It is certainly true that rough-and-ready utility calculations have led nations to war, and interest groups to violent confrontation. But such utility calculations have little to do with Bentham's or Mill's ideas, and even less with the principles of liberal utilitarianism.

A direct application of the liberal utilitarian theory produces three tentative results in this field. First, nonviolent civil disobedience can easily be justified, since the need frustration inflicted on others by it is not too serious - almost any reason is good enough to legitimize peaceful demonstrations, voluntary hunger strikes, the disregard of racially or sexually discriminating laws, and the like. Second, sabotage and violent civil disobedience, when directed against property but not against persons, can be justified if a truthful appeal can be made to lives which are to be saved by these activities. The mere fact that people have conflicting views on certain basic points does not, however, justify the destruction of other people's property, although some theorists have suggested that it should.

Third, it is very difficult to state with confidence whether or not terrorism and warfare can ever be unequivocally justified. When both war and peace (or terrorism and conformity) lead to equal or unpredictable losses of life and liberty, the utilitarian principle as such does not provide straightforward moral directives. Under such circumstances, the liberal utilitarian doctrine does not legitimize violent action, but it does not justify inaction which condones violence, either. This is an area where the liberal utilitarian theory does not pretend to have ready-made answers. My own view is that no sound moral theory can pretend to have such answers. The thing to be noticed here is that liberal utilitarianism does not stand for strict universal pacifism any more than it stands for hard-boiled opportunistic militarism.

Art, censorship and morality

The application of my theory to the questions of art and censorship highlights its similarities and dissimilarities with the teachings of Bentham and Mill. One of the most important likenesses between the three is that no secular utilitarian theory recognizes the absolute validity of traditional values, or the 'sacredness' of doing things as they have previously been done. In the context of art, this means that works considered offensive by some (or even by the majority) should not be censored, at least not because of their offensiveness.

The most important departure of my theory from the main utilitarian line is my emphasis on the indirect and cumulative consequences of human behaviour. This feature of the theory can be exemplified by some remarks concerning the harmfulness of pornographic films. Although the offensiveness of pornography provides no valid argument for its abolition, it is possible that the gradual influence of pornographic works on the human (and especially male) psyche is harmful enough to justify censorship. On the other hand, of course, legal restrictions are not necessarily the most efficient tool for altering attitudes and ways of thinking. Education and social policy would probably prove to be better instruments for change in this area.[34]

Environmental crime and the limits of responsibility

But once the concept of indirect harm has been introduced into the discussion, better candidates for legal restrictions and moral condemnation than indecent art can be found. Large-scale negligence in environmental matters is a case in point. The ever-increasing production and consumption of energy in the West threatens to pollute irreversibly our natural environment, but since the process is relatively slow and inconspicuous, the responsibility does not seem to be attributable to anybody in particular. According to liberal utilitarianism, we are all responsible for the protection of the natural environment, and blamable for its cumulative and collective destruction.

There are, however, theorists who believe that people cannot be held morally responsible for their actions unless those actions are directly, visibly and deliberately harmful to others. Individual culpability, according to this doctrine, cannot be extended to collective wrongdoing where the efforts of one individual cannot by themselves change the final outcome. The main argument for this view is that if human obligations are extended too widely, people lose their sense of duty in immediate and personal situations, that is, in dealing with their families, friends and fellow patriots. In environmental matters the logic would be the following. If individuals are held responsible for the collective environmental crimes of humankind, they may feel that the situation is unfair, and reject the idea of individual responsibility altogether. The next step may then be that they do not recognize the wrongness of more conspicuous environmental criminality either, but happily condone, say, the dumping of toxic waste in the sea.

It is, of course, impossible to predict what the actual consequences would be, if people assumed an extended view concerning their responsibilities. The intuitive superiority of this solution over the narrow concept of obligation can, however, be elucidated by an example which has been drawn from the sphere of law.[35]

There was recently a controversial criminal case in Finland in which three young men were charged with violently attacking and seriously injuring an innocent passer-by in the heart of Helsinki. All three defendants claimed that they had been drunk at the time of the beating, and, consequently, could not remember who had initiated the attack, nor who had thrown the most fatal blows. The court found it impossible to determine who had actually inflicted the worst injuries, and acquitted all defendants, although it was clear that at least one of them was guilty of serious physical assault on the passer-by.

In the public discussion that followed the court's ruling, many people argued, justly I believe, that even if the verdict was legally sound, its moral correctness can be challenged. One line of argument is to say that anybody who does not intervene when an innocent person is under attack is partly responsible for the outcome of the assault. Another possibility is to argue that all those who take part in activities which foreseeably lead to physical damage to third parties should be made answerable for the consequences, at least to some extent. The point of both arguments is that although the law presumably must mainly operate with the concept of active, direct responsibility, moral judgements, in their turn, can - and sometimes must - be based on negative or indirect liability as well. This is probably the case when it comes to our environmental obligations.

Animals, trees and future generations

Granted that our natural environment ought to be protected, the question remains as to how far one should go in the direction of sacrificing one's immediate wishes for the sake of furthering nature-related values. Within liberal utilitarianism the answer depends on the axiological basis that is given to preservationist ideals.

Traditional Western ethics maintained that the value of nature is derivable from God's creation, and that nature should be protected to the degree that the Bible tells us to do so. This theocentric morality has now widely given way to anthropocentric ideas, which state that all value in the universe ultimately derives from the attitudes and preferences of humankind. According to this latter view, it would not be wrong to let the natural environment be destroyed unless the destruction led to marked unpleasantness in human terms.

The most extreme axiological view in today's environmental discussion is *biocentrism*, an ethical theory which emphasises the intrinsic value of all life-forms.[36] Biocentric ethicists state that the natural environment ought to be protected for its own sake - it is our duty to find out what constitutes a good life for trees, butterflies and mosquitoes, and then to treat them accordingly.

My own view is that the biocentric theory is ill-considered and its application leads to unnecessary paradoxes. Consider, for instance, Albert Schweitzer's 'dilemma'. He wondered if it is justifiable that he, the European doctor, vaccinates African natives and thereby saves their lives, when he at the same time terminates the lives of innumerable germs and viruses. Respect for life may be a good ideal, but its application must surely not be pressed this far.

It follows from these remarks that the needs which constitute the value foundation of liberal utilitarianism must be seen as subjective rather than objective needs. Otherwise the theory would not discriminate between the good of people and trees any more than the biocentric model differentiates between the worth of various life-forms. The liberal utilitarian theory must be based on needs which are capable of being perceived and possessed with due awareness by the beings who have them. Intrinsic value, in the model, is not to be attributed to the lives of plants or lower animals, but to the lives and experiences of human beings and other higher animals who either live now or will, we predict, live in the future.

Notes

1. Smart, 1961.
2. Brandt,1979.
3. Hare, 1981.
4. Singer, 1979.
5. Rawls, 1972.
6. Nozick, 1974.
7. All the theoretical themes discussed in this article have been analysed further in Häyry, 1994a.
8. Cumberland, 1672.
9. Hume, 1751.
10. Hutcheson, 1725.
11. Mill, 1829.
12. Brandt, 1979.
13. Berkeley, 1712.
14. Tucker, 1768-77.
15. Paley, 1785.
16. Stephen, 1873.
17. Bentham, 1789.
18. Mill, 1861.
19. Sidgwick, 1874.
20. Moore, 1903, p. 188.
21. Harsanyi, 1982.
22. Brandt, 1979.
23. Hare, 1981.
24. Häyry, 1994a.
25. An additional premise here is, of course, that the hedonistic standing of the *lions* will not be significantly altered by the decision.
26. Godwin, 1793.
27. Smart, 1987.
28. Mill, 1861.
29. Stephen, 1874.
30. Different forms of paternalism have been discussed in detail in Häyry, 1991.
31. Mill, 1859.
32. The opinions of Mill scholars are, however, divided on this point.
33. I have examined the liberal utilitarian responses to crime in Häyry, 1992.

34. These themes are discussed in more detail in Häyry and Häyry, 1995.
35. I have previously used this example in Häyry, 1994b, p. 2.
36. A solid defence of biocentric ethics can be found in Taylor, 1986.

References

Bentham, J. (1789), *An Introduction to the Principles of Morals and Legislation*, edited by Burns, J.H. and Hart, H. L. A., reprinted with new introduction, Methuen: London and New York, 1982.

Berkeley, G. (1712), 'Passive Obedience', reprinted from *The Works of George Berkeley Bishop of Cloyne*, vol. 6, edited by Luce, A. A. and Jessop, T. E., Thomas Nelson and Sons Ltd: London, 1953.

Brandt, R. B. (1979), *A Theory of the Good and the Right*, Clarendon Press: Oxford.

Cumberland, R. (1672), 'De Legibus Naturae', partly reprinted from Raphael, D.D. (ed.), *British Moralists 1650-1800 I. Hobbes-Gay*, Hackett Publishing Company: Indianapolis and Cambridge,1991a.

Godwin, W. (1793), *Enquiry Concerning Political Justice and its Influence on Modern Morals and Happiness*, third edition first published 1798, edited by Kramnick, I., Penguin Books: Harmondsworth, Middlesex, 1985.

Hare, R. M. (1981), *Moral Thinking: Its Levels, Method and Point*, Clarendon Press: Oxford.

Häyry, H. (1991), *The Limits of Medical Paternalism*, Routledge: London and New York.

Häyry H. and Häyry M. (1995), 'Artistic value as an excuse for spreading cinematographic filth', *The Journal of Value Inquiry* 29, pp. 469-93.

Häyry, M. (1992), 'A defence of the utilitarian theory of punishment', in Gragg, W. (ed.), *Retributivism and Its Critics*, Franz Steiner Verlag: Stuttgart.

Häyry, M. (1994a), *Liberal Utilitarianism and Applied Ethics*, Routledge: London and New York.

Häyry, M. (1994b), 'The negative and indirect global responsibility of philosophers', in *Philosophy Today* 16, reprinted from *Proceedings and Addresses of The American Philosophical Association* 67, 1994, pp. 69-70.

Harsanyi, J.C. (1982), 'Morality and the theory of rational behaviour', in Sen A. and Williams B. (eds), *Utilitarianism and Beyond*, Cambridge University Press: Cambridge.

Hume, D. (1751), *An Enquiry Concerning the Principles of Morals*, edited by Schneewind, J.B., Hackett Publishing Company: Indianapolis and C ambridge,1983.

Hutcheson, F. (1725), *An Inquiry into the Original of our Ideas of Beauty and Virtue*, Treatise II, partly reprinted from Raphael 1991a.

Mill, J. S. (1829), *Analysis of the Phenomena of the Human Mind*, London.

Mill, J. S. (1859), *On Liberty*, reprinted from Mill, J. S., *Three Essays*, edited by Wollheim R., Oxford University Press: Oxford and New York, 1975.

Mill, J. S. (1861), *Utilitarianism*, reprinted from Mill, J. S. and Bentham J., *Utilitarianism and Other Essays*, edited by Harmondsworth, A. R., Penguin Book: Middlesex, 1987.

Moore, G. E. (1903), *Principia Ethica,* Cambridge University Press: Cambridge.

Nozick, R. (1974), *Anarchy, State and Utopia,* Basil Blackwell: Oxford and New York.

Paley, W. (1785), *Principles of Moral and Political Philosophy*, partly reprinted from Raphael, D. D. (ed.), *British Moralists 1650-1800 II. Hume-Bentham,* Hackett Publishing Company: Indianapolis and Cambridge, 1991b.

Rawls, J. (1972), *A Theory of Justice.* Oxford University Press: Oxford.

Sidgwick, H. (1874), *The Methods of Ethics*, seventh edition first published 1907, Macmillan: London, 1922.

Singer, P. (1979), *Practical Ethics* Cambridge University Press: Cambridge.

Smart, J. J. C. (1961), *An Outline of a System of Utilitarian Ethics*, reprinted from Smart, J. J. C. and Williams, B., *Utilitarianism: For and Against,* Cambridge University Press: Cambridge, 1987.

Stephen, J. F. (1873), *Liberty, Equality, Fraternity*, second edition first published 1874, edited by White, R. J., Cambridge University Press: Cambridge, 1967.

Taylor, P. W. (1986), *Respect for Nature,* Princeton University Press: Princeton, New Jersey.

Tucker, A. (1768-77), *The Light of Nature Pursued*, edited by St. John Mildmay, H. P., London, 1805.

Kant and liberalism

Ruth Chadwick

Introduction

Commentators have found several difficulties with Kant's political philosophy, identifying tensions in his position on the French Revolution, disappointment regarding his position on women, and problems in making his sense of his interpretation of 'independence'. There are differences of opinion about the extent to which his political philosophy is to be explained by the principles of his moral philosophy, and about whether his work is susceptible of liberal or socialist interpretations. The tensions have been explained in various ways - one possibility is that Kant simply could not see beyond the conventions of his own time, and thus did not follow through his arguments to their own logical conclusions; a second is that he was cautious about what was feasible in the real world; a third, that his political philosophy is to be explained by the phenomenal-noumenal distinction running through his work.[1]

In Kant's discussion of property, for example, Howard Williams notes that for Kant ownership is to be distinguished from physical possession. Property is a noumenon and not a phenomenon. The question then arises as to how private ownership can be grounded. Taking a view opposed to that of Locke, Kant argues that it depends on the prior consent of all. In the actual world, however, for property to become an empirical reality coercion is likely to be necessary.[2] Kant says, for example, in *Theory and Practice:*

> ... we leave aside the question of how anyone can have rightfully acquired more land than he can cultivate with his own hands... and how it came about that numerous people who might otherwise have acquired permanent property were thereby reduced to serving someone else in order to live at all.[3]

The origin of property from a moral point of view must be distinguished from the actual establishment of private property in the empirical world. The use of coercion depends on the notion of a universal will sanctioning it, as an a priori idea of pure practical reason. Says Williams, 'He sanctions the use of force because property-holding is the basis of civil society, and he cannot conceive of a genuinely human society which is not a *burgerliche Gesellschaft*'.[4]

Susan Mendus does not think that Kant's political philosophy can be explained by seeing him as an apologist for bourgeois society, but identifies a discrepancy between the moral philosophy, where Kant supports the view that all rational beings are to be regarded as ends in themselves, and his views on women in the political philosophy, where women are excluded from active citizenship.[5] For Mendus the tensions in this particular area of the political philosophy arise not simply from pure prejudice but from the *logic* of the individualism to which he subscribes. The core of these views, she argues, is to be found in the discussion of marriage, where the reciprocity between husband and wife in the sexual relationship is not translated into equality. The wife is to be subject to the husband and thus gain her true freedom. Mendus says that the dilemma is thrown up by individualism itself, which dictates, as a central tenet, that '*someone* must dominate, *someone* must give way'.[6] This is the only way an atomistic view can cope with social units.

For Lewis White Beck[7], writing about the tensions in Kant's views on the right to revolution, the explanation is to be found, not so much in a cautious approach to the political circumstances in which he found himself, as in the formalism which we do indeed find in the moral philosophy. Frederick II, who ruled Prussia from 1740 to 1786, regarded himself as an enlightened ruler, and Kant praised this quality highly in Frederick but, as Sullivan comments, 'did not overestimate Frederick's capacity for tolerance'.[8] Kant's opposition to revolution however did not arise out of sensitivity to the limits of Frederick's tolerance but rested on a point about contradiction:

> ... before such resistance could be authorised, there would have to be a public law which permitted the people to offer resistance: in other words, the supreme legislation would have to contain a provision to the effect that it is not supreme, so that in one and the same judgement, the people as subjects would be made sovereign over the individual to whom they are subject. This is self-contradictory, and the contradiction is at once obvious if we ask who would act as judge in this dispute between the people and the sovereign.[9]

On the other hand, Kant had a teleological view of history, which enabled him to distinguish between revolutions towards the better and towards the worse. The *reaction* of onlookers towards the French Revolution, rather than the action of the revolutionaries themselves, is cited as evidence for that fact that

> man has a moral character, or at least the makings of one. And this does not merely allow us to hope for human improvement; it is already a form of improvement in itself.[10]

The ideal constitution, according to Kant, was republican, but to revolt to achieve it was not permissible. A constitution cannot contain within itself the grounds of its own destruction, and the actions of revolutionaries are inconsistent with the maxim of publicity. Comparing Kant with Hegel, Beck identifies Kant's problems as the inability to resolve the conflict of duties satisfactorily. The formalistic adherence to obedience to those in power, he says, always wins over our duty to improve the lot of mankind. But, Beck says, 'Both obligations are rational and natural, and it takes deep moral and historical insight to adjudicate their conflict'.[11]

Some have argued that the contradictions in his work allow for a Marxist interpretation, although Marx and Engels were fairly scathing about Kant's willingness to settle for good will:

> The state of affairs in Germany at the end of the last century is fully reflected in Kant's *Kritik der praktischen Vernunft*. While the French bourgeoisie, by means of the most colossal revolution that history has ever known, was achieving domination and conquering the Continent of Europe, while the already politically emancipated English bourgeoisie was revolutionizing industry and subjugating India politically, and all the rest of the world commercially, the impotent German burghers did not get any further than 'good will'. Kant was satisfied with 'good will' alone, even if it remained entirely without result, and he transferred the *realization* of this good will, the harmony between it and the needs and impulses of individuals, to *the world beyond*. Kant's good will fully corresponds to the impotence, depression and wretchedness of the German burghers, whose petty interests were never capable of developing into the common, national interests of a class and who were, therefore, constantly exploited by the bourgeois of other nations.[12]

Howard Williams, on the other hand, considers the possibility that Kant's political thinking is 'too much tinged by absolutism' to be placed in the same class as liberal thinkers such as Mill and Hobhouse, but argues that his thought has to be viewed in the German context - as identified by Marx and Engels - and does not doubt Kant's claim to be a key liberal thinker *in Germany*.[13]

It is the aim of this article to explore those aspects of Kant's work which establish his credentials as a liberal, with particular reference to his discussion of freedom, equality and independence, but first there is a preliminary clarification to be made about what counts as liberalism.

Liberalism

The lack of agreement over what counts as 'liberalism' constitutes an initial difficulty. As Stephen Mulhall and Adam Swift point out in the preface to their book, *Liberals and Communitarians*, 'one theorist's reasons for his belief in the right to freedom of expression may be quite different from another's, or two theorists both regarding themselves as liberals may have quite different conceptions of, for example, something apparently so central as autonomy or the proper relation between the state and the individual'.[14] They hold, however, that 'it may be possible to recognise as constitutive of liberalism a commitment to a vague and general value such as the freedom or autonomy of the individual, and to relate this to the substantive political concern that individuals should have freedom of conscience, of expression and association'.[15]

Roger Sullivan recognises the diversity of liberalism but suggests that Kant made a significant contribution to classical liberalism through his opposition to the 'old despotisms' and through his support of the characteristics of liberalism identified by Gray: individualism, egalitarianism, universalism and meliorism.[16] Howard Williams, in *Kant's Political Philosophy*, follows Manning's account of liberalism as involving 'three elements of consistency' in its symbolic form: belief in the rule of law, the undesirability of coercion and belief in progress.[17]

Kant supported the rule of law and founded this on an original contract. W. H. Walsh identifies some tensions in his position here, however:

> he attempts to explain political authority partly in terms of the general will and partly in terms of the original contract. Insofar as he insists on the contract... he is advocating a version of political liberalism which lays particular emphasis on the rule of law; insofar as he grounds supreme political authority in the will of the people as a whole, he is obviously flirting with more radical doctrines.[18]

The original contract however is not regarded as being historically based, but this is irrelevant. It is a regulative idea. Sullivan in fact regards Kant's most significant contribution to the development of classical liberal theory as his claim that the justification of the state ultimately rests on moral grounds.[19]

There is coercion in Kant's commonwealth but this is reciprocal coercion 'which is necessarily consonant with the principle of universal freedom'.[20] The head of state alone has the authority to coerce others 'without being subject to any coercive law himself'.[21] This is necessary to preserve the commonwealth and thereby promote freedom and autonomy.

Allusion has already been made to the belief in progress, as discussed in *The Contest of Faculties* and which is in accordance with Kant's teleological view of history. In *Theory and Practice he says:*

> ... the human race is constantly progressing in cultural matters (in keeping with its natural purpose), it is also engaged in progressive improvement in relation to the moral end of its existence. This progress may at times be *interrupted* but never *broken off*.[22]

A defining feature of liberalism is sometimes described as neutrality towards ideas of the good life - linked with a concept of freedom as freedom to pursue the individual's view of the good. A belief in progress, partly connected with the freedom to pursue ideas, freedom to experiment and freedom of expression, goes along with this. There are thus several criteria on which we may assess Kant as a liberal: neutrality towards the good, autonomy, freedom of the individual. His position on equality will also be relevant. Gray, for example, identifies the egalitarianism of liberalism as lying in its conferring equality in moral status.[23] It will be found, however, that it is Kant's discussion of independence that is most revealing.

Neutrality and autonomy

Kant does appear to adopt a neutral position towards views of the good life. He says the

> *first* consideration lies precisely in that legal constitution which guarantees everyone his freedom within the law, so that each remains free to seek his happiness in whatever way he thinks best, so long as he does not violate the lawful freedom and rights of his fellow subjects at large.[24]

Just as the moral law is derived from the autonomous rational being and not imposed by any authority, so in political philosophy Kant adopts the liberal position that individuals should be free to pursue their own conception of the good. He claims in *On the Common Saying: This may be true in Theory, but it does not apply in Practice* that

> Man's *freedom* as a human being, as a principle for the constitution of a commonwealth, can be expressed in the following formula. No-one can compel me to be happy in accordance with his conception of the welfare of others, for each may seek his happiness in whatever way he sees fit, so long as he does not infringe upon the freedom of others to pursue a similar end.[25]

Kant utterly rejects paternalism, both in morality and politics. Paternalism keeps the subjects in the position of 'immature children' and is 'the greatest conceivable despotism'.[26] In *What is Enlightenment*? Kant defined Enlightenment as 'man's emergence from his self-incurred immaturity'.[27] Rational beings, having the capacity for autonomy, should have the courage to use their own understanding.

Equality

The autonomy of rational beings grounds a moral equality in so far as they are all ends in themselves. Richard Lindley has argued in fact that this was Kant's most important contribution to liberal theory - the principle of equal respect for individuals, based on their possession of a will.[28] In the political philosophy, however, Kant does not explicitly ground political equality on the equality of rational beings as ends in themselves but speaks instead of members of the commonwealth. Their equality consists, as outlined above, in 'rights of coercion in relation to all the others, except in relation to the head of state'.[29] This is an interpretation of equality before the law, as discussed above.

Kant goes on, however, to discuss the permissible forms of *in*equality in society. He does not see that there is necessarily a problem about material inequality:

> This uniform equality of human beings as subjects of a state is, however, perfectly consistent with the utmost inequality of the mass in the degree of its possessions[30]

and broadens this out to a point about personal attributes

> ... whether these take the form of physical or mental superiority over others, or of fortuitous external property and of particular rights.[31]

He gives particular examples of the poor depending on the rich, the child being bound to obey its parents and the wife her husband; the labourer serving the one who pays for his services.

Kant also has a conception of equality of opportunity, as commonly found in the liberal interpretations of equality:

> there emerges this further formula: every member of the commonwealth must be entitled to reach any degree of rank which a subject can earn through his talent, his industry and his good fortune.[32]

This line of thought, associated with a liberal theory of justice in accordance with merit or desert, leads Kant to distance himself from hereditary privilege, for 'birth is not an action on the part of the one who is born'.[33] Even this is qualified, however, to the effect that the opposition to hereditary privilege is confined to rank and not wealth. Those who do not achieve fortunate social and material status may accept this provided that they are aware that the fault lies in themselves.

This aspect of Kant's thought, which may sound rather harsh, expresses a linkage between autonomy, respect for persons, and the idea of 'just deserts'. As Tom Campbell points out, 'respect for agents also involves evaluating the choices and actions to which the exercise of agency capacities give rise'.[34] Kant on the one hand, however, appears to recognise there may be circumstances in which the need to survive undermines the capacity for choice, while on the other hand wanting to maintain a view of the individual as responsible for his fate.

Independence

It is Kant's discussion of independence that is the most interesting and the most troubling of the trio of freedom, equality and independence, partly because of the problems in making sense of it, and partly because of its implications for where Kant's political sympathies lay. Independence is concerned with who has the right to make law, rather than equality before the law. It cannot be that an individual will can legislate for another - this would be at variance with both moral autonomy and political freedom. What is required is unity in the will of all members.

> And the prerequisite for unity, since it necessitates a general vote (if freedom and equality are both present), is independence. The basic law, which can come only from the general, united will of the people, is called the *original contract*.[35]

It appears, however, that the right to vote on the legislation is not open to everyone, but only to citizens:

> The only qualification required by a citizen (apart, of course, from being an adult male) is that he must be his *own master (sui juris)*, and must have some *property* (which can include any skill, trade, fine art or science) to support himself.[36]

The words in the first parenthesis 'apart, of course, from being an adult male' have far-reaching implications. As Mendus points out, whereas males seem to have the possibility, given equality of opportunity and effort on their part, to rise from the status of dependency to independence, women seem permanently barred from this.[37] For present purposes I shall not pursue this particular topic, however. What I am concerned with are the criteria, apart from gender, which distinguish independence from dependence.

Kant proceeds to make a distinction that has puzzled commentators, between different categories of ways of earning a living.

> In cases where he must earn his living from others, he must earn it only by *selling* that which is his, and not by allowing others to make use of him.[38]

As an example, Kant contrasts the barber and the wigmaker; distinguishes the labourer from the artist or tradesman. Whereas the former allows someone to make use of him, the latter does a piece of work which belongs to him until he is paid for it, and *exchanges* property with the person who commissions the work.

Kant's reasoning here is obscure and he himself says it is 'somewhat difficult' to define precisely what entitles someone to claim to be his own master. Interestingly, barbering seems to be a popular example in political philosophy. Robert Nozick uses it to reply to Bernard Williams' position on equality. Nozick's view of barbering sees no contradiction between barbering and a fairly high degree of autonomy. Nozick speaks of a barber choosing to allocate his services where he will:

> If someone becomes a barber because he likes talking to a variety of different people, and so on, is it unjust of him to allocate his services to those he most likes to talk to? Or if he works as a barber in order to pay tuition at school, may he cut the hair of only those who pay or tip well? Why may not a barber use exactly the same criteria in allocating his services as someone else whose activities have no internal goal involving others?[39]

This reads rather differently from the picture of the barber as allowing himself to be used. There are clear echoes in Kant here of the position he takes in his moral philosophy concerning allowing oneself to be used as a means and concerning selling parts of the body. Kant takes a very strong line on the use of the body - prostitution, for example, is a breach of one's duty to oneself, but also to sell part of the body, even a single finger, for money, is ruled out on his view. We are entitled to sell what is ours, but my body is not mine, it is me.[40] To think otherwise is to involve oneself in the contradiction of regarding oneself at the same time as both subject and object.[41]

One objection that is commonly raised against the 'allowing oneself to be used' argument of Kant's is that it is difficult to draw a sharp line between selling one's physical labour on the one hand, and selling one's body, as in prostitution (or surrogate motherhood), or part of it, as an organ. Kant's position as expounded in *Theory and Practice* makes it clear that he would have been unlikely to be moved by such an argument. The analogy between the two does not help the seller of the body; it worsens the case of the physical labourer, whom Kant is disposed to regard as allowing himself to be treated as a means.

As a contrast to the point made about Nozick and barbering above, Howard Williams points out that to suppose that the tradesman is not 'used' is stretching the point - there seems nothing at all odd about employing the language of 'use' in this context.[42] Williams takes the view that what Kant wants to rule out is exploitation. An argument that exploitation and independence are incompatible would make sense. The question then arises, however, as to whether to be free of exploitation is a sufficient or only a necessary condition of being independent, and whether it is sufficient to be *de facto* free of exploitation of whether the structure of one's position must be such that it is necessarily free of the possibility of exploitation.

It is not clear, however, that Kant has room for a concept of exploitation. The whole emphasis is on how one acts with regard to oneself - *allowing* oneself to be used. In the *Doctrine of Virtue* he says 'Be no man's lackey'.[43] This is true both in the discussion of selling the body and its parts, where nothing is said about the morality of the purchaser; and it is true in the discussion of the barber versus the wigmaker. There is no suggestion that the man who uses the services of a barber is in a position to exploit him. Hence the emphasis on the individual being happy with his condition so long as he is aware that the fault lies within himself. The stress on equality of opportunity does not go along with support for any action to bring about social change. He wants to leave it 'exclusively to the ability, industry and good fortune of each member of the commonwealth'.[44]

I have argued elsewhere that Kant's position on selling bodily parts depends ultimately on a view about what is intrinsically degrading.[45] Analogously here it seems that the position put forward, which Kant himself admits is difficult to sustain by argument, depends finally on a view about what ways of living are suitable to a 'free man' - the examples he gives are, as we have seen, open to widely different interpretations. This is, of course, not unknown elsewhere in the liberal tradition. The whole notion of the 'liberal professions', notable in the British liberal tradition in particular, depends on a view about what is appropriate to a free man, with its emphasis on professional autonomy, fee for services rather than wage earning; association with values and an ideal of service rather than simply being competence-based.

Kant's distinction is however interestingly different from the liberal professions tradition. In the latter, a distinction is drawn between a profession and a trade. Being a wigmaker was not among the liberal professions of medicine, the church and the law. Kant's distinction appears to depend on being able to withhold: he 'does a piece of work which belongs to him until he is paid for it'. Property is absolutely central to the argument. This is what enables him to avoid being used - he can presumably sell the wig elsewhere if the customer does not produce the money to facilitate the transfer of property, even though, as Kant admits, the 'customer' may in fact have given the requisite hair. The barber on the other hand cannot take back the haircut.

What about Kant's own profession, viz. the life of the scholar? How might that fit? It is not immediately apparent how it might be dealt with in Kant's terms as in *Theory and Practice*. Consideration of this particular point takes us away from consideration of the criteria addressed there, such as being one's own master and the ability to retain property, towards claims about intrinsic values. In the *Lectures on Ethics* he speaks about it without referring to the criterion of independence, but calls on other values:

> Other occupations concern themselves with physical things, which are merely means to human life, but the scholar's main preoccupation is the acquisition of knowledge. This would seem to constitute an intrinsic difference, a real difference of value.[46]

Belief in the superiority of the philosophical life has, of course, a long history among philosophers. Kant is compelled however to consider Rousseau's counter-argument, however, that scholars actually pervert the end of humanity. Kant concludes that scholars as a class promote the end of humanity but that no single member of the class can claim this, and adds that 'after all, an artisan adds his quota to the world's welfare just as much as the scholar... all men are equal, and only he who has superior morality has superior intrinsic worth'.[47]

Conclusion

Consideration of Kant's political philosophy has revealed some characteristics that are distinctively liberal, such as belief in autonomy and the freedom of the individual, equality of opportunity, belief in progress, neutrality towards ideas of the good. There are some strong elements of conservatism however, such as the refusal to countenance revolution, and the denial of equality of opportunity to women. It is difficult to find evidence of sympathies of a socialist sort in Kant. Despite his recognition that some people may have little choice about what they need to do in order to survive, the basis for seeing concerns about exploitation in his work is not as strong as some commentators might wish, in the light of the very strong line of thought about individuals being responsible for 'allowing themselves' to be used. He says:

> ... can be considered happy in any condition so long as he is aware that, if he does not reach the same level as others, the fault lies either with himself (i.e. lack of ability or serious endeavour) or with circumstances for which he cannot blame others, and not with the irresistible will of any outside party. For as far as right is concerned, his fellow-subjects have no advantage over him.[48]

There is no support for social action to bring about change, except through argument.

As regards the explanation of the tensions in Kant's work, some of them do appear to be susceptible of explanation by the phenomenon-noumenon distinction, such as his views on property, but the discussion of independence suggests that he does ultimately fall back on views about what is intrinsically valuable, and what is 'fitting' to a 'free *man*'. In this, as in his emphasis on placing responsibility with the individual, his work is not at variance with his moral philosophy, which likewise makes the duty to oneself prior, and relies on a notion of what is intrinsically degrading to, or supportive of, human dignity. The most telling aspect of Kant's liberalism is the ultimate belief in autonomy and not only the possibility but also the necessity of individual choice, along with which we find individual responsibility.

Notes

1. See Mendus, 1992.
2. Williams, 1992.
3. Kant, 1970b, p. 78.
4. Williams, 1992, p. 396.
5. Mendus, 1992.
6. Ibid., p. 386.
7. Beck, 1992.
8. Sullivan, 1989, p. 233.
9. Kant, 1970d, p. 145.
10. Kant, 1970c, p. 182.
11. Beck, 1992, pp. 407-8.
12. Marx and Engels, 1992, p. 226.
13. Williams, 1983, p. 127.
14. Mulhall and Swift,1992.
15. Ibid.
16. Sullivan, 1989, p. 234.
17. Williams, 1983, pp. 125-6.
18. Walsh, 1967, p. 322.
19. Sullivan, 1989, p. 240.
20. Kant, 1970d, p. 135.
21. Ibid., p. 75.
22. Ibid., p. 88.
23. Gray, 1986.
24. Kant, 1970b, p. 80.
25. Ibid., p. 74.
26. Ibid.
27. Kant, 1970a, p. 54.
28. Lindley, 1986.
29. Kant, 1970a.
30. Kant, 1970b, p. 75.
31. Ibid.
32. Ibid.
33. Ibid., p. 76.
34. Campbell, 1988, p. 156.
35. Kant, 1970b, p. 77.

36. Ibid., p. 78.
37. Mendus, 1992.
38. Kant, 1970b, p. 78.
39. Nozick, 1974, p. 234.
40. Cf. Chadwick, 1991.
41. Kant, 1963, p. 165.
42. Williams, 1983, p. 146.
43. Kant, 1964, p. 101.
44. Kant, 1970b, p. 78.
45. Chadwick, 1991.
46. Kant, 1963, p. 242.
47. Ibid., p. 243.
48. Kant, 1970b, p. 77.

References

Beck, L. W. (1992),'Kant and the right of revolution', in Chadwick, R. F. (ed.), *Immanuel Kant: Critical Assessments,* vol. III: *Kant's Moral and Political Philosophy,* Routledge: London.

Campbell, T. (1988), *Justice,* Macmillan: Houndmills.

Chadwick, R. F. (1991),'The Market for Bodily Parts: Kant and duties to oneself', in Almond B. and Hill D. (eds), *Applied Philosophy: Morals and Metaphysics in Contemporary Debate,* Routledge: London.

Gray, J. (1986), *Liberalism,* University of Minnesota Press: Minneapolis.

Kant, I. (1963), *Lectures on Ethics,* translated by Louis Enfield, Harper & Row: New York.

Kant, I. (1964), *The Doctrine of Virtue,* translated by Mary J. Gregor, University of Pennsylvania Press: Philadelphia.

Kant, I. (1970a) "An Answer to the Question: 'What is Enlightenment?'", in Reiss, H. (ed.), *Kant's Political Writings,* Cambridge University Press: Cambridge.

Kant, I (1970b), "On the Common Saying: 'This May be True in Theory, but it does not Apply in Practice'", in Reiss, H. (ed.), *Kant's Political Writings,* Cambridge University Press: Cambridge.

Kant, I. (1970c), 'The Metaphysics of Morals', in Reiss, H. (ed.), *Kant's Political Writings,* Cambridge University Press: Cambridge.

Kant, I. (1970d), 'The Contest of Faculties', in Reiss, H. (ed.), *Kant's Political Writings,* Cambridge University Press: Cambridge.

Lindley, R. (1986), *Autonomy,* Macmillan: Houndmills.

Marx, K. and Engels, F. (1992), 'Political liberalism', translated by Dutt, C., reprinted from R. F. Chadwick (ed.), *Kant: Critical Assessments,* vol. I: *Kant Criticism from his Own to the Present Time,* Routledge: London.

Mendus, S. (1992), 'Kant: An Honest but Narrow-Minded Bourgeois?' in Chadwick, R. F. (ed.), *Immanuel Kant: Critical Assessments*, vol. III : *Kant's Moral and Political Philosophy*, Routledge: London.

Mulhall, S. and Swift, A. (1992), *Liberals and Communitarians*, Blackwell: Oxford.

Nozick, R. (1974), *Anarchy, State and Utopia*, Blackwell: Oxford.

Sullivan, R. J. (1989), *Immanuel Kant's Moral Theory*, Cambridge University Press: Cambridge.

Walsh, W. H. (1967), 'Kant' in P. Edwards (ed.), *Encyclopedia of Philosophy*, Macmillan: New York.

Williams, H. (1983), *Kant's Political Philosophy*, Blackwell: Oxford.

Williams, H. (1992), 'Kant's concept of property', in Chadwick, R. F. (ed.), *Immanuel Kant: Critical Assessments*, vol. III : *Kant's Moral and Political Philosophy*, Routledge: London.

Hume on the laws of nations and the relaxation of rulers' morality

Arto Siitonen

Introduction

In Section xi of Part II of the third book of his *Treatise of Human Nature*, David Hume shortly addresses himself to the problems of international justice. The Section is titled 'Of the laws of nations'. Part II consists of twelve sections, its title being 'Of Justice and Injustice'. It is the largest part of Book III ('Of Morals') of the *Treatise*. The other two parts of this book concern themselves with virtues and vices. It is in this virtuous context that Hume presents a large theory of justice.

The study of the laws of nations could be the peak of Hume's theory of justice. However, there is still one section in Part II, viz. 'Of chastity and modesty'. This is an addition written by Hume in order to remove all scruples that may be left in respect to his 'system concerning the laws of nature and nations' (sect. xii, p. 330).[1]

Some difficulties are indeed connected with Hume's system. He has a rather controversial view on the liberty of rulers and states as to transgressing justice. In Section ix, Hume makes two claims concerning the morals of the rulers: (1) There are two different species of morality, incommensurable as to their standards, one for the citizens and the other one for their governors. (2) It is not possible to determine exactly the relation between these two species of morality. Let me call the principle which Hume is defending 'a cynical maxim'. According to it, the princes and ministers are more often allowed violations of justice, and for more trivial motives, than private persons.

One may wonder whether Hume does present his maxim as a description of facts or also as a normative claim. He does not clearly distinguish between the dimensions of national and international politics, and one may ask what is the relation of his maxim to the principle of *raison d'etat*.

In respect to Hume's views, one may present the following questions, two of them systematical, the rest historical: Are Hume's claims correct? Are Hume's arguments acceptable? How far is Hume's reasoning in accordance with the

Machiavellian spirit? Has Hume's view been rendered obsolete through the developments in international politics, economy, technology, as well as through the emergence of global problems and of new critical social and political consciousness? Or has it rather been reconfirmed in the present world?

1. The 'Shocking Proposition'

Section xi of Part II of the *Treatise* is preceded by a section (vii) on the origin of government plus three sections concerning allegiance (of its sources, of its measures, and of its objects). Part II begins with reflections on justice, property and promises.

Hume wrote his *Treatise* in a time when the centuries old monarchy was still strong but was already being constrained by the rule of law. Thus he could claim that 'the three fundamental rules of justice, the stability of possession, its transference by consent, and the performance of promises, are duties of princes as well as of subjects'. (sect. xi, p. 328 f). He introduces his idea of two moralities in connection with the duties which neighbouring states bear to each other. Although nations resemble individuals in certain respects, their mutual relations are regulated by different maxims and rules than the relations between individuals, Hume claims. Nations may and must cooperate, but they may also have discord and even go to war against each other. There are rules concerning diplomacy, commerce and warfare (e.g. declaration of war, abstaining from poisoned arms), which are respected by civilized states.

Hume thinks that the principles of international law are extensions of the notion of justice which regulates the relations between individuals. Correspondingly as the common interest of maintaining peace in society brings individuals under the rule of government, the shared interest of peace, commerce and mutual succour compel nations to look for assistance from each other. However, the extended application of the principles of justice means a weakening thereof and leads to a relaxation of morality. Hume's words in this connection are the following:

> There is a maxim very current in the world, which few politicians are willing to avow, but which has been authoriz'd by the practice of all ages, *that there is a system of morals calculated for princes, much more free than that which ought to govern private persons.* 'Tis evident this is not to be understood of the lesser *extent* of public duties and obligations; nor will any one be so extravagant as to assert, that the most solemn treaties ought to have no force among princes. For as princes do actually form treaties among themselves, they must propose some advantage from the execution of them; and the prospect of such advantage for the future must engage them to perform their part, and must establish that law of nature. The meaning, therefore, of this political maxim is, that tho' the morality of princes has the same *extent*, yet it

> has not the same *force* as that of private persons, and may lawfully be transgressed from a more trivial motive. (Sect. xi, p. 329).

Hume refers to this maxim as 'a shocking proposition'. Under the concept of proposition he may be supposed to understand that part of the text which is underlined by him, or also the part of his text where he explains the meaning of the maxim. Whether extent or force, it is clear that there are two moralities, dictating different kinds of standards by which to evaluate the violations of justice:

> *M1*: *Standard 1* concerning a transgression of justice in the private commerce of one subject with another.
>
> *M2*: *Standard 2* concerning a transgression of justice among princes and republics.

As to the defensibility of the maxim, Hume says:

> However shocking such a proposition may appear to certain philosophers, 'twill be easy to defend it upon those principles, by which we have accounted for the origin of justice and equity. (Sect. xi, p. 329).

Easy to defend? This is doubtful, because despite Hume's explications, it is not even clear at the outset what exactly is the difference between the moralities thus introduced, and what actually is the content of the rulers' morals. To the former question, Hume tries to answer as follows:

> Shou'd it be asked, what proportion these two species of morality bear to each other? I wou'd answer, that this is a question, to which we can never give any precise answer; nor is it possible to reduce to numbers the proportion, which we ought to fix between them. (Sect. xi, p. 330).

Here again Hume takes recourse to the practice: 'The practice of the world goes further in teaching us the degrees of our duty, than the most subtile philosophy which was ever yet invented' (Ibid) Well, but a representative of subtile philosophy is puzzled by the obscurity of this message.

Why is the difference between the two moralities supposed by Hume to be so shocking to most politicians and to certain philosophers? And who would these philosophers be? Presumably he is thinking of those speculative idealists whom he attacks in so many pages of his *Treatise*. These are thinkers who do not take human nature into proper account. To the most innocent ones of them, Hume's proposition may well have or might have been conceived a shocking message. For politicians, on the other hand, this whole topic is annoying because it has an unpopular air.

In discussing Hume's view on the laws of nations, it may be difficult to keep the systematic problem of morality separated from the historical contingencies of eighteenth century Britain. To the background of the systematic problem belongs the difference between justice as established within the boundaries of a civil state and justice as to be constructed in order to regulate the relations between such states. To this problem belong also the relations between governors and their subjects and the relations between governors and governors, as well as the relations between the states which the governors represent. In order to give a modern reading to the problem, we have to substitute Hume's 'princes' by: the prime minister and her/his cabinet, plus the members of parliament - and in respect to such countries as the present USA also the president. This manoeuvre brings in new contingencies, but anyhow we must read Hume's text from the point of view of the modern world, not only as a document of the peculiarities of his time. Let us then proceed to a scrutiny of his arguments.

2. On Hume's arguments in favour of the proposition

Hume has to explain why rulers obey the same laws of justice as their subjects and why there are nevertheless cases in which violation of justice should be judged differently when committed by a ruler than when done by a private citizen. According to Hume, there are two kinds of obligation to justice, viz. natural and moral, the former being the foundation of the latter. The natural obligation is given by the interest to maintain society. There are actions which tend to the peace of society, and there are other actions tending to its disturbance. The former are praiseworthy, the latter to be blamed. This is uniformly the case within kingdoms as well as in respect to their mutual relations. Thus 'a prince, who voluntarily, and of his own accord, breaks his word, or violates any treaty' (sect. xi, p. 329 f) is to be disapproved.

After these considerations comes the but-clause. For individuals, it is advantageous and necessary to have intercourse with other individuals; human nature would not subsist otherwise. Hume means here the whole social net which connects individual persons and protects them. But for different states, the intercourse is neither so necessary nor so advantageous as that among individuals. This weakens the natural obligation to justice among states. Therefore, the moral obligation, arising from the natural one, 'must partake of its weakness' (sect. xi, p. 330). Hume's conclusion is that we have to allow a privileged status to a prince or minister who deceives another in comparison to a private gentleman who acts correspondingly.

This sounds rather fantastic. A prince should not voluntarily break his word, but if he does it, he is not to be blamed as strongly as a private gentleman - provided that the word was given to another prince. The structure of Hume's argument is the following:

1. Moral obligations rest on natural obligations.
2. The natural obligation to justice is binding to individuals as well as to states.
3. The intercourse between individuals is advantageous and necessary to each one of them.
4. The intercourse between states is advantageous and sometimes necessary to each one of them.
5. In comparison to the intercourse between individuals, that between states is less necessary and advantageous.
6. Therefore, the natural obligation to justice among different states is not as strong as among individuals.
7. Therefore, the moral obligation to justice is weaker among states than among individuals.

---

8. Accordingly, the rulers are not to be blamed on deceiving other rulers as strongly as individual citizens on deceiving other citizens.

Just what is the extent of this extra liberty to deception admitted to rulers, Hume does not specify. Neither does he deliver strategic or tactical considerations on the geographic details and military potentials of different states. Presumably, a ruler of a large and strong country would allow her/himself more liberties in this respect than rulers of small or weak countries.

At the end of the section, Hume repeats his reasoning in a somewhat different fashion. According to him, the moral rules concerning natural and civil justice arise from conventions and from the interest in the preservation of peace and order. This explains why the diminution of the interest produces 'a relaxation of the morality' (sect. xi, p. 330). Made explicit, the argument runs as follows:

1. Human beings have a strong interest in maintaining peace and order in their mutual relations.
2. States have a strong interest in maintaining peace and order in their mutual relations.
3. In comparison to the interest of individuals, the interest of states in maintaining peace and order is weaker.
4. Interests are natural obligations to justice.
5. Moral obligations rest on natural obligations.

---

6. Thus, the princes and republics are more easily allowed to transgress justice than individuals.

Should be allowed or are in fact allowed? Due to Hume's appeal to 'the practice of all ages', it seems that the conclusions of Hume's arguments are rather to be interpreted as reports of what is the case than as requirements. It is in accordance with this consideration that the conclusion in the reconstructed argument has been given a fact-stating air above. However, this construal is not so unproblematical in respect to the conclusion of the first-mentioned argument. In the reconstructed fashion, it says: 'are not to be blamed' (cf. above). This should capture the mode of Hume's actual text in this connection. Hume says as follows: '... we must necessarily give a greater indulgence to a prince or minister, who deceives another; than to a private gentleman, who breaks his word of honour' (Sect. xi, p. 330). Whether this is factual or normative, depends on the meaning of the words 'must necessarily give'. They may mean that the prince or minister has a right to deceptive behaviour - that he should be allowed to deceive another prince or another state's minister. Or they may convey the following meaning: if we accept the premises, we must abstain from criticizing such behaviour of the rulers which we would think unbearable if attributed to private citizens.

If the latter interpretation is chosen, Hume's theory of international law fits coherently together with the main bulk of the book - which is concerned with human nature. According to Hume's theory of knowledge, an appeal to custom does not justify but psychologically explains our practices of inductive reasoning and of associatively connecting occurrences into chains of causes and effects. Correspondingly, the well established practice does not justify but makes it understandable that something is allowed rulers that is prohibited otherwise.

The fourth premise of the second argument stems from Section ii of Part II ('Of the origin of justice and property'), where the concept of interest is defined by Hume as 'the *natural* obligation to justice' and distinguished from 'the *moral* obligation, or the sentiment of right and wrong' (p. 270).

In Hume's arguments, the most questionable premises are the fifth in the first and the third in the second one. It may have been true in Hume's time that states were less dependent on each other than individuals, but this idea has lost much of its credibility in the present day's world. Correspondingly, it has become questionable whether the states have less interest in peace and order than individuals.

However, granting the controversial premises to Hume for the sake of argument, we may raise the question: do the conclusions follow from the premises? Would it rather be the case that because of the fragility of international relations, it is expected from the rulers and from the states that they try to recompensate the weaker natural obligation to justice by committing themselves to efforts of strengthening the moral obligation? Or would it be so that because the interest of tyrants in peace and order has been weaker than the interest of their subjects, the rulers of civilized states will be expected to look for all means possible for guaranteeing a peaceful international cooperation? Deception hardly belongs to these means. Even if moral obligations would rest on natural obligations, the diminishing power of the latter could nevertheless strengthen the former.

This is wishful thinking, Hume could say. But the point of the present criticism is that his premises are questionable and even if they were accepted, they do not adequately sustain the conclusion which he so dramatically has presented as 'a shocking proposition'.

3. The extra argument from analogy

What have chastity and modesty to do with international relations? A reader who comes to the final section of Part II of Book III, may wonder the change of topics: Hume returns to the theme on virtues and discusses two characteristic excellences of the female sex. It is as if he had anticipated objections to his theory on the liberties of rulers, because he says that 'some may not think' that 'the universal approbation or blame' which follows from the observance or transgression of the laws of nature and nations has been 'sufficiently explained from the general interests of society' (Sect. xii, p. 330).

The theme is precarious: while the previous section was connected with a privileged right to transgression of duties, the present section concerns the rights and duties of men and women and compares transgression of conjugal fidelity on the part of husband to those on the part of wife. Hume thinks that ideas concerning male and female virtues and expectations on sexual behaviour stem from anatomy, education, conventions and from interests of the society. The fact is that men (and women?) do not apply the same laws with the same force to the representatives of the male sex as to those of the opposite sex. Hume writes a quite explicit text on 'copulation of the sexes', on generation (which goes from the man to the woman), on temptations and pleasures.

According to Hume, there is an analogy between the relations of sexes on the one hand and the relation of international community to civil society on the other hand. His reasoning goes as follows (sect. xii, p. 333):

> As to the obligations which the male sex lie under with regard to chastity, we may observe, that according to the general notions of the world, they bear nearly the same proportion to the obligations of women, as the obligations of the law of nations do to those of the law of nature. 'Tis contrary to the interest of civil society, that men shou'd have an *entire* liberty of indulging their appetites in venereal enjoyment: But as this interest is weaker than in the case of the female sex, the moral obligation, arising from it, must be proportionately weaker. And to prove this we need only appeal to the practice and sentiments of all nations and ages.

Here again one may discern a logical transition from natural obligation to the corresponding moral obligation, as in the arguments of the previous section. This time Hume's reasoning goes as follows:

> The natural interest of society on male chastity is weaker than that on the female chastity.
>
> ---
>
> The moral interest on male chastity is weaker than that on the female chastity.

Whether the derivation of weaker moral interest from a weaker natural interest be justified, was already questioned above. Moreover, one may wonder whether time has undermined the credibility of the premise as well as of the conclusion of the present argument. Even 'chastity' itself, with the moralistic connotation included in it, has become a questionable concept. Whether this concept is applied, or whether it is substituted by a more neutral concept, the use of the concept with asymmetric standards for men and for women is no longer as unquestionable as it may have been in Hume's time. The interest on chastity is founded on reasons of health and well-being, physical as well as mental. These reasons are basically the same for both sexes. The tradition of double morality, with two different sets of standards for males and females, has of course not disappeared. However, there is a strong stream of thought challenging the validity of this tradition.

It is interesting to note that Hume thinks his case can be *proven*. His appeal to the sentiments and practices of all ages and nations made a strong point in the time and place where he presented it - London 1740. However, at the end of the 20th century a cultural situation has emerged in which sentiments are changing, even if practices still drag behind. A modern reader is hardly inclined to accept Hume's claim as a proof. It may rather be considered as a document of the past ways of thinking.

This criticism, important as it may be, does not yet go to the heart of the matter of the chastity and modesty section. The main claim made by Hume is that there are two different kinds of relations which both exemplify double standards of morality and are in this respect analogous to each other. He even speaks of proportion; this is supposed to be 'nearly the same' between the obligations

$$\frac{\text{of men}}{\text{of women}} \quad \text{and} \quad \frac{\text{of the international law}}{\text{of the law of nature}}$$

This appears puzzling not only to mathematicians. Hume's words exclude the use of the identity sign here and the idea that an equation would be in question. But then he can speak of proportion only figuratively. Moreover, it sounds inconsistent that Hume in the previous section claims that the proportion between the rulers' and the citizens' morality cannot be reduced to numbers and in the present section says that 'nearly the same proportion' holds between two heterogeneous proportions. How should he know this? The concept of proportion were better not applied at all in section xii. Hume's actual claim is that rulers have an analogous relation to their subjects as men to women, analogous in the sense that rulers and men enjoy certain extra liberties which subjects and women do not have. This sounds patriarchal.

4. Towards a consistent ethics code for the international community

From the subjection of women by men, we may return to the subjection of citizens by rulers. Hume's claim that the system of international law allows a relaxation of rulers' morality is far from refuted. The actual world order of the closing 20th century seems to widely reconfirm Hume's cynical maxim, although one may find gaps in Hume's reasoning. In speaking of reconfirmation, one does not think only on gross transgressions of justice by tyrants, but also on the *Realpolitik* taking place behind the curtains of diplomacy and sometimes openly practiced in contrast to all pious speeches.

According to Hume, the laws of nations are 'superadded to the laws of nature' (sect. xi, p. 329). These extra laws 'do not entirely abolish the latter' (ibid.), which means that the basic laws of justice are binding to princes and subjects. But, he thinks, there are maxims which abolish some principles of justice which are followed by citizens. Such a maxim calculates for princes a much freer system of morals than that which is valid for their subjects. At the end of the section, Hume speaks of transgression of justice among princes *and republics*.

As originally formulated by Hume, the maxim concerns rulers' morality. In the complementary reasoning, he adds republics - or states or nations - to the trespassers. One may distinguish these two aspects more clearly than Hume, according as the principle "l'Etat c'est moi" was never true. This gives us two different discussion topics: (i) questions concerning the professional ethics of the political leaders, (ii) questions concerning the world order and a sustainable ethics code of international relations. Let us start with the former.

(i) In comparison to the moral and other privileges enjoyed by princes and ministers during the past centuries, 'the practice of all ages' has become problematical in the modern - and postmodern - world. Admittedly, power gives privileges and extra rights to governors, but is it any more sanctioned by the practice that their system of morals would differ from that calculated for private persons? You need not be thoroughly informed of the sex and other scandals such as Lockheed, Watergate etc., in order to realize that in many cases the governors' freedom to moral excesses has been seriously questioned. Indeed, critical journalists, alert citizens, active organizations and elections seem to render in some respects the system of morals calculated for the rulers even less free than the system which regulates their subjects. One may speak of a developing ethics code for the political profession which is comparable to other systems of rights and duties of professionals. This code does not enjoy a privileged status; it makes up just one of several mutually exclusive special moralities. It would follow from this that the rulers are not more often allowed violations of justice and for more trivial motives than private persons. Any morals code may entail extra clauses for such violations - think, for instance, police officers chasing a car which exceeds the speed limit. The governors' code would not be freer than that of others; it would only be different, the freedoms conceded to rulers being counterbalanced by freedoms denied them. Accordingly, one may conclude that in modern democratic society, the morality of governors has the same force as that of private persons and may not be lawfully transgressed for a more trivial motive.

(ii) The distinction between a country's internal affairs and foreign policy is no longer as clear-cut as it used to be. The human rights issue has shown that there are questions of justice which require internationally valid standards for their treatment. It is increasingly difficult for rulers to treat their subjects as second class citizens. This issue was never heard of in the time when Hume wrote his *Treatise*. It traces back to the French Revolution. Human rights are grossly violated all over the world today, but the claim to grant and to observe human rights cannot be made void. Even lip-service and hypocrisy do not corrupt the struggle which Amnesty International and other related organizations are leading in favour of suppressed individuals and of a more righteous world. A morality calculated for politicians which would allow them to violate human rights is no more feasible. This is a definite change in common morality; the wheels of history cannot be turned back.

Hume is right in that nations or states as actors are not comparable in all respects to individuals. It is indeed a tricky conceptual problem to determine the meaning of a state's deeds and to explicate which kind of legal subject a state is. International law has developed during the two hundred years since Hume's time; however, strength, power and resolution still determine justice as it is applied to international relations. A ruler who would betray another ruler and in so doing would save his or her country is generally considered a hero. There is no court of justice which would have enough power to enforce judgments in such cases. Here the hard problems begin.

Hume may be thought to have had Machiavelli's *Il Principe* in mind when he introduced his cynical maxim. His words are not specific enough to ease the task of a modern scholar, but the similarity to the Italian is close enough in order not to be a coincidence. According to Machiavelli, a wise prince cannot and should not keep his word if this would harm him and if the reasons upon which a promise is based are no longer valid.[2] Also Hume speaks of breaking one's word and of deception. Hume's word 'shocking' means the reaction of those who have an illusory picture of the political game or of those who participate in it but pretend not to know its nature.

Although Hume's arguments can be attacked, his basic pattern of explanation is still worthy of consideration. According to him, the general interests of society explain why certain standards have been assumed and how they are applied. Concerning international relations, we may substitute 'interest to national security' for the expression 'the general interests of society' in order to see how the explanation works. Through this substitution, we have reached a basis on which to determine the proportion between the rulers' morality and the citizens' morality. In questions of national security, the rulers are in fact vouchsafed a special morality with extra rights denied to average citizens. These rights concern access to secret information and actions undertaken to save the state. The rulers are expected to be tough enough in order to be able to keep their state independent and autonomous. International politics is power-play, like today's icehockey. However, rulers are also expected to improve international cooperation and understanding. Their interest in maintaining peace and order should be even stronger than the corresponding interest of citizens. There is no question about any relaxation of the rulers' morality. The world needs rulers who have strong moral integrity and who are committed to honour human rights and to avoid war and hostilities as much as possible.[3]

These requirements are in accordance with Hume's idea of sympathy. He speaks in the *Treatise* of an expanding circle of sympathy (cf. e.g. Book III, Part II, sect. ii). It is true that he thinks that sympathy gets weaker when distance grows. But his thought also allows the possibility that the moral perspective grows with the expansion of sympathy. Commerce between people and nations expands the sympathy. The interest of peace and liberty, so much stressed by Hume, will be conducive in the construction of an internationally binding order of justice.

Notes

1. All quotations are from *Treatise of Human Nature* reprinted from Hume 1964.
2. 'Non può, pertanto, uno signore prudente, né debbe, osservare la fede, quando tale osservanzia li torni contro e che sono spente le cagioni che la feciona promettere.' Machiavelli 1987, p. 80.
3. Cf. Hampshire 1989. Hampshire speaks of 'rationally controlled hostilities' which are 'the normal condition of mankind' (p. 189). He characterizes 'Machiavelli's problem' as 'the conflict between personal honour and public responsibility' and thinks that it 'has only a complicated answer, at least on a philosophical level' (p. 177).

References

Hampshire, S. (1989), *Innocence and Experience*, Harvard University Press, Cambridge, Mass.

Hume, D. (1964), *The Philosophical Works*, edited by Green, T. H. and Grose, T. H., vol. 2. (Reprint of the new edition, London 1886). Scientia Verlag: Aalen.

Machiavelli, N. (1987), *Il Principe, Epoca! I Libri del Punte Esclamativo*, XVIII (Quomado fidos a principibus sit servanda): Milano.

Rorty on liberalism and postphilosophy

Arto Tukiainen

Richard Rorty writes in the introduction to his book *Contingency, Irony, and Solidarity*,

> I borrow my definition of 'liberal' from Judith Shklar, who says that liberals are people who think that cruelty is the worst thing we do. I use 'ironist' to name the sort of person who faces up to the contingency of his or her most central beliefs and desires – someone sufficiently historicist and nominalist to have abandoned the idea that those central beliefs and desires refer back to something beyond time and chance.[1]

Two disparate comments on these two definitions that seemingly don't have much to do with each other, but which nevertheless occur in the text as I quoted them, one immediately below the other, as if they had some inner connection in the personality of a 'liberal ironist', who happens to be the figure Rorty wants to sketch in his book. 1) Rorty's definition of liberalism as the idea that cruelty is the worst thing we do seems rather inclusive. In fact, it looks like a definition of morality, for if morality can be said to have a point or a purpose, it must be something like the avoidance of cruelty. I don't know if anyone really *wants* to define morality (why does anyone want to define liberalism?), but if someone proposed that morality is the idea that cruelty is the worst thing we do, we would not feel that bad, would we? We don't praise a person as properly moral if he thinks that cruelty is not terrible; and the more someone abhors cruelty, the more moral he must be. If this definition of morality has its weaknesses, so does Rorty's definition of liberalism. Maybe morality is not always the idea that cruelty is the worst thing we do, but maybe liberalism cannot be always identified with that notion either. I shall in any case take Rorty's definition as it stands. And assuming that the parallel view of morality appeals to us, it follows that moral thought is composed of different versions of liberalism: there is no moral outside to the liberal tradition. Antiliberals are immoralists. 2) In Rorty's account the connection between irony and the realization of the contingency of one's own personality or selfhood – which for Rorty equals the contingency of one's own beliefs and desires, or of the vocabularies in which one describes them – is very important. Recognizing the contingency of one's selfhood results in irony, or at least seeing how contingent one's existence is considerably increases one's chances of being ironic about oneself. As further evidence for this connection we may quote a later statement in the same book. Rorty says of ironists that they are 'never quite able to take themselves seriously because always aware that the terms in which they describe themselves are subject to change, always aware of the contingency and fragility of their final vocabularies and thus of their selves'.[2]

Rorty thinks that playful ironism is an essential ingredient of what he calls postphilosophy, which is an effort to compare and contrast different self-descriptions and self-definitions, different ways of making our lives make sense, without imagining or even hoping that one of the vocabularies we use could be true to our real essence, where 'real essence' is something that cannot be altered by redescription and redefinition in another vocabulary or language game.[3] Since the postphilosopher is aware of the contingency of – and therefore ironic about – the vocabularies we employ to express and define our selves, the point of his work is not to find the truth about those selves and thereby fix the movement of the vocabularies of the self, but to collect different ways of speaking about human lives and everything that pertains to them, such as politics and physiological theories. In a postphilosophical culture the drive that makes us 'read through libraries, and to add new volumes to the ones we found' is not the hope of finding the true self-descriptions, but simply 'the hope of offering our descendants a way of describing the ways of describing we had come across – a description of the descriptions which the race has come up with so far'.[4] The postphilosopher is a historicist all-round intellectual who

> ...passes rapidly from Hemingway to Proust to Hitler to Mary Douglas to the present situation in Southeast Asia to Gandhi and Sophocles. He is a name-dropper, who uses names such as these to refer to sets of descriptions, symbol-systems, ways of seeing. His specialty is seeing similarities and differences between great big pictures, between attempts to see how things hang together. He is the person who tells you how all the ways of making things hang together hang together.[5]

An interesting feature of postphilosophy is that its protagonists don't wish to take sides in intervocabularic disputes in anything more than a strictly playful or educative purpose, the purpose of seeing, or enabling others to see, how things appear from the point of view of some particular vocabulary. Neither do they believe it is useful to defend some definite conclusions within the vocabularies they describe and compare, because those conclusions will almost certainly look bad or even despicable from within some other vocabulary, some other 'great big picture'. As metaphilosophers they talk *about* vocabularies rather than *within* them. Since their job is to describe and compare different ways of speaking and writing, the normative task of telling how people ought to speak or think tends to fall out as redundant. As Rorty emphasizes, otherwise than a metaphysician (which for Rorty is another name for a philosopher), the ironist postphilosopher doesn't think that arguments – logico-linguistic efforts to convince someone of the truth of a philosophical position – are that valuable:

> The metaphysician thinks that there is an overriding intellectual duty to present arguments for one's controversial views – arguments which will start from relatively uncontroversial premises. The ironist thinks that such arguments – logical arguments – are all very well in their way, and useful expository devices, but in the end not much more than ways of getting people to change their practices [i.e., language games, vocabularies] without admitting they have done so. The ironist's preferred form of argument is dialectical in the sense that she takes the unit of persuasion to be a vocabulary rather than a proposition. Her method is redescription rather than inference. Ironists specialize in redescribing ranges of objects or events in partially neologistic jargon, in the hope of inciting people to adopt and extend that jargon.[6]

The ironist's unit of persuasion is an entire vocabulary rather than a single proposition within some vocabulary, and his method is redescription rather than inference. Such redescription is what much of Rorty's own work has been. In the 1989 book, say, he compares Plato with Kant, Kant with Freud, Freud with Hegel, Davidson with Nietzsche, Bloom with Davidson, Baudelaire with Nabokov, Nabokov with Orwell, Rawls with Sandel, Derrida with Heidegger, and Heidegger and Derrida with Proust and Nietzsche. In his 1991 book, Rorty contrasts Dewey with Heidegger, Heidegger with Kundera, Kundera with Dickens, Habermas with Lyotard, and Foucault with Plato. He passes from one writer and vocabulary to the next with considerable ease and rapidity, in much the same way as a contemporary tourist travels around the world in a couple of weeks. He is on the move. He is curious about everything, and remembers to connect every name and scene with all the others. But this descriptive work is about all he does. The only arguments he gives, the only inferences he makes, concern the reasons why postphilosophy seems like a worthwhile activity in the first place. Even here his arguments must be more like persuasive redescriptions than logical inferences, because there is no knock-down argument for a view as comprehensive as anti-essentialism about the human selfhood. One of Rorty's favorite strategies of persuasion is retelling the story of twentieth century philosophy in such a way that it begins to seem as if all the 'important figures' (Dewey, Wittgenstein, Heidegger, Derrida, etc.) agreed with his own estimation of the value of doing philosophy, which happens to be a fairly low one. The rhetorical implication is that if we want to avoid being hopelessly parochial, it is better to start some postphilosophical project and not worry so much about philosophy itself. Rorty seeks to create the impression that he himself is waiting at the point toward which the major intellectual energies of our century have been directed. This inescapably brings to mind the Hegelian notion of the tide or tendency of history: we-here are on top of things, we are the point, the meaning, the high-point of history, its very summit.

One should stress the inference from contingency to irony to postphilosophy. These three names or concepts form a continuous line: the idea of the contingency of one's vocabularies gives rise to irony about them, and irony breeds postphilosophy. They also constitute an onion, a Russian doll: within the postphilosopher one finds the ironist, and within the ironist the thought of contingency.

Liberalism and ironist postphilosophy: my first thesis will be that Rorty can reconcile these two aspects of his personality – which here means something like a 'system of beliefs and desires' – only by splitting that personality in two parts, parts that don't communicate with each other very fluently. Rorty as an ironist postphilosopher and Rorty as a liberal don't mesh too well: the doll-onion, and more particularly its two upper layers, repels the liberal, and vice versa. This is the view I shall propose in the first section of this chapter.

If the remarks of that first section track the truth, then it will seem that as an intervocabularic enterprise postphilosophy is, and has to be, committed to neither liberalism nor antiliberalism exclusively, or, what comes to the same, to both liberalism and antiliberalism to some degree – fifty-fifty, if one likes exact figures. My aim in the second part of the chapter would therefore be to find clues of antiliberal attitudes in Rorty's text. If Rorty is indeed a postphilosopher, as he says he is, there should be textual evidence not only of liberalism, but also of antiliberalism. I shall try hard to unearth Rorty-the-antiliberal. If I don't succeed, I will have to conclude that the initial appearances are true: Rorty indeed suffers from a mild multiple personality disorder.

Let us first see what Rorty has to say about his commitment to liberalism.

I

As an ironist Rorty believes that liberalism is merely (or 'merely', if you like) one contingent vocabulary or a family of vocabularies among others. One cannot answer the question 'Why avoid cruelty?' in a way that would appeal to someone who doesn't already feel liberal, just as one cannot convince an atheist of the existence of God by theoretical arguments, or prove the existence of an immortal soul to anyone who doesn't already agree with much of one's own world-picture. For ironists 'there is no answer to the question "Why not be cruel?" – no noncircular theoretical backup for the belief that cruelty is horrible'.[7] In the end the liberal can only refer to reasons that non-liberals don't recognize as such:

> There is no *neutral*, noncircular way to defend the liberal's claim that cruelty is the worst thing we do, any more than there is a neutral way to back up Nietzsche's assertion that this claim expresses a resentful, slavish attitude, or Heidegger's that the idea of the 'greatest happiness of the greatest number' is just one more bit of 'metaphysics,' of the 'forgetfulness of Being'. We cannot look back behind the processes of socialization which convinced us twentieth-century liberals of the validity of this claim and appeal to something which is more 'real' or less ephemeral than the historical contingencies which brought those processes into existence.[8]

Here Rorty seems to be quite right. We feel that Plato didn't really convince us in his discussion of the Gyges's ring, Hobbes in his argument against the Foole, Kant in his reflections about the inconceivability of someone rationally choosing an egoistic life strategy, or Gauthier in his theory that constrained maximization will appeal to a purely self-interested agent. Neither do we believe that there is any non-circular argument to prove that nationalistic chauvinism (religious fundamentalism, political arrogance and aggression, etc.) is irrational: for liberals themselves it is irrational, but unless one is willing to beg the question, there is no proving this point to the chauvinist. Since circular justifications are all we are going to get, the figure of a cruel egoist or nationalistic fanatic will continue playing the Other of the moral game. This is what Rorty means when he says that there is 'no neutral, noncircular way to defend the liberal's claim that cruelty is the worst thing we do.'

And *yet* the postphilosopher is in Rorty's view free to call himself a liberal. Locutions like 'since I am a liberal' and 'we liberals' are among the most frequently used in his 1989 book. (See, for instance, the words 'us twentieth century liberals' in the above quotation.) How come? Why does Rorty think it is possible for someone to be a liberal ironist? The pattern of Rorty's argumentation seems to be the following. First Rorty generously recognizes that he cannot really defend his liberal attitudes without begging the question: there is no non-contingent reason why we should be kind instead of cruel. We just happen to have been educated to utter liberal judgements in circumstances that seem to call for moral comment, and there is no conclusive reason or argument why we should stay within this vocabulary instead of entering some antiliberal one. Then Rorty goes on to say that this doesn't really matter: let us define ourselves as liberals even if we know that in the end our liberal language-games and the moral judgements they involve are quite contingent. Rorty is well aware of the contingent, non-rational sources of his liberal views. His liberalism is foundationless; but it is so quite self-consciously. Rorty wants to say, 'Let us be ironic about liberalism – *but let us still be liberals*'. Even if we cannot find any conclusive reason for not being cruel to each other, we should nevertheless avoid cruelty. In fact, one should not even ask, as Nietzsche did, 'What has the suffering of my fellow humans to do with me?' just as one should not ask, as theists do, 'Why don't you believe in God?'.[9] Rorty says that

> ...we heirs of the Enlightenment think of enemies of liberal democracy like Nietzsche or Loyola as, to use Rawls's word, 'mad.' We do so because there is no way to see them as fellow citizens of our constitutional democracy, people whose life plans might, given ingenuity and good will, be fitted in with those of other citizens. They are not crazy because they have mistaken the ahistorical human essence. They are crazy because the limits of sanity are set by what we can take seriously. This, in turn, is determined by our upbringing, our historical situation.[10]

But doesn't it seem as if the ironist postphilosopher, insofar as he really is an ironist postphilosopher, *shouldn't feel quite at home* in the liberal vocabulary? He is always on the move, restlessly playing the liberal vocabulary against its Others, finding and inventing new outsides and margins to it, like a tourist, or better, like a permanent traveller. For the postphilosopher, it appears, there is something *unheimlich* about liberalism, something that reminds him of repression and measures of exclusion. Since he is aware of the radical contingency of the liberal vocabulary, the postphilosopher reads about ancient Egyptian customs and the reception of Nietzsche's works in late 19th century Russia rather than consults the latest commentaries on Mill's book on liberty. Rather than defending some current version of liberalism, he compares it with some others. Instead of claiming that Rawls is right, he contrasts Rawls's theory with Sade's novels or ironizes the veil of ignorance by treating it as an interesting metaphor. And instead of criticizing Nozick's criticism of Rawls, he opts out of the discussion altogether, preferring the distant metaphilosophical attitude. The purpose of his work is not to find the truth about liberalism, but to see how it hangs together with some other vocabularies. Why doesn't Rorty think this way? Why does he call himself a liberal?

Let us return to the idea of contingency. A non-ironist like Rawls could say, and does say, 'I know the liberal vocabulary is socially and historically contingent. *So what?* I want to see how things seem from within that vocabulary'. A philosopher may quite consistently stay within the language game of liberalism, and issue judgements that are perceived as correct according to the criteria of validity which define that game. He can acknowledge that his intuitions and judgements are historically and socially contingent, and yet 'stand for them unflinchingly', as Rorty quotes Isaiah Berlin's quotation of Joseph Schumpeter:[11] the liberal judgements and intuitions are appropriate to *us*, where the scope of the 'us' is defined by the historical and social borders of the liberal vocabulary. Rorty comments on Rawls's project: 'Rawls is not attempting a transcendental deduction of American liberalism or supplying philosophical foundations for democratic institutions, but simply trying to systematize the principles and intuitions typical of American liberals'.[12] In Rorty's view Rawls is a sociologist or social psychologist who wants to define, rather than defend, the principles that guide the moral judgements of American liberals. Rawls knows quite well that the liberal intuitions he wants to systematize are contingent and in the end foundationless, but doesn't care about that fact. It is rather like in the first person case: at bottom one finds it extremely difficult to be ironic about one's own happiness and well-being, even if one cannot answer the question 'Why should I care about my own life?' in a way that someone who seriously *doubts* the legitimacy of that concern would recognize as valid. In the end there is no 'because' or 'therefore', but only the fact of self-concern itself. As one can express this, there is no proof of the rationality of self-concern. It *just is so* that our own lives should attract our serious care and attention: pain is bad, pleasure is good, and that's that. Similarly *it just is so* that even if there is no compelling reason why we should not be cruel, we should nevertheless not be cruel. How could anyone be ironic about extreme cruelty? Isn't it obvious that cruelty must be avoided? One would like to say that the pains and sufferings of other people are bad in themselves, or that other people are ends-in-themselves. There is no non-circular justification for these thoughts – but let us still think this way.

It is quite all right for a *philosopher* to say this, for he doesn't wish to infer from the contingency of a final vocabulary to the appropriateness of being ironic about it. He may even state that liberalism is not a contingent vocabulary *at all*, because it articulates the truth of people as ends-in-themselves, and this truth is independent of the liberal vocabularies we happen to use. People as ends-in-themselves are here what Rorty would call a 'truth out there', Derrida a 'transcendental signified', and Sellars a special case of the 'myth of the given': a fact that any vocabulary must recognize or at least leave room for on pain of being irrational. The liberal philosopher may think that people are ends-in-themselves no matter how you describe them. This idea constitutes what Rorty says liberalism doesn't have: a metaphysical foundation. Cruelty ought to be avoided because of the non-contingent fact that people are ends-in-themselves.

But what about a postphilosopher like Rorty? Can he continue being a postphilosopher without loosening his grip on liberalism? I think not, simply because postphilosophers want to be ironic about all final vocabularies they perceive as contingent. Postphilosophy is an inherently ironic project. Since liberalism is contingent vocabulary, their irony doesn't end when liberalism begins. And the point is that you cannot be thoroughly ironic, thus thoroughly postphilosophical, about liberalism and yet call yourself a liberal. An ironist about liberalism is someone who doesn't take other people very seriously, and in particular doesn't think that their status as ends-in-themselves is any stronger than the liberal vocabulary itself. Since it just *happens* that we use the liberal vocabulary, it just *happens* that people seem ends-in-themselves. From this the postphilosopher infers that it is best to be ironic about both liberalism and its claim that people are ends-in-themselves.

As Rorty says, 'the issue is one about whether philosophy should try to find natural starting-points which are distinct from cultural traditions, or whether all philosophy should do is compare and contrast cultural traditions'.[13] Postphilosophers choose this latter strategy. So if Rorty is a postphilosopher, he doesn't take sides in the dispute between liberals and antiliberals. He merely compares and contrasts these two cultural traditions. This is why Morton Gurewitch writes, no doubt ironically, 'The liberal ironist is a heroic intellectual who counters the platitude that irony and solidarity are mutually antagonistic'.[14] The antagonism of ironistic postphilosophy and a liberal commitment to human solidarity is a 'platitude'. This is why resisting it requires a 'heroic intellectual'. Ironists are the sort of people who don't really commit themselves to any social cause or programme, but prefer to keep their distance. (For example, Anatole France had to temporarily shed his ironic attitude when he got horrified about the Dreyfus affair and defended the poor man against injustice.) They are on-lookers rather than participants; they smile rather than act. Rorty's liberal ironist is, if not a conceptual impossibility, then at least an empirically unlikely character.

Another way to make this point is that Rorty seems to be opposed to pragmatist wisdom in making a sharp distinction between theoretical reflection and practical engagement. In theory, he says, there is no reason to be a liberal instead of an antiliberal; but in practice we should still be liberals. But liberalism is a view about how we should live our lives. If there is no reason to believe in it, then why act on it? While a philosopher thinks that we have a good reason to be liberals instead of antiliberals, a postphilosopher like Rorty's doesn't. And while the former are able to keep their actions in line with their words, the latter isn't. He must think that while liberalism is not any better than antiliberalism in theory, it is better in practice. And I wonder whether it is rational to think that way.

Or let us focus on Rorty's expression 'postmodernist bourgeois liberalism'.[15] 'Postmodernist' roughly means 'postphilosophical'; liberalism means that cruelty is the worst thing we do. But what about 'bourgeois'? Bourgeois common sense has two conflicting features. On the one hand, it claims that you should be a decent citizen, a liberal person who doesn't interfere in other people's lives, and who occasionally gives alms to the poor. But the bourgeois also have another side, which is the idea that you should promote your own interests. And promoting one's interests doesn't always coincide with promoting the liberal ideology. Sometimes it requires being cruel to others, using them to one's own advantage, leaving them suffer, etc. Rorty would like to see the bourgeois as good-hearted liberals only, and this, I think, is his peculiar blindness. Rorty is blind to the fact that the society in which he lives – the society in which we all live – and its bourgeois tradition is not merely one of liberalism, but of self-interest as well. So one cannot be a postmodernist bourgeois liberal. If one wants to be a postmodernist, one has to manage with the bourgeois part and its two sides: self-interest and liberalism. Rorty's references to Nietzsche and Loyola are slightly beside the point, because those character types don't probably appeal to his readers, educated and fairly broad-minded as they are. Very few of us like Nietzschean overmen or religious fanatics (nationalistic chauvinists, political extremists, etc.). But quite many of us like money and power.

Rorty doesn't follow the lines of his postphilosophical thinking to their logical conclusion: persistent irony about all final vocabularies, including liberalism. Despite his seemingly jovial attitude, Rorty is still a bit too serious about cruelty. I think we can understand this seriousness: one easily becomes serious about a final vocabulary that surrounds one from all sides, and the rhetoric of the American public culture, if not the reality of the American society, is indeed very liberal. But this doesn't remove the fact that liberalism is still a quite contingent vocabulary, a vocabulary we should learn to be ironic about. Irony about liberalism doesn't of course mean repudiating it, and favoring some antiliberal vocabulary instead. It rather involves refusing to take sides in the discussion between liberalism and its alternatives, i.e., vocabularies which don't involve the idea that cruelty is the worst thing we do. On the one hand, since postphilosophers don't think that reasons of cruelty must be weaker or 'less real' than ones of non-interference, generosity, and kindness, they wish to see to it that philosophy doesn't overmoralize their lives. Liberalism as the claim that cruelty is the worst thing we do cannot avoid such overmoralization, because it requires that agents always act decently, just as any football coach always requires that his trainees play good and even outstanding football. Cruelty can only appear as the irreducible Other of liberal thinking, and postphilosophers don't simply say No to this Other. They wish to enlarge their selves with the non-liberal vocabulary of cruelty too. It is not always true that cruelty is the worst thing we do. But on the other hand, postphilosophers also think that the liberal reasons of kindness are real. Cruelty should indeed be avoided, and for reasons that have nothing to do with the self-interested fear of getting caught and being excluded from cooperative schemes for mutual advantage. It should be avoided because of distinctly moral reasons, reasons that articulate the notion of other agents as ends-in-themselves. Even if the postphilosopher doesn't think that the liberal final vocabulary should escape irony, he doesn't believe that the self-definition 'we *anti*liberals' should do so either. In sum, the postphilosopher doesn't assume an extreme point of view: contrary to what Rorty says, he is neither a complete liberal nor a complete non-liberal. As a moderate person he stays at the borderline between these two extremes.

Ironism, we may note in passing, has its own particular form of cruelty: redescribing another person's life against his will. Rorty writes,

> Ironism, as I have defined it, results from awareness of the power of redescription. But most people do not want to be redescribed. They want to be taken on their own terms – taken seriously just as they are and just as they talk. The ironist tells them that the language they speak is up for grabs by her and her kind. There is something potentially very cruel about that claim. For the best way to cause people long-lasting pain is to humiliate them by making

> the things that seemed most important to them look futile, obsolete, and powerless. Consider what happens when a child's precious possessions – those little things around which he weaves fantasies that make him a little different from all other children – are redescribed as 'trash ', and thrown away. Or consider what happens when these possessions are made to look ridiculous alongside the possessions of another, richer, child... Redescription often humiliates.[16]

Or think what happened when the first European pilgrims saw the naked savages of Africa: they started redescribing the natives in terms that made it look as if their brutish lives had to be worthless and fit for nothing so long as they kept on defining themselves in their own terms. Or consider how easy it is to cause suffering to someone who struggles to keep his head in one piece with some religious or therapeutic vocabulary by suggesting that there is no way he could rationally choose between different final vocabularies or self-descriptions. Saying that all those good-looking, life-saving vocabularies are quite contingent may be a cause of great pain. It humiliates.

Having said all this, we have to observe that Rorty 1) is somehow aware of the incompatibility between postphilosophy and liberalism, and 2) has a solution to this tension or contradiction. First he wonders whether it really is possible to be both an ironist and a liberal, both 'Nietzsche and J.S. Mill'. Then he proposes that we should think of ironism as the private side of our lives, and be liberals in the public domain. Private irony, public liberalism.[17] While we should continue standing by each other in the public domain, it is none of the other people's business what we do in our private lives: if someone like Rorty wants to be ironic about liberalism at home, then other people ought to keep their distance and not intervene.[18]

In fact, Rorty occasionally writes as if irony about *anything at all* were a private matter:

> But even if I am right in thinking that a liberal culture whose public rhetoric is both nominalist and historicist is both possible and desirable, I cannot go on to claim that there could or ought to be a public culture whose public rhetoric is *ironist*... Irony seems inherently a private matter. On my definition, an ironist cannot get along without the contrast between the final vocabulary she inherited and the one she is trying to create for herself. Irony is, if not intrinsically resentful, at least reactive. Ironists need something to have doubts about, something from which to be alienated.[19]

As Roy Bhaskar notes, Rorty's idea of the private ironist brings to mind a lonely intellectual, 'writing a diary no one can read'.[20] While the Rortyan ironist plays with all sorts of final vocabularies at home, he suddenly turns into a serious, commonsensical, literal-minded citizen at the front door, wearing a grey tie and flannel trousers. He spends his days diligently doing what everyone else does, but wastes his nights musing about how ironic it is that he should be doing all that, and not something entirely different. He combines private irony with public professionalism, romantic intellectualism with efficiency in the pursuit of pregiven social goals.

But it cannot be that all kinds of ironic commentary are private matters, because just like its philosophical complement, postphilosophical discourse is a public venture, and according to Rorty's account philosophers should become postphilosophers, and thus ironists. Should postphilosophers really keep their discourses to themselves, and never show them to anyone? Should they refrain from contributing to literary supplements and attending conferences? In particular, what if the public rhetoric of some society is decidedly antiliberal? What if it is racist, sexist, oligarchic, Stalinistic, Pol Potian, or aggressively nationalistic? What if it is cruel in one or several of the great number of ways in which people can be cruel to each other? Should one refrain from irony even then? I don't think so, and neither does Rorty, if I have understood him correctly. He wants to apply to postphilosophical literature what Salman Rushdie said about all literature: literature claims the right to speak of everything in all conceivable ways.[21] On this view literature should have the right to irony, i.e., to expose the contingency of all those final vocabularies we think are essential to our own self-understanding, to think otherwise, to describe it all in another way, to add a few new voices to the conversation of mankind, to resist the totalizing pretensions of all vocabularies. Literature, including postphilosophy, is of course a private institution in the sense that both the writing and the reading processes typically take place in circumstances we can call private. But in another sense literature is a perfectly public institution: people write for public consumption, and anyone can either buy or borrow copies of the books he judges interesting. We cannot even suspect that Rorty wants to repress the ironic voices, can we? It is surely symptomatic that Rushdie expressly refers to Rorty's *Philosophy and the Mirror of Nature*, and approves of Rorty's criticism of foundationalism (which is the idea that our vocabularies are something more than human contingencies), whether religious, political, or philosophical. How could this Rorty now suddenly think that all irony is a private matter? How could he have joined the reactionary forces? Or could Rushdie really have made a mistake in referring to Rorty's book? It is not easy to believe that a person who speaks of liberalism and the virtue of tolerating a multiplicity of different opinions so well and so beautifully thinks of irony as a private matter.

So let us agree that some kind of public irony is both possible and desirable. The question is whether public irony about liberalism in particular should be banned, or whether we should cease being postphilosophers when it comes to liberalism as a public ideology. Referring to the kind of cruelty through redescription in which ironists are especially gifted, Rorty says that according to the 'liberal ironist' (which is the sort of ironist I claim does not exist in a pure form, untainted by antiliberalism)

> we need to distinguish between redescription for private and for public purposes. For my private purposes, I may redescribe you and everybody else in terms which have nothing to do with my attitude toward your actual or potential suffering. My private purposes, and the part of my final vocabulary which is not relevant to my public actions, are none of your business. But as I am a liberal, the part of my final vocabulary which is relevant to such actions requires me to become aware of all the various ways in which other people whom I might act upon can be humiliated.[22]

One suspects that Rorty doesn't here pay sufficient attention to the indeterminacy of the criteria we use to make the distinction between private and public spheres. Quandaries arise. Whether some place or activity is private or public is often debatable, and when it is, one doesn't know whether one is entitled to postphilosophical irony or not. This point is not intended as a criticism of Rorty's position, but rather as a friendly reminder of what everyone – including Rorty himself, I am sure – knows.

I have two worries that have nothing to do with the occasional difficulty of making the distinction between the private and the public domains. The first is normative, the second psychological.

1) Why is the public-private split so important when we want to know whether it is desirable to be ironic about liberalism? For instance, why not cruelly redescribe other people in public? More generally, why not be ironic about liberalism in public? Postphilosophers want theirs to be a public venture. Rorty desires to align the distinction between philosophy and postphilosophy with the distinction between the public and the private domains, but that is an alignment any postphilosopher refuses to accept. Postphilosophy is not merely a private matter, just as criticism of religious fundamentalism is not something you must practice in the private sphere. According to liberalism itself criticism of liberalism may be a private matter, but postphilosophers are not liberals. In our view public cruelty is not that objectionable if it is not directed at us.

2) Is it really possible for one and the same person to so divide his psychic energies that he switches from a friendly liberal to an ironist posthilosopher the moment he comes home and draws the curtains? Or better, can anyone do this without splitting his personality in parts that don't remember each other, i.e., without suffering from a multiple personality disorder?[23] Assuming the answer is No, then there are two possible ways to proceed, two possible paths. A: Rorty's personality doesn't constitute a well-integrated whole. One of its sub-systems keeps producing liberal propaganda while another revels in postphilosophical fantasies. There is no single Rorty, but two: Rorty-the-liberal and Rorty-the-postphilosopher. B: We have missed some piece of textual evidence of Rorty's

antiliberal views. Maybe Rorty is both a liberal and an antiliberal after all; maybe we just haven't read his book carefully enough.

The doubt number two is the essential one, for *if* it is psychologically possible for someone to be both a good liberal and a good postphilosopher, then it is presumably possible for him to rationally maintain the position that while irony is a private matter, liberalism must be our public attitude. The idea that postphilosophical irony is a private matter is not an impossible one, *given* that one is psychologically capable of alternating between liberalism and postphilosophy. But, to repeat, if someone is able to do this, then I will urge that he must be deranged, because he is not a unified character, but is rather composed of two personalities.

Let me now pursue path B. I want to know whether Rorty's 1989 book doesn't give us any reason to believe that its author has an antiliberal side, too. Without such a side, I claim, we are obliged to think that Rorty is an MPD-case.

II

Sometimes Rorty appears to think that some varieties of cruelty are not very objectionable. He writes that

> our responsibilities to others constitute *only* the public side of our lives, a side which competes with our private affections and our private attempts at self-creation, and which has no *automatic* priority over such private motives... Moral obligation is, in this view, to be thrown in with a lot of other considerations, rather than automatically trump them.[24]

Or consider this statement: 'This book tries to show how things look if we drop the demand for a theory which unifies the public and private, and are content to treat the demands of self-creation and of human solidarity as equally valid, yet forever incommensurable'.[25] Rorty uses terms like 'solidarity', 'liberalism', and 'justice' more or less interchangeably. So when he here says that solidarity constitutes the public side of our lives, he could as well has spoken of liberalism as our public attitude.

These statements make it seem as if Rorty wanted to continue being a postphilosopher by claiming that cruelty should be avoided only to the extent to which we regard ourselves as members of the public domain. While liberalism is our public attitude, our private lives are somehow associated with non-liberal vocabularies. 'Somehow associated', because Rorty's statements admit of at least two interpretations. He doesn't indicate whether he thinks that active cruelty is not necessarily that bad if it occurs in the proper privacy, or whether he thinks that not helping one's private friends is not that bad. That is, I am not quite sure whether Rorty tolerates active private cruelty or accepts private omissions of kind actions.

Both interpretations support the view that Rorty doesn't wish to call himself too liberal. There are limits to his liberalism. Sometimes cruel motives may rationally trump liberal ones.

Then there is a third interpretation that would effectively undermine our interpretation of Rorty as a postphilosopher, namely the interpretation where Rorty is John Stuart Mill: occasionally we are morally entitled to say to our neighbors that it is none of their business what we do. If this is all Rorty means to say, then we can hardly call him a postphilosopher, for postphilosophers need a positively antiliberal side, and not merely the idea that we are morally entitled to a domain of privacy where our own likings are the sole determinant of what we have a reason to do. Unless extreme utilitarians, all liberals grant the existence of such a domain. We don't after all call a person cruel just because he sometimes prunes his roses, plays backgammon, writes an ironic diary, or drinks beer, even if he could do something morally useful instead of engaging in these communally useless activities. People like that may still think that cruelty is the worst thing we do: they don't conceive of themselves as cruel on account of the fact that they don't constantly appear as public benefactors or moral saints. So let us ignore this dull interpretation. According to our preferred mode of reading, Rorty endorses the claims of antiliberalism to some extent. He thinks that cruelty is not always the worst thing we do.

I just wonder how useful it is for Rorty to speak of liberalism as the public side of our lives, and of our need for private perfection and self-creation as that which entitles us to be less than perfectly liberal. First of all, the distinction between public and private domains doesn't seem to be doing any useful work here: one cannot seriously believe that Rorty is willing to accept cruelty simply because it occurs in privacy, where 'privacy' means something like 'at home', 'in the family', or 'among friends'. What rational difference does it make whether one is cruel in public or private? Isn't one cruel just the same? Secondly, why does Rorty speak of our need for poetic 'self-creation' as the source of antiliberal motives? Why doesn't he say, as seems natural and not so euphemistic, that antiliberal motives are ones of cruelty and egoism? Rorty had better speak of cruel instinct, heartless indifference, and straightforward egoism as the sources of antiliberal reasons for action. Instead of the distinction between private and public areas, and between self-creation and liberalism, we have the simple distinction between cruelty and kindness, or between egoism and altruism. Paraphrased, Rorty's statement goes as follows: 'our responsibilities to others constitute only the altruistic side of our lives, a side which competes with our egoistic drives and our egoistic attempts at self-assertion, and which has no automatic priority over such egoistic motives'. If one wants to capture the idea that most of us have friends or spouses or children whom we don't want to see suffer, one can speak of nepotistic desires or group-centric affections instead of egoistic drives. In any case, the essential contrast is between I-here or we-here and you-there instead of privacy and the public sphere.

So there is some textual evidence that Rorty is not as liberal as his frequent references to 'we liberals' seem to indicate. This evidence is not abundant, and that is why I am not sure whether I should make use of it all. But it is there anyway. Rorty is a bit like Sade, only conversely so. The writings of these authors give us the vague idea that they do not support liberalism and antiliberalism quite wholeheartedly. The general thrust of their texts points toward liberalism (Rorty) and antiliberalism (Sade), but there are also some hints of antiliberalism and liberalism, respectively. While Rorty is not quite sure whether cruelty really is always the worst thing we do, Sade has his own troubles with the possibility of perverse pleasures. (If cruelty is never wrong, then how can one obtain perverse pleasure by being cruel? Perverts need norms to transgress.)

One still has the uncomfortable feeling that Rorty's text is not very consistent. The textual evidence about Rorty's (wish for) non-liberal or antiliberal attitudes somehow seems *too scarce*, given all his talk about playful postphilosophical irony. Why isn't there more of that evidence? Why is Rorty so silent about his cruel, antiliberal thoughts? Or are we ultimately obliged to assume that he is quite simply confused and inconsistent? This inconsistency can be thought to emerge at two different levels, that of the wish and that of reality, as well as between these two levels. At the level of wishes the contradiction would be between Rorty's desire to be a postphilosopher and his desire to be a liberal. At the banal level of reality it would be between his postphilosophy and his liberalism. It could also exist between his desire to be postphilosophical and his actual liberal personality, or between his wish to be a liberal and his actual postphilosophical ego-structure.

One can think of interpretations of Rorty's work that make the contradiction between his (wish for) postphilosophy and his (wish for) liberalism appear either less obvious or even non-existent. First, perhaps Rorty is just being prudent in not advertizing his antiliberal side in public very voluptuously. One can here recall Hobbes's story about the man who 'hath sayd in his heart, there is no such thing as Justice; and *sometimes also with his tongue*'.[26] Hobbes called him a Foole. It could be that only foolish postphilosophers tell about their antiliberal thoughts and dispositions in books and articles, because the readers will then exclude them from their midst, or at least become reserved and mistrustful. This is not quite certain, however. In fact, my judgement is that a postphilosopher may gain as well as lose by openly declaring his ironic views, first of all because people don't always believe what they read, and secondly because consistently postphilosophical views may get so popular that their protagonists are praised in all conceivable ways, assuming a society that doesn't repress literary expressions of cruel sentiments. Sade's antiliberal books are read everywhere. Were Sade alive, he would profit from them in many ways. Rorty might be more cautious, of course. He might judge that some inconsistency between postphilosophy and liberalism is a small price to pay for not having to cope with all the suspicions which confessing one's flirt with cruelty may generate. On this interpretation there is a contradiction between what Rorty says about postphilosophy and what he says about liberalism, but this contradiction is made less severe by the fact that cruel people may wish to conceal their thoughts from public curiosity.

One selfish advantage of not confessing one's antiliberal views is that postphilosophers like Rorty can best disseminate their writings in liberal societies, especially ones that don't practice antiliberalism by suppressing inofficial voices and descriptions. If literature indeed wants to speak of everything in all conceivable ways, as Rushdie proposes, then postphilosophers will not have an easy time in totalitarian regimes, regimes that organize themselves around some antiliberal final vocabulary. Freedom of speech in particular is an important background requirement of a successful career as a postphilosopher.

But maybe Rorty doesn't really conceal anything; perhaps he is only being enigmatic and allusive. An interpretation along these lines offers itself if we place extremely heavy emphasis on the crucial statement according to which 'our responsibilities to others constitute only the *public* side of our lives, a side which competes with our private affections and our private attempts at self-creation, and which has no *automatic* priority over such private motives'. Rorty could here be thought to be hinting that he will refrain from abusing his neighbors (including us) in public, and confine his cruel exploitations to the private sphere. The distinction between public and private matters would now assume a significance we didn't appreciate before. Instead of proposing that it is all right for him to be somewhat cruel in all domains of life, he says that we don't have to be afraid, because he will only be cruel in his private life. There is a private Rorty and a public Rorty, a daytime Rorty and a night-time Rorty. While the former is a liberal, the latter is not. By making this move Rorty is able to avoid the threatening inconsistency between liberalism and postphilosophy, and *yet* not make his fellow-citizens worried. This is the most subtle interpretation I can find/invent. On the one hand, since Rorty doesn't want to contradict his postphilosophy by being a complete liberal, he lets go of complete liberalism. But on the other hand, since he doesn't want to make us worried about his cruel side, he hints that he will only be antiliberal at home.

So we have at least three interpretations of Rorty's views. The simplest one is that we should discount or ignore the textual evidence that suggests that Rorty has any antiliberal dispositions. This interpretation is supported by the fact that this evidence is meager in comparison to all the textual evidence to the contrary. The vast mass of Rorty's text claims that Rorty is a kind person, Punkt. The problem with this simple interpretation is that it makes Rorty seem confused and incoherent: one cannot be a postphilosophical ironist and a good liberal at the same time. So maybe we should be charitable and consider the alternatives? The second interpretation doesn't entirely remove the contradiction but only makes it less obvious and less blatant by claiming that since Rorty is a prudent, cautious person, he doesn't want to publicly confess his cruel thoughts and feelings, but withholds them from his readers. The text is peculiarly silent about Rorty's antiliberal side, but if we are allowed to think that Rorty doesn't always write down everything he knows about himself – if his book is not a diary – then we may suspect that he just doesn't want to say what he really thinks, that he conceals himself. Our third interpretation makes the contradiction disappear. According to this interpretation Rorty says that since he will only be antiliberal in his private life, we don't have to be afraid. Even if this last interpretation is the most charitable, its plausibility is reduced by the fact that it requires substantial speculation on a few lines in a large book.

Is there such a thing as the correct interpretation of Rorty? Can we ever know what Rorty really meant to say, what his intentions were? Or do we here have a few possible interpretations, interpretations among which only feeling and vague intuition can decide?

These doubts about the rational underdetermination of interpretation – about the possibility of finding the uniquely correct interpretation – get even more intense if we return to our assumption that Rorty wants to be a postphilosopher. Perhaps we should reconsider this assumption. *Does* Rorty really want to be a postphilosopher? What if he doesn't? What if he prefers the philosophical attitude as far as liberalism is concerned? Then we would have an inconsistency, or at least a difference that calls for an explanation, between what he says he is doing and what he actually is doing. If Rorty really wants to drop his postphilosophy when it comes to liberalism, then why does he not say so? This clearly creates a presumption against the notion that Rorty doesn't describe himself as a postphilosopher about liberalism. The author's own words are after all the primary source of evidence about his beliefs.

***

Even after all these interpretative hypotheses and caveats the suspicion of Rorty's not having a unified personality remains. The evidence of Rorty's antiliberalism is very, very scarce in comparison to all the evidence of his liberalism. Rorty just doesn't seem to be cruel enough. For this reason one is still prone to think that there is an inconsistency between his postphilosophy and his moral views. It is as if Rorty's ego was not one consistent, self-contained system, but a collection of more or less incompatible personality fragments. There may be enough thematic and stylistic unity in it to justify the belief that someone with a single ego or personality wrote the whole book; but just as Europe has many traditions of thought that communicate with each other less than transparently, the man we call Rorty has an ego with contents that sometimes seem like different personalities. My final clinical judgement is that Rorty should be seen to suffer from a mild multiple personality disorder. The source of this disorder is the struggle, which is not a simple antithetical opposition but rather an oblique incompatibility, between the ironist postphilosopher and the kind liberal. To be consistent, Rorty should either affirm both liberalism and antiliberalism, or deny his postphilosophical views; but since he cannot make up his mind between these two, he keeps on oscillating between them in a slightly confusing way.

Notes

1. Rorty, 1989, p. xv.
2. Ibid., pp. 73-4.
3. See Rorty, 1982, introduction, and Rorty, 1989, chapters 1 and 4.
4. Rorty, 1982, p. xl.
5. Ibid., p. xl.
6. Ibid., p. 78.
7. Ibid., p. xv.
8. Ibid., pp. 197-8.
9. See ibid., p. 87, and Rorty, 1991, p. 198.
10. Rorty, 1991, pp. 187-8.
11. Rorty, 1989, p. 46.
12. Rorty, 1991, p. 189.
13. Rorty, 1982, p. xxxvii. Emphasis deleted.
14. Gurewitch, 1994, p. 35.
15. Rorty, 1991, p. 198.
16. Rorty, 1989, pp. 89-90.
17. Ibid., p. 85.
18. Rorty, 1991, p. 198.
19. Rorty, 1989, pp. 87-8.
20. Bhaskar, 1991, p. 90.
21. See Rushdie's speech on the occasion of Herbert Read's death in 1990. Since religious fanaticism prevented Rushdie from delivering the paper himself, it was read by Harold Pinter. I myself read the Finnish translation of that speech in the first 1996 issue of *Parnasso*.
22. Rorty, 1989, pp. 91-2.
23. According to the 1994 statement of the International Society for the Study of Dissociation, the diagnostic criteria for multiple personality disorder are the following. 'A. The presence of two or more identities or personalities or personality states (each with its own relatively enduring pattern of perceiving, relating to and thinking about the environment and self). B. At least two of these identities or personality states recurrently take control of the person's behavior. C. Inability to recall important personal information that is too extensive to be explained by ordinary forgetfulness. D. The disturbance is not due to the direct physiological effects of a substance (e.g., blackouts or chaotic behavior during Alcohol Intoxication) or a general medical condition (e.g., complex partial seizures). Note:

In children the symptoms are not attributable to imaginary playmates or fantasy play.' Quoted in Hacking, 1995, p. 19.

24. Rorty, 1989, p. 194.
25. Ibid., p. xv.
26. Hobbes, 1973, p. 74.

References

Bhaskar, R. (1991), *Philosophy and the Idea of Freedom*. Blackwell: Oxford.

Gurewitch, M. (1994), *The Ironic Temper and the Comic Imagination*. Wayne State University Press: Detroit.

Hacking, I. (1995), *Rewriting the Soul*. Princeton University Press: Princeton.

Hobbes, T. (1973), *Leviathan*. Everyman: London. Originally published in 1651.

Rorty, R. (1982), *Consequences of Pragmatism*. Harvester Press, Brighton: Sussex.

Rorty, R. (1989), *Contingency, Irony, and Solidarity*. Cambridge University Press: Cambridge.

Rorty, R. (1991), *Objectivity, Relativism, and Truth*. Cambridge University Press: Cambridge.

G. H. von Wright's critique of liberal society

Mikko Salmela

The paper is a critical presentation of Georg Henrik von Wright's critique of Western culture and especially liberal society. Von Wright claims that the ecological and social problems of industrialized liberal societies stem from a foundational crisis in Western culture. The background of this crisis lies in the modern distinction between science and religion, reason and faith, and fact and value. These separations have enabled great scientific and technological progress. This progress has not, however, been accompanied by a similar kind of progress in morals. Thus the emancipation from Christian morality has, according to von Wright, led us to moral skepticism or even moral nihilism. His own attempt to provide a foundation for the cultural values is based on a form of ethical rationality that bears resemblance to the Aristotelian notion of 'phronesis'. Von Wright tries to evaluate subjective preferences by weighing harms and benefits connected with achievement of optional ends. This is possible inasmuch as we know the causal consequences and prerequisites connected with attaining optional ends. I argue that this von Wrightian 'value-rationality' cannot provide a foundation for objective cultural values. This is because it in the last resort leaves the content of 'the good of man' dependent on the subjective preferences alone. Therefore, the objective constituents of 'the good of man' that von Wright has advocated must be justified in some other way.

1. Von Wright's unknown cultural philosophy

Georg Henrik von Wright's international esteem is based on his works in analytical philosophy and philosophical logic. He is known as the author of *The Varieties of Goodness*, *Norm and Action*, *Explanation and Understanding* and several articles, especially on deontic logic, which was invented by him. There are only a few people outside Scandinavia, however, who know that on the other side of this cool analyst and logician there lies a profound and influential critic of culture. Along with such philosophical rebels as Derrida, Nietzsche, and Wittgenstein, von Wright has set himself the task to philosophize with a hammer, to destroy established ways of thinking.

> In the history of thought there are times when the best a philosopher can do is to destroy (Wittgenstein), to deconstruct (Derrida), or as Nietzsche said, to 'philosophize with a hammer' -in the hope that when everything is resolved soil is revealed where something essentially new and fresh can grow. I am inclined to think that we are living in such times.[1]

Von Wright's cultural philosophy has remained hidden, because the critical essays he has published since the 1950s have only appeared in his native Swedish along with Finnish translations. Although these essays cover a wide range of subjects from Dostoevski to the Myth of Progress, they focus on one recurrent theme: the threatened future of Western civilization. Neither liberalism nor liberal society are included in von Wright's *explicit* targets. Yet his critical remarks on the Western form of life identify some vital issues in the liberal agenda, both in theory and in practice. It is, therefore, consistent to read von Wright's appraisal also as a critique of liberal societies. Problems arise with the liberal, subjective view of values. Von Wright claims that subjectivism has given rise to cultural crises and to a number of specific social and environmental problems of our time.

2. The foundational crisis and its genealogy

The fatal problem of Western culture lies in the justification of basic cultural values. Ends and means used in pursuing them lack legitimation. 'The traditional values [of Christianity] that should justify our deeds and aspirations have been renounced, denied, and partly dispelled from view', claims von Wright.[2] The crisis is a modern phenomenon. Yet it has a long historical background in the intrinsic inconsistencies that our culture carries within its dualistic legacy inherited from the Hellenic and Judaeo-Christian cultures.

The ideological roots of Western culture lie in the collision of Hellenic rationality and Judaeo-Christian belief in authority. This collision gave rise to our modern culture that divided reason and faith into their own spheres of competence, science and religion. This basic division was also established in the philosophical separation of facts and values into two unbridgeable logical categories. It is just this isolation of reason into factual research that, according to von Wright, made possible the rise of instrumental rationality in our culture.

Instrumental rationality is characteristic of the modern tendency to limit deliberation to means only, while questions concerning the ultimate ends of human life are being neglected or dispelled from view.[3] Instrumental rationality is a natural companion to science, because judgements concerning instrumental value are purely factual. The objective truth of instrumental judgements of value rests on the causal connexions between phenomena. To quote von Wright's own example, if I want to make a hut habitable I must heat it. The example represents the form of instrumental rationality that von Wright has studied himself, namely practical inference.[4] As the Aristotelian origin of practical inference reveals, instrumental rationality has not been unfamiliar to other cultures either. The application of scientific knowledge to instrumental purposes is, however, characteristic of our modern Western culture alone. It is the basis of modern technology.

Technological applications of scientific knowledge have enabled the explosive growth of material living standards in the industrialized countries during the past few centuries. The huge improvement in material welfare has not, however, been accompanied with a parallel progress in morals. Science has refuted empirical beliefs held by Christianity, thereby also reducing its moral authority. Various theories of philosophical ethics have attempted to replace Christian morality with a rational foundation of objective values. Yet there is no agreement on this foundation so far, and von Wright entertains little hope for the future. Scientific and instrumental rationality are the only established forms of rationality in our modern culture, but they are not suitable for moral purposes. Instead, their dominance has put forward a widely accepted view that normative judgements of intrinsic value remain outside of rational research and argumentation, founded on irrational beliefs and attitudes only. To quote von Wright, 'we have approached the belief that value judgements differ from factual judgements: that they merely express emotive attitudes that reflect the opinions, aspirations, and wants of individuals and groups'.[5]

The rejection of intrinsic values outside the range of rational deliberation has, together with the decay of Christian morality, led Western societies to a state of moral vacuum or even moral nihilism. In a moral vacuum there is no generally approved set of norms and values available. This lack of objective norms and values is also liable to produce moral nihilism: indifference toward moral considerations and the ruthless pursuit of egoistic wants. Both a moral vacuum and moral nihilism characterize life in our liberal societies, claims von Wright.[6] These moral conditions of modernity also provide a causal explanation for the various environmental and social problems of our time.

The main problem of our civilization, which is dominated by scientific and instrumental rationality, is our inability to evaluate the ultimate ends of human life. The ever more efficient technological exploitation of nature -justified by the over 3 000-year-old, already abandoned Judaeo-Christian myth- threatens the ecological balance of the Earth with *nemesis naturalis*, the revenge of nature.[7] To support this gloomy prognosis von Wright points to the greenhouse effect caused by pollution, erosion caused by over-extensive pasturing and the cutting of forests; the extinction of several species; the exhaustion of natural resources; and fast-expanding growth of the world population. Great as the ecological problem is, even greater, however, is the threat posed by distressed human nature. Von Wright warns that "if *nemesis* beats down human technological hubris, it is because his own 'nature' does not stand any more but rises against those living conditions that man has created for himself'.[8]

Von Wright characterizes the social problems of industrialized liberal societies as various forms of alienation. Modern man is alienated from nature, which he exploits; from his neighbours, against whom he competes; and from social decision-making, whose formal democracy is being suppressed by governmental bureaucracy and the ever increasing intervention of market forces. Demands for efficiency and productivity invade all levels and structures of society as political institutions lose their control over the unified 'technosystem' of the market, science and industry. Life in our liberal societies has become an increasingly restless and stressful struggle for well-being, observes von Wright. The struggle for power and the ability to consume does not, however, have any winners: the winners as well as the losers end up experiencing the vanity and insignificance of their solitary lives. Some compensation and escape from the frustration and hopelessness of modern life is provided by alcohol, narcotics, and various irrational, mystical doctrines that spread under the heading of 'New Age'. Crime and terrorism represent the most extreme and violent form of escapism.[9]

Von Wright claims that modern societies are quite helpless in facing these environmental and social problems. Instead of tackling the basic structures and ends of modern society and the economy, they try to devise counter-technologies to eliminate problems that threaten the undisturbed functioning of industry and economy.[10] The price for economical growth will, however, be paid with the moral decay of our societies, warns von Wright. The civil rights and liberties of liberal societies become hollow words as

> the individual will become alienated from impersonal social machinery ruled by arbitrary bureaucrats. His lifeworld will become so restricted that his 'real freedom' will shrink to a narcissistic dedication to the external symbols of status and welfare provided by consumption and material ownership.[11]

Von Wright's critique of liberal society displays some striking similarities to the communitarian criticism of Alasdair MacIntyre and Charles Taylor. Von Wright's claim of a moral vacuum is related to MacIntyre's more sophisticated thesis of the incommensurability of moral concepts. Von Wright seems to agree with MacIntyre that the emotivist denial of objective moral criteria has become the main standpoint in modern discussion.[12] Even more equivalent to von Wright's position is Taylor's analysis of modern morality in *The Ethics of Authenticity*. Taylor is worried about 'the hold of moral subjectivism in our culture. By this I mean the view that moral positions are not in any way grounded in reason or the nature of things but are ultimately just adopted by each of us because we find ourselves drawn to them. On this view, reason can't adjudicate moral disputes'.[13] Von Wright shares Taylor's concern for individual autonomy and authenticity suffering from the pressures of instrumental rationality, governmental bureaucracy and the market economy. These problems also dominate the critical theory of Theodor W. Adorno and Max Horkheimer. Von Wright accepts the basic argument of *Dialectic of Enlightenment* that modern instrumental rationality is rapidly turning freedom into its opposite.

> It is not merely that domination is paid for by the alienation of men from objects dominated: with the objectification of spirit, the very relations of men- even those of the individual to himself- were bewitched. The individual is reduced to the nodal point of the conventional responses and modes of operation expected of him.— Through the countless agencies of mass production and its culture the conventionalized modes of behavior are impressed on the individual as the only natural, respectable, and rational ones. He defines himself as a thing, as an element, as success or failure. His yardstick is self-preservation, successful or unsuccessful approximation to the objectivity of his function and the models established for it.[14]

Put somewhat less provocatively these lines could be von Wright's.

It is rather difficult to evaluate von Wright's critique of liberal society. His claims are often general and extensive, yet he provides either no or only a few arguments to support them. Take, for instance, the claim that there is a causal connexion between a moral vacuum or nihilism and the various social and psychological problems of our time.[15] Von Wright provides no argument to show and explicate the causal connexions between these phenomena. Yet it is not possible to deny that there are no causal connexions at all, because even if there are some, they may be so subtle and complicated that we cannot follow them. This seems to be a general problem of cultural criticism. I therefore find it more promising to focus on von Wright's own attempt to overcome the assumed moral crisis of Western civilization. His attempt is based on Aristotelian ethical rationality and the notion of 'the good of man' attached to it.

3. 'Value-rationality' and 'the good of man'

'Value-rationality' is a form of practical, ethical rationality that von Wright has tried to revive in his own thinking. Although the notion of value-rationality originates from Max Weber, being a translation from his 'Wertrationalität', von Wright connects it rather to the form of rationality that Aristotle calls *phronesis*, in the meaning of 'a true and reasoned state of capacity to act with regard to the things that are good or bad for man'.[16]

Von Wright translates *phronesis* in various contexts by such expressions as 'practical reason', 'practical wisdom', 'deliberation', 'value-rationality', or more extensively, 'comprehension of the right way of life'. All these expressions point to the kind of rationality that enables us to evaluate the influence of human activity on our total wellbeing. Whereas the Aristotelian notion of *prohairesis* is equivalent to instrumental rationality, choice of optional means to some given end, *phronesis*, on the other hand, is concerned about the deliberation of optional ends of human life. These ends are of a specific kind since they are not aspired to as a means to some further goals but as intrinsic constituents of the good human life or 'the good of man'.[17] Von Wright introduces this concept as the central notion of *The Varieties of Goodness*. He then suggests that the proper synonym for 'the good of man' is 'welfare' in a broad and comprehensive sense that covers both happiness and wellbeing.[18] Later, however, he links it rather to 'happiness' in the Aristotelian sense, 'as a 'quality' of a man's life over a substantial part of it'.[19]

Von Wright argues that we need value-rationality to complement and direct instrumental rationality. The hold of instrumental rationality is a problematic feature in our culture,

> because it tempts us to separate the questions of ultimate ends from the sphere of rational argumentation and thus to suppress the other form of rationality connected with ends, not as means to other, perhaps only faintly comprehended ends, but as relevant to the purpose that philosophers have called 'the good of man'.[20]

The task of value-rationality is thus to bring the utmost ends of human life, buried under the instrumental way of thinking, into conscious, rational deliberation.

The point of von Wright's value-rationality is simply to qualify the preferential choices of an agent with knowledge of the causal consequences and prerequisites connected with attaining the optional ends of human action. Von Wright accepts the modern subjective view of human ends. Yet he sees that subjective choices can be more or less rational. 'Ends fall under rational control on account of their consequences', remarks von Wright.[21]

Von Wright considers the achievement of an end as a positive value. Means used in order to attain the end, in contrast, denote a negative value. Rational deliberation is the procedure in which we simply compare the 'magnitude' of these values. As von Wright puts it, 'we do this always while asking ourselves whether an end is (or was) worth pursuing. In other words, we ask whether an end is worth its price or not'.[22] A reasonable agent does not pursue ends that require means that cost more than attaining them would pay, states von Wright. His own example is a man who has ruined his health because of his professional and social ambition and now regrets his former preferences. His 'foolishness' was that he did not anticipate the way he might have had to change his preferences. Consideration of his 'real' preferences would, however, have been possible had he clearly paid attention to the causal consequences that will follow from his action, claims von Wright. Now it was only the actualization of these causal connexions that taught him practical wisdom about the price of his end.[23]

It is precisely by causal connexions that von Wright sees objective reality controlling the rationality of human ends. This kind of practical wisdom requires, however, complete knowledge over the causal connexions related to optional actions. Leaning on this knowledge, we should be able to evaluate and anticipate how the actualization of our ends will affect our valuation of these ends. Von Wright admits that this is a problem of all theories of teleological ethics as he says that we all have to face some irrevocable and oppressive decisions, knowing the importance of the decision without being able to determine all its consequences and hence its influence on our good.[24] Another problem of value-rationality that can, to some extent, be tackled is the weakness of will.

Weakness of will, *akrasia*, is a serious practical problem connected with value-rationality. This problem concerns especially strongly wanted and easily attainable ends, whose harmful side-effects will occur only in the distant future. One chooses an optional action whose consequences are wanted in the short run, but whose long-term consequences turn it into an unwanted one. One can fall into such irrationality whether for lack of self-discipline or because of one's shortsightedness. In the latter case one simply lacks the capacity for clear articulation of one's preferences.[25] The ability to deliberate one's own ends is not, however, enough. This is because many of our modern problems depend on the globally uneven distribution of benefit and harm.

In his latest papers von Wright has tried to apply the notions of value-rationality and the good of man on a social and global level. The causal connexions related to our ends usually concern not only our good but also the good of people living in other social groups, countries or future generations. Von Wright has, therefore, characterized the modern crisis as a global conflict of wants and needs: the satisfaction of our wants in the industrialized countries puts at risk the satisfaction of the needs of the majority of the world population, including future generations.[26]

Von Wright has attempted to base the duty to take care of the good of other people on practical reason. The argument rests on the symmetry and universalizability of our ends. If we want to derive benefit from such primary goods as happiness, friendship, health and loving care, we have to be able to generalize these wants. We must be ready to allow the same constituents of good life for other people as well, regardless of their temporal or local existence. 'It is logically impossible that everyone gets the love he needs unless there is someone to give it', argues von Wright in his support of altruism and the love of one's neighbour.[27] Furthermore,

> if it is rational to think that loving care should be generalizable, it is also the demand of practical reason that we should try to develop it in ourselves and in people we educate. This demand is expressed in the highest command of Christianity to love one's neighbor as oneself. This is the right kind of self-love in a generalized form.[28]

4. Evaluation

Von Wright maintains that enlightened reason has not been able to provide the foundation for a generally accepted code of moral norms and values. Instead, it has drifted into a subjective view of values as mere expressions of emotive attitudes. If this comment is meant to be an accurate evaluation of modern moral philosophy, it neglects the efforts of several thinkers with inequitable cynicism. This clearly cannot be the case. Von Wright may, on the other hand, deplore the poor success of philosophical ethics in replacing the decline of Christian morality. This is partly true but the claim is still exaggerated. Philosophers, including such liberal theorists as John Locke, Adam Smith, Immanuel Kant, John Stuart Mill, or John Rawls, have certainly shaped our moral consciousness with their ethical ideas, even though it is impossible to determine the exact measure of their influence. I suppose that von Wright would agree with this too. He might then reformulate his position to claim that the liberal tradition has not provided a sufficient moral foundation that could have enabled us to avoid or to solve the pressing problems of our time. But is von Wright's value-rationality able to serve this purpose any better?

Von Wright points out that causal connexions related to the achievement of an end constitute an objective factor in subjective decision-making. From this position he tries to bridge the gap between facts and values. Values cannot, however, be part of this bridge, because the process described by von Wright is only concerned with the clear articulation of the factual elements involved in the decision. The valuation of optional ends is left to deliberation and the decision of each subject alone. In this way the purpose of value-rationality proves to be only to clarify the knowledge of causal connexions related to optional ways of action, in so far as this kind of perfect knowledge before action is possible at all.

The justification of objective values seems in the end to return to the independent deliberation of human ends. The justification of ends belonging to the good of man is reduced, whether in the conditions of perfect or imperfect knowledge of causal connexions, to the decisions of a valuing subject. The question remains: what reason does a valuing subject have to prefer one good to another?

Von Wright has tried to solve this problem by introducing a distinction between 'intrinsic' and 'reasoned' preferences. Intrinsic preferences are based on merely liking better, and are equivalent to tastes. I may prefer oranges to apples, because I like oranges better. Compared to intrinsic preferences, von Wright's definition of reasoned preferences is only negative, because he considers 'reasoned' all preferences that are founded on some other reasons than mere liking better. An example of a preference for reasons could be a preference to take a train rather than to take a flight, because travelling by train is safer and cheaper than flying, even though one would like flying better.[29] Leaning on this distinction between intrinsic and reasoned preferences von Wright tries to give a more adequate account of the good of man.

Von Wright introduces another distinction between the 'overall' and the 'merely personal' good of man. The latter notion depends on intrinsic preferences alone. The broader notion of the overall good of man must, instead, be explicated in terms of preferences, *some* of which are reasoned preferences 'of a specific kind'.[30] The reason for these specific kinds of preferences is, according to him, that they enhance another person's happiness, his 'merely personal' good. And, to quote von Wright's conclusion, 'to prefer to enhance another person's happiness rather than one's own is an aspect of the sentiment we call love'.[31]

These conceptual clarifications do not, however, totally succeed in removing the problems involved in preferential choice concerning the good of man. If each subject is allowed his or her own deliberation and decision of his or her good, von Wright is not able to attain the objective values he longs for in his cultural philosophical essays. This conclusion is also confirmed in *The Philosophy of Georg Henrik von Wright*. "In the last resort the subject's own judgement decides whether something is or was good for him and thus counts as a positive 'constituent' of his good", maintains von Wright.[32] In a recent interview he admits even that 'I'm inclined– to favour subjectivism to objectivism, and I'm at least inclined to be suspicious and skeptical toward any kind of objectivism in ethics'.[33]

There seems to be a noticeable cleavage between von Wright's cultural and analytical enterprises. Von Wright the cultural critic declares that we need objective values in order to overcome the foundational crisis of our culture. On the other hand, there is von Wright the analyst who is reserved or even resistant to objectivism in ethics. Von Wright has been ready to admit that he is well aware of these two 'personalities' in his philosophical profile. It is also perfectly consistent to be an adherent of ethical subjectivism and yet to deplore that this position does not favour objective values of culture. The problem is, however, that von Wright has not been quite content with his subjectivism.

Von Wright has tried to provide an ethical position that could be called 'reasoned subjectivism'. Value-rationality is a method of excluding arbitrary ends from other subjective preferences. Yet von Wright seems, at times, to think that this critical method can even yield some objective values. Von Wright talks about such 'necessary', or 'natural' ends, or 'needs' as survival, health, welfare, happiness, friendship, and loving care. He thinks that these ends are necessary constituents of the good human life, because it is either logically impossible or perverted and thus irrational not to value them.[34] These objective constituents of the good life cannot, however, be founded on value-rationality, a method of weighing harms and benefits connected with the achievement of optional ends. This is because value-rationality only appears to be a negative method: it cannot provide a sufficient reason for everyone to adopt those positive values -survival perhaps as a biological end apart- that von Wright has advocated. Justification of those values seems rather to point at another well-known form of rationality: to the constituents of the good life according to *common sense*.

Notes

(Quotations from von Wright's texts not originally in English have been translated by the author and revised by Mark Shackleton.)

1. von Wright, 1989a, p. 163.
2. von Wright, 1983a, p. 182; von Wright, 1987, p. 61.
3. von Wright, 1985, p. 180; von Wright, 1987, p. 17.
4. e.g. von Wright, 1983b, pp. 1-18.
5. von Wright, 1992, p. 188.
6. von Wright, 1987, p. 75; von Wright, 1992, p. p. 188.
7. von Wright, 1977, pp. 13-5; von Wright, 1983a, pp. 183-91; von Wright, 1987, pp. 74-8.
8. von Wright, 1987, p. 135.
9. von Wright, 1983a, pp. 186-7; von Wright, 1987, pp. 75-6, 110-21, 134-8; von Wright, 1992, p. 163-8.
10. von Wright, 1987, pp. 134-5.
11. von Wright, 1992, pp. 166-7.
12. MacIntyre, 1985.
13. Taylor, 1995, p. 18.
14. Horkheimer and Adorno, 1994, p. 28.
15. von Wright, 1987, p. 75; von Wright, 1992, p. 188.
16. *The Nicomachean Ethics of Aristotle,* 1140b 4-5, quoted from the translation by Sir David Ross.
17. von Wright, 1985, pp. 180-4; von Wright, 1987, pp. 21, 131; von Wright, 1989, p. 161; von Wright, 1992, p. 171. Von Wright's interpretation of Aristotle's practical reason as an ability to deliberate different optional ends related to good life is not, however, completely coherent with Aristotle's own account. As von Wright remarks also by himself, Aristotle denies independent deliberation of ends. In *The Nicomachean Ethics* (1112b 12) Aristotle writes that 'we deliberate not about ends but about means'.
18. von Wright, 1963, pp. 86-7. Von Wright admits that there is a broad sense in which all the three terms can be regarded as rough synonyms and alternative synonyms for 'the good of man', but he maintains that more commonly this is not the case. Instead, he suggests that "welfare' is a comprehensive term which covers the whole of that which we also call 'the good of man' and of which happiness and well-being are 'aspects', or 'components', or 'parts'.
19. von Wright, 1989c, p. 781. Von Wright also provides an outline of a happy life: a human being is happy 'when his basic ('welfare') needs are satisfied, when his work gives him fulfillment, when he does not envy his

neighbour, and when great misfortunes do not befall him, such as serious illness or the untimely death of beloved person'.

20. von Wright, 1985, p. 180.
21. von Wright, 1985, p. 181.
22. von Wright, 1985, p. 175.
23. von Wright, 1963, p. 181; von Wright, 1983a, pp. 83-4; von Wright, 1985, pp. 181-2.
24. von Wright, 1963, pp. 106-13; von Wright, 1983a, pp. 83-4; von Wright, 1985, pp. 181-3.
25. von Wright, 1963, pp. 112-3.
26. von Wright, 1985, pp. 185-8; von Wright, 1989, pp. 165-6.
27. von Wright, 1985, p. 196.
28. Ibid.
29. von Wright, 1985, pp. 173-4; von Wright, 1989c, p. 786. Von Wright admits that many reasoned preferences are 'anchored', in the way of psychological motivation, in likings. To prefer safety to comfort may be a purely subjective tendency. Von Wright argues, however, that this need not always be the case. We may, for example, choose to do our duties although we would rather like to amuse ourselves.
30. von Wright, 1989c, pp. 786-9. Von Wright tries to bring together both intrinsic and reasoned preferences in his notion of the overall good of man. He does not, however, even try to meet the question concerning the proportion between intrinsic preferences and reasoned preferences in the overall the good of man. He passes the question by stating that 'whether a man will be better off (overall), if he consistently, instead of seeking his own (personal) good, lets his actions be guided by love of his neighbour, is a question that can not be decided on conceptual grounds'. Von Wright is compelled to put the question aside because of his general view on philosophical ethics. Philosopher's task is limited to conceptual investigation of moral notions and their criteria of application alone. 'It is not the task of the philosopher, *as* a philosopher, to censure people or society. His task is to reflect on the conceptual standards used in moral censuring and social criticism', maintains von Wright (1989b, 51). Conceptual clarification may provide more adequate tools for moral and social criticism, as von Wright readily remarks. Yet it cannot provide a sufficient basis for a normative theory of ethics. Von Wright,'s own pursuit of normative theory based on value-rationality illustrates this problem well.
31. von Wright, 1989c, p. 789.
32. von Wright, 1989c, p. 796.
33. von Wright's interview with Mikko Lahtinen, Sami Pihlström and Jarkko S. Tuusvuori in March 1995.
34. von Wright, 1985, pp. 167, 178; von Wright, 1989, p. 154.

References

Aristotle (1954), *The Nicomachean Ethics of Aristotle*, translated and introduced by Sir David Ross, Oxford University Press: London.

Horkheimer, M. and Adorno, T. W. (1969), *Dialectic of Enlightenment*, translated by John Cumming,, Herder and Herder: New York.

MacIntyre, A., (1985), *After Virtue*, Duckworth, 2nd edition: London.

Taylor, C. (1995), *The Ethics of Authenticity*, Harvard University Press: New York.

von Wright, G.H. (1963), *The Varieties of Goodness*, Routledge & Kegan Paul: London.

von Wright, G.H. (1977), 'What is Humanism, The Lindley Lecture', University of Kansas, October 19, 1976, University of Kansas, Department of Philosophy.

von Wright G. H. (1983a), *Humanismi elämänasenteena* (Humanism as an Outlook on Life), suomentanut Kaila, K., Otava: Helsinki.

von Wright, G. H. (1983b), *Practical Reason, Philosophical papers,. vol. I*, Basil Blackwell: Oxford.

von Wright, G. H. (1985), *Filosofisia tutkielmia* (Philosophical Studies), suomentaneet Nyman, H., Nyberg, T. ja Uusitalo, J., Kirjayhtymä: Helsinki.

von Wright, G. H. (1987), *Tiede ja ihmisjärki* (Science and Reason), suomentanut Leikola, A., Otava: Helsinki.

von Wright, G. H. (1989a), 'Arvot ja tarpeet' (Values and Needs) in Malaska, Kantola & Kasanen: *Riittääkö energia - riittääkö järki?*, Gaudeamus: Helsinki.

von Wright, G. H. (1989b), 'Intellectual Autobiography' in Hahn, L. E. & Schilpp, P. A. (eds), *The Philosophy of Georg Henrik von Wright*, The Library of Living Philosophers, vol. XIX, La Salle, Open Court, pp. 2-55.

von Wright, G. H. 1(989c), 'A Reply to My Critics' in Hahn, L. E. & Schilpp, P. A. (eds), *The Philosophy of Georg Henrik von Wright*, The Library of Living Philosophers, vol. XIX, La Salle, Open Court.

von Wright, G. H. (1992), *Minervan pöllö, esseitä vuosilta 1987-1991*, (The Owl of Minerva, Philosophical Essays from 1987 till 1991), Otava: Helsinki.

von Wright, G. H. (1995), Interview with Mikko Lahtinen, Sami Pihlström and Jarkko S. Tuusvuori, *Niin & näin*, vol. 2/1995, 4-14.

In defense of a moral concept of democracy

Tapio Puolimatka

The concept of a moral democracy has become a focus of attention in recent discussion on democratic theory. This interest has been raised by the realization that democracy cannot be conceived merely as a system of institutional arrangements like a multiparty system, a regular secret ballot, universal adult suffrage, a parliament with a fixed term, an independent judiciary, etc. It is essentially a system of values like justice, freedom, and respect for personal autonomy. Furthermore, democracy presupposes citizens with certain kinds of dispositions, with democratic virtues (White, 1995; Sartori, 1987; Tarrant, 1989).

The epithet 'moral democracy' may be misleading in that the realm of values and norms does not coincide with the realm of morality. The principles guiding public action have a basis in various non-moral as well as in moral values. The epithet can be justified by the central importance of the moral foundations of democracy and of the moral dispositions of the citizens.

The concept of moral democracy does not suggest that governments should be involved in the moral reformation of citizens, indeed, it has proved to be dangerous to assign moral functions to government in that sense. The realm of politics is not that of ethics, although one of the main tasks of government is to maintain justice. The concept of moral democracy points to the central importance of the moral foundations of democracy, the sense of which has been eroded by an economic-like view of politics (Sartori, 1987, pp. 241-2).

Although moral democrats' thinking is very diverse, these thinkers are unified in regarding democracy as a normative concept involving a certain constellation of values. My aim in this essay is to make suggestions about how the theory should be developed.

1. The moral basis of democracy

The concept of democracy in its etymological sense as rule by the people can be understood in various ways (a great many, everybody, people as an organic whole, the majority). In practice democracy means the will of the majority. That is sometimes understood in a purely descriptive sense. But such a descriptive sense is not sufficient. If the majority decides to enslave the minority against the latter's will, the system can hardly be called democratic, even if the enslaved minority maintains the right to vote. Therefore, democracy cannot be conceived as an absolute majority principle expressing whatever the majority happens to prefer or choose (Sartori, 1962, p. 19). An acceptable meaning of democracy has to include a moral aspect, the protection of the rights of the minority. This protection of the rights of the minority cannot be dependent on the whims or preferences of the majority. It has to be based on an independent moral framework.

While democracy is a normative concept involving a moral ideal, it has a descriptive aspect as well. In a sense democracy is an ideal which is never fully realized in practice. The name 'democracy' in its etymological sense of 'rule by the people' is somewhat misleading, since in the real world democracies tend to be polyarchies, as R. A. Dahl calls them. Nevertheless, it is an ideal which we constantly need to keep in mind. Although 'democracy' is misleading for descriptive purposes, it cannot be replaced. Ideals and reality should not be confused, but they may interact (Sartori 1962, p. 4).

The fundamental value of democracy is that of respect for human dignity, which assumes such ideals as justice, truth, liberty and equality. The political activity of the state should always be guided by the moral ideal of the sanctity of the individual. It may be problematic to justify the ideal, especially in the absolute form in which it is required as the foundation for the democratic order. Nevertheless, without it, democracy lacks an adequate moral basis. Democratic structures and procedures should concretize fundamental democratic values.

John Madison's view of democracy is an example. The ethical goal of democracy is to form a political system which does not tyrannize over its citizens but respects their fundamental rights. The basic axiom in Madison's political thought is an ethical one: natural rights ought to be respected (cf. Dahl 1953, pp. 10-2). A respect for fundamental rights is the equivalent to a political practice which does not tyrannize over citizens. To this ethical premise Madison joins an empirical one according to which a republic is a necessary although not a sufficient condition for creating a non-tyrannizing society. He looks for an answer to the question of which procedural solutions help towards the creation of such a society (see Hamilton & Madison & Jay, 1952).

2. The independence of the moral framework

The sanctity of the individual as the moral foundation of democracy has been understood within two basically different epistemological and ontological frameworks. Two different views on value compete for supremacy within liberal democratic theory. Differences in the epistemology and ontology of value lead to different interpretations of the two basic principles of liberal democratic theory: a) individualism, b) a view that the relationships between citizens are moral relationships.

The reductive naturalist view (started by Hobbes, as he is standardly interpreted) rejects traditional concepts of society, justice and natural law, and derives political rights and responsibilities from the wills and contracts of disassociated individuals. This view is based on moral antirealist and value relativist presuppositions. Political reality is constructed of atomistically understood individuals with various preferences, or interest groups representing these preferences; democracy is understood as a value-neutral procedural device for mediating conflicts. Since individuals are treated as atomistic points of utility preferences, their agreements and compromises define the moral principles guiding the relationships.

The rival view is moral realist and value objectivist: it regards individual worth as a moral ideal setting requirements also for the political system. The individual has an intrinsic worth regardless of his usefulness to the community, and the moral requirements derived from the sanctity of the individual are regarded as objective and universal. The principles guiding the moral relationships between citizens are inherent in the sanctity of the individual. Political procedures do not merely mediate between various preferences expressed in society, their application is constrained by objective moral requirements of freedom, equality and justice. The democratic ideal in this form assumes that some societal states of affairs are more valuable than others, and that there are rationally and morally compelling reasons for preferring the democratic view of the human being and society to its alternatives.

This essay builds on the latter tradition, which assumes that there is an intrinsic relationship between democracy as rule of the people and values which are independent of the preferences of individuals. The democratic process presupposes moral standards which do not derive their validity from the shifting preferences of individuals, but which serve as the basis for the moral evaluation of policies.

Criticism of the injustices perpetrated by those in positions of power involves a contrast between moral ideals and the existing political corruption. In addition to acquiring an insight into these factors, criticism aims at changing or even removing the conditions of a false or distorted consciousness (Connerton, 1978, pp. 18-20). This assumes standards which serve as a nonarbitrary basis for such evaluation. Thinking in a genuinely critical sense cannot be conceived without assuming a framework of objective criteria. The critical challenge to the corruption of political power is morally meaningless without a background of moral truth and objective values, which provide nonarbitrary criteria for evaluation and judgment.

3. The moral responsibility of the citizen

Democratic government is supposed to be responsive to the wishes of the people. But it obviously makes a great difference whether these wishes are morally responsible or irresponsible. The democratic process is not well served either by constituency or by government corruption. Democratic citizens should be morally committed to the fundamental values of democracy - freedom, equality and justice. Without such a moral commitment democratic procedures can be used for antidemocratic ends. Morally committed citizens are needed to counteract tendencies towards apathy, corruption and exploitation.

If the democratic citizen is understood merely as a rationally deliberating individual, an essential dimension of democratic citizenship is not accounted for. Deliberative rationality can be used to subvert and destroy society. Thus, the choice between constructive and subversive action is a moral one, since to choose a better society is rational within the framework of moral values.

The critical disposition characterizing the democratic citizen is not mere intellectual proficiency. Such proficiency does not preclude the citizen's being creatively destructive and intelligently subversive. Critical proficiency can be used to destroy democracy. Individuals may rationally (in the narrow sense) prefer an undemocratic alternative insofar as they have better chances of attaining positions of power in such a society. The subversion or dehumanizing of a society are not, however, compatible with the democratic ideal, even if rational standards are not formally violated. Such actions are not consistent with the moral commitment to freedom, equality and justice.

The human ideal which is central to democracy suggests that the citizen should exhibit an autonomous political will which is socially constructive. Such a political will presupposes conative and valuational integrity. This ideal involves a moral commitment to democratic values.

One way of expressing the need for moral commitment in political action is to speak of a healthy sense of public selfhood. This sense requires the cultivation of what Rawls calls the 'very great virtues', such as 'tolerance and being ready to meet others halfway, and the virtue of reasonableness and the sense of fairness' (Rawls, 1985, p. 17). The exercise of these virtues must be directed towards the fulfilling of those interests that work toward the well-being or a larger community. The perspective of public selfhood orientates the individual citizen to consider the interests of other people, as well as of the community as a whole. The concept of the public interest should not merely consider the individual interests in an optimal compromise from the perspective of utility, but considerations of moral worth should determine the concept.

4. Political participation

Moral democratic theory should regard the individual moral worth of the citizen as an objective and intrinsic value and derive the value of citizen participation from this notion. Citizen participation is regarded as something owing to individuals, as their right, and as conducive to the development of their full human potential.

Certain moral democratic theories regard citizen participation as valuable because of its educative effect on the citizens themselves. They regard the virtues of a political system as bound up with its effects on the characters of its citizens (Lively, 1975, p. 132). This approach has been challenged by arguing that political participation has no noteworthy educational effect on citizens.

Moral democratic theory may also justify the value of citizen participation in terms of the quality of the governmental decisions that emerge as a result of it. It informs decision makers about relevant points of view, and works as a check against governmental corruption. This approach partly measures the virtues of a political system in terms of governmental performance (Lively, 1975, 132). Some revisionists oppose political participation on the grounds that it leads to worse government than can be achieved with a more apathetic citizenry.

The crucial controversy centres around the question whether the active political participation of critical and morally committed citizens is a necessary precondition for democracy. The democratic concept of the rule by the people is inherently a moral notion, insofar as people are understood as moral beings. Understanding citizens as inherently moral beings with moral freedom in the context of objective values and norms requires a strong concept of citizen participation with the notion of moral responsibility attached to it.

A meaning crucially included in the democratic ideal of the citizen is that of oppositional thinking, 'an activity of unveiling or debunking' (Connerton, 1978, pp. 16-7). All public acts are subject to individual scrutiny insofar as each citizen has a moral responsibility which she cannot evade by referring to public opinion or the prevailing consensus on what is morally desirable and praiseworthy. As a consequence, political decisions have to stand the scrutiny of a wide variety of critical viewpoints. Such a critical practice is founded on the conviction that any person is corruptible if she possesses uncontrolled power or if she has any hope of possessing such power.

5. Democratic freedom and the moral character of citizens

Democratic freedom depends on the moral character of citizens. The relationships between citizens are moral relationships and the quality of the life of each person is largely determined by the way she is morally treated by others. Unless the sanctity of their person is respected by others, citizens will need protection by law enforcement. The more prevalent the moral violations of the sanctity of persons in society, the more law enforcement officers need to interfere in the moral relationships between citizens. The more they interfere, the more extensive their powers become and the area of their control is extended. The more their area of control is extended, the wider becomes the area of their potential control over the lives of citizens. Law enforcement is centrally controlled. Ultimately this tends to make society more totalitarian.

This means that the powers of law enforcement can be restricted to the extent that citizens can be morally trusted. Once the moral foundations of society disintegrate, increased powers of control have to be given to law enforcement to prevent the exploitation of the poor and powerless by the rich and powerful and the disintegration of society into anarchy. Once such increased powers are given to law enforcement in a situation of moral disintegration, they will also be increasingly misused. This will make certain kinds of political and moral corruption more prevalent, since power becomes more centralized and more vulnerable to corruption.

6. Moral ideals and political corruption

Since moral democratic theory understands democracy as a normative rather than as a descriptive concept, it contrasts the democratic ideal with the reality of empirical democracies. The ideal is not determined by the empirical situation, but by what is worth pursuing. The fact that empirical democracies do not correspond to the democratic ideal is no reason to reject it. On the contrary, the need for the ideal is emphasized especially when reality diverges from it. The fact that many empirical democracies provide examples of citizen indifference and irrationality does not mean that enlightened political participation is not an ideal. The failure to practise the virtues of democratic citizenship is all the more reason to focus attention on the ideal. The moral democratic ideal, therefore, is not determined by the political reality prevalent in democratic societies. On the contrary, empirical democracies have to be evaluated on the basis of the democratic ideal.

At the same time the commitment to democratic values should not deteriorate into unfounded idealism. It should be balanced by political realism. Democracy is not promoted by illusions; illusions confronted by the realities of political practice lead to disillusionment. And 'disillusionment is an erratic state of mind' which leads to errors in political assessment. (Sartori, 1987, p. 48)

Citizens frequently fail to live up to the democratic ideal. They should be realistic about their failures and be ready to recognize them. To camouflage one's failures by a defensive moral rhetoric means to create an illusionary picture of oneself. Authentic citizenship presupposes the honesty to face the truth about oneself in the light of the ideals one regards as supreme. Any dishonesty naturally distorts the person's view of herself and her interaction with other people, which then makes it hard to achieve genuine social progress. Those who have an illusionary picture of themselves cannot see social problems in their true depth nor realistically evaluate the means for their improvement. They lack the capacity to assess their own social activity and its impact on society. If citizens lose sight of the ideal in order to justify the practice, the practice further degenerates. If they lose sight of the reality of the political corruption and see it in the light of the ideal, they are unable to assess their political activity in its true significance.

Commitment to moral values is not always genuine. The worst atrocities have been committed by persons who thought they were benefiting mankind. Mass murderers have regarded themselves as the world's benefactors. Furthermore, this corruption is never restricted to certain special persons.

Values convey a sense of meaningfulness. The more captivated one becomes by the moral ideal, the more clearly one sees and experiences one's own moral failures. A morally honest person cannot regard her failures as insignificant. It is morally repulsive to think of a Hitler or a Stalin easing their conscience in spite of their victims. The same applies in a more restricted way to anyone who has caused unnecessary suffering to others. Unless citizens maintain a grip on both the ideal and their personal reality, they will fail to reach personal integration. This endangers both a reflective consciousness and a moral vision, since no one can risk ultimate disintegration. As a result they cannot realize some of the essential dimensions of democratic citizenship. This seems to be the crucial dilemma for the moral constitution of the democratic citizen.

7. The moral foundations of democratic procedures

According to the moral democratic vision, democracy consists primarily of a value constellation and only secondarily of a set of procedures. Democracy depends on a moral framework which is independent of subjective desires and preferences or social compromises and agreements. Even optimal structural and procedural solutions are inadequate by themselves to guarantee the proper functioning of democracy. Democracy depends on citizens who take the moral framework seriously. Democratic procedures as such do not guarantee that human rights are respected, if a considerable proportion of the citizens does not respect human dignity.

Mere outward procedures do not in this view make a society democratic. One of the questions worth considering in this respect is: How far can political reality withdraw from the democratic ideal without society ceasing to be democratic? According to the moral democratic vision one should not regard as democratic a society with formally democratic political procedures but without critical and morally committed citizens. If ordinary citizens are manipulated to the extent that they cannot make autonomous political decisions, they cannot be said to exercise political power.

Once democracy is understood as a moral ideal, it is not defined primarily in terms of systemic properties such as the number of competing groups, etc. This does not mean that the systemic effects of e.g. widespread popular participation can be ignored (Ståhlberg & Helander, 1984, pp. 35-7). However, instead of viewing democracy predominantly in terms of systemic properties, the democratic ideal emphasizes people as ends-in-themselves rather than as objects or means to an end (Kant, 1959, 2nd sect.; Scheffler, 1985, pp. 37-8, 85). Democracy is thus a normative concept which sets an ideal for political reality, its procedures, institutional arrangements as well as its political actors. The proper functioning of democracy assumes that a considerable proportion of the citizens practise relevant moral virtues of an enlightened political participation including a concern for justice, equality and freedom.

Although the moral democratic viewpoint is not dominated by the systemic viewpoint, it cannot ignore the factual preconditions of democracy. Systemic stability and effectiveness are relevant considerations although they should not eclipse moral considerations of the sanctity of the human individual. Political procedures have to be evaluated in terms of their factual consequences while not losing sight of the character of democracy as a value system which sets criteria for the procedures. The realistic considerations of system stability and effectiveness are not incompatible with the moral vision of the person as an end-in-himself.

Genuine ideals are capable of interacting with the world. An ideal is not constructive unless it is capable of modification in the light of experience and evidence. Sartori (1987, p. 71) suggests that 'to the extent that an ideal is converted into reality, to the same extent it must become feedback monitored'. The attempt to apply the democratic ideal of self-governance in a maximal form is counterproductive. We need intermediary principles like representation to realize it in practice in the form that it is realizable.

8. Prescriptive pluralism

A crucial element of moral democratic theory is prescriptive pluralism. It implies that 'the independence of non-political bodies with respect to the state has a normative justification and hence that such independence ought to be safeguarded in law and public policy' (Chaplin, 1993, p. 25).

A classical example of a prescriptive pluralist is Johannes Althusius. He broke with the universalistic conception of the state and outlined an anti-universalistic view according to which each type of social association has its own peculiar structure which also governs its relationships to other forms of social association. 'Every type of social relationship has its proper laws peculiar to it, whereby it is ruled. And these laws are different and divergent in each kind of social relationship, according to the requirement of the inner nature of each of them' (Althusius, 1610, cp. I). While provinces and districts may properly be called 'members of the state', individuals, educational institutions, voluntary associations etc. cannot be so called (Althusius, 1610, cap IX, p. 115). Unless both the state and other social institutions are conceived of as possessing a structural principle which forms the basis of their empirical manifestations, it becomes impossible to differentiate them from each other or to identify each of them.

The basic claim of prescriptive or normative pluralists is that the state should not be understood as an all-encompassing social body of which the other institutions form a part. Rather, the state is one social institution among others with a restricted sphere of competence. Democratic freedom, equality and justice are incompatible with a 'power state' which has unlimited political power, that is, which has the competence to determine the scope of its own competence. The competence of the state is normatively delimited by its structural principle, which has to be justified from a value-perspective. Justice, equality and freedom cannot be realized in social practice without instituting certain kinds of societal structures, for example, of the state.

Although states have acquired various forms in the course of history, the values to be realized through the state-structure are not historically relative. There is something relatively constant in the value of justice even though it is part of the process of cultural unfolding. In a similar manner, there are also some constant structural elements in effective ways of realizing these values in social practice, even though cultural disclosure is expressed in these structures as well. The democratic state should be a differentiated organization, which integrates its citizens into a community of justice, equality and freedom.

Prescriptive pluralists are motivated to reflect on the normative significance of non-political bodies in response to the social atomization brought about by the disintegration of communal institutions (like the family) as well as by the tendency towards political centralization characteristic of the modern state. They criticize modern society for 'its isolation of individuals from supportive social bonds found in pre-modern societies without offering adequate replacements, and its exposure of these isolated individuals to the encroachment of an increasingly powerful state' (Chaplin, 1993, p. 27).

Prescriptive pluralism may be justified on the basis that many human values can be realized only in the context of associational pluralism, which provides variegated opportunities for the development of social interaction. Democracy means a political system built on the free interaction between individuals as opposed to a system which sets up barriers to free intercourse and association.

9. The educational foundation of democracy

Tarrant (1989, pp. 82-4) suggests that moral democracy implies the concept of dynamic equality as contrasted with the 'passive' equality of the market democrats. Essential to the former is the fact that the citizen's possibility of furthering her interests through democratic procedures depends on her educational opportunities. Dynamic equality, therefore, implies the right to education.

Implicit in the concept of dynamic equality is the presupposition that people are capable of cognitive and moral development upon which education can have a positive effect. This implies that 'provision shall be made within the institutions of society, especially the political system, for the means of human improvement' (Tarrant, 1989, p. 82). In its developed form moral democratic theory perceives every citizen as an individual whose educational development enables her to take part in discussions about the good society (Tarrant, 1989, p. 161). For moral democrats, fostering the development of citizens is intrinsically valuable.

Israel Scheffler (1985, pp. 121-6) points out that education is not ancillary but essential to democracy: 'A society committed to the democratic ideal is one that makes peculiarly difficult and challenging demands on its members; it accordingly also makes stringent demands on those processes through which its members are educated' (Ibid., p. 122). Public policy cannot be changed through reasoned persuasion and informed consent unless citizens are appropriately educated. The capacity to reshape one's dispositions is the capacity to learn, and a society of learners is what the democratic vision implies. The demands made upon education are not ancillary but essential to the democratic vision. Education is not an instrument through which rulers mould the minds of the ruled, rather it is meant to strengthen the critical powers of the mind so that citizens may take part in the processes of critical discussion on which the social structure depends. Without education citizens lack the capacity to take part in the process of shaping public policy, which would deprive them of the exercise of their basic democratic right. (Ibid.)

Dewey (1963, p. 87) brings out the relationship between the three foundational elements of democracy, its moral, structural and educational aspects. Interaction between individuals presupposes respect for other persons, an effort to understand them and to relate to them. The moral component of social interaction is closely combined with the intellectual one: 'Interest in learning from all the contacts of life is the essential moral interest' (Dewey, 1955, p. 418). Democratic procedures apply these kinds of moral, intellectual and social values to the political process.

Conclusion

This essay suggests that moral democratic theory in its most coherent form centres around the notion of the sanctity of the individual, from which are derived the values of freedom, equality and justice, as well as those of political participation. These values have to be understood within the contexts of moral realism and objectivism about values. Once moral ideals are taken as the essence of democracy, a strong conception of moral and political corruption emerges. The norm for democracy is independent of the reality of empirical democracies, although their application is not.

Values and norms are the foundation of democracy in two ways. First of all, democracy presupposes citizens who are committed to democratic values. Second, it presupposes structures and procedures which concretize these values. Once societal structures and procedures are understood in terms of values, a prescriptive pluralism emerges. The state structure is not seen as an all-compassing structure but one determined by the value of justice and limited in its scope by other relatively independent societal structures. The power state which has the competence to determine its own competence is regarded as inherently totalitarian.

Since democracy is based on the notion of the sanctity of the individual, it should be conducive to the full development of individual potential. Education is therefore central, not merely ancillary, to democracy. Citizens cannot protect their interests without adequate education, nor does the democratic system function properly without critical citizens.

References

Althusius, J. (1610), *Politica Methodice Digesta*, Groningen.

Chaplin, J. P. (1993), *Pluralism, Society and the State*, Unpublished Doctoral Dissertation. University of London.

Connerton, P. (1978), 'Introduction', in Connerton, P. (ed.), *Critical Sociology*, Penguin Books: Harmondsworth.

Dahl, R. A. (1953), *A Preface to Democratic Theory*, University of Chicago Press: Chicago, Ill.

Dewey, J. (1955), *Democracy and Education*, Macmillan: New York.

Dewey, J. (1963), *Experience and Education*, Collier Books: New York.

Hamilton, A. & Madison, J. & Jay, J. (1952), *The Federalist*, edited by Hutchins, R. M., William Benton: Chicago, Ill.

Kant, I. (1959), *The Foundations of the Metaphysics of Morals*, translated by Lewis White Beck. Bobbs-Merrill: Indianapolis, Ind.

Lively, J. (1975), *Democracy*, Blackwell: Oxford.

Puolimatka, T. (1995), *Democracy and Education. The Critical Citizen as an Educational Aim*, The Finnish Academy of Science and Letters: Helsinki.

Rawls, J. (1985), 'Justice as Fairness: Political not Metaphysical', *Philosophy and Public Affairs* 14, no. 3.

Sartori, G. (1962), *Democratic Theory*, Wayne State University Press: Detroit.

Sartori, G. (1987), *Democratic Theory Revisited*, Chatham Press: Chatham, NJ.

Scheffler, I. (1985), *Of Human Potential*, Routledge & Kegan Paul: London.

Ståhlberg, K. & Helander, V. (1984), 'Influence and Participation', in Anckar, D. & Berndtson, E. (eds), *Essays on Democratic Theory*, The Finnish Political Science Association: Tampere.

Tarrant, J. M. (1989), *Democracy and Education*, Avebury: Aldershot.

Liberal identity and moral individualism

Sirkku Hellsten

Introduction

Does the liberal requirement for value pluralism lead inevitably into communitarian ethics or are the liberal values of autonomy, tolerance and equality actually based on an objectivistic and teleological account of justice? This question leads us to one of the main quandaries of modern liberal democracy, that is, how to promote value pluralism without simultaneously falling into radical value subjectivism or cultural relativism. This liberal quandary is related to the practical problems which follow from the cultural diversity of our belief and value systems. It is also connected with the intellectual and theoretical legitimization of liberal democracy as such. Consequently, the main questions discussed in this article are the following: to what degree a liberal democracy must require its individual citizens to commit themselves to shared values and purposes? To what degree a liberal state can and should support cultural diversity and to what degree it must require cultural integration? And furthermore, is liberal value pluralism any more value *pluralism* if it is grounded on an objectivistic account of universal values that are always to be promoted within a liberal society?

The problems in the intellectual justification of liberal value pluralism as well as in the practical actualization of the requirement of tolerance are both closely tied with the problems which individual citizens may have when they are trying to understand what the liberal ideal of an autonomous, moral and political agency really requires from them in practice, as citizens of liberal democracies. After all, on the one hand, the requirement for pluralism demands that liberal society allows and even encourages cultural diversity and many different ways of living. On the other hand, clear moral conflicts arise when some of the different cultural beliefs and traditions themselves turn out to be the enemies of liberal values of tolerance, autonomy and equality.

In this article I want to show that in order to promote its core values and to maintain its legitimacy a liberal political order has to be able to provide such a social and political circumstance in which its individual citizens, first, learn to separate the liberal metaphysical ideals from the empirical facts of their political reality and, secondly, in which they want to commit themselves also in practice to the actualization of these liberal ideals. This means that in order to find the proper limits of tolerance and in order to set guidelines for cultural integration within a liberal state we have to first learn to understand how the idea of moral and political agency has to be reflected in the building of our personal moral identities. I suggest that the only proper way to do is to turn from mechanical, methodological individualism to moral individualism.

The purpose of the view which I have named moral individualism is then simply to once again bring out open the objectivistic values involved in the metaphysics of the positive concept of freedom which has provided the moral foundation of Western democracy since the *polis* of the Ancient Greek - until the naturalist and reductionist liberal economics replaced the teleological value of human dignity with the economic rationality. With the concept of moral individualism I am then trying to find a way to redefine the objectivistic moral foundations of Western democracy. The aim is not to introduce a new political ideology to replace the modern liberal world view but to recapture the insight of the Ancient Greeks on politics which saw the unity of politics, ethics, education and metaphysics.

The purpose is not to suggest that state should be involved in the moral reformation of its citizens. Instead it is to emphasize that also in modern liberal reasoning we can find the human ideal which requires that the individual citizens have to display an autonomous but still socially constructive moral and political will. This shows that the concept of democracy *per se*, even by its liberal definition, is not only descriptive but has also normative and teleological elements in it; elements that are often forgotten in the modern mechanical, procedural individualism. This is simply to state that the concept of democracy defined as the self-government of autonomous individuals asserts clearly in itself what is the good that is to be promoted within a democratic order, and that democratic process presupposes moral standards which do not derive their validity from the random preferences of atomistic individuals, but which serve as the basis for the moral evaluation of state policies.

It also adds moral perspective to liberal individualism by explicating what kind of characteristics and moral dispositions are presumed from the individuals as citizens as well as what are those intrinsic democratic values that these individuals have to be committed to. Simultaneously it demands that the duty of a democratic state is to provide such a cultural and political atmosphere which encourages individuals' critical judgement and moral behaviour. In political practice this means that in order to maintain its legitimacy a liberal regime has to promote individuals' moral and political agency by linking the individual rights, which we now take granted, with duties and by emphasizing that freedom has to be balanced with responsibility. It also means that the requirement of tolerance as well as material property and market economy can have only instrumental value in actualizing individuals moral autonomy and commitment to moral behaviour.

Moral agency and liberal democracy

The theoretical background for the quest for liberal moral identity is in the problems of the modern welfare liberal concept of justice as it is presented by John Rawls in his *A Theory of Justice* (1972) and *Political Liberalism* (1993). Rawls's welfare liberal deontology is of central interest in this context because it integrates two quite different Western liberal traditions in a somewhat controversial manner.[1] Methodologically Rawls's liberalism has its roots in the Anglo-American naturalistic and empiricistic tradition of classical economical liberalism, which originally promotes the concepts of negative freedom, market economy, and the minimal state. Rawls's own normative agenda, however, clearly appears to have more in common with the continental idealistic liberal humanism and its metaphysical assumption on the individuals' potential for a moral agency. This means that Rawls's liberalism then promotes the idea of positive rather than negative freedom, and has clearly more collectivist views on political distribution than the classical liberal economics would consent to.[2] If applied to practice Rawls's welfare liberal reasoning would produce a state that would not be very different from the continental and Northern European style of welfare state.[3] Rawls's attempt to bring together these methodologically and normatively two quite different liberal traditions, however, leads modern welfare liberalism into circular reasoning which, for its part, tends to confuse liberal values with political facts much in the same way as they lately have been confused in the political practice of the Western welfare liberal states. This confusion between values and facts leads welfare liberal reasoning to a cul-de-sac: firstly, the central values of liberalism such as autonomy, equality, tolerance and individual rights can be interpreted either as values (to be attained) or as facts (which already exist) depending on what other purposes (political, economic, and so on) we have. This makes liberal policies to lose their normative direction. Secondly, the integration of the two different liberal traditions creates an internally contradictory image of an individual as a moral and political agent. A Rawlsian image of a fully rational and reasonable political decision-maker is, on the one hand, based on the naturalistic and reductionistic assumptions of human nature. This means that it conceives individuals egoistic competitors whose personal morals are more or less directly derived from their natural will for self-interest and self-preservation. On the other hand, this same ideal decision-maker implicitly presents the teleological idea of the true nature of human beings as moral and political agents with responsibility on others.

This complex constellation of methodological subject makes it difficult to see whether contemporary political liberalism is mere political rhetoric used to maintain prevailing power relations; whether its function is to describe the structure and functioning of a modern market economy or whether it actually promotes a particular, objectivistic and comprehensive view of the good that welfare liberal democracy is based on, and also built to promote in practice. The attempt to integrate the two different liberal approaches to human nature in an abstract, intellectual image of an ideal decision-maker also provides a complicated model for a modern individual as an autonomous moral and political agent. This ideal decision-maker that is divided into an empirical egoist, and to the ideal of universal human morality makes it difficult to distinguish liberal values from local political and cultural facts. This means that the image of an ideal decision-maker not only describes the cultural identity of modern individuals living in a Western market society but it also attempts to provide us with the metaphysical, teleological idea or rather ideal we, as individual citizens, should strive for in our own lives in order to maintain the legitimacy of our liberal political order. If we now assume that this methodological subject presents an ideal prototype for an individual who is to survive in a materialistic consumer society we come to accept that such features as the egoistic market rationality, consumption and disinterest in others are justified, maybe even desired, features in a modern identity. Simultaneously we lose the connection with the objectivistic, humanistic values which are, at least implicitly, built-in the idea of positive freedom that welfare liberal democracy was meant to promote.

It is obvious that in political practice it makes quite a difference whether we start with the naturalistic and empiristic view, which takes as a given fact that modern individuals are isolated and self-interested market competitors, who care for no one but their own interests; or whether we start with the humanistic metaphysical assumption which believes that in every individual human being there is potential for moral responsibility and solidarity. If we start with the naturalistic view, the result is radical value-subjectivism and the justification of an egoistic society of isolated strangers. But if we start with the idealistic view we have found the objectivistic values that are built in the humanistic justification of a welfare liberal democracy.

From theory to practice: the communitarian connection

We can now build a bridge from this brief methodological analysis of the Rawlsian welfare liberalism to the actual problems of liberal pluralism in the politics of the Western world. In fact, particularly in the contemporary political practice of European welfare states we can find the Rawlsian tendency to integrate the two very different liberal traditions into a symbiosis that in the end leads to the political crisis in a welfare democracy. This means that the moral foundation of welfare liberalism is lost and that even such central liberal values as autonomy, tolerance and equality can, in political practice, to be turned against their original goals and used to justify also suppression of individual will, intolerance and inequality. Also the idea of property rights, material welfare and market economy which all originally in the humanistic tradition had merely instrumental value in guaranteeing individuals' economical independence that was needed for the development of one's moral capacities as a citizen of democratic state, are now frequently given intrinsic value. All in all, this political development is gradually leading into a situation in which the modern liberal welfare states are no longer governed by morally active, able and autonomous citizens but instead are led by the 'invisible hand' of amoral and impersonal market forces.

The intellectual justification of liberal political order, however, conceives that liberal democracy can maintain its legitimacy only when its individual members can identify themselves as self-governing moral and political agents who share the common membership in a society that is based on the practical promotion of the metaphysical ideal of a moral and political agency. Nevertheless a modern liberal state quite often fails to provide such an intellectual and social atmosphere in which its individual members would truly commit themselves to the actualization of this liberal metaphysical ideal. Instead they tend to enforce their own original cultural identities. The failure to separate liberal metaphysical ideals from features of Western market economies leaves us then easily believing in arbitrary value-subjectivism and relativism instead of promoting true value-pluralism.

In our search for the true liberal identity the communitarian criticism of the liberal view is of great help. All such theorists as Alasdair MacIntyre (1984, 1988), Michael Sandel (1982), Charles Taylor (1979, 1989) and Michael Walzer (1982, 1988), who are labelled as communitarians, criticize Rawls's liberalism for its use of an abstract contractarian method in its attempt to derive the universal principles of liberal justice. For the communitarians the idea of the fictive original position which presents individual decision-makers as fully rational and reasonable moral and political subjects, who are behind the veil of ignorance and thus are detached from their own ends, values and social ties, is too abstract. The communitarian critics see that this Rawlsian methodological subject and the idea of the original position distort our view on moral subjectivity, that is, a person's identity as such a subject. Communitarians claim that the liberal image of a methodological subject appears to have nothing to do with real life decision-making situations in which the communal values and social ties affect the autonomy of the moral and political choices which individuals as citizens make. We are then left to wonder from where we have gotten the values among which we are 'free' to choose? What kind of moral and social identity - if any - does a fully rational and reasonable decision-maker behind the Rawlsian veil of ignorance have? How can someone who does not know his or her own values or goals make an autonomous and rational choices in the first place? Doesn't the very idea of rationality and reasonableness require knowledge on the options available? What happens to the ideas of individuality and individual's autonomous moral agency when the starting position presents an abstract collection of identical decision-makers?

Should the communitarians stop here, we maybe could agree with them that the abstract contractarian method hardly succeeds in describing our liberal social reality. However, with their second argument the communitarians seem to undermine the validity of this first claim. This is because they also argue that the individual members of modern liberal states are exactly the type of subjects described by the liberal theory: alienated, asocial and self-interested agents. The citizens of liberal societies cannot identify themselves as morally and politically participating members of a democratic state. They cannot conceive themselves as functional and constitutive parts of the liberal political order as a whole. This second communitarian claim holds then that contemporary Western societies are really the homes of radically isolated individuals, rational egoists, and existential agents, men and women protected by their inalienable (property) rights, but who have lost their true identity with the alienation from their traditional cultural values and social ties. It now appears that the communitarian critique of welfare liberalism must present a contradictory set of arguments. On the one hand, it points out that the liberal methodological subject mispresents our political reality. On the other hand, it claims that a liberal society cannot do otherwise but produce just these atomistic and isolated individuals in real life.[4] The question is now, whether these two claims which are mutually inconsistent can be true at the same time; and whether liberal political theory actually simultaneously succeeds in and fails in describing the moral identity of a modern individual living in pluralist and multicultural liberal society?[5]

This is when the idea of moral individualism steps in. The communitarian contradictory set of arguments gives us the background for the problems that the modern societies have in defining and in realizing the liberal moral identity. When we take the image of an ideal and autonomous decision-maker as our starting point we have a distorted picture of individuals who are cut loose from all social ties and common value systems. These abstract images of self have lost all their individuality and their uniqueness as real moral and political agents who everyday encounter ethical problems that can be solved only with the use of practical, rather than theoretical, reason. However, since theory and practice always interact, the more the Western intellectual culture relies on this abstract image of the subject, the more the Western political culture enforces the development of such individual decision-makers who are isolated from each other, asocial and egoistic.

The original idea of liberal subject, in the humanistic tradition (of Kant and through Kant also in Rawls) is in moral personhood which is in itself based on metaphysical account of a moral agency and thus is not directly connected to any particular culture as such (it is not directly connected for example to the Western consumerism and competitive market ideology). Instead it is to rise above particular cultural values and social ties. Its purpose is to reflect an individual's capacity as a self-reflective moral and political agent (as a human being in the metaphysical sense). Liberal identity in a multicultural and pluralist society should then not be directly equated either with the stereotypes of modern Western egoist (sometimes even ethically nihilistic) and competitive market culture or any other particular *cultural* identity. Instead, liberal moral identity means the realization and actualization of one's own moral agency and moral responsibility. In other words, the true liberal identity is related to the metaphysical idea/ideal that the humanist tradition has on a moral agency.

State neutrality and ethical impartiality

The abstract theoretical formulation of the liberal methodological subject was originally meant to support the idea of state neutrality. State neutrality demands that a liberal state does not promote any particular ends or goals, but rather it must remain impartial in order to enable its citizens to pursue their own ends, consistent with a similar liberty for all. The idea of liberal subject that is freed from any particular set of values and beliefs is thought to support the idea of such a liberty. In political reality this emphasis on impartiality requires that a liberal state must be governed by principles of political justice that do not presuppose any particular conception of 'the good life' whether this good is described in cultural, religious, ideological or in other terms. Instead a liberal state must advocate pluralism and tolerance as far as possible when it comes to different value and belief systems, ethical views and ways of living. As for liberal justification everyone is seen as an autonomous moral agent and should therefore be allowed to choose his or her own belief system, values, ends and ways of living. A liberal state must treat its citizens with equal concern and respect and thus any individual's conception of the good life should not be considered to be nobler or superior to another. If any individuals with certain communal or cultural backgrounds voluntarily persist in maintaining particular traditions and values of their culture, they should have the right to do so without inference from the liberal state.[6]

This requirement of neutrality and tolerance combined with the promotion of individual autonomy has made the question of cultural integration one of the most difficult questions for the liberal political order. On the one hand the liberal requirement of tolerance promotes the liberal value system and liberal world order, thus often claimed gradually to lead towards a Western cultural imperialism: the globalization of Western culture. On the other hand the liberal requirement of value pluralism leads, within liberal societies, into a 'communitarian' fragmentation that promotes the belief and value systems of individuals' from different cultural backgrounds and traditions. The liberal promotion of value-pluralism appears then to guide liberal societies into opposite directions. It promotes (what is considered to be) Western culture but by doing this it also allows, and even encourages, the maintenance of other cultural heritage and traditions. Since liberal pluralism in itself aims towards impartiality, the liberal state needs the existence of different values systems in order to provide the basis of value choices for its citizens. This liberal value-pluralism which is based on the idea of state neutrality shows that the deep structure of a liberal society is in fact 'communitarian'. Its individual members are always socially situated and thus find their personhood and moral identity rather as members of certain communities than as members of morally neutral liberal political order. The problem is that these cultural influences within liberal society can sometimes turn against the very ideals of pluralism and tolerance. Therefore, when we discuss the requirement of tolerance, the citizens of liberal welfare society tend to face a curious dilemma. When immigrants and refugees from different cultural backgrounds try to adapt to their new societies without losing their own cultural identity and traditions, the requirement of tolerance and autonomy insists the liberal state and its citizens not to interfere. Nevertheless, some cultural traditions in themselves oppress these very same liberal values. We have to then ask, do the people from different cultures have a right to maintain their traditions just because they have been, for whatever reason, valued practices in a particular community. Should we and how could we accept, for instance, such views and practices which violate the very principles of equality and individual autonomy; principles which are promoting tolerance to begin with? What should we do when some different cultural traditions conflict with our legislation or with our personal moral intuition and judgement?

Morally neutral liberal state does not provide us with any solution here.[7] When value pluralism is justified by the liberal promotion of individuals' autonomy, modern liberal states tend to see this autonomy as an existing fact rather than as a metaphysical ideal. In practice this means that if individual members of our societies themselves want to hold on to some even harmful traditions or intolerant and suppressive cultural structures, and this requirement is based on the demand of respect for individuals' assumed moral autonomy, we cannot interfere - at least as long as we really assume that they have been truly autonomous choices. If we take moral autonomy and equality to be empiristic facts about human nature, we inevitably violate the idea of autonomy and equality if we prevent someone from following his or her apparent will and apparently voluntary choice - no matter how abhorrent this choice may seem to us. However, if we considered moral autonomy from the teleological and originally humanistic point of view which takes moral autonomy to be the human potential that can and should be actualized within liberal political order, we could justifiably interfere when our aim is to secure an individual's development towards an autonomous moral agency. The real task of the liberal democracy is then to build a society that not only respects supposed moral autonomy, but succeeds in securing such a circumstance in which this autonomy can be reached to begin with.

If we, as members of liberal societies, do not take this task seriously, the promotion of tolerance can easily lead us to relativist thinking. Relativism, for its part, can result either in direct conflict or in moral indifference. The reason why ethical relativism is the enemy of liberal pluralism is because it leads us easily to believe that our cultural identity also determines our moral identity. Whether we speak about the liberal identity, or some other cultural identity within liberal society, we easily connect the cultural tradition and the adopted values with an individual's autonomy as a moral agent. Cultural and moral identities are, however, two distinct ideas. Even if there are always important social attachments and cultural influences which, at least partly, constitute one's values and one's social identity, cultural or social background does not, or at least it should not, fully determine one's moral identity. If we are to promote the liberal values of autonomy and freedom, one's cultural background should not decrease an individual's ability for autonomous reflection, critical moral judgement and for the correction of one's ethical beliefs (or the beliefs of one's society). Thus, in order to overcome these natural tendencies to reason egocentrically and sociocentrically, liberal reasoning and ethical pluralism both promote an individual's capacity to engage in self-reflective questioning. It shows that our belief and value systems are irrational, by definition, if we are incapable of abandoning some mere beliefs even if we can prove them wrong by rational and justified reasoning. Critical thought and moral identity must be predicated on discovering the insights of opposing views as well as on discovering the weaknesses of our own beliefs. Relativistic view has little to do with the social and political goal of the liberal requirement of tolerance. After all, the liberal ideal of the neutral state was originally meant to minimize the restrictions of the freedom of will and to promote moral autonomy - not to permit also their suffocation.

From cultural identity toward moral identity

Value-pluralism should never be equated with subjectivism or relativism. The maintenance of value pluralism in liberal political order requires that we as the citizens learn to make a distinction between the idea of cultural identity and the ideal of moral personhood. In a liberal society the most important task of its citizens is then to focus on the development of moral personhood (their own individually and of the society as a whole).This can be done only if the liberal societies recognize, firstly, their empirically communitarian ethical structure and secondly, their metaphysical and objectivistic humanistic ideals. However, if we do not find a way to integrate the individualistic and communitarian features which both occur in a liberal society, we shall either end up with subjectivism introduced by the liberal atomist and disinterested image on subject or we shall be left with cultural relativism by the communitarian 'embedded and situated' subject. The idea of an atomist subject directs us to equate our cultural identities with our moral identities. This is inevitable because liberal states do not, in general, educate their citizens in the matters of morals, and thus individual citizens gain their moral identities through their social and cultural backgrounds. The liberal requirement of pluralism enforces communitarian ethics and this, for its part, leads liberal societies easily toward social fragmentation and ethical indifference and even moral incapacity. Without any shared, common idea of what the good is that the liberal society is to promote, the smaller internal groups with their own set of values tend to conflict not only with each other but also with the liberal political ideals of equality and autonomy. Individual members of a liberal society, who have gained their moral and social identity through these smaller groups and communities tend also to be loyal to these smaller groups and feel themselves as members of such groups. Thus, their commitment to a liberal state, and their identity as a self-governing members of a liberal democracy, is only secondary. True liberal moral identity can, nevertheless, be realized only, when individuals can identify themselves as actual political and moral decision-makers and learn to critically evaluate and revaluate the values they have adopted within a liberal society and as members of whatever social collectives they happen to belong to at any given time. Individual citizens have to be able to separate their autonomously chosen values from those they have been indoctrinated in by their socialization, if they are to fulfil the liberal promise of autonomy.

Pluralist liberal democracy does not work without individual, self-governing agents who can identify themselves as such agents. If the members of liberal societies remained merely cultural agents with their inherited set of values, the legitimacy of liberal democracy would be lost. If pluralism of values is really desired in a liberal order every individual living in this society has to commit himself or herself to the actualization of this pluralism. In order to be able to do this one has to have a strong moral identity as well as ability and will to critically judge between different value systems. Furthermore, one has to learn to make the difference between good and bad, right and wrong in his or her own actions and choices. If we are to move from the abstract and procedural individualism of liberal political theory towards moral individualism, we have to note that in a liberal society the liberal and communitarian views on value-pluralism rather complement each other than conflict with each other. In other words, if we set the concept of the liberal methodological subject aside and focused on the realization and actualization of the metaphysical ideal of liberal moral identity, we realize that there is no open conflict between individualism and collectivism, that is, between the universalist principles of constitutional liberal democracies and the particularist claims of ethnic communities within them to preserve the integrity of their habitual ways. Instead the promotion of liberal pluralism based on the actualization of individuals' moral agency, on the one hand, presumes and, on the other hand, promotes communitarian approach to ethics.[8] If a liberal state is to be neutral between different value and belief systems, the values the individual citizens 'choose' and the beliefs they adopt are always provided by some social collectives with a common set of values. A neutral liberal state cannot promote value-pluralism unless there already exist different sets of values to choose from or to adapt to. In order to fulfill its promise of value-pluralism, a liberal society needs communitarian ethical foundations.

However, communitarian ethics alone is not enough and therefore the idea of moral individualism attempts to bring the liberal and communitarian lines of reasoning closer together by suggesting that value-pluralism requires that even if we recognize the existence of different value systems, there is no *a priori* demand for their acceptance merely as such systems. Instead, moral individualism emphasizes that value-pluralism demands not only emphatic but also critical assessments of differing perspectives. Value pluralism requires that different belief and value systems can be critically evaluated and assessed and that the basis and validity of their norms can be questioned. If we can prove certain cultural practices to be contradictory, incoherent, and even harmful, we have grounds for rejecting them. If it is ethical value-pluralism we are after, rather than relativism, we can then agree that our cultural traditions and our value judgements should be continuously evaluated, because there is always something good and something bad in every system of beliefs and values as a whole. Only then we can promote harmonious and fruitful cultural integration in which we all can learn from each other.

Without giving up on tolerance, it is possible to challenge the consistency of the practices, norms and prohibitions prevailing in a particular community or culture as a whole. For instance when refugees are looking for rights and equality, they should be ready to give up those traditions of their own culture that violate these principles. In these cases one can point out that since the moral code of society is self-contradictory, the requirement of consistency prevents rational individuals from accepting the dictates of the system.[9] It should be also kept in mind that the moral system under consideration can be conceptually extended. While it is true that moral judgements are always relative to ethical theories or shared opinions, it is by no means the case that only existing socio-cultural entities should be defined as the source of valid moral judgements. Even if we accept that our social environment affects our values, there is no reason why cultural traditions should be equated with moral standards and why our moral identity should be fully determined by our cultural background.[10] Liberal moral identity is thus no more and no less than the recognition of one's moral capacities and their active realization in everyday decision-making. This is the liberal moral identity that is to be realized within a liberal political order regardless of one's cultural background and earlier traditional beliefs and values.

What makes liberal societies different from some other political orders should then be in the promotion of proper ethical value-pluralism that in itself encourages the development of an individual's moral judgement. It promotes the individual's moral autonomy without requiring one to abandon his or her cultural heritage. It offers an evolving understanding of meaning and morality that depends on the interaction, first, between oneself and one's society and, second, between people from different cultural backgrounds. In order to develop our moral identities, we need to clarify our values and beliefs. The only way to do this is to openly investigate different sides of an issue. We have to respect the existence of divergent beliefs and values, but instead of accepting or rejecting them offhand, we have to focus on assessing the validity of opposing views and different belief and value systems. This process of ethical inquiry is central to an individual's moral development. It is no less important to communal and cultural development. A richly-varied and secure cultural structure does not have intrinsic moral status of its own. Instead it has instrumental value because it provides the context for our choices. An individual's autonomous choices for the good life require not only freedom from coercion, but they also require a degree cultural diversity which gives us a change to reflect our own set of values with those of others. In multicultural societies, the diversity of choice can therefore provide concrete, living alternatives, life experiments that will facilitate our intellectual growth and moral development. A multicultural atmosphere can also provide us with a multiplicity of choices and opportunities. At its best, the influence of our cultural background supports the development of our moral identity by making us aware of all the options available to us. It may help us intelligently examine not only the values adopted by other people, but also our own values. However, if a cultural identity is misinterpreted as meaning the same as our moral identity, it can stifle individual will and prevent one's moral autonomy from developing at all. The shift from methodological individualism toward moral individualism means then taking into account the fact that the realization of liberal identity is not in the actualization of the Western materialist egoism or ethical nihilism, but it is in the recognition of the metaphysical ideal of moral agency and in one's strife for its actualization in practice, that is, in finding one's moral identity.

Conclusion

Liberal political emphasis on autonomy, equality and pluralism protects individual citizens against the suppression of the liberal state. It, however, can consistently disregard the values and ties of communities that people are born with and thus make a liberal democracy to become an uncritical booster of a fragmented civil society which is prone to naive collectivism that often undermines the metaphysical moral ideals of liberal democracy. This happens, for some of those social collectives within the modern state that are protected and promoted by the liberal requirements of tolerance, equality and autonomy, can themselves be enemies of these very same values. Contemporary liberal reasoning works then well only in such (should there be any) societies which already truly respect equality and promote the realization of moral autonomy. When we talk about individuals within liberal political order who nevertheless are members of such communities in which the boundary of the self is strictly limited to such existing norms and traditions which do not respect the presumed autonomy of an individual, problems are evident.

In conclusion I must note that in order to avoid these problems we have to reinterpret the requirements of liberal individualism and value pluralism. This means that liberal states have to take seriously the challenge they have in providing such a cultural and political circumstance in which individual citizens learn to identify themselves as moral and political agents who together form the state and its policies and are committed to the democratic values of justice, equality and tolerance. In everyday social situations this view could be promoted when individuals' practicing of virtue and practical moral judgement were once again more clearly honored and rewarded by our Western culture. Only the inspiring and encouraging political and social attitude can make moral life more attractive to the individual agents, because our moral capacities develop only in a cultural and political environment which respects virtue and motivates us to behave morally. The teleological turn in the idea of moral individualism means then merely that also in political theory it should be taken into account that we as individual citizens should not lose our sight of the ideals of liberal democracy (whether we talk about the ideal citizens or the ideal state) and settle with justifying the practice, because this lets the liberal values to turn against their original goals. In order to avoid the degeneration of modern welfare liberal democracy and our individualistic culture we therefore have to turn to moral individualism that finds the actualization of human dignity in self-restraint and in human universality rather than in random subjectivist liberation, market rationality and in personal idiosyncracy. If this value which liberal theory gives to the development of one's moral agency and moral identity were set within a teleological framework, it would describe - and also prescribe - the metaphysical aspects of 'the good life' that a liberal political order is to promote in practice. What we have to keep in mind then is that the liberal state is not neutral or indifferent between conceptions of good and bad. There is always room for more than one concept of good in the liberal society as long as there is some commonly accepted concept of good. The open, critical, but emphatic dialogue between different belief and values systems within liberal society helps us to adopt 'the best' from different cultures and to realize our liberal identity as an autonomous moral agent; autonomous meaning here an individual's ability to separate his or her moral agency from the cultural agency.

Notes

1. See for instance Locke, 1980, Rawls 1972, pp. 3-45, 1993, pp. 3-42, Reiman, 1990. Within the liberal contractarian tradition there are two major intellectual and political trends: classical liberalism or libertarianism, which is seen to promote negative freedom and welfare liberalism which advocates the positive concept of freedom. Both of these approaches are liberal at the core, i.e., they promote liberal values of freedom and individual rights, but politically and economically they present very divergent and sometimes even incommensurable views. Libertarianism requires economic freedom; freedom from state constraint. It has its roots in John Locke's classical liberalism, in its advocacy of individual rights and particularly the property rights. Libertarianism sees that political liberty and the freedom of the markets are the most important things in society, so that restrictive laws, taxes, welfare, state economic control

should be eliminated or at least minimized. This libertarian right wing-position is presently theoretically formulated by, for instance, Friedrich van Hayek, Robert Nozick, and David Gauthier.

2. The liberal right wing sees that this is leading us toward social democracy, and in the worst case, towards socialist politics. Rawls himself, however, emphasizes individuals' rights and demands that the state should be neutral when it comes to values and different moral views. This means that he rejects the collectivist idea of the common good and the educational purpose of the state (like in Plato, Aristotle, Kant and even in Locke) or that the state in itself is our moral purpose (unlike for instance in Hegel and up to a degree in Rousseau).

3. Rawls's (1972, 1993) deontological welfare liberalism states that in order to realize the equality (as the realization of one's capacity to moral agency) we can - and often need to - allow more state interference in the distributional policies. This means that it allows more government interventions in order to free people from ignorance and misery, or for solving other social problems such as poverty. Rawls's liberal deontology is based on the Kantian moral emphasis that gives right priority over the good and the subject priority over the goals. Rawls's welfare liberal theory is, however, a pragmatic attempt to combine 'the egalitarian features' of the continental humanism with the contemporary Anglo-American procedural justice and formal individual rights. This attempt has drawn Rawls's theory so far from the Anglo-American liberal tradition that many proponents of classical liberal economics and neo-liberalism find it difficult to recognize or to accept that Rawls's welfare liberalism is still presenting a form of liberal reasoning. The reason why Rawls's theory is controversial and why the libertarians find it difficult to accept as liberal theory in begin with can be found in its promotion of positive freedom

4. See Walzer, 1990, pp. 9-11.

5. See Walzer, 1990, pp. 9-11.

6. Gauthier, 1986, Locke, 1980, Green, 1995, pp. 260-1, Rawls, 1972, pp. 3-45, 1993, pp. 3-42.

7. Pluralism sees that there is an irreducible diversity of ultimate values (goods, excellences, options, reasons for actions, etc.) And in a neutral state when these values come into conflict or competition with one another there is no overarching standard or principle, no common currency or measure, whereby such conflicts can be arbitrated or resolved. Gray, 1995, pp. 68-9. On cultural relativism see Howard, 1993, pp. 315-338 and Williams, 1972, pp. 33-5.

8. However, in modern political theory as well as in Western political reality we tend to take very one-sided views in political categorizations. If something is said to be liberal it cannot be communitarian, and thus, if something appears to have communitarian (often equated with collectiv-

ism) features in it, it must conflict with the liberal view. This is a fallacy that makes us see everything either in black or white and to miss the various shades of gray. This dichotomous thinking fails to grasp the complexity of the whole and is partly due to the problems that both the liberal and the communitarian lines of reasoning face in their attempts to justify the promotion of value-pluralism.

9. See M. Häyry, 1992, p. 55.
10. See also M. Häyry, 1992, p. 55.

References

Gauthier, D. (1986), *Morals by Agreement*, Clarendon Press: Oxford.

Green, L. (1995), 'Internal Minorities and their Rights' in Kymlicka, W. (ed.), *The Rights of Minority Cultures*, Oxford University Press: New York.

Howard, R. (1993), 'Cultural Absolutism and the Nostalgia for Community', *Human Rights Quarterly*, vol. 15, No. 2, pp. 315-38.

Häyry, M. (1992), 'Moral relativism and the philosophical criticism of other cultures', *Science Studies*, vol. 15, No. 1, pp. 53-56.

Kant, I. (1990), 'Social Contract as an Idea of Reason' in Lessnoff, M. (ed.), *Social Contract Theory*, (orig. 1785) Basil Blackwell: Worcester.

Locke, J. (1980), *Second Treatise of Government*, second edition, ed. Macpherson, C. B. (orig. 1690) Hackett, Cambridge: Indianapolis.

MacIntyre, A. (1984), *After Virtue*, 2nd edition. University of Notre Dame Press: Indiana.

MacIntyre, A. (1988), *Whose Justice? Which Rationality?* Duckworth: London.

Rawls, J. (1972), *A Theory of Justice*, Oxford University Press: Oxford.

Rawls, J. (1993), *Political Liberalism*, Columbia University Press: New York.

Reiman, J. (1990), *Justice and Modern Moral Philosophy*, Yale University Press: New Haven and London.

Richardson, H. S. (1990), 'The Problem of Liberalism and the Good', in Douglass, Mara, Richardson (eds), *Liberalism and the Good*, Routledge: New York and London.

Sandel, M. (1982), *Liberalism and the Limits of Justice*, Cambridge University Press: Cambridge.

Walzer, M. (1980), *Radical Principles. Reflections of an Unreconstructed Democrat*, Basic Books: New York.

Walzer, M. (1983), *Spheres of Justice*, Basic Books: New York.

Walzer, M. (1987), *Interpretation and Social Criticism*, Harvard University Press: Cambridge.

Walzer, M. (1990). 'The Communitarian Critique of Liberalism', *Political Theory*, vol. 18 No. 1, pp. 6-23.

Williams, B. (1972), *Morality*, Cambridge University Press: Cambridge.

Women vs. emotions, community and the moral law or why would any sensible woman want to uphold communitarian ideals?

Heta Häyry

JACK: My dear fellow, what on earth is there in that? Some aunts are tall, some aunts are not tall. That is a matter that surely an aunt may be allowed to decide for herself. You seem to think that every aunt should be exactly like your aunt! That is absurd!

- Oscar Wilde, The Importance of Being Earnest.

Many women working in the fields of philosophy, the social sciences and the humanities seem to think that the cluster of moral and political ideas now usually labelled as 'communitarian' represent the best ethical thinking in today's Anglo-American academic world. I cannot for the life of me understand why. To me, the situation is clear. All types of thinking that find the basis of ethics in emotions, community values or 'natural moral laws' belong to the era in European history when women were systematically oppressed and mistreated, and I find it incredible that any sensible woman would want to glorify that dark period by upholding the ideals put forward by the (primarily male) philosophers of the communitarian movement.

In what follows I shall explain what I mean by these remarks, and why I think that they are valid and important. I shall begin by making a few observations about the history of ethics, and about the place of women in the main traditions of moral philosophy. I shall then proceed to sketch the most important present-day doctrines of social and political philosophy, and clarify their connections with the earlier European lines of thought. This will make it possible to see how communitarian thinking, far from showing the way to a bright future for practical philosophy, can best be seen as a reactionary doctrine which aims, among other bad things, at keeping women in or returning women to their traditional roles in social and political life.

The historical schools of ethics and their views on women

Historically, the first systematic, or philosophical, form of European moral thinking was secular and teleological. Aristotle[1] thought that all beings have an essence, or nature, or end (TELOS) which is their ideal form, or a state towards which they are bound to develop. The TELOS of men, according to Aristotle, is to live virtuously in a good society, and to cultivate their intellectual capacities. The TELOS of women, on the other hand, is to serve men, as women do not have sufficient rational capacities to make virtuous choices or to strive towards intellectual perfection. The husband should rule over his wife as a statesman rules over the people, because:

> [The] male is more fitted to rule than the female, unless conditions are quite contrary to nature. [In] most cases of rule by statesmen there is an interchange of the role of ruler and ruled, which aims to preserve natural equality and non-differentation. [But] between male and female this kind of relationship is permanent.[2]

Equality and freedom are, then, in any serious sense alien to Aristotle's thinking due to the biological hierarchies and social stratifications that he held so dear.

Christianity did little to improve the lot of women,[3] and the 'natural' distinction drawn between women and men by Aristotle was carved in stone by Thomas Aquinas, who, following a great many Church Doctors preceding him, irrevocably fused together the Aristotelian idea that women are driven by desires, not by reason, and the Christian view that desires are the root of evil. In point of fact, Aquinas was quite puzzled as to why God had created woman at all, and came to the conclusion that she must be a freak in nature:

> As regards the individual nature, woman is defective and misbegotten, for the active force in the male seed tends to the production of a perfect likeness in the masculine sex; while the production of woman comes from a defect in the active force or from some material indisposition, or even from some external influence.[4]

In the end, Aquinas defined the TELOS of both women and men as an afterlife of everlasting joy, but he insisted that in this life women should, due to their imperfection, obey absolutely their fathers, husbands and other male authorities, because this order of things is detectable in the divine law of nature, the natural law.

The sixteenth and seventeenth centuries saw the rise of two new types of ethics. The first of these, deontological thinking, was based on the idea that it is not really ethical to strive for an afterlife of great personal joy, because the motivation in this model is blatantly egoistic. Instead, the moral law should be respected for its own sake, either because it is given to humanity by God, or because it is dictated to men by reason. Immanuel Kant, the best-known eighteenth-century representative of the deontological school, believed that all moral agents should be guided by the 'categorical imperative' he had invented, which states that we must always act as if by our own actions we were making exceptionless laws for all humanity. We should, according to another Kantian formulation of the categorical imperative, always treat humanity, in ourselves as well as in others, also as an end in itself, never as a mere means to benefit others.[5]

Kant's general model seems to be quite impartial, and it is therefore somewhat surprising to note that he drew a clear distinction between the rights of women and the rights of men in the political arena. Kant insisted, for instance, that 'not everyone is equally qualified to have the right to vote', only those whom he called 'active citizens'. These are persons whose livelihood depends only on their own industry, not on the beneficence and protection of others. By contrast, the people Kant called 'dependents' are supported by others, and they therefore 'lack civil personality' and with it the right to vote. This group, in Kant's model, includes children, servants, labourers and women, who must all be placed under the 'legal tutelage' of active male citizens. As Kant regards this position as degrading, dependents are generally granted the permission to 'work up' to an active status, but this permission is denied women.[6]

Another strand of deontological thinking can be traced back to the theory of natural rights introduced in the seventeenth century by John Locke. Partly following other political philosophers of the contractarian tradition, Locke argued that civil government ought to be based on, and serve, the rights of individual human beings to protect their life, liberty and private property. The only inviolable moral law in this model is that individuals are not allowed to interfere with the liberty of others if the liberty in question can be consistently enjoyed by all.

Locke's liberalism does not, in theory, restrict the participation of women in public affairs. As a matter of fact, Locke admitted that families, which form the core unit of the social contract, could be headed by the mother as well as by the father, and that 'paternal authority' should be replaced as a political concept by 'parental authority'.[7] But when he analysed the matter further, he came to the conclusion that the father is, after all, the natural head of the family:

> But the husband and wife, though they have but one common concern [the continuation of the species], yet having different understandings, will unavoidably sometimes have different wills too. It therefore being necessary that the last determination (*i.e.*, the rule) should be placed somewhere, it naturally falls to the man's share as the abler and the stronger.[8]

In the end, then, political sovereignty as well as the all-important right to private property belong, by natural entitlement, to men rather than women.

The second type of ethics which saw the light of day in the beginning of the modern era can be labelled as consequentialist, and it was initially formulated by the Scottish Enlightenment philosophers Francis Hutcheson and David Hume.[9] The classical model of consequentialism was, however, put forward by Jeremy Bentham whose doctrine, which came to be called utilitarianism, consisted of three basic principles.[10] First, human actions (including both positive acts *and* omissions, or deliberate failures to act) can be deemed right if, and only if, they produce the greatest possible happiness to the greatest possible number of human and other sentient beings. Second, happiness means pleasure and the absence of pain and suffering. And third, individuals should be treated equally, so that in the happiness calculations 'everybody [is] to count for one and nobody for more than one'.[11]

Unlike Kant, Bentham did not make any ethical or political distinctions between women and men per se, and he therefore saw no intrinsic reason to oppose, for instance, women's right to vote. He wrote:

> In certain nations, women, whether married or not, have been placed in a state of perpetual wardship: this has been evidently founded on the notion of a decided inferiority in point of intellects on the part of the female sex, analogous to that which is the result of infancy or insanity on the part of the male. This is not the only instance in which tyranny has taken advantage of its own wrong, alleging as a reason for the domination it exercises, an imbecility, which, as far as it has been real, has been produced by the abuse of that very power which it is brought to justify. Aristotle, fascinated by the prejudice of the times, divides mankind into two distinct species, that of freemen and that of slaves. Certain men were born to be slaves, and ought to be slaves. - Why? Because they are so.[12]

Assessing the political realities of his own time, the turn of the nineteenth century, Bentham did not actively advocate women's political rights because he felt that this would have been counterproductive, but he fought, instead, for the franchise of all men as the most immediate step towards universal suffrage.[13]

Half a century later John Stuart Mill, Bentham's acutest disciple, took consequentialist thinking to its natural conclusion by arguing in his feminist classic *The Subjection of Women* that legislation should recognize no significant differences between women and men, and that even where distinctions exist, individuals should, nonetheless, be treated equally.[14]

A common misconception regarding the history of ethics

Many contemporary feminist writers tend to acknowledge only parts of the story that I have sketched here, and to ignore certain historical points which I feel are important. Susan Mendus, for instance, who in her article "Kant: 'An honest but narrow-minded bourgeois'?"[15] levels a good criticism at Kant's views concerning women, then goes on to associate the flaws of his thinking with individualism in a way that leaves at least me totally flabbergasted.

Mendus sets off soundly by noting that women are not excluded from active citizenship in Kant's model merely because the time is not ripe for their acceptance in this role, or because they have not yet received enough formal education to understand the requirements of the position. Instead, Kant makes it clear that women can *never* become active members of the society, because they are women. As a matter of fact, he suggests that further improvements in the status of women and especially further education would be dangerous for social life.[16]

As Mendus points out, Kant sets three necessary conditions for active citizenship. The person striving for this position must be his own master, he must have sufficient possessions to support himself, and he must be male. Women, therefore, cannot become active citizens as long as they are women. As Mendus writes:

> By contrast with the formulation in the *Metaphysic of Morals* [where the general permission to 'work up' is granted], we are invited [in *Theory and Practice*] *first* to enquire into the sex of the individual and *then*, if the individual is male, to ask whether he satisfies the independence criterion. Of course, in this way, women, so to speak, never get past the starting post. They become, not persons occupying particular social positions, but occupants of the position 'woman', which, by definition, fits them only for passive citizenship - and, unlike servants, they cannot hope to occupy a different position in the future. Thus they are eternally denied that possibility of advancement, which is open even to the lowliest of men.[17]

Given that Mendus condemns Kant's ideas, as the tone of the analysis suggests, it would seem that her sympathies lie with the liberal Enlightenment tradition which grants individuals an equal right to the free and unrestricted enhancement and use of their faculties, talents and abilities, as long as they do not violate each other's fundamental rights or unduly harm one another.

It is, therefore, quite surprising to learn that Mendus attributes the problems exemplified by Kant to individualism, which may or may not be properly considered a part of Kant's thinking, but which definitely forms the basis of enlightened liberalism. What is more, Mendus even manages, in the process, to throw mud at Mill, who can hardly be placed in the same category with Kant as regards the rights of women. She asserts:

> All individualist theories share this difficulty: in construing persons as essentially independent, free and equal, they support an atomistic model which cannot readily accommodate those social units, such as the family, which

> transcend mere atomism. The choice then is between abandoning individualism and construing the family as itself a single unit, with the husband as the head and decision-maker. [This] dilemma is thrown up by individualism itself, which dictates, as a central tenet, that *someone* must dominate, *someone* must give way. Even in Mill (champion of the emancipation of women), this problem arises, forcing him to appeal to woman's nature as a guarantee against the destruction of the patriarchal family.[18]

Shifting her attention to the difficulties of contemporary feminism, Mendus continues:

> [Even when] individualism is feminist individualism, it still cannot escape its own internal demands. Thus the modern feminist may insist that at least sometimes the head of the family may be female, but it is never in doubt that *someone* must be the head and decision-maker. The language of domination and subordination is central to individualism and cannot be dispensed with except by abandoning individualism itself.[19]

This, I think, is one of the most extraordinary statements that I have ever read. Mendus seems to suppose, quite seriously, that if we put our trust in individuals as separate entities with equal rights, we are also bound to believe in somebody's natural superiority and leadership in any given social unit, including the family. I can see no grounds whatsoever for believing that such a connection exists. If individuals who are endowed with equal rights think that they need a leader for a limited task, they can nominate one, but there is absolutely no need to let this arrangement degenerate into permanent structures of 'domination and subordination'. In the case of the modern family, even the nomination of a temporary leader seems rather far-fetched, since the unit is usually small and the tasks it is supposed to perform are not all that complicated. Surely two adults can in a just liberal society come to an agreement concerning their expectations, values and desires - and if they cannot, they can always go their separate ways.

As I see the matter, the demand for domination and subordination which is detectable in Locke and manifest in Kant is more probably inherited from the ancient and medieval antagonists of liberalism and individualism - Aristotle, Aquinas, and their followers. Locke's 'law of nature' and Kant's 'moral law' bear an uncomfortably close resemblance to the 'natural law' of the medieval tradition, which dictates the hierarchical structure of the universe, including women's subordination to men. Although Locke and Kant can in many respects be seen as detached from the natural law tradition, the traces of the model are apparent in their theories. Therefore, if we wish to advance beyond Kant's appalling views on women's status in society, we have to reject the collectivism that he assumed from the teleological tradition, not his illusory individualism. Unfortunately, however, many philosophers today agree with Mendus, and opt for the communitarian solution.

The emergence of communitarianism and some difficulties with the model

In the late nineteenth century traditional moral doctrines came under attack by philosophers who demanded that ethics should either be based on scientific observations, or rejected as a form of metaphysical speculation. This attack was followed by half a century of metaethical studies, accompanied with a deeply felt contempt towards all efforts to create normative theories of morality. As a consequence, even today specifically ethical theories remain underdeveloped in view of contemporary moral problems, and many academics think that solutions should rather be sought in the direction of social and political philosophy.

After the rise and fall of fascist and socialist thinking in Europe, the most popular approaches to moral and social questions have been liberalism and communitarianism. When I use the term 'liberalism' here, I refer to the doctrine in its ethical and ideological form, and disregard the political and economical creed which has its origin in the work of John Locke, and is nowadays more commonly called libertarianism.[20] It was liberalism in the sense that I mean that brought to the fore, seriously for the first time in history, the ideals of equality, social mobility, the pursuit of happiness and well-being, and freedom from religious oppression and from narrow-mindedness in general.

The liberal way of thinking makes it possible to extend the sphere of civil liberties to many groups that other ideologies ignore, among them women. Liberalism in this sense emphasizes that all human beings ought to be treated equally, and that individuals should be allowed to improve their minds and utilize their talents according to their own capacities without restrictions which are based on imaginary 'natural' differences. The rejection of the originally Aristotelian idea of fixed social roles makes way for the universal recognition of the freedom and autonomy of individuals to choose their own actions and their own life-styles, and to overlook - if they so choose - the opinions of their families, the supposed values of their ancestors and the disapproval and indignation of their neighbours. The only constraint set on human activities in this model is that individuals must not inflict harm on their fellow beings unless it is necessary to do so to prevent even greater harm.

Philosophers who have been dubbed communitarian - like Michael Sandel, Alasdair MacIntyre, Charles Taylor and Michael Walzer - share the view that liberalism should either be rejected or at least made to respect more traditional values than freedom, equality and general well-being.[21] These communitarians believe that human beings are not primarily individuals who are alone responsible for their self-determined choices, but members of their societies and communities, occupiers of their socially and culturally determined roles, and moral agents whose ethical values are defined by the linguistic and historical context in which they live. Liberalism, according to these critics, is an immoral doctrine in that it does not recognize the need of human beings to belong to groups and to form their identities and ethical responses within these groups.

There seem to be three main reasons why communitarian thinking appeals to many women philosophers and social scientists. The first is that some women resent the allegedly 'cold', 'hard', 'instrumental' or 'superficial' values of liberalism, and want to put in their place 'warmer', 'softer' and 'deeper' values which are directly linked with the proper ends of humanity, and which are therefore more appropriate to women as creators and preservers of life. The second reason appears to be that communities, which are neither voluntary nor human-made associations, are not based on covenants or contracts, and can, subsequently, be seen as a part of the private rather than the public sphere. This is pertinent because women's activities have traditionally been confined to private matters. The emphasis put on communities promises women more influence as the natural bearers of children and their moral educators than doctrines which mainly operate on the male-dominated social and political levels. The third reason for preferring communitarianism is the one sketched by Mendus in the above - namely, that this line of thought can transcend the atomistic liberal concept of personhood.

All these points can, however, be contested. First, as Marilyn Friedman has noted, there is no guarantee that communitarians support any particular set of values which a given group could be inclined to assume. They refer, characteristically, to clans, tribes, cities and nations, but where, Friedman asks, are

> the International Ladies Garment Workers' Union, the Teamsters, the Democratic Party, Alcoholics Anonymous, or the Committee in Solidarity with the People of El Salvador?[22]

Some of these communities do indeed cherish 'warmer' and 'softer' values than some forms of liberalism (some do not), but these are not the kind of associations in which Sandel, MacIntyre, Taylor and Walzer place their trust.

An additional difficulty is to find out what exactly is the true community, tradition or way of life for each of us. Friedman elucidates this problem by referring to Adrienne Rich's essay 'Split at Root',[23] where the author writes about her experiences growing up between two possible primary communities. Her mother was a Christian, her father a Jew who suppressed his ethnicity, and her Jewish identity was denied her - only later in life did she find the vocabulary to describe the Holocaust and other matters which were as important to her as the Christian values that she had grown up with. The question that examples like this pose to the proponents of communitarianism is, how are we to discover our one true identity when so many of us have several viable alternatives to choose from?

Second, it is important to realize that the roots of all genuinely communitarian theories are in teleological or deontological thinking. MacIntyre, for instance, relies openly on Aristotelian ideas - presumably including the distinction between women and men on the grounds that the female of the species is less intelligent than her male counterpart. A clear division according to gender becomes visible every time MacIntyre lists possible roles and positions in society. Taylor, in his turn, operates, roughly speaking, within a Hegelian framework, which means that for him societies and communities consist of historically fixed roles with their strict corresponding duties that individuals are bound to perform. The categorical obligations of the Kantian model are here assigned to human beings as the predetermined holders of their basically Aristotelian positions in society.

The third reason for preferring communitarianism is flawed mainly because it rests on an inadequate view regarding liberal thinking. Communitarians seem to believe that everybody who prefers freedom of thought and action to communities bound by tradition claim, in fact, that individuals make all their choices atomistically, in complete isolation from other people. This, of course, is untrue. Liberalism in my sense is quite compatible with the recognition of the fact that all my choices are *influenced* by my past history, my family and the society in which I live. All liberalism states is that although I am influenced by my past, I can in the majority of cases refuse, if I so choose, to yield to the pressures of history. There are, I think, traditions, including the subjection of women, which should not only be ignored but also actively challenged.

Even the communitarians themselves seem to acknowledge the possibility of revolt when they criticize what they see as the individualistic and liberal follies of our time. But then, for them we are not only influenced by our past, but *determined* by it. Thus, supposedly, their true communal identities *force* them to reveal the mistakes made within the Western culture during the last two centuries. But in this case, do they belong to a tradition which has somehow miraculously missed the intellectual and social progress which has taken place in the last two hundred years, including women's liberation? In many crucial respects, I sincerely believe that they do.

Enforced community values as a threat to sensible women

One principle that all communitarians insist upon is that political authorities should commit themselves to the enforcement of a set of community-based values. The state, in other words, should not be axiologically neutral, and it should not let the citizens decide for themselves what values they want to uphold - like many liberal theorists have maintained. An examination of this principle uncovers the lethal threat imposed on all sensible women by communitarianism.

There are three possible sets of values that the state can undertake to enforce within the communitarian model. The first set is built on the assumption that nations could be culturally homogeneous. If they could, then the values enforced by the state would be shared by all citizens, and it would be impossible to criticize them. The problem with this alternative is that societies are not, in fact, homogeneous, and attempts to pretend that they are can only lead to the glorification of conservative attitudes, unreasoned chauvinism, and the oppression of minorities and women. Since most communitarians recognize the worth of religious and ethnic minorities, this is fortunately not the route they are likely to take.

The second option is to enforce the particular values of culturally distinct communities within the state. This can be done, for instance, by setting quotas for ethnic groups in public offices, and by encouraging types of education which aim at preserving the traditional habits and customs of these groups. Some communitarians seem to support practices like these.

I can easily see why the - traditionally male - leaders of religious and ethnic groups prefer this model to the neutrality of the state in cultural and gender-related matters. Not only can they go on treating women like subhuman beings, they can also turn to the government for material help in their struggle against liberal and egalitarian ideals. When values are set above individuals in the political sphere, the ones who suffer are the individuals who have not been given the opportunity to choose the values in question. In traditional communities this means, among other groups, women.

The women philosophers who place their trust in communitarian thinking probably want governments to choose the third possibility and to enforce values which are important to women and increase their influence in both private and public matters. These values are often defined in terms of women's 'natural' role as peaceful child-bearers, with an emphasis on the political importance of family affairs.

My question is, what would the result of the official enforcement of values like these be? It should, I think, be remembered that according to communitarian theorists individuals are not allowed to choose their values, nor the groups they belong to. The values enforced by the state are not negotiable in the sense that people could decide whether they want to occupy a traditional role in society or not. It follows from these premises that if you are a woman, and if women are natural child-bearers, and if the state is duty-bound to enforce this natural link, then you can be legally coerced into having children. Or if you are a woman, and all women are life-preserving and peace-loving creatures, you can be legally prevented from joining the army.

I know that many women do not see these prospects as particularly threatening, because the norms and restrictions they predict are consistent with their own preferences. They themselves *want* to have children, and they themselves *want* to avoid military service, so it does not matter to them that women who think differently (and whom they therefore see as perverted) are forced to fit the mould.

Other women probably do not regard the rules enforced by communitarian governments as threatening, because they believe that women who think differently can make their own choices even if the state encourages the dissemination and preservation of traditional values. These women have simply mistaken communitarianism for liberalism. When the state does not dictate what your self-regarding values must be, you can make your own choices, but when the state takes an interest in your personal values, the decisions are no longer yours to make.

During this century enforced community values have decreased so radically in affluent Western societies that many women tend to forget how harmful they really are. It is perhaps a healthy reminder for those women to consider the fate of their sisters in traditionally governed countries like Saudi Arabia, and to remember that communitarian theories do not even enable their supporters to criticize the total subjection of women under the religious fanatics of those countries.

I rest my case, and conclude that I cannot think of any good reasons for sensible women to uphold communitarian ideals.[24]

Notes

1. Plato and many others, of course, preceded Aristotle, but it is difficult to find a full and systematic account of individual and social morality before him.
2. The quotation is from Aristotle's *Politics,* 1981, 1259a37.
3. See, e.g., Armstrong, 1986.
4. The citation from Thomas Aquinas's *Summa Theologica,* (IV, Part I. Quaest. XCII, art 1,2) quoted in Armstrong, 1986, p. 62.
5. Kant, 1983.
6. Kant's position is discussed by Roger J. Sullivan, 1989, p. 376 n. 26.
7. Locke, 1690, Book II, 53.
8. Citation from *Two Treatises of Government* (II, 82), Locke, 1690, p. 156-7.
9. Hutcheson, 1725; Hume, 1983.
10. Bentham, 1982.
11. 'Bentham's famous dictum' concerning impartiality was never explicitly formulated by Bentham himself - the citation is from Mill, 1861, p. 336.
12. Bentham, 1982, p. 245 n. f4. His reference is to Aristotle's *Politics*, I.V.
13. See, e.g., Dinwiddy, 1989, p. 82.
14. *The Subjection of Women* (1869) has been reprinted, for instance, in John Stuart Mill, *Three Essays*, edited by R. Wollheim, (1975).
15. Mendus, 1992. p. 370-411.
16. Ibid., p. 384.
17. Ibid., p. 375.

18. Ibid., p. 385-6.
19. Ibid., p. 386.
20. See, e.g., Nozick, 1974; Narveson, 1988.
21. See, e.g., MacIntyre, 1981, 1988; Sandel, 1982; Taylor, 1990; Walzer, 1982.
22. Friedman, 1989, pp. 275-90, 283.
23. Rich, 1986.
24. My thanks are due to Dr Mark Shackleton for checking my English.

References

Aristotle *Politics* (1981), translated by Sinclair, T. A., revised and re-presented by Saunders, T. J., Penguin Books: Harmondsworth, Middlesex.

Armstrong, K. (1986), *The Gospel According to Woman: Christianity's Creation of the Sex War in the West*, Pan Books: London and Sydney.

Bentham, J. (1982), *An Introduction to the Principles of Morals and Legislation* (1789), edited by Burns, J. H. and Hart, H. L. A., reprinted with new introduction, Methuen: London and New York.

Dinwiddy, J. (1989), *Bentham*, Oxford University Press: Oxford and New York.

Friedman, M. (1989), 'Feminism and modern friendship: dislocating the community', *Ethics* 99, pp. 275-90.

Hume, D. (1983), *An Enquiry Concerning the Principles of Morals* (1751), edited with an introduction by Schneewind, J. B., Hackett Publishing Company: Indianapolis and Cambridge.

Hutcheson, F. (1725), *An Inquiry into the Original of our Ideas of Beauty and Virtue*, Treatise II, partly reprinted from Raphael, D. D. (ed.), *British Moralists 1650-1800 I. Hobbes-Gay*, Hackett Publishing Company: Indianapolis and Cambridge, 1983.

Kant, I. (1983), *Kritik der praktischen Vernunft* (1788) with *Grundlegung zur Metaphysik der Sitten* (1786), edited by Thom, M., Reclam: Leipzig.

Locke, J. (1690), *Two Treatises of Government*, introduction by W.S. Carpenter, London: J. M. Dent & Sons Ltd, 1924.

MacIntyre, A. (1981), *After Virtue*, Duckworth: London.

MacIntyre, A. (1988), *Whose Justice? Which Rationality?*, Duckworth: London.

Mendus, S. (1992), "Kant: 'An honest but narrow-minded bourgeois'?", in Chadwick, R. (ed.), *Immanuel Kant: Critical Assessments Vol. III. Kant's Moral and Political Philosophy*, Routledge: London and New York.

Mill, J. S. *Utilitarianism* (1861), reprinted from Mill, J. S. and Bentham, J. *Utilitarianism and Other Essays*, Harmondsworth, Middlesex: Penguin Books, 1987)

Mill, J. S. (1869), *The Subjection of Women* has been reprinted, for instance, in Mill, J. S., *Three Essays*, edited by Wollheim, R., Oxford and New York: Oxford University Press, 1975.
Narveson, J. (1988), *The Libertarian Idea*, Temple University Press: Philadelphia.
Nozick, R. (1974), *Anarchy, State, and Utopia*, Basil Blackwell: Oxford and New York.
Rich, A. (1986), *Blood, Bread and Poetry*, Norton: New York.
Sandel, M. (1982), *Liberalism and the Limits of Justice*, Cambridge University Press: Cambridge.
Sullivan, R. J. (1989), *Immanuel Kant's Moral Theory*, Cambridge University Press: Cambridge.
Taylor, C. (1990), *Sources of the Self*, Cambridge University Press: Cambridge.
Walzer, M. (1982), *Spheres of Justice*, Basic Books: New York.

2. FACING THE WORLD: THE LIBERAL STATE AND ITS POLICIES

Limits of corporate personhood: a new philosophy of the corporation

Jukka Kilpi

Milton Friedman's 'The Social Responsibility of Business Is to Increase its Profits' is a classic piece of business ethics which opens the discussion about corporate personhood in many textbooks.[1] It is usually followed by articles which then refute Friedman's thesis, often by arguing that the corporation is more than a mere aggregate of individuals or an agent of stockholders. Friedman's critics give different reasons why the agency[2] or aggregate view he represents is mistaken, but their common credo is that the corporation has a distinct personality of its own which has responsibilities and rights similar to those we attach to natural persons. I shall begin with Friedman's paper, proceed to the strengths and weaknesses of the main rival theories, and finally, present a new philosophy about the kind of personality corporations have.

Milton Friedman: no corporate personhood

> ... in his capacity as a corporate executive, the manager is the agent of the individuals who own the corporation or establish the eleemosynary institution, and his primary responsibility is to them.[3]

According to Friedman, the corporation has no morally relevant personality as such but is only a technical medium to further the interests of the aggregate of individuals who own it. It can have no moral responsibility apart from the purpose for which it has been set up, that purpose usually being profit-making. If the managers who decide on behalf of the corporation assume roles which do not support the profit motive, they are actually imposing taxes without a warrant from the owners. They surpass the area of their legitimate governance by introducing some of the functions of government to the running of business. This is contrary to the interests of those whose agents they are. It is also subversive as it extends the scope of the political mechanism to an area where it does not belong.

It should be noted that Friedman is not advocating ruthless, unlimited profiteering without regard to any rules. He is not saying that the corporation should try to maximize its profits by breaching the law or contractual obligations. Friedman's view is distorted when it is claimed that he leaves the ethical guidance of business completely to economics.[4]

What Friedman is propounding is that the framework of rules that governs business activity, as well as other human activities, should be left up to the political process to decide, and that individuals should be free to pursue profit within the field a democratic government has marked off for business. This division of powers preserves a lot of room for ethical thought, both in regard to the nature of rules which are politically decided, and in regard to the manner in which profit ought to be pursued under these rules. It is another matter that Friedman's work as an economist tells us that he would favour a fairly loose framework of control, but this is not a necessary consequence of his normative argument in his paper on corporate social responsibility.

The corporation as an agent for an aggregate of owner-individuals is the core of Friedman's normative argument. This conception of the corporation enjoyed wide acceptance among legal theorists[5] and economists[6] when he wrote his article. However, new ideas have taken over legal and economic theory since the 1970s. I shall draw on them later when I develop my own proposal for corporate moral personhood.

Law and economics apart, there are also philosophical objections to Friedman's position. They point out that corporations and their actions cannot always be reduced to individuals and their conduct. Peter French was the pioneer in applying the tools of analytical philosophy into business ethics. The results of his analysis are diametrically opposed to Friedman's views.

Peter French: full-fledged corporate personhood

> In short, corporations can be full-fledged moral persons and have whatever privileges, rights and duties as are, in the normal course of affairs, accorded to moral persons.[7]

French starts from the fact, evident in language, that corporations have intentions. He then focuses on corporate decision-making processes, which he calls CID-structures, and says that they introduce permanence into the corporate entity, thus making it able to stand on its own regardless of changes in its constituency (owners, managers, creditors, etc.). To French corporate nature is non-eliminatable, irreducible to an aggregate of individuals. A corporation has intentions and rights of its own, and is a moral person and a moral agent.[8]

The definition French uses for agency is a Davidsonian one. The following quote from French, in which he refers to Daniel Dennett, sums up which entities are entitled to a Davidsonian agency:

> For an entity to be treated as a Davidsonian agent it must be the case that some of the things that happen (some events) are describable in a way that makes certain sentences true, sentences that say that some of the things the entity does were intended by the entity itself.[9]

French's argument goes smoothly. It is no wonder that it has received wide recognition. Nevertheless, it has also been subjected to crushing criticism.[10]

The critics underline that while corporate actions can be described as intentional, it is always natural individuals' minds which possess the intentions. The corporation is an eliminatable subject, not a moral person. As we will see, these philosophers do not necessarily exclude corporate social responsibility, but their broadside against French should be enough to sink the idea of full-fledged corporate moral personhood.

French was led astray by his over-reliance on the narrow definition of personhood he borrows from his peers. He commits a fallacy when he first grants full ontological, and subsequently all-encompassing moral, existence to every entity which we describe as intentional. We may **ascribe** properties to entities without assuming that the ascribed properties exist in those entities in any ontological sense. We ascribe the properties of a car to a toy without transforming the toy into a car, we ascribe God's will to empirical events without changing the causal order of nature, and we ascribe intentions to corporations without altering their existence as legal fiats.

True sentences that ascribe intentions to corporations may be enough to make them Davidsonian agents, but those sentences are insufficient to make corporations into full-fledged persons or moral agents. The nucleus of moral agency is autonomy, which is the capacity to produce and possess not only intentions but moral judgements. Without the help of agency vested in natural persons, corporations could never perform their intentional and autonomous functions; this is why intentions and agency can be ascribed to them but can never be possessed by them. People acting on behalf of corporations exist and are persons regardless of definitions, but corporations exist and have traits of personhood only because we as persons find it convenient to describe them in a certain manner. Through our ascriptions we define the corporation into existence and confer it with a personality.

French claims that he has provided grounds 'for holding corporations *per se* to account for what they do, for treating them as metaphysical persons *qua* moral persons'.[11] His fundamental mistake is his adherence to orthodox conceptual analysis, which forgets the role that Kantian agency plays in the constitution of the world and moral judgement. The orthodox analysis of the concepts denoting objects ignores the constitutive interplay between the perceiving subject and the sensibilia. As a consequence, mysterious entities without any empirical reference gain reality only because they have linguistic plausibility, which is seen to warrant them as potential targets of perception. Time-travel, reincarnating persons, ontologically real possible worlds, and swampmen are well-debated examples of weirdos artificially inseminated by contemporary analytical philosophy. French conceives them a new next-of-kin: the corporation as a full-fledged moral person. His orthodox analysis of normative concepts ignores the constitutive interplay between the moral agent and the moral judgement and, as a consequence, real corporations are obscured into mysterious personhood.

Thomas Donaldson and Kenneth Goodpaster: versions of stakeholder theory

The failure in establishing the corporation as a full-fledged moral person does not mean that it is a mere aggregate of its constituents. The proposition that social responsibility arises from social power is simple but strong. Corporate actions affect us. They cannot always be reduced to any particular natural person's actions, and their impact may be felt by persons who are not constituents of the corporation. Because corporations affect persons, they have moral obligations to the persons affected.[12]

We have accepted that intentions are ascribed to corporations and that their actions affect persons. Therefore, it would be difficult to deny that moral obligations could be attached to them over and beyond the obligation to maximize profits. But this does not take us very far. What is the nature of corporate morality? Is it captured by a negative stipulation that self-interested pursuits should not cause unjustified harm, or does it amount to positive duties which require the pursuit of profits to be constrained by more noble causes? More philosophical analysis and argument is needed to specify how much morality corporations can be loaded with.

Stakeholder theories are a recent attempt to explain the source of corporate moral obligations and to define their extent and contents. These theories understand the corporation as a broad concern for all who have a stake in corporate policy. In addition to shareholders, the interests of consumers, employees, and the community at large count.[13] Two distinguished philosophers arguing for this view are Thomas Donaldson and Kenneth Goodpaster. I shall put Donaldson's work under scrutiny first.

Donaldson uses a hypothetical social contract to illustrate the answer to the question 'Why should corporations exist?' His point is that corporations are productive organisations which enhance the welfare of society through the satisfaction of consumer and worker interests. This is the moral foundation of the corporation. It is enforced by all stakeholders' hypothetical approval, and therefore the corporation has a moral obligation to take their interests into account.[14]

Donaldson's explanation for obligations towards stakeholders has charm, but it stumbles into serious theoretical difficulties. Their source is the hypothetical nature of the social contract sanctioning business:

> The distinctive basis of the 'social contract theory' is that under such a theory obligations arise only if they have been voluntarily assumed, and Donaldson has no reason to believe that corporations have assumed voluntary obligations. The doctrine of tacit consent cannot help Donaldson.[15]

After this passage, Paul Hodapp details the reasons why business persons cannot plausibly be said to have given the tacit consent required by the social contract theory. I leave this discussion aside. I think it is clear that a hypothetical social contract cannot play the same normative role for corporations as it may play for natural persons.

If the spirit of Rawlsian contractualism[16] is followed, hypothetical arrangements do not decide the moral nature of individual agents. On the contrary, their moral nature controls the outcome of the contractual set-up, the outcome being general moral principles whose application is left to actual contractual arrangements. In the case of natural persons, a Rawlsian social contract acts as a philosophical tool which reflects the contractors' moral personality, thereby exposing the moral principles that ought to prevail between them. This is achievable because the contractors are autonomous agents whose agency furnishes the hypothesis with enough material to bring forth substantive normative conclusions.

In the case of the corporation the same model is implausible. A hypothetical contract cannot tell us what sort of corporations we ought to have because a corporation does not exist until we have actually contracted it into existence. Our moral agency may be the source of our right to create corporations, but it can never be the source of a corporation's right to exist in its own right. Because corporations lack moral agency of their own, they lack the moral personality necessary for having moral responsibility allocated to them through hypothetical contracts.

Thus, Donaldson is right that the moral foundation of the corporation is a contract, but he errs in focusing on the hypothetical contract. The moral foundation of each and every existing corporation is always an actual contract:

> ... corporateness simply coincides with the qualities of a separate legal entity.[17]

The coincidence is no accident. Corporations lack inherent moral potentials, therefore actual contractual and legal arrangements are the material used to determine their moral obligations. Hypothetical procedures cannot illustrate moral potentials that do not exist without actual contracting first taking place.

Donaldson is also right in assigning moral weight to the interests of all stakeholders of the corporation, but these interests do not necessitate a hypothetical contract. They are well served if actual contractual undertakings of the corporation are given appropriate attention. Donaldson has helped us by raising contract to the centerpiece of corporate moral essence, and by pointing out the importance of all stakeholders, but he has fallen short of providing an adequate theoretical explanation of these characteristics.

Kenneth Goodpaster has presented an alternative theory that seeks to establish the corporation's moral responsibility to stakeholders in general.[18] He does not assign full personhood to the corporation, but uses an analogy to relate it to the individual person. This leads him to the following conclusions:

> Organizational agents such as corporations should be no more and no less morally responsible (rational, self-interested, altruistic) than ordinary persons.
>
> We take this position because we think an analogy holds between the individual and the corporation. If we analyze the concept of moral responsibility as it applies to persons, we find that projecting it to corporations as agents in society is possible.[19]

The crux of Goodpaster's argument is the finding that we may project moral responsibility to corporations. We may indeed do so, as our common language and legal, social, and economic practices evidence. Goodpaster is careful not to claim that this makes the corporation a person in a literal sense, yet he claims that they 'should be no more and no less morally responsible'. Where is the difference then?

Goodpaster's analogy holds because it is true that we project, attribute, and ascribe moral responsibility to the corporation. His conclusion that the corporation is 'no more and no less' morally responsible than a human individual does not hold for exactly the same reason. When we project moral responsibility upon an entity which is not, as such, a moral agent, a plethora of problems emerge. Do we create new responsibility by projecting, or does it transfer some of our existing burden to others? What if the amount of responsibility projected by us differs from that projected by others? Can we project away all our personal moral constraints? Once projected, do the responsibilities vested in the non-personal entity change somehow, for instance, by the effect that many individuals unknown to each other and unaware of each others' actions participate in the projection? Questions like these are not answered simply by assuming that the corporation's responsibilities are the same as the individual's. The two agents clearly differ in kind; why should the contents of their responsibilities not differ?

The merit of Goodpaster's analogy is that it captures the source of corporate moral agency, that is, projection of responsibilities. Its flaw is that it fails to show how the moral obligation to pay respect to stakeholders' interests springs from that source. Even if we are capable of projecting moral properties to corporations, why should we do so? In particular, why should our projections indicate moral concern for stakeholders' interests?

Patricia Werhane: secondary agency

> ... a corporation functions as a unit, dependent upon, but distinct from, its constituents. Because a corporation is capable of secondary action, it is a secondary moral agent but is not morally autonomous.[20]

Patricia Werhane's book *Persons, Rights, & Corporations* is a careful study which contains detailed criticism of the major theories of corporate personhood, and a constructive corporate ontology. Werhane refutes French by pointing out the difference 'between ascribing goals to an organization and determining what are the intentions and goals of an organization'.[21] The descriptions of corporate actions in terms of intentions do not make the corporation a moral person.

On the other hand, Werhane denies that the corporation is merely a fiction standing for an aggregate of individuals. Corporations have an impact on the world, and our language refers to them as the cause of that impact. In corporate decision-making the causal role of an individual is distinct from corporate action. The aggregate theory fails to explain this. Having rejected the two extremist views, Werhane moves towards stakeholder theories. She explicitly underwrites Donaldson's idea of social contract[22] and, although she criticises Goodpaster for assigning too much moral character to the corporation, she adopts a position very similar to his analogy examined above:

> Corporations *function*, then, as if they were real, autonomous, individual entities.[23]

Werhane adds to these familiar ideas an ontological analysis exploiting her distinction between primary actions of natural persons and secondary actions of corporations. The latter are

> ... *secondary collectives*, whose actions are ontologically reducible to, but not identical with, actions of individuals performing on behalf of the corporation.[24]

Although this is not enough to blow life into corporate personhood, it entitles us to ascribe moral agency to corporations in order to ascribe moral responsibility to them. The crucial difference between corporations and persons is that corporations 'lack the autonomy necessary to perform primary actions'.[25] Nevertheless, since they are capable of secondary actions, we may ascribe responsibility to them, including moral responsibility.

Werhane's analysis is illuminating in many respects. She exposes the weaknesses of rival theories, makes their tenable concepts work together, and complements the picture by introducing new concepts. The resulting secondary moral agency explains how corporations can be held morally responsible without procreating new unnatural moral persons.

Can the success of Werhane's corporate ontology give wings to normative conclusions? She speaks of ethics in the language of rights, and says that the rights of corporations

> ... are derived from, dependent upon, and secondary to, individual rights, although they are not identical to them.[26]

Her normative view relies heavily on a Goodpasterian analogy. She claims that just as human beings possess moral rights because they 'are capable of independent (primary) action', corporations possess secondary moral rights "that they derive from their capacity to 'perform' secondary actions".[27]

Werhane finalizes her normative steps by saying that all moral rights are equal, and thus secondary moral rights are equal rights as well, though she makes the concession that their nature is 'somewhat different from individual or primary rights'.[28] One of the implications of the equal standing of secondary rights is that they, like their primary counterparts, impose duties upon their holders:

> If corporations have rights, they have obligations to respect the equal rights of persons as well as other corporations.[29]

Hence, corporations have moral obligations to all stakeholders, not just to their owners.

Here Werhane's ontological results do not support her normative claims. She sets aside too bluntly the complications caused by the fact that the morally relevant qualities of primary agents and secondary agents are significantly different. The former are autonomous, which may be used to justify the normative conclusion that they are entitled to some inalienable moral rights, but the latter are not autonomous. Why should the rights of non-autonomous agents be equal to the rights of autonomous agents? Why should secondary agents have any rights at all?

The analogy between natural persons and secondary agents is not enough to remove doubts raised by the moral difference between the two. Their unlikeness is manifest in autonomy - the source of a natural person's moral agency, rights and obligations. This is recognized even by Werhane who, in spite of her call for equality of rights, admits that secondary rights are 'somewhat different'. She takes heed of the difference when she specifies two peculiarities of corporate rights: they can never 'exceed any individual's entitlement to a right', and they are 'collective rather than aggregate rights'.[30] But this means that secondary rights clearly have inferior powers. Why is their equal standing now forgotten?

Werhane sorts out well the differences between primary and secondary moral agency, and between the rights peculiar to each kind of agency, yet her normative argument is built upon the equality of rights. The weak point of her reasoning is that she does not have an adequate justification for that equality, nor do her normative conclusions conform with it.

Werhane's shift from ontological analysis to normative discourse falters at a crucial step. This does not necessarily invalidate the applied ethics that follow in her book, but hinders the exploitation of the full potential of her otherwise penetrating analysis. I shall now make an attempt to further refine corporate ontology with the purpose of better explaining its connection to corporate ethics.

A new philosophy of the corporation

The outcome of the foregoing debate over corporate moral personhood is that the corporation is neither a mere aggregate of its owners, nor a full-fledged moral person. The language we use and the social and legal customs we have adopted bear witness to the fact that the moral responsibility for corporate actions cannot always be reduced to individual responsibility. Together with the fact that corporate actions cause impact on others this is enough to shoot down the aggregate theory. On the other hand, we have found that the attempts to make corporate bodies the source of their intentions run into difficulties. Most importantly, the corporation lacks autonomy which is the central precondition of moral personhood. These flaws in corporate character render it ineligible for the status of a full-fledged moral person.

On the positive note, we have been offered good reasons to focus on contracts in explaining the corporation. We have seen that the impact of corporate actions in society brings stakeholders' interests to the forefront. The moral responsibility for these actions has been given a plausible explanation in terms of being 'ascribed' or 'projected' to corporate agents. The analogy between the individual and the corporation seems to hold to some extent, but significant differences also remain between the two, justifying the characterization of the corporation as a secondary moral agent. The ensuing proposal for a new philosophy of the corporation is an attempt to increase the cohesion of these positive results in order to extract normative principles out of them.

Consider the following quotations from Eugene F. Fama and David Millon respectively:

> More recently the literature has moved toward theories that reject the classical model of the firm but assume classical forms of economic behavior on the part of agents within the firm. The firm is viewed as a set of contracts among factors of production, with each factor motivated by its self-interest.[31]
>
> Since around 1980, legal academics have developed a new theory of the corporation explicitly grounded on neoclassical economics. This theory conceives of the corporation as a 'nexus of contracts'.[32]

The view of the corporation as a nexus of contracts dominates economic and legal theory. Our philosophical analysis points in the same direction.

The corporation is a nexus of contracts. For what is it that makes it feasible for us to ascribe and project responsibility and obligations to secondary agents? It is the actual contractual arrangements, either explicit or implicit, that bring corporations into existence. Most often, in a modern society, the contractual arrangements creating secondary moral agents are explicit documents in a prescribed form - the articles, memorandum or charter of a corporation - but there is no necessity for them to be thus formalized.

For a secondary agent to exist, moral and legal attributes have to be attached to it. These attributes can, theoretically, be attached whenever natural persons reach a consensus that they act together for some particular aim. If they have so agreed, there is a conceptual entity on which actions, and responsibility for them, may be projected. If they have not so agreed, the projection of responsibility to a joint venture distinct from the acting individuals would target an entity which does not exist to the acting persons, and therefore the projection itself would be arbitrary.

It is a matter for an empirical judgement whether actual contractual arrangements creating the corporate entities capable of being the targets of projections do exist, and it is a matter for an ethical judgement what kind of contractual arrangements creating these entities are acceptable. We have faculties to settle both matters rationally.

A set of contracts is the ontological originator of the corporation. Because corporations lack autonomy the moral categories applying to them have to be generated by actual rather than hypothetical contracts. Actual contracts embody a corporation's undertakings, place it in a social context, and define its relations to other agents - both primary and secondary.

Just as the actions of natural persons may fall within the limits of law or step outside of them, so too may corporate actions. The actions of natural persons may be moral or immoral regardless of their lawfulness, so too with corporate actions. Is there any difference between the two? Yes, there is, because the nature of their moral agency is different. The rights of a corporation are always ascribed to it, and so are its duties. If no natural person ever ascribes any rights or obligations to a corporation a moral wrong is not committed. In fact, that particular corporation would be a moral vacuum which could hardly be said to exist. But a human being may exist even if everybody neglects her moral status as a person, and if that neglect leads to the termination of her existence a moral wrong has been done.

The moral limits of a natural person's actions are set by human rights and contractual commitments. Human rights are on the top of the moral hierarchy. An individual is protected by these fundamental trumps, as well as bound to pay respect to others' similar trumps, by virtue of her potential for autonomy alone. On the other hand, a corporation cannot claim any human rights. Corporate actions are limited by human rights and contractual obligations too, but the actor is protected only by the moral bearing of the contracts effectuating it.

However, the interpretation of contractual rights, duties, and obligations should not be, and never has been, confined to mere reading of the explicit text. In law, implications and unexpected circumstances call for judicial judgement. Part of the judicial judgement consists of moral judgement, as sources as diverse as common law and Ronald Dworkin's philosophy[33] show. More generally in life, the impact of corporate actions upon people leads us to moral ascriptions which may go beyond the law.

The new legal and economic theories of the corporation have carried the ballast of classical economics: their vision has been locked at the stockholder interest as the contractual core of the corporation. But there is more than one model of contract, as W.W. Bratton points out:

> Theories more relational than that employed by the neoclassical new theorists offer values protective of individuals who invest their labor and energies in business enterprises, including firms.[34]

The new philosophy takes heed of the relational abundance of the corporation. The set of contracts that constitutes the corporation defines and protects the rights of all parties to the web: owners, customers, corporations and the society.Thus, the new philosophy provides stakeholder interests an improved ethical foundation.

It would be irrational to claim that an entrepreneur or an executive had only the responsibility to pursue profits regardless of the legal and moral obligations present in the rest of the contractual body making up the company they run. The corporation cannot be indifferent to its obligations to other stakeholders of the web because those obligations are the material constituting it as a corporation! A corporation denies its own existence if natural persons acting on its behalf refuse to participate in the projection of obligations that the web of contracts they are serving demands.

This somewhat Hegelian language is not as mystifying as it may first appear. The corporation is a legal fiat, the content of its obligations is embodied in a set of contracts, and some of the obligations require moral ascriptions. The material we use to read the corporate essence is much more concrete than the material available to explain the moral essence of human beings. This means that the Hegelian expressions lack the metaphysical ambiguity that normally bothers them, and can thus explain how a Friedmanite quest for profits is compatible with wider corporate moral responsibilities.

The new philosophy appreciates the corporation both as a legal fiat and as a morally responsible agent. The outcome shows how secondary agency emerges as a result of us ascribing, projecting, or assigning moral properties which pay respect to interests of all those who have a contractual stake in the company. It owes a lot to stakeholder theories and Patricia Werhane's observations on secondary agency, yet it is a new theory in the sense that it accommodates the findings of these philosophers into one explanatory framework which is compatible with contemporary mainstream economics and jurisprudence, and is capable of contributing to the normative discourse.

Much of the debate on the corporation revolves round the distinctions public/private and aggregate/collective. The new philosophy reveals that these distinctions are not sharp and exclusive. Being based on contracts, the corporation always has a public exposure, but it cannot exist without private actions behind it. As for the distinction aggregate/collective, we have found that corporate actions are constituted by individual actions, yet may not be reducible to them.

The legal and moral connotations of the corporation exist by virtue of our autonomy, which has the potential to construct contractual entities. Limited liability corporation is a contractual vehicle for autonomous persons to exercise their potential for moral judgement and conceptual thinking. It is a vehicle for bringing about more sophisticated rights and obligations. Just as derivative contracts commodify certain aspects of rights of ownership of tangible objects, so too the limited corporation refines and splits promissory obligations into packages which are more suitable for the purposes of modern trade and production. We are furnished with means to exempt some of our intentional actions from the rigours of responsibility, yet that exercise is subject to constraints authorized by the nature of that potential itself. Our power to transcribe responsibility to artefacts cannot override moral notions that emerge straight from autonomy, or, as Patricia Werhane put it, corporate rights cannot exceed any individual's entitlement to a right.

Economic activity is made of intentional actions by human beings. Its peculiarity is that the actors have declared it a reserve free from some ethical constraints that apply elsewhere. The declaration is within their authority as long as it does not assault the universal moral values, that is, human rights which protect autonomy.

As a result, intentions which in everyday social intercourse would raise moral blame do not have that effect in a business context. A successful entrepreneur gets acclaim because she is more astute or lucky than the rest of us, yet her success may build on others' losses. If she had made less, someone might have had more! Good deals are often to the mutual benefit of the participants. But even when benefits are reaped from others' detriment, the beneficiary does not have to be ashamed for her fortune if it is achieved through voluntary contracting. It would be unethical if I hypnotized my neighbour to mow my lawn, but there is nothing wrong in hiring her to do it.

From our ethical space, which is filled with constraints, we carve out business as a less fettered area because it is a technical activity carried out for the production of the necessities of life. Through our experience we have learned that, in the long run, voluntary contracting delivers the best bounty. It means that those who are more cunning can get a licence to persuade the less shrewd to participate in unrewarding deals, but in return we have superior means to live by our will, commitments, and duties.

We are not only allowed to seek profit out of personal and corporate business. It is a necessity that we do so, even for a 'non-profit' venture. I understand 'profit' here in a weak sense: it stands for income at least equal to expenditure. A trade which defies the necessity of profit is doomed, and will go broke sooner or later. Of course, a business may decide to impose charitable and altruistic duties upon itself, but only after its profitability affords the benevolence. Virtue ethicists aim at the impossible when they try to subdue the necessity of profit to altruist moral considerations. Their efforts can only lead to virtual ethics, window-dressing from the side of business and lip-service from the side of philosophers.

Nevertheless, business ethics is no oxymoron: it participates in the determination of the borders of the reserve where concessional ethics for productive trades apply, and in the determination of the concessions specific to that reserve. The most important tools of any trade are money and credit, and they become obsolete without trust and ethical behaviour. Ethics is an ingredient of the social cohesion conducive to trust and confidence in a market economy: sound moral principles make sense to rational autonomous agents.

Notes

1. The original article was published in New York Times Magazine, September 13, 1970. References here are to Friedman, 1993.
2. 'Agency' is here understood in the sense of being entrusted with the concerns of another, which is a meaning different from the Kantian 'agency' standing for an originator of judgments and choices.
3. Friedman, 1993, p. 162.
4. This claim is made in DesJardins & McCall, 1990, p. 1.
5. Millon, 1990, pp. 220-9.
6. Fama, 1980, pp. 288-9.
7. French, 1993, p. 228.
8. Ibid., pp. 228-30; French et.al., 1992, pp. 14-5, 43.
9. French, 1985, p. 74.
10. Ladd, 1993; Pfeiffer, 1990; Velasquez, 1990; Werhane, 1985, pp. 34-40.
11. French, 1993, p. 235.
12. Versions of this impact-argument can be found in Davis, 1990, p. 166; Solomon & Hanson, 1985, p. 186 ff.; and Werhane, 1985, p. 4.
13. DesJardins & McCall, 1990, p. 98.
14. Donaldson, 1993, pp. 183-4.
15. Hodapp, 1990, p. 130.
16. Rawls, 1971.
17. Stoljar, 1973, p. 177.
18. Goodpaster & Matthews, 1990; Goodpaster, 1993.
19. Goodpaster & Matthews 1990, p. 105.

20. Werhane, 1985, p. 59.
21. Ibid., p. 36.
22. Ibid., p. 46.
23. Ibid., p. 50.
24. Ibid., p. 50.
25. Ibid., p. 57.
26. Ibid., p. 60.
27. Ibid., p. 61.
28. Ibid., p. 61.
29. Ibid., p. 61.
30. Ibid., p. 62.
31. Fama, 1980, p. 289.
32. Millon, 1990, p. 229.
33. Dworkin, 1977.
34. Bratton, 1989, p. 1526.

References

Bratton, W. W. (1989), 'The New Economic Theory of the Firm: Critical Perspectives from History', *Stanford Law Review*, vol. 41, pp. 1471-527.

Davis, K. (1990), 'Five Propositions for Social Responsibility', excerpted in pp. 165-70 in Hoffman W. M. & Moore, J. M. (ed.), *Business Ethics*, 2nd ed., McGraw-Hill Publ. Co: New York.

DesJardins, J. R. & McCall, J. J. (eds), (1990), *Contemporary Issues in Business Ethics*, 2nd ed., Wadsworth Publishing Company: Belmont, Cal.

Donaldson, T. (1993), 'Constructing a Social Contract for Business', reprinted from White, T. I. (ed.), *Business Ethics. A Philosophical Reader*, Macmillan Publishing Company: New York, pp. 167-187.

Dworkin, R. (1977), *Taking Rights Seriously*, Duckworth: London.

Fama, E. F. (1980), 'Agency Problems and the Theory of the Firm', *Journal of Political Economy*, vol. 88 no. 2, pp. 288-307.

French, P. A. (1985), 'Fishing the Red Herrings Out of the Sea of Moral Responsibility', in Le Pore, E. & McLaughlin, B. P. (eds), *Actions and Events*, Basil Blackwell, pp. 73-87.

French, P.A., Nesteruk, J., Risser, D. T., with Abbarno, J. (1992), *Corporations in the Moral Community*, Harcourt Brace Jovanovich College Publishers: Fort Worth, Fla.

French, P. A. (1993), 'The Corporation as a Moral Person', reprinted from White, T. I. (ed.), *Business Ethics. A Philosophical Reader*, Macmillan Publishing Company: New York, pp. 228-35.

Friedman, M. (1993), 'The Social Responsibility of Business Is to Increase Its Profits', reprinted from White, T.I. (ed.), *Business Ethics. A Philosophical Reader*, Macmillan Publishing Company: New York, pp. 162-7.

Goodpaster, K. E. and Matthews, J. B. Jr, (1990), 'Can a Corporation Have a Conscience?', reprinted from DesJardins, J. R. & McCall, J. J. (eds), *Contemporary Issues in Business Ethics*, 2nd ed., Wadsworth Publishing Company: Belmont, Cal, pp. 104-13.

Goodpaster, K. E. (1993), 'Business Ethics and Stakeholder Analysis', reprinted from White, T. I. (ed.), *Business Ethics. A Philosophical Reader*, Macmillan Publishing Company: New York, pp. 205-23.

Hodapp, P. F.(1990), 'Can There Be a Social Contract with Business?', *Journal of Business Ethics*, 9, pp. 127-31.

Ladd, J. (1993), 'Corporate Mythology and Individual Responsibility', reprinted from White, T. I. (ed.), *Business Ethics. A Philosophical Reader*, Macmillan Publishing Company: New York, pp. 236-51.

Millon, D. (1990), 'Theories of the Corporation', *Duke Law Journal*, pp. 201-62, vol. 1990.

Pfeiffer, R. S. (1990), 'The Central Distinction in the Theory of Corporate Moral Personhood', *Journal of Business Ethics*, 9, pp. 473-80.

Rawls, J. (1971), *A Theory of Justice*, Harvard University Press: Cambridge, Mass.

Solomon, R. C. & Hanson, K. R. (1985), *It's Good Business*, Atheneum: New York.

Stoljar, S. J. (1973), *Groups and Entities. An Inquiry into Corporate Theory*, ANU Press: Canberra.

Velasquez, M. G. (1990), 'Why Corporations are not Morally Responsible for Anything They Do', reprinted from pp. 114-26 in DesJardins, J. R. & McCall, J. J. (eds), *Contemporary Issues in Business Ethics*, 2nd ed., Wadsworth Publishing Company: Belmont, Cal.

Werhane, P. (1985), *Persons, Rights, and Corporations*, Prentice-Hall Inc: Englewood Cliffs, N. J.

Insiders and outsiders - ethical theorising in concrete business life

Marjaana Kopperi

In his article 'Corporate Roles, Personal Virtues: An Aristotelian Approach to Business Ethics', Robert C. Solomon criticises general attempts to define or develop the theory of business ethics:

> It has been standard practice in many business ethics courses and most standard textbooks, to begin with a survey of ethical theory. This means, inevitably, a brief summary of Kant and deontological ethics, a brief survey of utilitarianism with a note or two about John Stuart Mill, and a distinction or two between act and rule, pleasure versus preference utilitarianism, and some replay of the much-rehearsed contest between the two sorts of theories... But is this the theory of business ethics? Not only is the application to concrete business situations in question - and then the message to students is too often an unabashed relativism ('if you are a utilitarian, you'll do this, if you're a Kantian, you'll do that') - but it is not even clear whether there is, then, anything distinctive about *business* ethics. There is just ethics, or rather ethical theory, whatever that may be.[1]

Solomon maintains that attempts to derive ethical principles for business from the classical theories of Kant and Mill, for example, are doomed to fail. The problem with these major theories is their inapplicability to the specific conditions of everyday business life. These theories try to resolve practical issues by reference to an abstract principle or decision procedure, such as categorical imperative or general utility. But such a theoretical approach is insensitive to the concrete business context and to the particular roles inhabited by people in business. It dismisses personal values, involvements and responsibilities of an ordinary manager, executive or employee. As a consequence, the field of business ethics is dominated by what Solomon calls policy issues; questions concerning very general business practices and problems, such as pollution, advertising, employee rights and duties, and the social responsibilities of companies to their surrounding communities. What is missing from these policy discussions, he maintains, is an adequate account of the personal dimension of ethics.

Instead of these major theories, Solomon wants to promote what he terms an Aristotelian approach to business ethics. An Aristotelian approach begins with the idea that business ethics relate to individual responsibility and cultivation of character rather than to abstract principles and decision procedures. Unlike utilitarian and Kantian theories, it regards considerations of personal roles and responsibilities as its most important concern. The focus on individual and personal does not, however, mean 'private' or 'subjective'. Rather, the personal dimension in the Aristotelian sense refers to a person's account of oneself as someone occupying a particular place in a particular community. The Aristotelian approach regards the rights and duties, virtues and responsibilities of a person as derived from the shared ends of the community and determined by the specific role that he or she has in that community.

According to Solomon corporations today are real representations of such communities. They have shared ends, they invoke extraordinary emphasis on loyalty, they inspire teamwork and require cooperation.[2] And as any significant community, they have a share in the forming and shaping of the identities of their members. So, people working in these corporations seem to 'identify themselves in terms of their companies'[3] and see themselves 'as intimate parts of the business world with a keen sense of the virtues and values of that world'.[4]

Business ethics, when conceived in this way, takes the specific features and requirements of the context seriously. It determines what is morally right or wrong in the business world not by referring to the general moral principles and rules, but by considering how a person's actions correspond to the virtues and responsibilities relevant of his or her role in the particular corporation. The theory of business ethics in Aristotelian terms can then be defined as 'the theory of individuals in business roles'.[5]

The standard practice in many business ethics textbooks criticised by Solomon has often resulted in an overly theoretical approach. Theoretical framework and practical aspects of business life do not meet easily, which is evident to anyone reading these books. Discussion of major ethical theories on the one hand, and the everyday issues and problems of business life, such as advertising, employee rights or environmental issues on the other, seem to have only few if any mutual connections.

However, I think that the replacement of the utilitarian and Kantian theories with the Aristotelian one does not help in responding to these problems. The Aristotelian philosophy entails its own problems that are no less difficult than those generated by utilitarian or Kantian theories. Instead, I think it would be useful to cast a closer look at these theories in order to detect what is really fundamental in them and what really distinguishes the Aristotelian from the 'standard' approach. Actually, I believe that these rival approaches represent entirely different understandings about the role and nature of ethics on the whole.

These differences also result in divergent views about the role and tasks of ethics in concrete business life.

In this article I will first present an account of the nature of these theories, basing my view on the contemporary discussion of the subject. After doing this, I consider the implications of these theories in concrete business life. I argue that despite their differences these approaches are not necessarily exclusive options but, when properly understood, each has an important though different role in business ethics, as well as in concrete business life.

How does the Aristotelian approach differ from Utilitarian and Kantian ethics?

It might seem strange at first glance to connect utilitarian and Kantian theories in the way Solomon does. We are, after all, used to 'the much-rehearsed contest' between the utilitarian and Kantian sorts of theories, as Solomon remarks. Nevertheless, Solomon's distinction between Aristotelian ethics on the one hand and utilitarian and Kantian on the other is not without grounds, and, as a matter of fact, this distinction has recently become quite common in different ethical discussions. A considerable number of philosophers have felt that there is less difference than similarity between utilitarianism and Kantianism.[6] Despite of the differences between the two, utilitarian and Kantian theories are both representatives of the ethical tradition that derives its force from the Enlightenment thought and that, as a 'modern' mode of thinking, has been separated from the 'ancient' ones.[7]

One of the most important distinguishing features between ancient and modern ethical thought often pointed out in contemporary discussions is the way the domain of morality is defined.[8] Modern moral theory, it has been claimed, both in its utilitarian and Kantian forms, interprets morality exclusively in other-regarding terms. Modern theorists have defined morality as a matter of what one does or does not do to others, and as morally relevant situations only those where other people are involved. They focus on the articulating of the agent's responsibilities to others, whether these responsibilities are conceived in terms of contributing to the greatest good of the greatest number or in terms of treating others as ends and not merely as means.[9] Morality, according to this view, is concerned with social conduct, with issues such as justice, respect for other people's lives, well-being and dignity.[10] Issues related to one's own life, one's personal aims and desires, in turn, are not usually regarded as moral ones, insofar as they do not have significant effects on other people.

Opposing modern theories, most ancient ones are not primarily concerned with agents' responsibilities towards others, but rather with the agents themselves. The purpose of ethical inquiry in the Aristotelian, as in most other ancient theories, is to promote the good life, happiness and flourishing of the human being. Beginning from the general question 'how should I live' or 'what should my life be like', those theories proceed with articulating the constituent parts of human good. What is essential in these articulations is not the 'duty' or 'rights' or even 'good' as such, but 'my life'.[11] Thus ethical reflection within ancient theories aims at providing each person with an understandable picture about what one's good life or happiness or flourishing consists of, and thus helping one order his priorities in a way that enables the realisation of the good life.[12]

According to this view, the fundamental difference between ancient and modern understanding of morality concerns the role given to the self-regarding and other-regarding aspects of morality. Ancient morality begins with the consideration of aims, values and purposes of the agent, regarding other people as constitutive parts of the flourishing, self-realisation and happiness of the agent.[13] By contrast, modern ethics begins with the examination of people's interests and needs in order to determine their rights and duties towards one another.[14]

Taken in the business context, these rival approaches result also in different interpretations about the role of ethics. When viewed from the 'modern' perspective, what matters morally in the business world is the general obligation to respect the rights and interests of other people when advancing one's economic goals. Accordingly, business ethics requires that corporations or people who work there identify and respect the specific rights and interests of all the parties involved in a particular situation. In other words, it requires them to consider the effects of their actions on all those whose well-being is somehow at stake because of those actions. Given this sort of concern, the basic task of business ethics can be defined as one of weighing the different and often conflicting rights and interests of all the parties involved in specific circumstances.[15] This account is indeed often assumed in the 'standard textbooks' of business ethics.

The Aristotelian approach, in turn, requires the ethical inquiry to focus on the reflection of the good life of an individual, both in and out of the business context.[16] Of fundamental importance are questions such as 'what is a good corporation?' and 'what is the good life of an individual in the business world and in a particular corporation?' Answers to these questions are to be found by examining the values and purposes specific to the business world. Business life, as any other aspect of life, has its specific goals and distinctive practices that must be taken seriously when determining the ethical theory appropriate for the business world. People play different roles in different fields of their lives, and what the good life entails in each specific field is at least partly determined by the context itself. As Solomon points out, the good life has many facets. Consequently, the proper rights and duties, virtues and responsibilities vary from one field or context to another.

Business ethics defined in Aristotelian terms hence consists primarily of the reflection of the virtues and values, roles and responsibilities of individual persons working in the business world, as defined both by individual corporations and the business world as a whole. It is concerned with individuals as persons who 'identify themselves in terms of their companies'[17], who 'accept a set of particular obligations' and 'adopt a certain standard of excellence and conscientiousness that is largely defined by the job itself'.[18] In short, it is concerned with individuals as persons who see themselves as 'intimate parts of the business world with a keen sense of the virtues and values of that world'.[19]

Corporate values, personal roles

How can this Aristotelian approach then be applied in concrete business life? What does the demand of respecting the virtues and values of the specific context mean in *this* specific context?

Interestingly, the considerations Solomon regards as fundamental in business ethics seem to be well in use in the contemporary business world. Talking of the corporation as a community with shared values and of individuals primarily as persons occupying their specific roles in this community has become increasingly common in everyday business life. Corporations today have often explicitly defined aims and values, usually as part of different Quality Management Systems. They also have a determinate account of what it means to be a good company and what it means to be a good employee in such company. Personal responsibility, commitment, self-assessment and aspiration for excellence in performing one's duties are also issues to be emphasised in Quality Management philosophy. The commitment to these aims and values can help in creating and sustaining a flourishing corporate community with flourishing individual members as part of it. Naturally, the final objective of these activities is the success of the corporation with respect to its competitors.[20]

From the perspective of 'modern' ethics, this kind of approach might seem to have little to do with ethics. It could be argued that there is nothing specifically ethical in the pursuit of one's own aims. The activities that aim at the success and flourishing of the corporation can be classified as rational or prudential rather than moral concerns. It seems, at least from the modern point of view, that defining business ethics in the way Solomon does results in a certain 'disappearance' of the specifically ethical field in concrete business life.[21] If this is the result, it might be asked why speak of business ethics at all, why not speak instead of corporate values, shared ends or quality management as the representatives of the business world themselves have done.

Yet another more serious question can be raised about Solomon's account of business ethics. It might be argued that when concentrating on the explication of corporate aims and values and the creation of the corporate community, the rights and interests of the 'outsiders' are not taken into account seriously enough. A corporation may have a flourishing corporate culture with its shared aims and explicitly defined values. But does this guarantee that a corporation also takes care of the effects of its actions on people who are *not* considered members of the corporate community? Regardless of the flourishing corporate culture, the corporation might, for instance, ignore the pollutive effects of its operations with respect to its neighbourhood or local community. Or it might, as has become commonplace in recent years, differentiate its activities between core company and various subcontractors and their subcontractors - often located in third world countries - and, while directing the former according to the highest ethical and managerial principles as described above, takes no responsibility at all for the latter.

What is missing, thus, from Solomon's account of business ethics is the viewpoint of those outside the business world and the particular corporation. His Aristotelian approach is concerned with the virtues and values of the 'intimate members' of the corporate community but says nothing at all about those who cannot be regarded as such. Yet the operations of the corporation can affect also these 'outsiders'.

I think these problems are easier to avoid if business ethics is understood in terms of modern moral theory. As beginning from the recognition of the equal rights and interest of all human beings, 'the modern approach' is better prepared than the Aristotelian one to take also the people outside of the business world into account. The question still to be asked is how this modern approach can be applied in concrete situations of business life? Does the adoption of this approach necessarily require one to ignore the conditions of concrete situations and, instead, to employ mechanically some abstract decision procedures? I do not think so. Unlike Solomon, I think that an overly theoretical and abstract approach is not the necessary result of the modern approach, even though it has often been so. There are more context-sensitive ways to consider and weigh the interests of all the relevant parties.

Taking other people seriously - a stakeholder approach

One attempt to take the interests of others seriously is the 'stakeholder' approach advocated for instance by Kenneth Goodpaster. According to this view, a corporation must, when pursuing its economic goals, take not only the interests of the stockholders but also other stakeholders into account. The term 'stakeholder' is defined by Goodpaster as follows: 'A stakeholder in an organization is (by definition) any group or individual who can affect or is affected by the achievement of the organization's objectives'.[22] As examples of such stakeholder groups, Goodpaster mentions employees, suppliers, customers, creditors, competitors, governments and communities.

A stakeholder approach simply means that when making the decisions on its future operations, a corporation or its management must consider how these operations will affect its employees, customers and other stakeholders. This entails, for instance, the 'fact-gathering about the options available and their short- and long-term implications', and an 'analysis of these implications with specific attention to affected parties'.[23] Goodpaster maintains, however, that these activities as such cannot be regarded as specifically ethical ones. He remarks that the mere identification of different stakeholders says little if nothing about the ethical character of this exercise. Stakeholders can be determined for various reasons which are not always ethical. For example, they can be identified because of their potentiality to influence corporate goals and interests: 'A management team, for example, might be careful to take positive and (especially) negative stakeholder effects into account for no other reason than that offended stakeholders might resist or retaliate (e.g. through political action or opposition to necessary, regulatory clearances). It might not be *ethical* concern for the stakeholders that motivates and guides such analysis, so much as concern about potential impediments to the achievement of strategic objectives. Thus positive and negative effects on relatively powerless stakeholders may be ignored or discounted'.[24]

Unlike Solomon, Goodpaster finds it important to distinguish ethical concerns from other considerations relevant in the business world. The last sentence of the quotation shows clearly why. Without such distinction, the treatment of other people may depend on the aims, values and purposes of various individual and corporate agents. In other words, it may be the case that other people matter only insofar as they have a positive or negative role in the agent's life. Consequently, the rights and interests of those people irrelevant or unimportant to the agent may be ignored or discounted.[25] Considerations that regard other people in terms of the agent's own ends and values are not, according to Goodpaster, what is usually meant by *moral* concern. Moral concern, properly understood, requires that the rights and interests of other people are taken seriously because (all) people matter as human beings, as persons important in their own right.

Accordingly, what makes a concern ethical in the context of the business world is the recognition of the rights and interests of all the stakeholders, regardless of their position in or out of the business world. The rights of other people set limits on what individuals, corporations or other institutions can do in the pursuit of their goals: 'The conscientious corporation can maintain its private economic mission, but in the context of fundamental moral obligations owed by any member of society to others affected by that member's actions... Private institutions, like private individuals, can be and are bound to respect moral obligations in the pursuit of private purposes'.[26]

The identifying and weighing of the different, even conflicting interests of various stakeholders are certainly not easy tasks. How these interests are taken into account and whose interests count most in a particular situation are difficult questions that can perhaps be answered only case by case. In the complex conditions of everyday life, the mechanical applicance of a specific decision procedure might not be of much help, as Solomon maintains. However, I do not regard these procedures even as crucial for modern ethics. What is most important, instead, is the respect for other people's lives, well-being and dignity. It is the demand to take the rights and interests of other people seriously that is fundamental in 'modern' moral theory. These concerns can be recognised and these demands can be carried out without employing abstract principles or mechanical decision procedures.

The practice

Regardless of the above discussion, I do not consider modern ethical thought and the Aristotelian approach as exclusive options in business ethics. As a matter of fact, these theories can be seen as representing different sides of ethical thought: one emphasising the happiness, flourishing and good life of an individual, and another reminding that there are other people around whose interests must be taken into account in the pursuit of one's aims and plans. I think that both can contribute significantly to business ethics and practical business life. The application of the Aristotelian approach can help in creating a sense of community in the corporate context and developing individual members of these communities as persons who aspire for excellence in all their doings. As a result, it is hoped that both corporations and individuals will prosper and flourish. The 'modern' view in turn emphasises the viewpoint of the outsiders of the business world and the corporate community. It encourages people working in corporations to consider their decisions and operations from the viewpoint of all those affected by these decisions. I regard neither of these approaches too demanding to be included in the everyday practices of the business world.

Notes

1. Solomon, 1993, p. 202.
2. Ibid., p. 210.
3. Ibid., p. 207.
4. Ibid., p. 205.
5. Ibid., p. 204.
6. This argument is in different forms presented by Annas, 1993 and 1995; Louden, 1992; MacIntyre, 1981; Nussbaum, 1986; Taylor, 1989, to mention only a few.
7. See for instance Annas, 1995; MacIntyre, 1981.
8. Annas, 1993, pp. 27, 127-9; Annas, 1995, pp. 242-6; Friedman, 1988, p.149; Louden, 1992, pp. 5-7.
9. It has been a standard criticism against utilitarian theories that they demand too much of the agent when concentrating entirely on the other-regarding aspects of morality. Recently this charge has been extended to Kantian ethical tradition as well.
10. Taylor, 1989, p. 4.

11. Julia Annas (1993, p. 27) argues that 'to us, the question What should my life be like? may seem too particular to be a properly ethical question. Shouldn't ethics be about duty, or rights, or the good, rather than about my life?... A great deal of modern literature and psychology arises and revolves around the way people reflect about their lives, but thought about one's life is no longer seen as central to ethical philosophy, at least to ethical theory. At best the question is seen as marginal, to be answered when the main lines of the theory are already established.'

12. Annas, 1993, p. 161.

13. See Annas, 1993, p. 323; Irwin, 1990, p. 397. Though ancient ethical theories have this sort of self-regarding or prudential structure, it does not imply that they are egoistic, as is sometimes claimed. Julia Annas (1995, p. 242) discusses the issue, claiming that prudence in ancient ethics can be understood in a much broader manner than simply as a pursuit of one's immediate, unconsidered interest such as money or power. When so understood, 'the function of ancient ethical theory is to expand the agent's view of what prudence requires. In *The Republic*, for example, does Socrates not start from narrowly conceived notion of what is good for the agent... and proceed by getting the agent to expand his idea of what is good for him... Prudence can be seen as a correct view of what is in the agent's interest, and ethical theory guides the agent from an intuitive, restrictive view of what is in her interest (money, power) to a more expanded and elevated view (the virtues). The agent's view of what her interests are is enlarged and modified in a way which tracks the enlargement and modification of her view of what her happiness really consists of: but there is no change in the type of reasoning employed from beginning to end - it is simply prudence. On this view, the only reason for denying that ancient ethics employs prudential reasoning is an overly narrow view of what prudence must be, and dissolves once we realize the scope for expansion of the agent's view of what her interest are'. Nevertheless, Annas herself does not regard even this interpretation as correct. Other writers disagree. Terence Irwin (1995, p. 286), for example maintains that Greek and, in fact, also most medieval moralists, do argue prudentially (in the broad sense of the term): 'They encourage us to reason about what promotes our own happiness; in reasoning about this we reason about what achieves our own interest; and so our reasoning is prudential'.

14. A good example of this distinction is provided by Friedman, 1988, p. 153.

15. See van Luijk, 1994, p. 16.

16. Solomon, 1993, pp. 213-4.

17. Ibid., p. 207.

18. Ibid., p. 219. In this paragraph, as in several others, Solomon points out that the business world, however, is not independent from other aspects of human life as is sometimes claimed. He argues that business works in the framework of the larger community where its roles and responsibilities are defined. Nevertheless, Solomon does not explain where these definitions and considerations of the larger community are derived from.

19. Ibid., p. 205.

20. Similarities with Solomon's view can be easily detected when reading the brochures in which corporations present their Quality Management philosophies. Solomon's view of the business ethics could have been the basis of, for instance, the philosophy of ICL, as the following quotations from the booklet 'Quality the ICL way' show: 'The ICL Way binds ICL together as a coherent group of companies with common values' (p. 22). 'Everyone must be satisfied with their involvement in the Company and with their own personal development. They must be aware of the requirements of their job and of the values, vision and strategy of the organisation' (p. 45). 'ICL staff need to feel part of the vision, to be involved and to have a role to play' (p. 23). 'The achievements of managers are dependent on the achievements of their staff, and all managers must be committed to developing each employee to his or her full potential' (p. 26). 'Our main strength lies in the quality and skill of the people who work here, so real progress will only come about by constantly developing and improving skills' (p. 42).

21. It is worth noticing that this is not a problem for Solomon. He (1993, pp. 212-3) explicitly rejects interpretations that regard ethical or moral considerations as something qualitatively different from other concerns relevant in the business context. Business ethics should be closely related to and dependent on the general values and practices of the business world: ' the virtues that constitute business ethics should not be conceived of as purely ethical or moral virtues, as if (to repeat) business ethics were nothing other than the general application of moral principles to one specific context (among others)... The virtues of business ethics are business virtues but they are nonetheless virtues'.

22. Goodpaster, 1993, p. 230. Goodpaster himself uses here the definition given by R. Edward Freeman.

23. Goodpaster, 1993, pp. 232-3.

24. Ibid., p. 234.

25. It should be noticed, however, as pointed out above (see n. 13), that the reflection that begins from the first-person perspective is not necessarily egoistic. Other people, as well as the broad account of what the person's good life and happiness consists of, can be included in such reflection. What is crucial, however, is that other people are ultimately viewed from the perspective of the agent's own good: they matter because they form an

intrinsic part of the agent's happiness. This feature indeed has often been seen as a problem in ancient ethics which begins from the reflection of the agent's happiness and a good life. See the discussions of the subject in Annas 1993, pp. 127-9 and Chapter 14; Irwin 1990, Chapters 17-8. See also O'Connor 1988, p. 426.

26. Goodpaster, 1993, p. 245.

References

Annas, J. (1993), *The Morality of Happiness*, Oxford University Press: Oxford.

Annas, J. (1995), 'Prudence and Morality in Ancient and Modern Ethics', *Ethics* 105, pp. 241-57.

Friedman, R. Z. (1988), 'Morality and Morally Informed', in French, P. A., Vehling, T. E. Jr, Wettstein, H. K. (eds), *Midwest Studies in Philosophy vol. XIII, Ethical Theory: Character and Virtue,* University of Notre Dame Press: Notre Dame, pp. 149-50.

Goodpaster, K. (1993), 'Business Ethics and Stakeholder Analysis', in Winkler, E. and Coombs, J. (eds), *Applied Ethics: a Reader,* Basil Blackwell: Oxford, pp. 229-48.

Irwin, T. (1990), *Aristotle's First Principles,* Clarendon Press, Oxford.

Irwin, T. (1995), 'Prudence and Morality in Greek Ethics', *Ethics* 105, pp. 284-95.

Louden, R. (1992), *Morality and Moral Theory: a Reappraisal and Reaffirmation,* Oxford University Press: Oxford.

van Luijk, H. (1994), 'Business Ethics: The Field and its Importance', in Harvey, B. (ed.), *Business Ethics: European Approach,* Prentice Hall: Hertfordshire, pp. 12-31.

MacIntyre, A. (1981), *After Virtue,* University of Notre Dame Press: London.

Nussbaum, M. (1986), *The Fragility of Goodness: Luck and Ethics in Greek Tragedy and Philosophy,* Cambridge University Press: Cambridge.

O'Connor, D. K. (1988), 'Aristotelian Justice as a Personal Virtue', in *Midwest Studies in Philosophy vol. XIII, Ethical Theory: Character and Virtue,* University of Notre Dame Press: Notre Dame, pp. 417-27.

'Quality the ICL Way' (1994), *International Computers Limited,* Stevenage.

Solomon, R. (1993), 'Corporate Roles, Personal Virtues: An Aristotelian approach to Business Ethics' in Winkler, E. and Coombs, J. (eds), *Applied Ethics: a Reader,* Basil Blackwell: Oxford, pp. 201-21.

Taylor, C. (1989), *Sources of the Self: The Making of the Modern Identity*, Cambridge University Press: Cambridge.

The background requirements of markets

Olli Loukola

> Business underlies everything in our national life, including our spiritual life. Witness the fact that in the Lord's Prayer the first petition is for daily bread. No one can worship God or love his neighbor on an empty stomach.
>
> - Woodrow Wilson, in a speech (1912)

I

In this essay I will discuss free markets and their constraints which are embodied in 'background institutions', as they are sometimes called in contemporary business ethics literature,[1] and the background requirements that are used to justify them. It has, however, been difficult to find any systematic formulation of the nature and functions of these institutions in the literature and I believe that the reluctance to formulate and explicate them may lead to vague moralizing and disregard of the actual and potential interaction between state, markets and morality. These problems of modern markets and contemporary ethical theorising are especially vivid in the context of the transition of the post-soviet countries.

This is the task I will address: describing the background requirements of markets and explicating their nature and purpose; and evaluating their viability from a normative point of view as well as from considerations of efficiency. Since this is surely no minor task, in this essay I will merely set out the outlines of the problem.

II

Generally speaking, by the free market system I refer to the idea of *laissez faire*, the ideal of unrestricted capitalism, in which the role of the state is confined to certain minimum functions, as opposed to interventionist economies in which the markets are deliberately steered by the government towards some overall goal. In politics and economics this doctrine limits governmental interference to the minimum necessary for the maintenance of peace and property rights. It favors self-interest, competition, and natural consumer preferences as forces leading to optimal prosperity and freedom. In philosophy it may be characterized as deliberate abstention from direction or interference with individual freedom of choice and action. This ideology is nowadays most explicit in libertarian theory.

Contrary to what one might be tempted to believe, libertarians do not trust solely to the uninhibited working of the markets. Most of these theorists have supported some form of governmental regulation and control.

According to libertarians, one's own interest is the basic motive for economic activity, each pursuing his or her own interest, so that cooperative ventures begin and mutual benefits accrue. Yet certain limits have to be imposed on these strivings, since libertarian freedom is not unlimited. This creates the basic moral infrastructure that the libertarians are prepared to enforce and sanction: individual liberty, which is usually interpreted as negative liberty; or 'abstaining from violating the person, the estate or the reputation of the neighbor'.[2] This also sets limits on justifiable government action. The infrastructure of the society is to be founded on this restriction, that is, it establishes the background institutions which would be justified in *laissez faire* markets.

The sort of governmental background institution favored by libertarians on the basis of this varies. Adam Smith approved three forms of central government intervention, which are protection of the citizens, legislation and adjudication of law and the provision of public goods. To these Milton Friedman added the responsibility of protecting those citizens who are not competent to take care of themselves, like children and old people. Rather surprisingly, Friedrich Hayek, one of the pioneers of economic libertarianism, argued for considerable governmental interventionism[3]. James Buchanan allows only the functions of legislation and adjudication of law and the provision of public goods. Robert Nozick famously reduces the role of the state to its minimum that is, protection; and market anarchists like Murray Rothbard, David Friedman and Jan Narveson deny that the state should have any role at all. There seems then, to be considerable disagreement among libertarians about what the minimal institutions should be.

Instead of concentrating on the various justifications these writers have offered for their favorite background institutions, I will focus on the general background requirements for the operation of markets, which are expressed simply in a quotation of Peter Koslowski: 'One would want neither to live in a just society where there is nothing to buy nor in an efficient, rich society, which employs its resources for morally reprehensible purposes'.[4] I believe that these background requirements are embodied in the principles of efficiency and fairness, principles which in economic affairs are often thought to present an antagonistic contradiction. It seems also that these demands are acutely present in the two main strands of libertarian theory.

In a sense, libertarianism is merely a political theory. This means that libertarianism is interested only in those minimal rights, duties and/or restrictions that are necessary on two accounts: either to ensure general beneficial and efficient cooperation between diverse and disparate individuals; or in order to secure certain moral rights, like non-coercion and property rights. Libertarianism as such is not indifferent to moral matters, as sometimes has been claimed. It is that other matters – circumscribed by the aforementioned restrictions – such as personal goals, interpersonal commitments or moral virtues are seen as private, as matters of personal discretion, as those, in which no one else has a right to interfere. Libertarian theory is profoundly subjectivist in the sense that these private values and principles – moral or any other – are a matter of individual choice. Negative freedom and minimal rights are enforceable by the state and any further interference would mean either prohibiting beneficial cooperation or treating individuals in an unjustified or immoral manner.

The question of whether this conception of minimal restrictions/rights arises from efficient and beneficial cooperation (that is, consequentialist considerations) or from some version of rights (that is, deontological considerations) is a great divide in the forms of libertarian theory[5]. I believe that this dichotomy also embodies the basic requirements of markets, that is, requirements of efficiency and fairness, though not in any straightforward manner. The most interesting line of reasoning in contemporary libertarian theory comes from rational libertarianism[6]. The starting point of this interpretation is deontological in the sense[7] that it takes as fundamental the 'right to our persons as our property';[8] on the other hand it fits nicely in the consequentialist interpretation when trying to justify this basic right by appealing to rational behaviour and social choice theory. As such, it's one of the grand dreams of philosophy to reconcile rationality and morality; a more humble dream is to justify fairness as the more efficient and reasonable way of co-existing in societies.[9]

The central question may now be rephrased as what sort of background requirements are **necessary** for the proper working of free markets? A related question is then whether they are also **morally justifiable** or perhaps even **morally necessary**. At face value, the problem is thought to be a balancing act: at one end of the tightrope lurks the interventionist danger of losing the efficiency of the market process and at the *laissez faire* end the danger of leaving people to pay an unreasonably high price for their failures in market transactions. I agree with Koslowski when he states:

> The question of the morality of capitalism cannot be: is capitalism moral? The question must be: is capitalism justifiable under the conditions of human nature and the scarcity of resources? The morality of capitalism can be justified only by the nature of the object, that is, the function of the economy and the possibilities it offers for human self-realization.[10]

In other words, the ideal economic arrangement would be one which combines efficiency and just operation, one which truly creates wealth for its subjects and yet respects each of them as individuals. A telling indication of the importance of these two principles is that both doctrines, interventionism and *laissez faire*, utilize them to justify themselves and criticize their rivals.

There are at least three major structures which are generally thought to impose restrictions or sanctions on behavior in economic affairs. The first system, 'the rules of the market', is thought to be an integral part of the process itself; the second, 'government control', is clearly interventionist and the status of the third, which I will loosely term 'public demands', is ambiguous. At face value, the first one seems to ground its demands on considerations of efficiency, while the other two are based on fairness. Again, the situation is not at all this straight forward. Arguments from fairness as well as efficiency are intermingled within each structure. How these structures work, and to what extent they satisfy the demands of efficiency and fairness, will be my next questions.

III

The first control structure is the market system itself, that is, the laws of the market. The basic idea here is that in the market there are certain self-imposed constraints, which belong among the dictates of economic prudential rationality, or 'theorems of prudentiality'. The thing causing controversy here is the status of the market compared to society at large, that is, the question of their relative interdependence. Yet the question seems not to be that market advocates or their critics would conceive of markets as a distinct or autonomous sphere of human action. Neither party wishes to conceive of markets as an independent realm with its own functions, laws and purposes. The question is rather about logical precedence. For libertarians, the market is not a detached but the central sphere of human action and market rationality is not a special, but more like the paradigm case of human rationality. For market critics the situation is reversed: the market is merely instrumental for the rest of or for the 'proper' sphere of human life – whatever that turns out to be. As such it is to be subsumed under the rules and purposes of that life. This fundamental ontological orientation is, I believe, the source of well-known controversy over the role of the market. How we solve this issue, has far-reaching ramifications.

In libertarian theory the primacy of the market is, as I mentioned earlier, justified on two accounts. Consequentialist or economic libertarianism claims that markets function most efficiently when they are restricted the least and that central planning is doomed to fail because of the unavailability of the relevant information. Deontological libertarianism has usually invoked a concept of Lockean-type natural rights, the most important of which is ownership. Yet the vague and intuitionist character of such rights renders this version of libertarianism implausible.[11]

In the tradition of rational libertarianism the concept of rationality and consequently the laws of the market have been drawn from the work of Thomas Hobbes. Important contemporary work has been done by David Gauthier; of interest here are also the writings of Jan Narveson.

Hobbes has become the forefather of modern public choice theory and rational moral theory, and it has been claimed that he was the first to present the Prisoner's Dilemma, one of the central paradoxes of individual choice. According to Narveson, Hobbesian human nature is such that

> People concerned about their own well-being... will have to accept these rules, as being rationally called for by a combination of four things: (1) their interests; (2) their powers; (3) the proclivities and capabilities of their fellows; and of course (4) the characteristics of the nonhuman environment. People wishing to do well will see the benefits of association with their fellows, and will see the need for such association to be along peaceful and cooperative lines rather than the reverse. The need in question will be perceived, in Hobbes' account, as arising from the evident rough equality of the human capacity for destruction and violence, and the evident impossibility of getting on if others are free to use those destructive capacities. In short, Hobbes argues that the general shape of the rules of human interaction are not self-evident and certainly not matters of some special sort of 'intuition', but rather, pretty straightforward inferences of common sense about the four factors mentioned.[12]

The structure of this situation is such (in game-theoretical terms, social cooperation is not stable, thus leading participants to defect) that according to Hobbes' famous solution there is no **moral** way out of it. The **political** way out this dilemma was, for Hobbes, the 'Sovereign', an essential device for securing the actual benefits of the rule of natural law.[13] By utilizing the Hobbesian dilemma, Narveson tries to offer a moral defence of the free markets.

The problem in both the libertarian project and contemporary business ethics is to evaluate the limits of morality and determine whether political solutions to the Hobbesian problem in the markets becomes necessary. Is there a need for a political solution or are the internal constraints – rational and/or moral – of markets sufficient?

In business ethics vocabulary the situation may be described differently. The Hobbesian problem is patently present in the markets and especially in the concept of competition. Competition is the single main factor which is thought to remedy the ills accruing within the market process, and its core notion I have sometimes expressed as the denial of the Kalashnikov method. The idea here is simple: if you use violence and force, cheat and betray people, under normal circumstances you will be out of business after a while. Soon no one will do business with anyone who uses a Kalashnikov; and those who do will also use a Kalashnikov. In the long run then, it does not pay to do business with a Kalashnikov.

This idea lies at the heart of most theories of business ethics, just as H. B. Acton distinguishes between 'competition' and 'rivalry':

> The essence of competition is that each competitor strives after what he wants. The essence of rivalry is that each competitor strives to outdo the others... [C]ompetitive markets are not places where people fight, nor places where they pursue their rivalries... [A]ttempts to outwit one another in what is called 'oriental' bargaining are not features of developed markets, but can only make sense for parties who are ignorant of conditions of supply and demand. Rivalry comes in when political considerations are important, as with pre-emptive purchases in time of war. But in general, economic behavior in competitive markets is a peaceful sort of thing. Piracy and confiscation are uncommercial activities and trade flourishes when goods can be inspected and moved without danger from marauding bands. Exchange... is morally preferable to spoliation or entreaty.[14]

The moral lesson here is clearly that markets should not be an unlimited Hobbesian war. We have no problems separating fair competition from rivalry, where one 'breaks one's opponent's legs'. There is a moral solution to the Hobbesian problem; at the same time it is also a rational solution, since it not only respects individuals, but is also reciprocally advantageous. Morality and rationality seem to coincide here, thus fulfilling the promise of the laws of the market: it is rational to be moral.[15]

In order to examine these issues we must determine the character of human action in the markets, its point and purpose. To start with, we must examine what sort of bonds – rights, duties or obligations – are possible determinants of the relationships and legitimate actions within the market realm. If either of the two background principles are violated, that gives us a *prima facie* reason for intervening.

A popular solution has been to conceive of the market as a competition, a game or a similar rule-governed social activity. But is it plausible? A paradigmatic analysis of the concept is offered by Alasdair MacIntyre.[16] A practice (or a game) is a coherent and usually a complex form of human cooperation. It is socially established, meaning for example that everybody knows that the practice exists, knows what its goods and purposes are, how one can join in, what joining entails and what the rules and the obligations of the practice are. It is a form of activity which has its peculiar goods and ends. Participating and obtaining goods from it entails learning the rules and regulations of that game, all legitimate and illegitimate moves and maneuvers. A practice has its own standards of excellence, or virtues, which detail the best means of realizing the ends involved in the practice in question.

It is possible to gain two kinds of goods by participating. First, there are external goods, which are contingent and attached to practices because of contingent social circumstances: money, status, prestige or the like. A chess-player may be highly valued in Latvia, but if one wants to gain similar prestige in Brazil, one should concentrate on football. There are thus alternate ways of gaining these external goods.

Second, there are goods internal to a practice which cannot be had in any other way nor from any other practice. They are internal because we can only specify them in terms of that practice and illuminate them by examples taken from it. These goods are also internal in the sense that to recognize and identify them you must have participated in the practice. Attaining them therefore calls for something like a **commitment**, e.g, a disposition in which the bond or tie to the practice is strong.[17]

Committing oneself to the practice of the market and its virtues and orations about the good that it does to one's material as well as spiritual well-being was the way old American business tycoons talked about business around the turn of the century. This seems also to be the way some business ethicists would like people to respond to it today[18]. And when we recall the favourite libertarian model of human transaction, e.g. 'voluntary undertaking', the case here becomes more interesting. If the libertarian project aims at reducing market transactions to voluntary individual undertakings, contracts and fair cooperation, surely then this practice model is appropriate for explicating the rights, duties and obligations arising in such circumstances? If people in market transactions were thus engaged to their ventures and enterprises, they would honour their responsibilities and fulfill their obligations. And isn't this just what we mean by commitment? With this concept the problem of free riding also disappears, since where there are commitments, there is no free riding. It just wouldn't make any sense to talk about free riding when one has voluntarily chosen to participate and is free to opt out whenever one wants.

This is an ideal and would certainly be an advantageous situation in terms of morality as well as efficiency. But isn't this is a privileged attitude to markets? For most people the market is the means for material wealth, not commitment in any sense of the word. In accord with the definition of practice, is it possible to talk of markets in the sense that 'everybody knows... what its goods and purposes are, how one can join in, what joining entails and what the rules and thc obligations... are'? For instance, what are the goods and purposes of the market; and is there really a way out in the game of markets? In modern societies people and their labour are undoubtedly in the market in order to make a living, not to opt in or out of their favourite game.[19]

In the game of the market people should more likely – and perhaps more realistically – be conceived of as attaining external, not internal goods; they do aim at money, status, prestige or the like. And when a true desire to participate is missing, it is possible to cheat, defraud or free ride. Where one merely wishes to obtain external goods, where one has no commitment to the practice itself, cheating and free riding become tempting options. At least, that is, until business ethicists have fulfilled the old dream of all moralists and taught people to become so moral that they are disposed to live virtuously in each and every sphere of their lives.

Commitment (and corresponding virtues) would naturally be highly desirable in business; yet this principle seems much too strong; it is elitist and far too demanding. We are approaching the area of supererogacy, where acts are morally praiseworthy, but cannot be morally entailed. Much more down-to-earth principles within the limits of human weakness are needed.

To conclude then, the central problem of this control structure is the possibility of misconduct and the unfairness accruing from it. The Kalashnikov method does work in the short run and it does not seem possible to construe a binding commitment that would stop free riding in this context. If one is out to make a good profit in a short time, the market mechanism will not have enough time to react. One can often cheat, and obtain goods until one is caught; and a clever cheat scrams before that. A cheat may repeat the swindle with new players, who are not yet competent enough to recognize it. By the time they do, the Kalashnikov user may already have done considerable harm to a number of people. In real life, the question is naturally not only of mere cheating. It is also that of various types of wrongdoing, exploitation and manipulation, false rhetoric and information, coercion and domination, and the like.

But surely it is also a problem of efficiency: in markets, where free riding is frequent and cheating is a common policy, there are less cooperative ventures and overall costs are greater. Exchanges are not stable and security has to be guaranteed; all thus ending up in increased expenses and a fewer number of transactions.

Uninhibited markets may yet be efficient when compared to centrally-planned ones. But this situation is morally deficient if it does not respect individuals, if it exposes individuals to hazards, which although short term are no less disastrous. This is the primary justification for interventionism; that Hobbes was right, that the moral solution is not enough and a political solution is necessary.

IV

Short-term users of the Kalashnikov and free riders are prohibited through government control mainly by the creation and enforcement of laws them efficiently and the punishment of violators. At one extreme, a minimal state restricts interference to mere enforcement of individual liberty and penalizing breaches of contract. But at the other extreme, a full-blown interventionist state uses extensive measures not only to correct these and other market failures, but also to further some overall goals by using general taxes and welfare programs, fiscal and monetary policies, special taxes and subsidies, anti-trust actions, and the producing of public goods. Since only a few of these activities may be justified by the prohibition of Kalashnikov users, free riders or other market failures, the rest surely call for further justification. Usually this has been done by construing positive or welfare rights.

There are two central critiques against interventionism put forward by libertarians. The first critique of interventionism is given by libertarian economists and it is based on the sheer impossibility of successful central planning.[20] It may be boiled down to two central arguments, the incentive and the epistemic. According to the former, in a planned economy the structure of incentives becomes artificially distorted. The latter explains the failure of central planning not only as a calculational impossibility, but also because of the non-explicable character of economic knowledge.

John Gray reconstructs these arguments from the perspective of individual autonomy. Thus the incentive argument claims that planning institutions obstruct individuals from acting upon their projects and purposes, and the epistemic argument that they prevent individuals from using and benefiting from their personal knowledge. They both claim that the planning institutions constrain or diminish the autonomy of individuals. They do this partly by compelling individuals to act for purposes that are not their own, and partly by depriving them of the opportunity to engage in projects animated by their own knowledge.[21]

These arguments provide a powerful case against interventionism in favor of free markets on the grounds of efficiency and knowledge. Yet it is important to notice, as Gray does, that these arguments do not say that economic planning is impossible or that markets could not be simulated or replicated; they merely state that

> ... in the absence of an effective price mechanism that can only be provided by market institutions, there will inevitably be massive waste and malinvestment... In short, the upshot of the epistemic argument is not that central planning institutions always fail, but that even their success carries heavy and unnecessary human and economic costs.[22]

They do not tell us what sort of governmental interference – if any – is needed for the efficient working of the markets, but they do give us suggestions of the ones that will hinder it.

These arguments evidently support the background principle of efficiency. What then is the status of the principle of fairness? Gray adopts a harsh policy: they tell us nothing about the moral character of the markets:

> These arguments are ... deficient. As they stand, they are morally virtually empty, even if they have some ethical implications and presuppositions. They tell us that only the markets can deliver the goods to us, but they leave the moral criticism of the market economy unanswered. Critics of the market might accept all that has been argued here about the indispensable efficiencies of the market and yet attack it on ethical grounds. They might argue that

> unfettered markets promote greed and envy, shatter communities and debase cultural value... they might deny that markets promote individual autonomy... focus critically on the distributional effects and preconditions of market economies, holding that they necessitate or reproduce structural inequalities in life-chances that are morally unacceptable... draw our attention to the situation of those people, lacking in skills and resources, whose plight prevents them from fully participating in the market or enjoying many of its benefits. Such critics of the markets might, in other words, accept all... and yet deny that the market economy has any real ethical standing.[23]

In other words, they are amoral in the sense that they firmly establish the fact that pure interventionist measures are doomed to fail sooner or later; yet this obviously says nothing about the morality of the markets themselves. I do not, however, agree with Gray about the 'virtual moral emptiness' of these arguments. Surely avoiding 'heavy and unnecessary human and economic costs' is also a solid moral reason for abandoning central planning, and not just a contingent 'ethical implication'. But then again, Gray is correct in that, as such, the moral demand that no one is made to suffer unreasonably remains to be fulfilled.

The moral justification for the markets comes in libertarian theory mainly from its deontological section. Following Locke, individual natural rights are construed and they are to be moral rights in the full sense, and are to protect individuals from interference and coercion. Since, as I mentioned earlier, this starting point is more or less groundless – heroic and appealing in a similar manner as human rights are, but nevertheless without a solid argumentative basis – we seem to be left with the option of trying to show that it is rational to be moral.

V

I will pose this central question of rational libertarianism from another perspective. This is the alleged third control structure of the markets, that is, 'public demands'. In contemporary business ethics it has become customary in the cases of unethical action to call for social responses like general disapproval and moral criticism, consumer movements, boycotts, media, all kinds of informal and indirect methods of influence. However, its true status and role is debatable; occasionally results of these activities are encoded in the law, as consumer protection, non-discrimination and the like, thus adjoining them to the area of interventionism. At other times, in pro-market theories, such restrictions have been accounted for as belonging to the realm of business practice, as 'back-firing effects' of the Kalashnikov-method. This is the type of activity which, at best, is thought to be in accord with the actual functioning of the markets, thus not harassing the mechanism of the market. It also satisfies the liberal ideal of 'voluntary undertaking of action'. At face value, it seems to combine both the background principles, efficiency and fairness.

But if the thesis of the intermingling of rationality and morality is sound and the central sphere of human action and rationality is the market, then we should be able to merge or reduce this third structure to the first one, to the 'laws of the market'.[24] I believe that the most interesting contemporary exposition to this line of argument is given by Narveson. This is clearly his project; when discussing the ideal market situation he states that

> ... the degree to which the conditions [of ideal market] are realized or realizable in the real world... [I]t is here that morality must enter the picture. We approximate the 'ideal market' in the real world by *reinforcing* the internalizations that define it.[25]

How rational libertarianism fares in this task remains to be judged.

Notes

1. See for instance, de George, 1990, pp. 315-6.
2. These attitudes described by Adam Smith bring out the central idea in the libertarian concept of negative freedom vividly. It has to be noted that Smith himself found this stance insufficient for the purposes of just conduct.
3. See Hoppe, 1994, pp. 127 – 30, where he claims that Hayek's views of market and state cannot be distinguished from those of a modern Socialdemocrat.
4. Koslowski, 1994, p. 237.
5. See for instance, Barry, 1983.
6. The term rational libertarianism is from Danielson, 1996, p. 219.
7. I am not sure whether deontological starting point is central in this tradition; see for instance de Jasay, 1989, who clearly belongs to this line of reasoning, yet does not purport to vindicate any deontological basic values.
8. Narveson, 1996, p. 66.
9. By no mere coincidence, it has also been one of the central canons in contemporary business ethics to try to show that in business there is a 'positive relation between ethics and profits' or that 'ethics can be a competitive advantage'. See for instance Bowie, 1996, p. 365.
10. Koslowski, 1994, p. 237.
11. For this critique, see for instance Narveson, 1988 and Danielson, 1996.
12. Narveson, 1996, p. 265.
13. Ibid., p. 267.
14. Acton, 1982, pp. 236 – 7.
15. The basic work here is Gauthier, 1986.

16. MacIntyre, 1984, pp. 175-9.
17. Webster's Dictionary defines *commitment* as: '1 a: an act of committing to charge or trust'; '2 a: an agreement or pledge to do something in the future'; '2 b: something pledged' (*pledge* being among other things: 'the state of being held as a security or guaranty'; 'something given as a security for the performance of an act'; 'a binding promise or agreement to do or forbear'; or even, 'a promise to join a fraternity, sorority, or secret society'); '2 c: the state or an instance of being obligated or emotionally impelled [... to a cause]'.
18. See especially Solomon, 1993.
19. See also van Luijk, 1994, pp. 23-5.
20. For these arguments, see Gray, 1995, pp. 69-75, Loukola, 1996 & 1997; for more thorough background, Cubeddu, 1993.
21. Gray, 1993, pp. 73 – 4.
22. Ibid., p. 74.
23. Ibid., pp. 75 – 6.
24. It may be argued, if such a reduction does not seem possible, that the reason is that people have false moral beliefs, misconceptions or moralizing attitudes because they have misconstrued or misunderstood the role and methods of the markets because of ideological convictions, propaganda, excessive fear of new and unknown or similar reasons (as in developing free market societies). But to what extent libertarian theory is entitled to appeal to considerations based on universalist claims, like 'false', 'ideological conviction' or 'excessive fear'? That is, in this context, with their strict division between private and public spheres?
25. Narveson, 1988, p. 189.

References

Acton, H. B. (1982), 'The Ethics of Competition', in Machan, Tibor (ed.), *The Libertarian Reader*, Rowman & Littlefield: New Jersey.

Barry, N. (1983), 'Review Article: The New Liberalism', *The British Journal of Political Science*, 13.

Bowie, N. (1996), 'The Moral Foundation of Capitalism', in Gasparski, W. W. & Ryan, L. R. (eds), *Human Action in Business. Praxiological and Ethical Dimensions*, Transaction Publishers: New Brunswick.

Cubeddu R. (1993), *The Philosophy of The Austrian School*, Routledge: London.

Danielson, P. (1996), 'The Rights of Chickens: Rational Foundations for Libertarianism?' in Sanders J. T. & Narveson, J. (eds), *For and Against the State. New Philosophical Readings*, Rowman & Littlefield Publishers: Maryland.

De George, R. T. (1990), *Business Ethics,* (third edition), MacMillan Publishing Company: New York.

Gauthier, D. (1986), *Morals by Agreement*, Oxford University Press: Oxford.

Gray, J. (1993), *Beyond the New Right. Markets, Government and the Common Environment,* Routledge: London.

Hoppe, H. -H. (1994), 'F.A. Hayek on Government and Social Evolution: a Critique', in Frei, C. and Nef, R. (eds), *Contending with Hayek. On Liberalism, Spontaneous Order and the Pot-Communist Societies in Transition,* Peter Lang AG: Bern.

de Jasay, A. (1989), *Social Contract, Free Ride. A Study of the Public Goods Problem,* Clarendon Press: Oxford.

Koslowski, P (1994), 'The Ethics of Capitalism' in Harvey B. (ed.), *Business Ethics: European Approach,* Prentice Hall: Hertfordshire, pp. 236-47.

Loukola, O. (1996), 'Background Institutions and Free Markets' in Gasparski, W. W. & Ryan, L. R. (eds), *Human Action in Business. Praxiological and Ethical Dimensions,* Transaction Publishers: New Brunswick.

Loukola, O. (1997), 'Gone with the Wind? Morality on the Post-Soviet Markets' in Lewicka-Strazałecka, A. and Loukola, O. (eds), *Science in Society II: Science Policy and Ethics,* IFiS Publishers: Warszawa, forthcoming.

van Luijk, H. (1994), 'Business Ethics: The Field and its Importance', in Harvey B. (ed.), *Business Ethics: European Approach,* Prentice Hall: Hertfordshire.

MacIntyre, A. (1984), *After Virtue*, University of Notre Dame Press: Notre Dame.

Narveson, J. (1996), 'The Anarchist's Case', in Sanders J. T. & Narveson, J. (eds), *For and Against the State. New Philosophical Readings,* Rowman & Littlefield Publishers: Maryland.

Narveson, J. (1988), *The Libertarian Idea*, Temple University Press: Philadelphia.

Solomon, R. C. (1993), *Ethics and Excellence. Cooperation and Integrity in Business,* Oxford University Press: Oxford.

Moral and immoral views on paying taxes

*Bruno S. Frey & Manfred J. Holler**

Strong empirical evidence suggests that, contrary to standard criminal choice theory, deterrence does not increase tax compliance. A model based on a peculiarity of the mixed-strategy Nash equilibrium in 2-by-2 games is used to explain this observation theoretically: The strategy choice of a player is not affected by the changes in his or her payoffs induced by deterrence. Moreover, as empirical observations suggest that increased deterrence tends to undermine tax morale, it follows that tax policy should not so much try to deter but should make an effort to raise or at least citizens' tax morale.

1. Introduction

On the occasion of the meeting of the European Public Choice Society at Turin in April 1992, the authors of this paper discovered that they had two alternative models which explain why higher penalty rates do not decrease tax evasion (see Roth, Scholz, and Witte, 1989, for this result). The size of the deterrence effect (in the few cases where it has been found statistically significant) is very small, and less consequential than the impact of other factors (see, e.g., Paternoster, 1989). Calculation based on empirical magnitudes for the United States show that 'taxpayers would have to exhibit risk aversion far in excess of anything ever observed for compliance predicted by expected utility theory to approximate actual compliance' (Alm, McKee and Beck, 1990, p. 24). As a reaction to similar calculations for different periods, other authors go so far as to state that 'most of the theoretical work to date is not particularly useful either for policy analysis or empirical study' (Graetz and Wilde, 1985, p. 357).

The standard economic theory of tax evasion was first formulated by Allingham and Sandmo (1972) based on Becker's (1968) model of criminal choice[1]. Taxpayers are assumed to maximize expected utility which depends on noncompliance detection probabilities, the magnitude of punishment and incomes and tax rates. While the effects of higher income and higher tax rates on tax evasion depend on additional factors (in particular relative risk aversion), virtually all models subscribe to the notion underlying the economics of crime; an increase in the probability of being detected and punished ceteris paribus decreases tax evasion. Rational taxpayers should react to the higher cost of cheating by cheating less.

The empirical findings, however, suggest that deterrence does not work as expected in the important case of tax evasion. This challenges the standard criminal choice model developed in, as well as the compliance policy advocated by, standard economics. The authors of this paper were therefore quite excited when they found out that they had two models available to meet this challenge; they decided to write a joint paper and submit the result to a scientific journal for publication. Manfred Holler presents a game theoretical model based on a peculiarity of the mixed-strategy Nash equilibrium in 2-by-2 games. In the mixed-strategy equilibrium, the strategy choice of a player is not affected by the changes in his or her payoffs; thus, payoff changes induced by deterrence have no effect on tax compliance. On April 29, 1985, presented an earlier version of this model at the Department of Philosophy. Timo Airaksinen arranged a seminar and Georg Henrik von Wright chaired the session. (See footnote 1 in Holler (1986).) Bruno Frey argues that increased deterrence tends to undermine tax morale and thus countervails the deterrence effect which may result from an increase of the penalty if tax morale does not change.

When the paper was completed and submitted to a scientific journal, an anonymous reviewer argued that 'this is really two different papers which have merged into one. They are obviously related in that both are concerned with tax evasion and deterrence policy, but otherwise the connection between them is quite thin'. The editor of the journal concluded that the two parts of the paper should be integrated or developed separately and invited the authors to resubmit the paper if after considering the reviewer's position. However, the authors still consider it meritorious that the paper contains two very different models of human behavior which explain the same phenomenon. They also hope that the obvious parallelism between the rational choice model and the model of moral behavior, which characterizes the following analysis, contributes to the ongoing discussion of a rational theory of morale behavior (see, e.g., Binmore, 1994, for a recent contribution).

Section 2 presents a game theoretical model. It demonstrates that, in the case of a Nash equilibrium, a reduction of the payoffs to a taxpayer due to punishment has no effect on his or her choice if the Nash equilibrium is mixed. In section 3, we propose that more intensive monitoring and higher fines may crowd out tax morale so that an increase in deterrence may under some conditions have a perverse effect on compliance, i.e., tax evasion may increase. Section 4 discusses alternative tax compliance policies. Our results indicate the importance of citizens' morale for a successful tax policy.

2. A strategic approach to tax compliance

In this section, an explanation for the ineffectiveness of deterrence based on a game theoretic model is presented. The model assumes that the taxpayer sees himself or herself in a decision situation where (i) the outcome results from decisions of the taxpayer and the tax authority, (ii) the tax authority forms expectations about the behavior of the taxpayer, (iii) the taxpayer forms expectations about the behavior of the tax authority, (iv) taxpayer and tax authority know about (i), (ii), and (iii), and (v) they know their own strategy set and their preferences on the outcome of the tax game as well as the strategy set and the preferences of their opponent in the game (i.e., we assume complete information). The strategy set of the taxpayer (player TP), S1, contains two pure strategies: cheat (C) and not cheat (NC). The strategy set of the tax authority (player TA), S2, contains two pure strategies: deter (i.e., audit and punish if noncompliance is detected) (D) and not deter (ND). We allow for mixed strategies, i.e., we assume that (1) TP may expect TA to randomize on choosing between D or ND with probability q for D, and (2) TP may randomize on C and NC with probability p for strategy C. There are four outcomes, each implemented by one of the four pairs of pure strategies. The evaluation of the outcomes and the corresponding strategies are summarized by the payoff matrix in Figure 1.

Figure 1: The taxpayer / tax authority game

		Tax Authority (TA)	
		Deter (D)	Not Deter (ND)
Taxpayer (TP)	Cheat (C)	(a, α)	(b, β)
	Not Cheat (NC)	(c, γ)	(d, δ)

It seems plausible to assume the following ranking of the payoffs:

(A.I) (i) $b > a$, $b > d$, $c > a$, $c > d$ for taxpayers
and
(ii) $\alpha > \beta$, $\alpha > \gamma$, $\delta > \beta$, $\delta > \gamma$ for the tax authority.

Most payoff relationships are rather straightforward and need not be commented on any further. The relation c > d, however, does not seem to be obvious; it implies that TP prefers deterrence to non-deterrence in case that TP does not cheat - which parallels the pleasure potential smugglers enjoy at the border when they get searched by the custom officer but do not carry hot goods with them. Honest taxpayers may prefer deterrence for equity reason: they want tax cheaters to be punished so that such people do not enjoy advantage compared to themselves. The motivation corresponds to the notion of tax morale which, as we have argued in the previous section, tends to be undermined if the tax authorities do not treat taxpayers equally, i.e., in a fair manner.

The relation $\alpha > \gamma$ may express a catch premium given by the policy maker to the tax officials if they detect a cheating taxpayer. We will come back to this interpretation in section 4. There is, however, also a motivational interpretation of the relation $\alpha > \gamma$. Tax officials would feel superfluous and would become demotivated if taxpayers were completely honest. The tax officials can only justify their deterrence policy and the use of resources in fighting tax evasion (to themselves as well as to the public) if indeed some taxpayers cheat.

A policy maker, P, say the parliament or the government, cannot perfectly control the tax authority, however, it is assumed to be able to manipulate payoff a which results from cheating (C) and deterrence (D) within the limits given by (A.I). Alternatively, we will consider that P can offer a catch premium, implied by an increase of α. P's preferences on the outcomes of this game[2] follow the ranking (NC, ND) > (NC, D) > (C, D) > (C, ND), i.e., x1 > x2 > x3 > x4 in Figure 2. Thus, irrespective of the decision of the tax authority, P prefers the taxpayer to choose NC instead of C. This ranking of P's preferences also takes care of the fact that auditing and paying a catch premium are costly to P.

The informational structure of this game is characterized by the following assumptions: (i): P determines the level of a, before TP and TA make their strategy choices and (ii) the payoff matrix in Figure 1 is known to TP and TA before they simultaneously, i.e., without knowing the other's strategy choice, decide on their strategies. The interactive decision situation can be illustrated by the game tree in Figure 2.

The dotted line between the two nodes of TP expresses that TP does not know whether the tax authority TA has chosen D or ND when making his decision on C and NC. This structure depicts the imperfect information of TP in the game. The imperfect information of TA is captured by the sequence of the game tree: By assuming that TA is first to make its decisions, we exclude that TA knows which strategy TP selects. Obviously, there is a second tree which equivalently illustrates the strategic decision situation of our model. It results from exchanging TP and TA and the corresponding strategies in Figure 2.

The strategic situation in which an individual taxpayer and a tax official see themselves are considered as of one-shot, i.e., both agents assume that a previous specific decision situation will not repeat itself in future periods. This assumption can be justified by the structural anonymity of large numbers typical for taxation in larger communities, or by the strategic anonymity stemming from bureaucratic rules designed to minimize reputation effects, so that cooperation from repeated interaction is restricted. One of these rules is that the material of a specific taxpayer will never be checked by the same tax official in two subsequent years.

Figure 2: The principal-agent-controller model

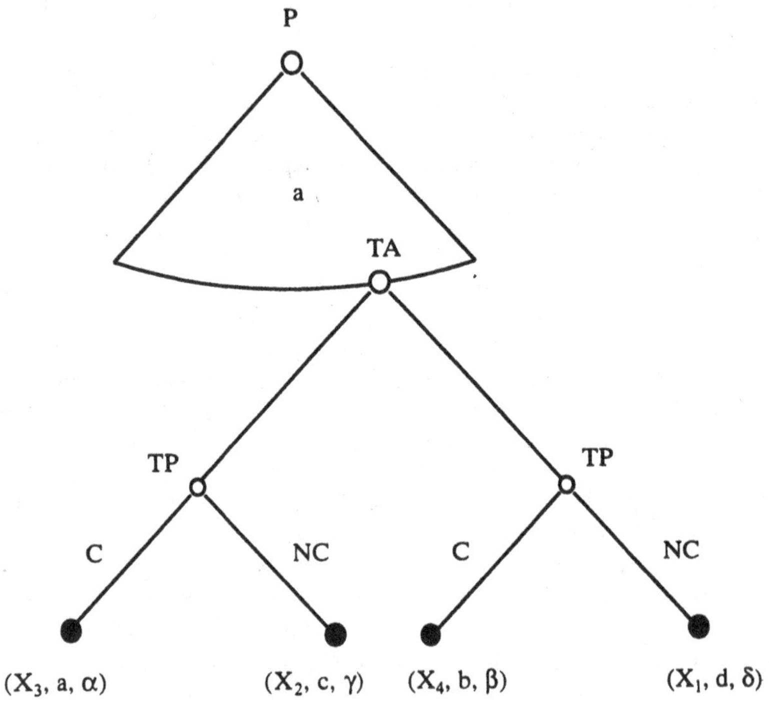

The principal's preferences: $X_1 > X_2 > X_3 > X_4$

If the political decision maker P can manipulate payoff a over a continuous interval of values, then Figure 2 expresses an infinite set of games consistent with our model. It is up to P to decide what game TA and TP play. In order to select the preferred game, P has to know what strategies TP and TA will choose in the various settings corresponding to alternative values of a. This problem is not easy to solve. To answer the question how TP will decide implies that TP can form expectations on how TA decides, given that TP is a (Bayesian) rational player. (See Tan and Werlang (1988).) The corresponding view holds for TA, provided TA is rational.

To form expectations is equivalent to applying solution concepts to the game in order to break down the complexity created by the interrelationship of the choices, via outcomes and payoffs, and the information of the players. Various solution concepts can serve as indicators for the players to grasp the strategic interdependency inherent to an interactive decision situation as described in Figure 1 and prepare for an analysis of the decision making. Given the constraints in (AI), the game in Figure 1 has no pure strategy Nash equilibrium (and thus, of course, no equilibrium in dominating strategies). The pure maximin strategy of TP is determined by the relative size of a and d while the pure maximin strategy of TA depends on whether $\beta > \gamma$ or $\beta < \gamma$ holds. Since we have no immediate justification for any of these relations, the application of the pure-strategy maximin solution seems somewhat vacuous. Given condition (A.I), we do not have to specify these relations. Let us assume that the payoffs of the players are of von Neumann Morgenstern type, and thus characterized by cardinality. This allows us to calculate mixed strategy pairs for the Nash equilibrium and for the maximin solution of the game in Figure 1. (Note since the von Neumann Morgenstern utility functions, U_i (i = TP,TA), satisfy the expected utility hypothesis[3], no distinction has to be made between 'payoffs' and 'expected payoffs' in what follows.)

If p is, as defined, the probability of TP selecting strategy C and q is the probability of TA selecting D, then the (mixed strategy) Nash equilibrium is characterized by the pair (p*,q*) such that

(1) $U_{TP}(p^*,q^*) \geq U_{TP}(p,q^*)$ for all $p \in [0,1]$ and
$U_{TA}(p^*,q^*) \geq U_{TA}(p^*,q)$ for all $q \in [0,1]$.

Condition (1) is fulfilled if q* satisfies

(2a) $qa + (1-q)\,b = qc + (1-q)\,d$

and if p* satisfies

(2b) $p\alpha + (1-p)\,\gamma = p\beta + (1-p)\,\delta.$

Satisfying (2a), q* makes TP indifferent with respect to all $p \in [0,1]$ and thus also for p*. That is, TA's strategy q* fixes the payoff value of TP to a constant value. The corresponding result applies to p*: TP's strategy p* fixes the payoff value of TA.

Solving (2a) and (2b) we get

(3a) $p^* = (\delta - \gamma / (\alpha - \beta - \gamma + \delta)$
(3b) $q^* = (d - b) / (a - b - c + d)$

From (3a) and (3b) the following result is immediate:

Result 1: In 2-by-2 (two-person matrix) games, player i's Nash equilibrium strategy is independent of i's payoff values if it is mixed.

The mixed strategy maximin solution, characterized by the probability pair (p^+,q^+), derives from the equations

(4a) $pa + (1-p)\,c = pb + (1-p)\,d$

(4b) $q\alpha + (1-q)\,\beta = q\gamma + (1-q)\,\delta.$

TP's strategy p^+, which satisfies (4a), fixes TP's payoff value and makes it independent of the strategy choice of TA. Similarly, TA's strategy q^+, which satisfies (4b), fixes TA's payoff value and makes it independent of the strategy choice of TP. Thus we have

(5) $U_{TP}(p^+,q) \geq \min U_{TP}(p,q)$ for all $q \in [0,1]$ and

$U_{TA}(p,q^+) \geq \min U_{TA}(p,q)$ for all $p \in [0,1]$.

Solving (4a) and (4b) we get

(6a) $p^+ = (d - c) / (a - b - c + d)$

(6b) $q^+ = (\delta - \beta) / (\alpha - \beta - \gamma + \delta)$

In order to calculate the payoffs of TP and TA for the Nash equilibrium and for the maximin solution, we plug p^* and q^* into (2a) and (2b) and p^+ and q^+ into (4a) and (4b), alternatively. We get

(7a) $U_{TP}(q^*) = (ad\text{-}bc) / (a\text{-}b\text{-}c\text{+}d) = U_{TP}(p^+)$

(7b) $U_{TA}(p^*) = (ad\text{-}bg) / (a\text{-}b\text{-}g\text{+}d) = U_{TA}(q^+)$

Thus we have

Result 2: In 2-by-2 (two-person matrix) games, player i's Nash equilibrium payoff is identical to i's maximin payoff if both solutions contain mixed strategies.

Result 2 (which is derived in Holler (1990)) says that the Nash equilibrium is 'unprofitable' (see Harsanyi, 1977, pp.104-107). It raises the question why, e.g., TP should play Nash equilibrium strategies if the expected payoff of the Nash equilibrium is identical to the payoff of playing maximin, i.e., identical to the payoff which TP can guarantee himself, irrespective of what strategy TA selects - while the Nash equilibrium payoff of TP is exclusively determined by TA's strategy choice. To justify p^* as a best reply assumes that TA plays q^*. That is, p^* is only optimal, if TA chooses q^*. In this case, however, any other p (including the pure strategies $p = 1$ and $p = 0$) would also be a best reply. The Nash equilibrium (p^*,q^*) is weak; thus it does not 'hurt' a player choosing an alternative strategy.

The maximin solution, however, prescribes strategies which are, in general, not best replies to each other. That is, given the maximin strategy of TA, TP could do better by choosing an alternative strategy to maximin, and vice versa. If the game is one-shot, then players have no possibility to revise their strategies. Does it matter under these circumstances that they might regret what they have done after implementing the maximin outcome? And if they regret and play the Gedankenexperiment of revisions in order to end up in a strategy pair of mutually best replies, i.e., the Nash equilibrium, what are the payoffs from the solution? The answer is: The same payoffs as in the maximin solution.

We do not further discuss here which solution concept is the right one (for arguments, see Holler, 1990; 1993) but accept both the Nash equilibrium and the maximin solution as a point of departure to discuss P's policy with respect to manipulating payoff a. Of course, the optimal policy of P in choosing a will depend on what solution concepts P assumes TP and TA will follow in case TP and TA think strategically, i.e., whether they are expected to be Nash players (choosing strategies in accordance with (3a) and (3b), respectively) or maximin players (choosing strategies in accordance with (6a) and (6b), respectively).

Case 1: Both TP and TA are Nash players. A decrease of a motivates TA to reduce the probability of deterrence, q^*, while the probability of cheating, p^*, remains unchanged. That is (C,D) becomes less likely while the probability of the strategy pair (C,ND) increases.[4] - This result is counter-productive for P since P prefers (C,D) to (C,ND).

Case 2: Both TP and TA are maximin players. A decrease of a motivates TP to reduce the probability of cheating, p^+, while q^+ remains unchanged. That is (C,D) becomes less likely while the probabilities of the strategy pairs (NC,D) and (NC,ND), both preferred by P to (C,D), increases. This result is favourable to P.

Case 3: TP is a maximin player and TA is a Nash player. A decrease of a motivates TP to reduce the probability of cheating, p^+, while TA will reduce the probability of deterrence, q^*. Thus (C,D) becomes even less likely than in CASE 1 and in CASE 2, given a is reduced by the same amount, while the probability of the strategy pair (NC,ND), P's preferred choice, increases. - This result is 'very favourable' to P.

Case 4: TA is a maximin player and TP is a Nash player. A decrease of a has no impact on the probabilities q^+ and p^* and thus leaves the behavior of both parties unchanged.

Figure 3: Changes of Maximin and Nash strategies induced by a reduction of payoff a

		Tax Authority (TA)	
		Maximin	Nash
Taxpayer (TP)	Maximin	$p+\downarrow$, $q+$	$p+\downarrow$, $q^*\downarrow$
	Nash	p^* , $q+$	p^* , $q^*\downarrow$

Figure 3 summarizes the effects of a decrease of a on the strategy choices which derive for alternative behavioral assumptions.

We can confront these four cases of strategic interaction with cases where TP is assumed to be a naive utility maximizer as implied by standard criminal choice theory. This case can, however, be summarized as follows: Because of a reduction of a, cheating becomes a less likely choice, i.e., the probability p of strategy C decreases, if TP assumes the probabilities of TA for choosing D and ND (q and 1-q) to remain unchanged. The latter assumption holds if TA is a maximin player or a naive utility maximizer, the latter assuming the probabilities of C and NC to be unaffected by the decrease of a. This result is positively evaluated by P. However, if TA is a Nash player, TA will reduce the probability of deterrence, q^*, which corresponds to an increase of the probability of non-deterrence. Depending on the magnitude of the probabilities (i.e., of the magnitudes of TP's payoffs in Figure 1, the probability of the strategy pair (C,ND), which is the least preferred result to P, will increase, decrease, or remain constant.

If, however, TP expects TA to be a Nash player then we are back to strategic reasoning and CASE 1: while D will become less likely due to a decrease of a, the Nash strategy of TP, p^*, will not be affected by a change of a. Moreover, any decision of TP will be a best reply to TA's Nash strategy q^*. Thus we have to conclude from the preceding analysis that deterrence does not work if taxpayers and the tax authority see themselves involved in a game situation chracterized by the strategies and payoffs represented in Figure 1 and by condition (A.I). This outcome is consistent with the empirical observations cited. However, given the equality of expected payoffs in Nash equilibrium and maximin solution we may argue that, for this game, maximin is a more plausible solution concept than Nash equilibrium.

A decrease of payoff a through deterrence then induces a decrease of the probability of cheating (i.e., p^+). This result corresponds to the result of standard criminal choice theory, although it is motivated by a rather different reasoning, but it is inconsistent with the quoted empirical observations. On the one hand, this falsifies the arguments which support maximin.[5] On the other hand, it questions the game model above which described the strategic relationships between taxpayers and tax authorities.

Let us follow the path of mainstream game theory, however, and accept the result suggested by the Nash equilibrium concept. Is there a strategy which frees the policy maker from the strategic trap which deterrence policy builds up? We may consider a catch premium, implied by an increase of a as an alternative to the unsuccessful deterrence policy of reducing a. The results of this policy (e.g., analysed in Holler (1993)) are summarized in Figure 4.

Figure 4: Changes of Maximin and Nash strategies induced by an increase of payoff α

		Tax Authority (TA)	
		Nash	Maximin
Taxpayer (TP)	Nash	$p^*\downarrow$, q^*	$p^*\downarrow$, $q^+\downarrow$
	Maximin	p^+ , q^*	p^+ , $q^+\downarrow$

Naive (non-strategic) policy suggests that an increase of α is followed by an increase of the probability q of auditing (implying an increase of expected deterrence) inducing a lower probability p of cheating. Indeed, the Nash equilibrium strategy of TP implies a reduction of p although q remains constant. If, however, TP follows the maximin solution concept, the probability of cheating remains constant since p^+ does not depend on α. It is, however, peculiar to see that TA will reduce the auditing probability, q, if α increases and TA follows the maximin recipe. That is, auditing becomes less likely - but the probability of cheating will remain constant, if TP follows maximin, or even decrease, if TP follows Nash.

To summarize: a decrease or an increase in the catch premium α and therewith a variation in deterrence is not a reliable policy for the tax authority to influence tax compliance. To ensure compliance within the postulated strategic framework, non-cheating (NC) has to be made a dominant strategy. Since (A.I) assumes $c > a$ the dominance of NC hinges on generating $d > b$. So far, however, $d < b$ expresses the benefits of tax evasion. Moreover, it seems that nothing can be done by the taxpayers to change this relationship. One possibility is to raise citizens' tax morale by so much that the monetary gain from tax evasion in the case of non-deterrence is overcompensated. If this holds, non deterrence is a best-reply strategy of the tax authority. Is it plausible to assume that the tax authority is able to increase d so that d > b follows? This question will be discussed in the following section.

3. Tax morale and compliance

Empirically oriented econometric, survey and experimental research has, at least in part, acknowledged the importance of tax morale[6]. What has so far not been considered is that deterrence in the form of both stricter auditing and higher punishment may, under specific conditions, systematically reduce **intrinsic motivation** to pay taxes, i.e., as an increase in a may reduce d. This makes tax morale an endogenous factor in a model of compliance (see, in general, Frey, 1992). Cognitive experimental social psychology has identified two general circumstances in which deterrence reduces intrinsic motivation: violation of a basic norm of reciprocity (see, e.g., Gouldner, 1960) and reduction of overjustification (see, e.g., Pittman and Heller, 1987).

Reciprocity implies that a taxpayer considers his or her particular tax balance. If the exchange between the tax paid and the government services performed are found to be equitable, the taxpayer is more inclined to comply to the law than if he or she evaluates the exchange to be unfair. An increase in deterrence disrupts this balance for an honest taxpayer. This feeling is strongest when a taxpayer who personally considers himself to have paid a fair due, is audited and fined; or when he or she notes that other taxpayers violating the tax law do not get punished. When such errors of type I (fining an honest taxpayer) and of type II (not fining a dishonest taxpayer) occur the intrinsic motivation to comply to tax law is undermined and a higher extent of tax evasion is observed than if no such moral effect existed.

Reduction of overjustification states that when people are extrinsically rewarded for a task which they are ready to undertake for their own satisfaction, the intrinsic reason is negatively affected or crowded out. As a result, when the extrinsic reward is discontinued, less of the task will be performed. (Such 'hidden costs of rewards' are reported and discussed in, e.g., McGraw (1978) and Deci and Ryan (1985); for experimental evidence see also Deci and Ryan (1980).) This implies that taxpayers, who consider themselves honest, feel 'overjustified' when their high tax morale is not required because the auditing and fining scheme of the tax authorities force compliance upon them anyway. Thus, when deterrence is raised, the taxpayers are rational to reduce their tax morale in order to regain the least cost equilibrium, i.e., to produce performance at the lowest possible costs.

Taking the effect of increased deterrence on tax morale into account within the framework of a standard economic model allows us to derive empirically testable propositions of the tax evasion phenomena.[7] In the following, we will discuss three propositions and relate them to empirical findings.

Proposition 1: The insignificant and/or ambiguous effect of deterrence on tax compliance can be explained by the fact that the effect of deterrence on tax morale has been disregarded.

To illustrate this proposition we use the following standard equation for tax compliance estimation as a point of departure:

$$(8) \qquad T = \alpha_0 + \alpha_1 D + ß Z$$

where T measures the extent of tax compliance, D represents deterrence (i.e., auditing an detection probabilities as well as the magnitude of punishment) and Z summarizes other influences on tax-compliance including income and tax rates. Criminal choice theory assumes that deterrence works, i.e. $a_1 > 0$.

Now we consider an alternative model in which tax morale M influences tax compliance and in which deterrence undermines tax morale (for simplicity, in a linear way):

$$(9) \qquad T = \alpha_0 + \alpha_1 D + \alpha_2 M + ß Z \text{ with } \alpha_2 > 0$$

$$(10) \qquad M = m_0 - m_1 D \text{ with } m_0, m_1 > 0.$$

Thus we get

$$(11) \qquad T = \delta_0 + \delta_1 D + ß Z$$

where $d_0 = (a_0 + a_2 m_0) > 0$ and $d_1 = (a_1 - a_2 m_1)$. If the deterrence effect is smaller than the undermining effect on tax morale ($a_1 < a_2 m_1$), deterrence reduces compliance ($d_1 < 0$). A number of studies have found a negative deterrence effect. It is no fluke that many of them are survey studies, which do pay attention to tax morale (e.g., Spicer and Lundstedt, 1976; Westat, 1980; Yankelowich et al., 1984). An Internal Revenue Service study (1973) - not based on surveys but on the effect 1967-69 audit histories of taxpayers on 1968-69 - reports tax liabilities: For three out of four medium-income and high-income classes (which have the best opportunities to conceal income), the audits were associated with lower reported tax liabilities, thus also observing a perverse effect of deterrence on tax compliance.

The negative effect can of course be attributed to many different causes (such as selection biases) but is consistent with a model in which, under specific conditions, the undermining effect of deterrence on tax morale (captured by $\alpha_2 m_1$)

dominates the effects of deterrence (expressed by $\alpha_1 > 0$) as suggested by standard criminal choice theory. Whether this relation applies cannot always be unambiguously shown. However, there is some empirical evidence which supports the following proposition.

Proposition 2: A cooperative relationship between taxpayers and tax authorities may lead to the same level of tax compliance as a coercive relationship based on deterrence.

In their comparative study of the European tax system, based on surveys of 1.000 individuals, Schmölders (1970) and Strümpel (1969) studied the effects of different enforcement levels on compliance and attitudes. They found a striking difference between Germany and Britain. The German system is strict and stresses coercive enforcement while the British one is relatively cautious, more lenient and the atmosphere between taxpayers and tax officials is more cooperative. However, the general level of tax compliance achieved in the two countries was quite similar. Indeed, Schmölders and Strümpel observed that tax morale in Germany was significantly lower than in Britain. - The reason why the two tax authorities pursued a different policy is based on historical and institutional conditions specific to the two countries. British citizens with their long democratic tradition and respect for private rights tend to resent intrusions by the tax authorities more strongly than do the Germans who are used to believe in authoritarian structures and in government doing what is good for them.

We can model the differences of aversion to deterrence on optimal compliance policy. Let us assume that tax authorities want to maximize tax compliance; and that tax compliance depends on both deterrence and tax morale so that

$$(12) \qquad T = T(D,M) \text{ with } T_D \geq 0, T_M \geq 0$$

$$\text{and } T_{DD} < 0, T_{MM} < 0$$

Tax authorities will decide on the quantity of auditing and punishment (i.e., deterrence) so that

$$(13) \qquad T_D + T_M(dM/dD) = 0$$

Obviously, it depends on the sign of dM/dD of whether the tax authority should increase, reduce or keep constant deterrence D. If, following the above discussion, we assume that $dM/dD = -m_1 < 0$ then rational tax administrators will employ less deterrence than in the standard criminal choice model.

From the analyses of Schmölders (1970) and Strümpel (1969) we conclude that the British had a stronger aversion to raising taxes by deterrence than the Germans, i.e., the product - $(dM/dD)T_M$ was larger for Britain than for Germany. If we assume a similar marginal effectiveness of deterrence on compliance T_D in both countries, the model suggest a lower optimal degree of deterrence in Britain than in Germany. This is consistent with the empirical evidence found by Schmölders (1970) and Strümpel (1969).

A generalization of this results is captured by

> *Proposition 3:* The cooperative atmosphere between taxpayers and tax authorities, resulting in high tax morale, is the larger, the more extensive the democratic participation possibilities are.

The amount of cooperation and trust between taxpayers and tax authorities varies greatly between nations; in some countries it scarcely exits, while it seems to be of considerable importance in countries such as Britain and the United States. For Switzerland, it has been shown by econometric cross section estimates that in cantons with more developed institutions of direct democratic participation (referenda and initiatives), in which a higher tax morale can be expected, tax compliance is **ceteris paribus** significantly larger (Pommerehne and Frey, 1992). Breaking the relationship of trust one-sidedly by imposing stricter auditing and higher fines, would make many taxpayers feel that their tax morale is not adequately recognized by the tax authorities. This induces taxpayers to reduce what they consider to be their 'excess' tax morale leading them to more strongly underreport their taxable income.

4. Tax policy and tax morale

Our analysis based on a game theoretical model suggests that deterrence is an ineffective policy to raise citizens' tax compliance. Moreover, if deterrence indeed reduces tax morale, as argued in section 3 of this paper, non-deterrence raises the payoff of the taxpayer because his high tax morale is acknowledged by the tax authority. If this effect is strong enough to compensate the monetary gains from tax evasion in the case of non-deterrence, then non-deterrence is a **best reply strategy** of the tax authority.

The policy maker may be well advised to strengthen tax morale instead of trying to increase tax compliance by payoff policies. To rely on moral persuasion may, however, result in a too optimistic policy and of course its success depends on the general level of morale existing in the tax-paying community. It was Machiavelli who stated that 'in the province of Germany it is quite clear that goodness and respect for religion are still to be found in its peoples' and 'when these republics have need to spend any sum of money on the public account... each person presents himself to the tax-collectors in accordance with the constitutional practice of the town. He then takes an oath to pay the appropriate sum, and throws into a chest provided for the purpose the amount which he conscientiously thinks that he ought to pay; but of this payment there is no witness save the man who pays' (1983, pp. 244-245). For his beloved Italy no such traits existed and Machiavelli therefore suggested oppressive policies and rules to the 'Principe' to be applied in order to stabilize society by tyrannical power. With respect to the strategic situation given by Figure 1, tyrannical policy coincides with increasing deterrence and manipulating the payoffs of the tax officers so that D becomes a dominating strategy and NC (i.e. compliance) becomes the only best reply.

Notes

*The authors are grateful to Rainer Eichenberger and Laszlo Goerke for helpful suggestions. Sections 2, 3, and 4 of this paper are identical with the authors' earlier manuscript entitled 'Tax Compliance Reconsidered'.

1. Reviews of the theoretical developments of microeconomic models of tax (non-) compliance are provided, e.g., in Witte and Woodbury, 1985, Cowell, 1985, 1990, and Roth, Scholz and Witte, 1989, with a large number of references to the literature. A stronger psychological orientation is given in Hessing et al., 1988 and Robben et al., 1990.
2. The discussed model is a version of the principal-agent-controller model as applied in Holler, 1993.
3. The von Neumann-Morgenstern utility function is defined by the fact that it satisfies the expected utility hypothesis (see, e.g., Harsanyi, 1977, p. 32).
4. A series of similar paradoxical results are discussed in Brams, 1992) and Tsebelis (1989, 1993). For a theoretical analysis, see Wittman,1985, 1993. It is immediate from Holler, 1990, that the paradoxical results which derive from mixed-strategy Nash equilibriua in 2x2 games are due to the linear functional relation of probability and utility which characterizes von Neumann-Morgenstern utilities and the corresponding weakness of the Nash equilibrium. Cheng and and Zhu, 1995, demonstrate that strikt Nash equiilibria for mixed-strategies exist if players have 'quadratic utility'. Then there are unique best replies and the results are no longer paradoxical.
5. See Holler and Høst, 1990, for empirical results and theoretical arguments which support maximin.
6. See, e.g., Tittle, 1980, Westat, 1980, Scott and Grasmick, 1981, Friedland, 1982, Lewis, 1982, Grasmick and Scott, 1982) Wärneryd and Walerud, 1982, Webley and Halstead, 1985, Graetz and Wilde, 1985, Graetz, Reinganum and Wilde, 1986. A pioneering study comparing the tax morale of various European countries was undertaken by Strümpel,

1969, and Schmölders, 1970, at the University of Cologne. Song and Yarbrough, 1978, measured the tax ethics among residents of a North Carolina city.

7. Previous games between taxpayers and tax collectors are surveyed in Cowell, 1990, ch. 6; path breaking is Graetz, Reinganum and Wilde, 1986.

References

Allingham, M. G. and Sandmo, A. (1972), 'Income Tax Evasion: A Theoretical Analysis', *Journal of Public Economics,* 1, pp. 323-38.

Alm, J.; McKee, M. and Beck, W. (1990), 'Amazing Grace: Tax Amnesties and Compliance', *National Tax Journal,* 43, pp. 23-38.

Becker, G. S. (1968), 'Crime and Punishment: An Economic Approach', *Journal of Political Economy*, 76, pp. 169-217.

Binmore, K. (1994), *Playing Fair (Game Theory and the Social Contract, Volume I),* Cambrisge, MIT Press: MA.

Brams, S. J. (1992), 'A Generic Negotiation Game', *Journal of Theoretical Politics,* 4, pp. 53-66.

Cheng, L. K., and Zhu, M. (1995), 'Mixed-Strategy Nash Equilibrium Based upon Expected Utility and Quadratic Utility', Games and Economic Behavior 9, pp. 139-50.

Cowell, F. A. (1985), 'Tax Evasion with Labour Income', *Journal of Public Economics,* 26, pp. 19-34.

Cowell, F. A. (1990), *Cheating the Government. The Economics of Tax Evasion,* Cambridge, MIT Press: MA.

Deci, E. L., and Ryan, R. M. (1980), 'The Empirical Exploration of Intrinsic Motivational Processes', *Advances in Experimental Social Psychology,* 10, pp. 39-80.

Deci, E. L. and Ryan, R. M. (1985), *Intrinsic Motivation and Self-Determination in Human Behavior,* Plenum Press: New York.

Downs, A. (1957), *An Economic Theory of Democracy,* New York: Harper & Row.

Frey, B. S. (1992), 'Tertium Datur: Pricing, Regulating and Intrinsic Motivation', *Kyklos,* 45, pp. 161-84.

Friedland, N. (1982), 'A Note on Tax Evasion as a Function of the Quality of Information about the Magnitude and Credibility of Threatened Fines: Some Preliminary Research', *Journal of Applied Social Psychology,* 3, pp. 103-18.

Gouldner, A. W. (1960), 'The Norm of Reciprocity: A Preliminary Statement', *American Sociological Review,* 25, pp. 161-78.

Graetz, M. J. and Wilde, L. L. (1985), 'The Economics of Tax Compliance: Fact and Fantasy', *National Tax Journal,* 38, pp. 355- 63.

Graetz, M. J.; Reinganum, J. F. and Wilde, L. L. (1986), 'The Tax Compliance Game: Toward an Interactive Theory of Law Enforcement', *Journal of Law, Economics and Organization,* 2, pp. 1-33.

Grasmick, H. G. and Scott, W. J. (1982), 'Tax Evasion and Mechanisms of Social Control: A Comparison with Fraud and Petty Theft', *Journal of Economic Psychology,* 2, pp. 213-30.

Harsanyi, J. C. (1977), *Rational Behavior and Bargaining in Games and Social Situations,* Cambridge University Press: Cambridge.

Hessing, D. J.; Kinsey, K. A.; Elfers, H. and Weigel, R. H. (1988), 'Tax Evasion Research: Measurement Strategies and Theoretical Models', in van Raaij, W. F., van Veldhoven, G. M. and Wärneryd, K. E. (eds), *Handbook of Economic Psychology,* Dordrecht: Kluwer.

Hirshleifer, J. and Rasmusen, E. (1992), 'Are Equilibrium Strategies Unaffected by Incentives?', *Journal of Theoretical Politics,* 4, pp. 353-67.

Holler, M. J. (1986), 'Moral Sentiments and Self-Interest Reconsidered', in Diekmann, A. and Motter, P. (eds), *Paradoxical Effects of Social Behavior: Eesays in Honor of Anatol Rapoport,* Physica-Verlag: Heidelberg and Vienna.

Holler, M. J. (1990), 'The Unprofitability of Mixed-Strategy Equilibria in Two-Person Games: A Second Folk-Theorem', *Economics Letters,* 32, pp. 319-23.

Holler, M. J. (1993), 'Fighting Pollution When Decisions are Strategic', *Public Choice,* 76, pp. 347-56.

Holler, M. J. and Host, V. (1990), 'Maximin vs. Nash Equilibrium: Theoretical Results and Empirical Evidence', in Quandt, R.E. and Triska, D. (eds), *Optimal Decisions in Markets and Planned Economies,* Boulder et al.: Westview.

Internal Revenue Service (IRS) (1973), quoted in Roth et al. (1989).

Lewis, A. (1982), *The Psychology of Taxation,* Oxford: Blackwell.

Machiavelli, N. (1983), *The Discourses*, edited by Bernard Crick, Harmondsworth: Penguin Books.

McGraw, K. O. (1978), 'The Detrimental Effects of Reward on Performance: A Literature Review and a Prediction Model', in Lepper, M. R. and Greebe, D. (eds), *The Hidden Costs of Reward: New Perspectives of Human Behavior,* Erlbaum: New York.

Paternoster, R. (1989), 'Desist from Four Types of Common Delinquency and the Rational Choice Perspective', *Law and Society Review,* 23, pp. 7-40.

Pittman, T. S. and Heller, J. F. (1987), 'Social Motivation', *Annual Review of Psychology,* 38, pp. 461-89.

Pommerehne, W. W. and Frey, B. S. (1992), 'The Effect of the Administration on the Tax Morale'. Presented at the Meeting of the International Seminar in Public Economics (ISPE), El Escorial, Spain, June.

Robben, H. S. J.; Webley, P.; Weigel, R. H. et al. (1990), 'Decision Frame and Opportunity as Determinants of Tax Cheating', *Journal of Economic Psychology,* 11, pp. 341-64.

Roth, J. A.; Scholz, J. T. and Witte, A. D. (eds), (1989), *Taxpayer Compliance,*

University of Pennsylvania Press: Philadelphia.
Schmölders, G. (1970), 'Survey Research in Public Finance - a Behavioral Approach to Fiscal Theory', *Public Finance,* 25, pp. 300- 6.
Scott, W. J., and Grasmick, H. G. (1981), 'Deterrence and Income Tax Cheating: Testing Interaction Hypotheses in Utilitarian Theories', *Journal of Applied Behavioral Science,* 17, 395-408.
Song, Y., and Yarbrough, T.E. (1978), 'Tax Ethics and Taxpayer Attitudes: A Survey', *Public Administration Review,* 38, pp. 442-52.
Spicer, M. W., and Lundstedt, S.B. (1976), 'Understanding Tax Evasion', *Public Finance,* 31, pp. 295-305.
Strümpel, B. (1969), 'The Contribution of Survey Research to Public Finance'; in Peacock, A. T. (ed.), *Quantitative Analysis in Public Finance,* Praeger: New York.
Tan, T. C-C., and da Costa, S. R. Werlang (1988), 'The Bayesian Foundations of Solution Concepts of Games', *Journal of Economic Theory,* 45, pp. 370-91.
Tittle, C. R. (1980), *Sanctions and Social Deviance: the Question of Deterrence,* New York: Praeger.
Tsebelis, G. (1989), 'The Abuse of Probability in Political Analysis: The Robinson Crusoe Fallacy', *American Political Science Review,* 83, pp. 77-91.
Tsebelis, G. (1993), 'Penalty and Crime: Further Theoretical Considerations and Empirical Evidence', *Journal of Theoretical Politics,* 5, pp. 349-74.
Webley, P. and Halstead, S. (1985), 'Tax Evasion on the Micro: Significant Simulations or Expedient Experiments?', *Journal of Interdisciplinary Economics,* 1, pp. 87-100.
Westat (1980), 'Self-Reported Tax Compliance: A Pilot Survey Report', Report to the Internal Revenue Service, March 21.
Witte, A. D., and Woodbury, D. F. (1985), 'The Effects of Tax Laws and Tax Administration on Tax Compliance: The Case of the U.S. Individual Income Tax', *National Tax Journal,* 38, pp. 1-13.,
Wittman, D. (1985), 'Counter-Intuitive Results in Game Theory', *European Journal of Political Economy,* 1, pp. 77-89.
Wittman, D. (1993), 'Nash Equilibrium vs. Maximin: A Comparative Game statics Analysis', *European Journal of Political Economy,* 9, pp. 559-65.
Wärneryd, K. E. and Walerud, B. (1982), 'Taxes and Economic Behavior: Some Interview Data on Tax Evasion in Sweden', *Journal of Economic Psychology,* 2, pp. 187-211.
Yankelovich, S. and White Inc. (1984), *Survey of Taxpayer Attitudes,* Washington, D.C Internal Revenue Service.

Technology policy in a democratic state

Ilkka Niiniluoto

Technology policy is usually understood as a system of organisations and activities which allocate public funds to stimulate and support research and development in industrial companies and firms. It might seem that such a state-centered conception is outdated, belonging to the era of nation states with planning economies: perhaps a liberal state needs no technology policy at all? In this paper, I argue that this would be a wrong conclusion. The development of technology is not only an economic phenomenon, a business enterprise in the free market, but rather its effects penetrate the whole culture and society. Technology is a thoroughly political form of activity which both depends on human valuations and influences social values. A rational liberal state needs more, not less, technology policy, but its main emphasis should be in democratic methods and decision procedures that allow the citizens to participate in the assessment and control of technological change. But this requirement does not mean that truth claims in science should be placed under democratic steering. Technological progress should be based upon objective scientific truth and humanistic ethical values. In this way, technology might be able to fulfil its great promise to enhance human positive freedom.

1. Is technology out of control?

Technological progress is a central factor influencing industrial economies. Research and science-based development are productive forces. This situation is not changing in the 'post-industrial' or 'post-capitalist' society with Big Science, high tech, information technology, computers, automatisation of production, mass media, and content industries. Technology continues to be the source of the wealth and competitiveness of nations. It is, therefore, natural that most developed countries have established national systems of science and technology policy in order to promote and accelerate technological invention and innovation. And to gain more power in this task, small countries have joined their forces to build larger economical and political units like the European Union.

On the other hand, technology also has dramatic effects on the natural and social environment. Many of them have been unintended by-products of the employment of new technical tools and machines. No one (except some visionaries like Karl Marx and Charles Chaplin) could foresee the revolutionary social consequences of steam engine, spinning wheel, work line in factories, cars, and computers. The damaging effects of our technological form of life to the health of nature (such as waste of resources, pollution of air and water, greenhouse effect, etc.) have only gradually been realized in the last decades. The scientists in the Club of Rome have argued that there are limits to the growth, green movements have arisen to conserve nature and to protect life, and many governments have endorsed the goal of sustainable development (cf. Niiniluoto, 1994).

It is thus clear that there is an urgent need to control technological change, both to promote and accelerate it in profitable directions and to assess its effects and to inhibit its dangerous growth.

Both of these tasks, acceleration and assessment, presuppose that technology is under human control. This view may be called *technological voluntarism*, as it claims that the emergence and change of technology depends on human will, i.e., can be influenced and directed by human evaluation and intervention.

There are powerful trends in the philosophy of technology which deny voluntarism. Usually they are based on the idea that modern technology has become an independent system or monster which follows its own 'inner logic' and directs 'technological imperatives' to us. Such *technological determinism* has been formulated, as a horror picture, by Jacques Ellul (1964). In a milder form, Langdon Winner (1977) has defended the thesis that technology has become 'autonomous', and today determines politics, rather than vice versa. But determinism has also been advocated by the spokesmen for *technocracy*, who suggest that for ordinary citizens it is simply the best to accept and passively follow the advice of the technical experts who know where technology is going by its own inner necessities.

Besides technological voluntarism and determinism, the third main alternative is to claim that technological change is indeterministic, chaotic, and unpredictable. One formulation of this view is *decisionism*: value choices are arbitrary, subjective, and situational. This position is in fact an extreme version of voluntarism. Jürgen Habermas (1970) criticises it by defending the possibility of rational discourse on values.

Another expression of the 'contingent' and 'heterogeneous' nature of technology is the *constructivist* approach in the STS-studies. Wiebe Bijker and John Law (1992) suggest that 'sociotechnology' constitutes a 'seamless web', where society and technology cannot (or should not) initially be distinguished, so that one of them does not dominate the other. In particular, this means that there are no predetermined trajectories for the evolution of technological projects (cf. Bijker, 1995).

I think all the three approaches have their insights and merits (see Niiniluoto, 1990), but they do not describe any inherent nature that technology has independently of us. Naive voluntarism is certainly an illusion. Technology is a powerful social system which, in Emil Durkheim's sense, has coercive power over us. Technological development does present its 'imperatives' to us, but they are always conditional on some value premises (about what should be desired or avoided), and therefore we always have the option to disobey them. Even though progress in technology may to some extent influence our goals and values, our choices need not be random, nonpurposive, or externally determined, but also the social needs and ends have to be publicly and freely discussed in a democratic community. I think we have to recognize that it is a matter of a major political decision whether we *allow* technology to develop in the deterministic or chaotic manner or whether we wish to find democratic ways of assessing and controlling it.

2. Democracy, liberalism, and freedom

The technocratic view surrenders the power in society to an elite which is assumed to guide others by their expertise without value choices and commitments. Another challenge to democracy arises from the position which admits that technological change is value-laden but claims that these values can be objectively known by a philosophical elite who can settle for others what is really good and right. This view, formulated already by Plato, has recently reappeared as value objectivism in environmental philosophy (see Skolimowski, 1981).

It is conceivable that some day the 'ecological imperatives' become so pressing that the Western model of democracy is unable to cope with them. This is not an issue to be discussed in this paper, which is focused on the prospects of technology policy in a *liberal democratic state*. In such a state, the citizens enjoy personal freedom and rights. They are allowed to have different preferences, and there are systematic procedures for guaranteeing that different valuations are taken into account in social decision-making. Also market economy in some form is the cornerstone of a liberal state. But these conditions still leave open many alternative ways of building a democratic state.

Modern political debates have centered on the relations between the state and its individual citizens. The Platonist, Hegelian, and Marxist traditions see the state as a kind of superindividual which is more real and important than its individual members. The Hegelians made a distinction between the family, civil society, and the state. The civil society (*bürgerliche Geschellschaft*) is the domain of social life where citizens enter as individual bearers of rights; in pursuing their needs their success requires co-operation. Here Hegel followed the Aristotelian view that man is not an atomistic individual, but a social being, a 'political animal'. Even though Hegel ultimately asserted that the potentials of a human personality - *Bildung*, self-consciousness, and morality (*Sittlichkeit*), through education and knowledge - can be fully realized only in a state, and thereby differed from the tradition of individualism, his conception of a civil society is an indispensable element of his social doctrines.

The modern individualist conception of human beings led first to the return of the doctrine of Thrasymachus, as described in Plato's *Republic*: justice is nothing but 'the advantage of the stronger'. For Macchiavelli, a ruthless prince gains power and prosperity for himself by exploiting his adversaries. Hobbes suggested that in the natural state 'man is a wolf to another man', and therefore the task of the state is to protect citizens from other citizens. The tradition of liberal democracy, from Locke to Mill, led to ideas of special political rights (such as freedom of thinking, universal suffrage), expressed in declarations, laws, and constitutions of nation states.

The Nordic model of welfare society is a sort of compromise between the Hegelian and liberalist traditions. It has involved a conception of a strong state, based upon democratic constitution, and large public sector which takes care of security networks, allowances, and many other welfare services to all citizens. But the Nordic model has also given room for a large 'third sector' - besides the state-centered public sector and the private business sector. In contrast, the Catholic model of welfare has given more emphasis to the family and the church, while the American model relies largely on private insurance policies and the economic market.

Since the 1980s, many Western countries have been struggling with economical problems of the welfare society, and *libertarian* views of the New Right have strongly influenced their politics. Deregulation, cuts in the public sector, commercialisation, privatisation, individual responsibility, initiative, and enterprising spirit are suggested as remedies against the nurturing and paternalising tendencies of the welfare society.

Libertarianism understands freedom in the negative sense as the absence of constraints. This view is often called 'neo-liberalism', even though it seems to be basically an old doctrine, a repetition of the ideas of the 19th century social Darwinism: the whole of society is seen as a field of merciless struggle and selfish competition, where the strongest and fittest survive. This view emphasizes man's will to power. The role of the state should be minimal: its task as a 'night guard' (Nozick, 1974) is to make sure that the conditions of free competition are maintained.

Today the welfare state is often blamed for excessive paternalism and domination which subjects its citizens to serfdom. This libertarian criticism confuses two notions of freedom: *negative freedom* ('freedom from') as the absence of constraints and prohibitions, and *positive freedom* ('freedom to') as the possibility and capability of doing something. (Feinberg, 1971) has argued that there is only one concept of freedom, since positive freedom can be defined as the absence of negative constraints. But I think it is artificial to describe, e.g., wealth as the lack of lack of money.) The basic rights of the citizens of liberal Western democracies include many negatively defined freedoms - such as the freedom of speech, thinking, trade. The view of a libertarian is restricted to this domain of rights. On the other hand, welfare society is characterized by principles of positive freedom as well - such as the rights to education, work, child care, aid to the elderly, and health care. The existence of such rights give opportunities and capabilities to the citizens (cf. Nussbaum and Sen, 1993). It is of course an important issue how large domain of positive freedom a society can afford to guarantee, but it is clearly a propagandist mistake to urge that such freedoms or rights would be examples of domination and serfdom.

A social organization may evaluated on two grounds. First, is it *effective* in producing the desired results, and does it perform this task *efficiently* in the cost-benefit sense? Secondly, is it *just* or at least more just than its alternatives? In my view, in the latter respect (cf. Rawls, 1971), the democratic welfare society fares better than the libertarian one which reduces questions of justice to negative freedom and efficiency in the market. Furthermore, the welfare society may on the whole be even more effective than its rival in producing individual and common goods (cf. Niiniluoto, 1995).

The mechanical policy of subjecting the whole public sector to accountability in terms of cost-benefit-efficiency has proved to be problematic in many cases (e.g., university, army, police, school): the desired 'results' are difficult to define and measure; the real costs (including increased working load, bureaucracy, unemployment, social insecurity, violence) are hard to count. The transformation of public offices and institutions into business corporations (e.g., post, train) has resulted in diminishing available services and to lower quality of life.

A special challenge is to analyze the conditions of the economic market. Sometimes a distinction between capitalism and market economy is made. *Capitalism* is the economic system that allows private ownership and fosters ruthless egoistic competition for one's own advantage. The only sense of justice is derived from Thrasymachus: the strongest and the greediest wins the weaker ones. The so-called casino economy is a form of uncontrolled capitalism in this sense. *Market economy*, on the other hand, should view economic competition as a means to common good (as in Adam Smith's assumption of the invisible hand). Free economic competition should mean freedom from manipulation (e.g., by big international companies). Further, market economy should be based upon principles concerning the ethical responsibilities of business enterprises with respect to the consumer and the natural and social environment. Potentially misleading talk about 'free trade' should then be replaced by the term *fair trade*.

3. Science and technology in the free/fair market

Different conceptions of liberalism may lead to various solutions concerning the relationships between science, technology, and the market.

For a libertarian, technology should be seen as a way producing and distributing commodities in the free market. Firms, based on private ownership, produce goods with the aim of maximizing profit, and the consumers have complete freedom in making their own choices according to their own needs and preferences. In deciding to buy commodities, the consumers are as if it were voting for alternative technological products, so that the whole procedure appears to satisfy the ideal of democracy as well.

Science, both 'strategic' basic research and applied research, serves as basis of technological development. For the libertarian, this motivates the treatment of scientific research and higher education as 'investments' which should yield economic profit in the short or at least not-too-long run. This means that both science policy and technology policy are understood to be parts of the economic strategy concerning commerce and industry. For example, the Finnish Council of Science and Technology Policy, in its programmatic *Towards an Innovative Society* (1993), a development strategy for Finland as a 'country of knowledge and competence', uses the economic concept of 'innovation system' to motivate the need of promoting R&D in Finland.

When technology is seen as an effective instrument of national economy, a purely libertarian approach, with its skepticism about the state, does not work quite well in practice. It turns out that there is an optimum amount of state intervention, in the form of public subsidies and funding, which keeps technological invention and innovation in progress even in private firms. Similarly, scientific education and basic research are too important for modern nations to be left entirely to the mercy of the market. For these reasons, non-extremist libertarian thinkers like James Buchanan (1986) are willing to allow the state to finance 'the enterprise of science 'as a public good (see Loukola, 1995).

Neo-liberal influences can be seen also in the currently fashionable competitive approach to scientific research and education. The success of science is not measured primarily by economic indicators, but in terms of quantities expressing numbers of publications and citations. Science is viewed as a sport where the competition is between individual researchers, groups, departments, institutes, universities, and nations. Research and universities should be goal-directed, cost-benefit effective, managerially directed, and accountable in such terms. This leads to what might be called *Matthew strategy* in science policy: give more to those who already have, and take away from those who have less. (I have used this term first in 1984 in analogy with Merton's (1973) descriptive term 'Matthew effect'. See Niiniluoto, 1987.)

John Ziman has described the recent trend in science policy as a change from the Mertonian ethos of Communalism, Universalism, Disinterestedness, Originality, and Skepticism (CUDOS) to Proprietary, Local, Authoritarian, Commissioned, and Expert work in science (PLACE). Ziman notes that the CUDOS norms have served to guarantee the progress and productivity of science by leaving space for personal creativity, openness to debate, and hospitability towards novelty. He illustrates vividly how the new PLACE principles are realized in the new global and national organization of Big Science, the research programmes of the European

Union, contract research in the universities and in industry, and the changing conditions of scientific careers. And he raises the important question, whether this reshaped system is still able to sustain the progress of scientific knowledge. Ziman expresses his strong misgivings about the new slogans and trends of science policy. Many of the new practices, he argues, are 'so ill judged that they could do lasting damage to the health of science and its efficacy as a social institution' (p. 252). In particular, 'accountability' lays stress on the narrowly instrumental aspects of science and is unfavourable to genuine scientific originality. 'Evaluation' is counter-productive if carried out too frequently. 'Selectivity' enforces the Matthew Effect and often leads to arbitrary decisions to 'close down small, but beautiful research operations'. The idea of producing 'trained research workers' as a kind of 'manpower' devalues the personal commitment that motivates good scientists. 'Exploitation' of academic research leads to the 'commercial patronage of university'. Emphasis on 'priorities' is a very serious threat to the integrity and credibility of the social sciences. Excessive 'competition' undermines the communal spirit of inquiry. 'Management' leads to bureaucratic top-down policies that are incompatible with personal and departmental autonomy.

On the whole, I think there is reason to agree with Ziman's analysis, but with three reservations. First, Ziman over-emphasises the 'individualism' of CUDOS against the 'corporate' or 'collectivized' spirit of PLACE. Science has been based on co-operation within the scientific community at least since the seventeenth century. Secondly, creative work within Humboldtian universities may very well be highly successful in quantitative terms. Thirdly, the strategy of building 'centres of excellence' may turn out to be useful for the whole research community, and thus justifiable by the Rawlsian difference principle (as suggested by Airaksinen, 1994).

In my view, the best way of philosophically defending the autonomy and integrity of scientific inquiry against reduction to the commercial principles of technology policy is provided by scientific realism (see Niiniluoto, 1984) and the conceptual distinctions between science and technology (see Niiniluoto, 1997) and between basic and applied research (see Niiniluoto, 1993). A step in the same direction is made by Timo Airaksinen's (1995) discussion of the role of 'theoretical virtues' in the professional practice of science (such as wisdom, creativity, clarity, consistency, and criticism), and their difference to the 'Franklinian virtues' in financing science and the 'Macchiavellian virtues' in profiting from science.

Support from other potential sources is not easily available. The communitarians, who pointedly criticise narrowly individualist and egoistic ethical principles, are overly skeptical about the prospects of science and Enlightenment (cf. Hellsten, 1995).

In the study of science, technology, and society (STS), the currently most popular view is that 'scientific knowledge has no privileged claim to truth', all theories and belief systems are 'on a common epistemological footing', the scientists are not guardians of objective knowledge but 'hired brains of special interests and lobbyists for their own' (see Cozzens and Woodhouse, 1995). The message of these STS-studies seems to be devastating: everything that you might have been afraid that could happen to science, is already true.

I agree that, in the study of the role of politics in shaping the scientific production of knowledge, it is important to be free from ideological prejudice in any direction. But the by now popular thesis that science has no rational or epistemological advantage over other practices of belief formation has itself become a prejudice in the STS-studies. If it were true, why should the society spend any funds at all to such an expensive activity as research - it would be cheaper and faster to consult fortune tellers using crystal balls and tarot cards.

Scientific research always takes place in a social context which influences its organisation, orientation, and sometimes even the content of knowledge. The results of research are fallible and revisable, but - as long as the methods of scientific inquiry are employed - they are constrained by what is *true* and what kind of *evidence* is available. The basic 'epistemic utilities' in the tentative acceptance of scientific hypotheses are such cognitive factors as truth, information, explanatory power, predictive power, accuracy, and simplicity (cf. Niiniluoto, 1984). Such criteria are relevant also in applied science (cf. Niiniluoto, 1993), which seeks instrumental knowledge that has practically significant applications and, hence, commercial value in the market.

The legitimate domain of technology policy is quite difference from that of science policy. Technology does not produce knowledge like science, but rather designs new artefacts, tools, and machines. They are not constrained by truth in the same way as knowledge claims, but by what is physically and economically *possible*. This makes technology 'value-laden' in a way which differs from science. Therefore, the criteria for the acceptance of technological products are different from the epistemic utilities in science. Commercial value in the market is one of such factors, in our society even the primary criterion for the innovation and diffusion stages in the life-cycle of artefacts. But it need not be the only relevant factor. This is basic issue of technology assessment.

4. Facts and values in technology assessment

Alex Michalos (1983) has argued that it is useless and even dangerous to appeal to a fact - value distinction in technology assessment. A deconstruction of such a distinction is also given by the constructivist approach. It denies the use of facts about artefacts as explanations of how they work: machines work because they have been chosen by relevant social groups (see Latour, 1987; Bijker, 1995; cf. Niiniluoto, 1997).

In my view, it is of utmost importance to make a clear distinction between the objective properties of an artefact and the value criteria in its assessment. For example, a car has a shape and colour, and its engine has efficiency measurable in horse powers. The behavior of the car (e.g., its ability to carry passengers, its maximum speed) is a function of these facts (see Sahal, 1987). To be sure, these properties are results of design, and in this sense depend on our decisions, but, when the car has been produced, they are as objective facts as the colour of a bird and the material constitution of a tree. In the same way, the 'technical norms' sought in applied research have a factual content about the relations between means and ends. The task of establishing facts about artefacts belongs to the scientific and technological experts.

The properties of artefacts make them *tools* which may have *instrumental value* relative to human purposes. Each technological artifact has an intended function, and its *effectiveness* or 'instrumental goodness' (cf. von Wright, 1963) depends on its ability to serve or fulfil this function. Intended functions are sometimes specific (e.g., spade), sometimes open-ended (e.g., computer). They may be culturally and historically relative: a tool may change when it is transferred to another social context or when it is placed into an exhibition in a museum.

By their effectiveness, technological tools open up new resources and possibilities of human action. Thereby they increase the domain of human *positive freedom*. Such increase of freedom may be a good or bad thing relative to human values. Such possibilities are created by utilizing some resources, and the use of tools has also often unintended and unwanted by-products and side effects. Besides the misuse of tools and their harmful effects on nature and society, such by-products include increased risks (see Shrader-Frechette, 1991). This suggests a straightforward utilitarian calculus of evaluating technological projects by their costs and benefits.

Each tool and the related novel possibility can be evaluated by several criteria. One of them is the monetary exchange value of the product, or its *economic* profit, which is the domain of economic theories (cf. Elster, 1983). This is the only criterion which is standardly applied, when technology is viewed as a part of the economic market. But effectiveness and economy are not the only dimensions of technology assessment. As products of design, artefacts have *esthetic* qualities, studied today in applied esthetics. The relations of tools to the health of their users is studied in *ergonomics*. The relations of human technologies to the health of natural environment are treated in *ecology*. Technology has also an impact which is *social* in the broad sense (legal, institutional, political). Further, technical tools and their effects can always be evaluated by *ethical* standards which concern their moral worth.

In the 1970s, several Western industrial countries developed systems of *Technology Assessment* (TA) for the evaluation of large-scale technological projects (cf. Durbin and Rapp, 1983). In the United States, the Office of Technology Assessment (OTA) was established in 1973 - and closed in the 1990s.

Technologists have sometimes misunderstood the nature of TA by believing that numerical indicators are always 'objective' and 'value-neutral'. They have also tended to ignore those dimensions that cannot be neatly quantified (see Shrader-

Frechette, 1983). The same problems are common in the use of numerical performance indicators of scientific progress: the numbers of exams and publications are easy to calculate, and questions about quality are easy to forget (see Niiniluoto, 1987). It is better to see such indicators as attempts to express and articulate values. There are specific issues in the 'measurement' of each dimension of assessment (such as esthetic or ethical value), and it is ultimately a value question as well to balance or weight the dimensions relative to each other. The situation is basically the same in science and technology, even though the relevant epistemic and technological utilities differ from each other.

In a democratic state, the citizens should have the right to decide how large percent of the GNP is spent on research and education, and whether public funds are allocated to military research or AIDS research. However, in matters concerning scientific quality and the scholarly significance of research, the scientific community should have autonomy in the society at large, and it should function as an expert system rather than a democracy. When a scientific project or publication is evaluated, the members of the scientific community do not vote about the issue, but the best expert in the field is asked to do the assessment. This is the basic idea of *peer review* in science.

Technological experts have also a special role in evaluating facts about technological constructs and rules, but their task is not to decide the value questions about the development of technological innovations. The decisionist strategy would lead to the libertarian market model of delegating decisions about the use of technological products to individual consumers. This populist idea in fact easily gives the power back to the technocrats, since human needs and hopes are constantly influenced and manipulated by marketing and advertising. Still, it may work well for some 'innocent' artefacts: when a rational person chooses his or her toothbrush, we have no reason to exercise paternalism over such a decision (see Häyry, 1991). And in some cases, market rationality may lead to socially desirable results, if the individuals have enlightened preferences (e.g., buy nonleaded gas or other 'eco-products').

But most commodities are not private affairs, as they may have harmful environmental and social effects. When it turns out that a deodorant affects the ozone layer, it becomes a dangerous tool. As Liisa Uusitalo (1986) has shown by applying game-theoretical models of 'free riding' to consumer behavior, what seems individually rational may lead to collectively irrational consequences - unless some moral or legal constraints on our actions are accepted. Most of us approve some restrictions on the selling of drugs and guns. (Unfortunately, Archie Bunker's logic still has some popularity: he suggested that, in order to prevent hijacking, every passenger should carry a gun in a plane!) Some decisions about large-scale technological developments are socially so important and difficult that they are handled in democratically elected boards. For example, in Finland the Parliament has made the decision about the freezing of the program of building of nuclear power plants.

Technologists should feel responsibility for the uses and effects of their inventions, and it is important that the engineers have agreed about codes of professional ethics. They should be ready to co-operate with other professions who have expertise in the different domains of valuations: medical doctors and psychologists in ergonomics, industrial designers and architects in esthetics, applied philosophers in ethics, sociologists and lawyers in the social studies, etc. These other professions should play an important role, when technology assessment is organized and administrated in a systematic way. But they in turn should be ready to work in co-operation with laymen, who are potential consumers of technological tools and methods. For example, consumer panels, including surgeons and women, have been used in the development of methods of treating breast cancer. In many issues about the quality of life, ordinary citizens are the best experts about their own attitudes and feelings.

Stanley Carpenter (1983) has argued that technology assessment as program is not sufficiently radical, since its own cost-benefit methods rely on technological and utilitarian ideas. He suggest that TA should be replaced by AT, i.e., Alternative Technology, advocated by 'green' environmentalist movements and proponents of 'appropriate', 'soft', and 'participatory' technology. I don't see that there is real contradiction between TA and AT. To promote democratic procedures in technology policy (see Shrader-Frechette, 1985), we need participation of many interest groups on several different levels. We need state and city councils, political organizations, international co-operation, legislation on the treatment of wastes in industrial production, bureaus protecting consumers for unfair commerce, self-reflection by technological professions, teaching of engineering ethics, public debate on environmental issues, value discussion about good life, and active citizens working in free groups and societies.

In brief, rational technology policy in a democratic state should be based upon co-operation between the public, private, and 'third' sectors. In this way, we might hope that technology would better redeem its promise to positively liberate human beings - in the terms of Macpherson (1983), not as Benthamite 'infinite consumers' and 'infinite appropriators' in the capitalist society, but as Millian 'exeters and enjoyers' of their own unique 'powers and capacities' in a liberal egalitarian democracy.

References

Airaksinen, T. (1994), *Arvojen yhteiskunta*, WSOY: Porvoo.

Airaksinen, T. (1995), 'The Virtuous Face of the Ethics of Science', in Garsparski and Airaksinen, pp. 13-26.

Bijker, W. E. (1995), *Of Bicycles, Bakelites, and Bulbs: Toward a Theory of Sociotechnical Change*, The MIT Press: Cambridge, MA.

Bijker, W.E. and Law, J. (1992), *Shaping Technology/ Building Society: Studies*

in Sociotechnical Change, The MIT Press: Cambridge, MA.
Buchanan, J.M. (1986), *Liberty, Market and the State: Political Economy in the 1980s*, Oxford University Press: Oxford.
Bugliarello, G. and Doner, D. B. (eds), (1979), *The History and Philosophy of Technology*, University of Illinois Press: Urbana.
Carpenter, S. (1983), 'Technoaxiology: Appropriate Norms for Technology Assessment', in Durbin and Rapp, pp. 115-36.
Cozzens, S. E. and Woodhouse, E. J. (1995), 'Science, Government, and the Politics of Knowledge', in Jasanoff *et al.*, pp. 533-53.
Durbin, P. and Rapp, F. (eds), (1983), *Philosophy and Technology*, D. Reidel: Dordrecht.
Ellul, J. (1964), *The Technological Society*, Alfred A. Knopf: New York.
Elster, J. (1983), *Explaining Technical Change*, Cambridge University Press: Cambridge.
Feinberg, J. (1971), *Social Philosophy*, Prentice Hall: Englewood Cliffs, NJ.
Gasparski, W. and Airaksinen, T. (eds), (1995), *Science in Society*, IFIS Publishers: Warsaw.
Habermas, J. (1970), *Toward a Rational Society*, Beacon Press: Boston.
Häyry, H. (1991), *The Limits of Medical Paternalism*, Routledge: London.
Hellsten, S. (1995), 'The Communitarian Approach to Science in Society', in Gasparski and Airaksinen, pp. 27-43.
Jasanoff, S.; Markle, G.E.; Petersen, J.C. and Pinch, T. (eds), (1995), *Handbook of Science and Technology Studies*, Sage: London.
Latour, B. (1987), *Science in Action*, Open University Press: Milton Keynes.
Loukola, O. (1995), 'On Libertarian Science Policy: Does Science Need Nurturing?', in Gasparski and Airaksinen, pp. 51-64.
Macpherson, C. B. (1983), 'Democratic Theory: Ontology and Technology', in C. Mitcham and R. Mackey (eds), *Philosophy and Technology*, The Free Press: New York, pp. 161-70.
Merton, R. S. (1973), *The Sociology of Science: Theoretical and Empirical Investigations*, The University of Chicago Press: Chicago.
Michalos, A. (1983), 'Technology Assessment, Facts and Values', in Durbin and Rapp: pp. 59-81.
Niiniluoto, I. (1984), *Is Science Progressive?*, D. Reidel: Dordrecht.
Niiniluoto, I. (1987), 'Can Evaluation Be Applied in Universities?', *Tiedepolitiikka* No. 3, pp. 11-8.
Niiniluoto, I. (1990), 'Should Technological Imperatives Be Obeyed?', *International Studies in the Philosophy of Science* 4, pp. 181-7.
Niiniluoto, I. (1993), 'The Aim and Structure of Applied Research', *Erkenntnis* 38, pp. 1-21.
Niiniluoto, I. (1994), 'Nature, Man, and Technology - Remarks on Sustainable Development', in L. Heininen (ed.), *The Changing Circumpolar North: Opportunities for Academic Development*, Arctic Centre Publications 6:

Rovaniemi, 1994, pp. 73-87.
Niiniluoto, I. (1995), 'Principles of Justice, Law, and Welfare Society', in E. Paasivirta and K. Rissanen (eds), *Principles of Justice and the Law of the European Union*, Publications of the Helsinki University Institute of International Economic Law: Helsinki, pp. 5-22.
Niiniluoto, I. (1997), 'Science vs. Technology: Difference or Identity?', in E. Kaukonen and Matti Sintonen (eds), *The Dynamics of Science and Technology*, The University of Tampere: forthcoming.
Nozick, R. (1974), *Anarchy, State and Utopia,* Basil Blackwell: Oxford and New York.
Nussbaum, M. and Sen, A. (eds), (1993), *The Quality of Life*, Oxford University Press: Oxford.
Rawls, J. (1971), *A Theory of Justice*, Harvard University Press: Cambridge, MA.
Sahal, D. (1987), *Patterns of Technological Innovation*, Addison - Wesley: Reading.
Shrader-Frechette, K. (1983), 'Technology Assessment and the Problem of Quantification', in Durbin and Rapp, pp. 151-64.
Shrader-Frechette, K. (1985), 'Technology Asseesment, Expert Disagreement and Democratic Procedures', in P. Durbin (ed.), *Research in Philosophy and Technology*, JAI Press: Greenwich, CT, pp. 103-29.
Shrader-Frechette, K. (1991), *Risk and Rationality: Philosophical Foundations for Populist Reforms*, University of California Press: Berkeley.
Skolimowski, H. (1981), *Eco-Philosophy*, Marion Bayars: Boston.
Toward an Innovative Society; A Development Strategy for Finland, Science and Technology Policy Council of Finland: Helsinki, 1993.
Uusitalo, L. (1986), *Environmental Impacts of Consumption Patterns*, Gover: Aldershot.
Winner, L. (1977), *Autonomous Technology*, The MIT Press: Cambridge, MA.
von Wright, G. H. (1963), *The Varieties of Goodness*, Routledge and Kegan Paul: London.
Ziman, J. (1994), *Prometheus Bound: Science in a Dynamic Steady State*, Cambridge University Press: Cambridge.

Technology, complexity, and social decision

Nicholas Rescher

(1) While technological innovation makes **particular** tasks easier to perform, its overall effect it to make life-as-a-whole more complicated. (2) For technical progress involves not only the generation of problem-solutions but also that of the problems themselves. And the rate of increase in problem complexity outpaces on that of solution complexity. (3) Coping with the complexity that comes in the wake of technological progress confronts us with the necessity of destabilizing leaps into the unknown. (4) This process militates towards decision quandaries and gridlock in social decision making. (5) The natural developmental dynamic of human technology (be it physical of intellectual) carries us out of our depths. It impels us into an area where the problem-field that confronts us may come to outrun the power of our cognitive capacities for problem resolution.

1. Technological progress makes life more complicated

We members of **Homo sapiens** are amphibious creatures: we inhabit two realms, the realm of nature and the realm of human artifice. The former domain is one where we **find** matters in place; the latter is a **construct** which we ourselves produce under the guidance of intelligence. But on both sides alike we encounter an unfathomable complexity. Nature has levels of depth extending beyond any point that our cognitive efforts can manage to attain, and human artifice also carries us ever further down the road of complexification.

Biological evolution under the aegis of natural selection makes for ever more specialized speciation, differentially selecting for those organisms who branch off towards a particular variety able to respond more effectively to the challenges of changing environmental conditions. Evolution accordingly makes for increasingly complex organisms.

And technological evolution has exactly the same tendency. In virtually every sphere of our human concerns we constantly encounter new obstacles. And new problems call for doing what we were unable to do before; they require new solutions which themselves call for new methods, new processes, new instrumentalities. Such escalating demands stimulate technical progress. We are driven to devising more complex systems that put increasing performative sophistication at our disposal. We here encounter the fundamental Law of Technical Progress: **Human artifice is caught up in a complexity tropism**. For reasons that are easy to understand because rational creatures are naturally inclined to try simpler solutions first, maintaining them until such time as it becomes advantageous to replace them. In consequence, all of our creative efforts—in material, social, and intellectual contexts alike—manifest a historical tendency moving from the simpler to the more complex.

We are generally inclined to think that technological progress makes life easier. It is faster and more convenient to cross oceans by plane than by sailing ship, to phone messages rather than mail letters, to type with word processors than write with quills. But while all this is true enough, there is the other side of the coin as well. Individual actions are generally simplified at the cost of complicating larger processes.[1] For not only does the gain in efficiency that technical progress brings in its wake provide us with more time to do things, but it also vastly increases the range of things that can be done and the intricacy of the means for their realization. The fact is that technological progress makes life vastly more complicated by widening the range of choice and opportunity, thereby increasing the operational complexity of process all about us. Technological progress helps in detail but always complicates matters in the large by posing new challenges to decision.

Anyone tempted to think that technology makes things simpler as it makes things better should compare a Ford Model-T with its contemporary successor. We pay for the advantages of sophisticated technology by confronting issues of operational choice and decision that are of ever increasing complexity. The complexities of information management and control in technologically sophisticated settings pose enormous demands. As technology advances, the problems of cognitive discrimination—just like those of visual discrimination—expand exponentially in line with the proliferation of possibilities.[2] And so, while technological progress—be it material or social—may indeed facilitate and ease the performance of particular tasks, its aggregated effect is to make large-scale processes more complicated.

New-gained technical capacity accordingly brings additional problems of management in its wake. Along the roadway of technological progress, ever more tracks branch off before us into different sections of the realm of possibility. More choices mean more decisions which require more information. Think, for example, of travel and communication, where modern resources mean that we become linked in an increasingly large and complex system of operation. With this increase, however, the problems of choice and decision become increasingly elaborate, with ever more choices to be made—and more switches to be thrown. Notoriously, one virtually has to be a rocket scientist to program one's VCR. A modern car has many thousands of parts, but a jet aircraft can have over four million and a space rocket over six million. Only technical experts can carry out repair or modifications: the era of string and sealing wax is over. And as regards operation, the same story holds. We are led inexorably into regions of greater operational difficulty.

In the course of scientific and technical progress, the management of complexity calls for ever greater sophistication, and thus in turn imposes problems of decision in the face of exploding information. The driver of a horse and buggy can afford to doze off, but the driver of a car can afford it far less, and the pilot of a supersonic fighter plane not at all. With more sophisticated camera equipment one will always need to make many more detailed decisions about locations the optimal perspectives from which to take a picture. And if we replace these human decision makers by automatic control devices, each must be many orders of magnitude more complex and sophisticated than its more rudimentary compeers. The problem of complexity management is now simply shifted from one of operating a system to one of managing the functioning of its cybernetic governance. The drug industry is subject to far more regulations today than the entire economy was fifty years ago. In combat, the pilot of a jet fighter makes for more operational decisions in five minutes than a sailing-era ships naval captain did in a day.[3]

But what of a 'return to the past'—a nostalgia-satisfying reversion to the conditions of an earlier, simpler age? The short answer is that this is simply impracticable outside the limited range of museum-piece environments in isolated backwaters. We would not have resorted to those complications in the first place if we had not been forced to them by the needs of the situation. In general, the price of a return is unaffordable.

To be sure this is a matter of how things stand in the large and in the whole. It is possible to preserve islands of simplicity in human affairs. But this is possible only in exceptional and highly localized conditions. Overall, the later position in the realm of artifice is bound to be one where complexity is unavoidable and uneliminable.

2. Problem complexity outpaces solution complexity

Of course, technology is not just part of the problem, it affords part of the solution as well. For while technological progress always poses new problems in the management of information and the control of operating procedures, it also of course helps with resolving issues of this sort. Safety engineering in all its forms—redundancy provision, fault detection sensors—together with the 'cybernetic' automation of control mechanisms, and above all the use of computers in information management and decision implementation, all afford powerful resources for problem resolution in technological contexts. Process controls too can be handled in substantial measure by technological means. Interestingly enough, the electronics in a contemporary automobile cost some two thousand dollars more than the steel used to produce the same car.

However, there yet remains the crucial issue of comparative pace. With technological progress, which grows the faster, the manifold of problems to be resolved or the reach and power of our instrumentalities of problem resolution? Now here it might seem that complex technology gives the advantage to problem resolution. After all, do not the cognitive resources that computers afford us offset the problems raised by increasing of complexity? Alas, not really.

First of all, it has to be recognized that computers help principally with information **processing** and do not equally address the problems information **acquisition**. And in the course of technological progress these become even more extensive and even more significant. Here the classic dictum holds good: as far as the efficacy of computational resources is concerned, garbage in, garbage out. Moreover, the fact remains that computers do just exactly what they are programmed to do. The level of complexity management they are able to achieve is determined through—and thus limited by—the levels of ingenuity and conceptual adequacy of their programming. No central bank places unalloyed confidence in its economic models. Then, too, there is the problem of unforeseen and unforeseeable interactions within the intricacies of the operating processes of computer functioning. These 'bugs' can result in malfunctions in computer operation even as they can produce accidents in other sorts of systems. And the more elaborate and complex our programs get—particularly in areas where novelty and innovation are the order of the day—the larger the prospect and chances for such mishaps. Maiden voyages are notoriously fertile in bringing unanticipated difficulties to light.

The fact is that as technical systems become more complex, their operation becomes even more so. And over time managerial complexity generally outpaces the growth of functional sophistication. For added complexity always imposes new difficulty in matters of process and procedure. And, as already noted in the preceding chapter, process concatenations always grow at a rate faster than the processes themselves.

Granted, computer automated problem solving is one of the wonders of the age. Computers fly planes, land rocket modules on the moon, win chess tournaments, develop mathematical proofs. All the same, we have to come face to face here with what might be called a **Hydra effect** after the mythological monster who managed to grow several heads to take the place for each one that was cut off. The fact is that there is a feedback symbiosis between problems and solutions which operates in such a way that the growth of the former systematically outpaces that of the latter. Accordingly, those sophisticated information and control technologies not so much resolve problems of complexity as enlarge this domain by engendering complexity problems of their own. Despite the enormous advantages that they furnish to intellectual efforts at complexity management, computers nevertheless do not and can not eliminate but only displace and magnify the difficulties that we encounter throughout this sphere.

Such a Hydra effect is closely related to the Principle of Question Propagation in matters of factual inquiry. The phenomenon of the ever-continuing 'birth' of new questions was first emphasized by Immanuel Kant, who maintained that: 'The solution of any factual (scientific) question gives rise to yet further unsolved questions'.[4] This opening up of new and deeper questions in the course of our inquiries into matters of empirical fact is a phenomenon that is empirically as well established as any encountered within our study of nature herself. Insofar as the history of science has any lessons to teach us, it forcefully substantiates this principle of question-proliferation in empirical inquiry. And it deserves emphasis that this circumstance of escalating diversity and complexity holds just as much for **practical** as for **cognitive** problems.

The long and short of it is that complexity management via computers will not remove the obstacles to managerial effectiveness exactly because the problems of complexity grow faster than do the means for their solution. Computers—the very instruments that enhance our capacity for complexity management—widen the scope of the field of action and thereby augment the complexity we face. The technical resources that enlarge our powers in the area of problem resolution not only do not manage to **reduce** the overall size of the problem field that confronts us, but actually manage to **enlarge** it. Technological progress engenders what might be characterized as the 'rolling snowball effect' because complexity breeds more complexity through engendering problem-situations from which only additional technical capacity can manage to extract us.

With the progress of science, technology, and human artifice generally, complexity is self-potentiating because it engenders complications on the side of problems that can only be addressed adequately through further complication on the side of process and procedure. The increase in technical sophistication confronts us with a dynamic feedback interaction between problems and solutions that ultimately transforms each successive solution into a generator of new problems. And these feedback effects operate in such a way that to all intents and purposes the growth rate of the problem domain continually outpaces that of our capacity to produce solutions. Both our problems and our solutions grow more complex in the wake of technological progress, but the crux of the matter lies in the comparatively greater pace of the increase in problem complexity.

The gigantism of the managerial machinery of the contemporary city or industrial enterprise or university is thus no accident. Designed for greater control over more complex problems, the administrative machine of such organizations is left ever further behind in point of performative efficacy. As the functional capacity of such institutions expands under the pressure of technological progress, the scope of management operations expands explosively. With the modern technology of communication and information management, bureaucracy is thus bound to increase irrespective of the particular operational tasks for whose management the bureaucracy is instituted.[5]

3. The intimidating impetus of the unknown: risk and destabilization

The growing complexity that emerges in the wake of technical progress always engenders unexpected difficulties. And with every step that we take towards coping with these difficulties, unforeseeable consequences generally arise. All along the line, the Law of Unintended Effects comes into operation. As technical sophistication increases, we penetrate ever further into a domain where we cannot see clearly along the road that lies ahead. We continually confront problem situations within which we not only cannot determine **optimal** solutions, but where even the identification of **desirable** solutions becomes problematic and imponderable.

This phenomenon is distinctly threatening. **Physical chaos**, it will be recalled, occurs when a system functions in so volatile a way that a minute difference in its initial condition—a difference so small as to lie beneath the threshold of observation and perhaps even of observability—can make for a vast difference for the state that ensues. **Cognitive chaos** is exactly the same sort of thing transposed to the region of information processing. It occurs whenever a minute variation in input information can produce great difference in its inferential consequences—that is, whenever an inferential outcome is enormously sensitive to small variations on informational input. The prospect of subjecting such processes to adequate cognitive control by way of principled understanding are somewhere between small and nonexistent. And it is just here that complexity makes itself felt.

As systems grow increasingly complex, they become more difficult to control, both intellectually and physically. The prospect of insufficient or misleading information grows along with system complexity and, other things equal, sophisticated systems need to have more elaborate processes. Prediction too becomes less practicable, save at the level of statistical indefiniteness. The activities of a primitive tribe are easier to predict than those of the U.S. Congress; extra-heavy atoms are less stable than extra-light ones; strategy is easier to manage with tic-tac-toe than with chess. Screws are more complex than nails, but thereby more limited. They do a better job at holding things together, but are less versatile (all sorts of things can be nailed together while screws require a porous material like wood). The general structure of the situation is depicted in Display 1. Simple systems are more versatile are flexible but less effective and efficient; complex systems are more specialized but less adaptable. Complex systems pay for greater efficiency and effectiveness through being more specialized, more closely attuned to the circumstantial specifics of the case. They are, accordingly, easier to destabilize—more vulnerable to the interventions of chaos.

Display 1: The tension between efficiency and versatility in systems control instrumentalities

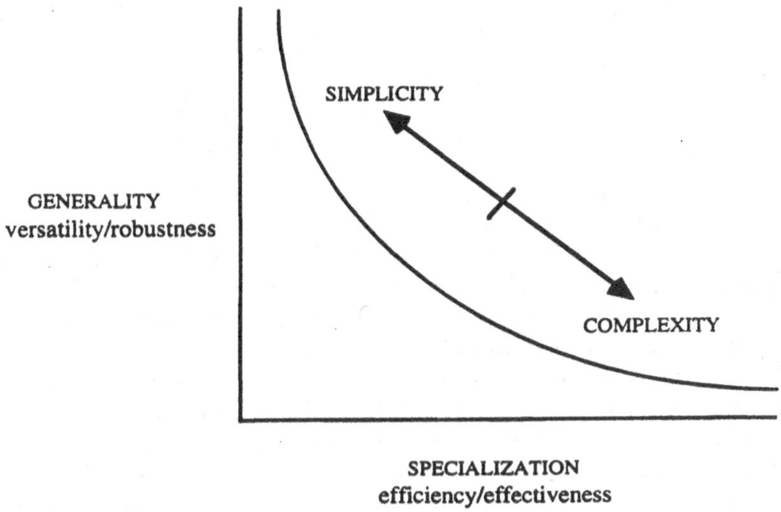

Note: The consideration that the generality (G) and specialization (S) of goal-directed systems stand in an essentially inverse relationship to one another ($G \approx 1/S$) means that the curve in question is in effect an equilateral hyperbola: $G \times S \approx$ const. We achieve increases in the one parameter at the cost of corresponding decreases in the other.

As the operations of a goal-directed system of any sort become more complex, there increasingly comes to the fore the importance of safety engineering — of devising contrivances that protect against potential for failure that is an inevitable accompaniment of increasing complexity. To be sure, part of that growing complexity may be invested in safety assurance—in building malfunction controls into the system operations and proliferating back-ups and redundancies. But problems are inevitable in this domain as well. The prospect of things going wrong will always slip 'through the cracks', and complex systems for this very reason grow increasingly error-prone and susceptible to malfunction understanding is somewhere between small and nonexistent. And it is just here that complexity makes itself felt.

The results of this situation are not difficult to discern. Increasingly complex systems pose ever greater prospects of mishap. Complex systems are inherently less amenable to successful comprehension, management, and control. It is evident that where double the number of steps must go right in a goal-pursuing context, we double the prospects of somethings going wrong, other things being equal.

Complexity generally enlarges the prospect of system failure—and where not in frequency, there in magnitude of effect. A washing machine can malfunction far more readily than a wash board—and with more extensive consequences. There is no clearer indication of the vulnerability that complexity engenders than the extent to which a single act of sabotage by a terrorist, or of dishonesty by a greedy or disgruntled employee, can inflict destructive damage on a large enterprise or an extensive organization.

Evolutionary biologists have insisted that organisms achieve their development at a price—that as the process of natural selection and adaptation ties a creature ever more firmly to the conditions of its environmental niche there comes an ever-increasing complexity. More 'highly developed' creatures thus pay for this status by becoming more complex, and this in turn creates a line of adaptability that renders them increasingly vulnerable. More primitive species—say viruses in comparison with humans—are vastly more adaptable and thereby far less at risk under environmental change. And this principle that complexity makes for vulnerability is clearly not confined to the biological domain.

Risk is a natural companion to complexity. It makes the (multiplicative) combination of two factors: the probability of failure and the magnitude of the consequences should failure occur. Increasing complexity generally enlarges risk. It does so not necessarily by increasing the probability of failure but by increasing the negative consequences should failure occur. (Precisely when particularly [risk] of failure is diminished we tend to increase our stake on success.) Increasing complexity thus tend to be associated with increasing risk.[6]

Our individual activity—say getting from home to work—is undoubtedly simplified by the technology of the automobile in contrast with that of the horse. But the entire system of automotive transport is something vastly more complex, penetrating pervasively into every aspect of our social and economic life. Local simplicity rides on the back of globally systemic complexity. The present day motor vehicle code of U.S. states is more complex than the whole of their transport legislation in the 1890s. And no American who has lived through the months of the Arab Oil Embargo can fail to realize the magnitude and power of the vulnerabilities to which such systemic complexification renders us subject.

This state of things engenders inevitable threats and dangers. Specifically, with the ongoing sophistication of human artifice we find that:

- with **cognitive** systems we face the threat of disintegration, disorganization, and cognitive dissonance.
- with **technical** systems we face the threat of breakdown and malfunction.
- with **social** systems we face the threat of gridlock and stalemate or—at the opposite extreme—of chaos and anarchy.

Throughout the domain of human creativity—alike in matters of cognitive, technological, and social engineering—we encounter an increasing complexity that carries with it the inherent risks of system malfunction.

The basic point that is at issue here is relatively straightforward. It is that in general and as a rule complex systems are by reason of their very complexity more expensive and more difficult to constrict, operate, and maintain. And they are also more risky to use—not necessarily by way of an increased likelihood of malfunction but rather through the increased seriousness of the consequences that ensue when a malfunction occurs. In sum, the increased complexity of our systems does not come cost-free; to achieve its undoubted advantages we have to pay a substantial price.

4. Concretization quandaries and decision gridlock

At the earlier, less sophisticated stages of technological progress, it was easier for people to understand the implications of change. For when changes occur in highly complex systems there is bound to be an obscurity of consequences. It becomes somewhere between difficult and impossible to say in advance just what the result of modifications and innovations will be. We all too frequently cannot see our way clearly through the accompanying ramifications to grasp the implications of innovation for their management. For effective decision making requires the timely processing of full information. And both of these factors —acquiring and processing information— tend to be more difficult and cumbersome in contexts of complexity. And the more complex the ramifications of a choice situation are, the more likely it is that any particular way of resolving it will be worrisome to some of the individuals or groups who have a stake in its outcome. Few of us have the engineering sophistication to be rocket scientists. But, effectively none of us today have the technical sophistication to be social engineers. And there is a real possibility that even all of us taken collectively do not have what it takes.

In particular, the measures that are required to cope with matters of social and economic policy become increasingly complicated and constantly more expensive to implement and difficult to operate. The complexities that have to be taken account of outrun the grasp of ordinary understanding. (Think, for example, of Hilary Clinton's health care program, not to speak of the Federal Tax Code.) The management of America's systems in the area medical or social or economic processes and programs has grown so difficult throughout the successive decades of the present century that the political system is nowadays close to throwing up its hands in frustration.

And so the very power of technical progress leads it to carry new disabilities and incapacities in its wake. The operational dynamics of complexity expansion means that as we increase our problem-resolving capacity we will inevitably —with the best will in the world— increasingly loose our grip on the overall effectiveness of problem control. In fact, none of us can form an accurate picture of how proposed changes of process and procedure in the management of complexity will work themselves out —both for the society at large, and for themselves and those in whom they take an interest. And even where we ourselves think that we can see the way clear, there will be precious few others who agree with us.

This state of affairs manifests itself in a striking and by now familiar phenomenon that might be called the **cacophony of experts**. The difficulties of rational problem solution in complex situations engenders a variety of plausible but competingly alternative possibilities. And in the absence of a single clean-cut resolution a dissonance of theories arise. Pundits come upon the scene with their competing wares—each with a case that seems plausible and persuasive but is nevertheless insufficiently clear-cut and decisive to drive its opponents from the field. The destabilizing effect of technological change thus paves the way to social discord and procedural impotence. Here sheer stagnation is the natural result of risk-aversive 'better the devil we know' thinking. All too often, life in our imperfect world proceeds in such a way that to all appearances certain abstractly desirable aims simply cannot be concretely realized by acceptable means. Let us inspect the ramifications of this process a bit more closely.

As noted above, technological progress increasingly complicates the processes of social choice and decision. In an environment of increasing technological complexity we must develop ever more sophisticated control processes to address new problems. Such changes affect different people, different groups, different constituencies differently. And just here the eventual effects of the measures we take to address the challenges become lost in a fog of impredictability. For every winner there are some losers and various others who—not being able to see the way clear—come to feel threatened. When people confront more complex problems they find it difficult and sometimes impossible, to think their way through to satisfactory solutions. Everyone feels put to risk by some aspect of the ill understood consequence flow of potential innovation. And in the face of this perplexity, people become fearful lest any step away from the status quo—unhappy though the existing state of things may be—will plunge them into disaster.

This sort of situation is an open invitation to gridlock.

What might be called a **concretization quandary** arises when it is—abstractly considered—a good idea to do **A** and the only way to do so concretely is by doing **A1** or **A2** or **A3** (etc.), while nevertheless doing each of these alternative **Ai** is a bad idea. In such situations there is no concrete way of realizing a generically desirable objective. A certain act that is generically positive can nevertheless be accomplished only in various particular ways each of which is something that is—individually—something negative.

Think here of the story of the princess whose father is a kingly ogre who will release her from his paternal thralldom only on the condition of her marrying the princeling of some neighboring kingdom. But it turns out that all of the available princelings are quite ineligible: one is too ugly, another too stupid, a third too loutish, and the like. For the princess, marriage is seemingly a good idea. Yet each of the actually available alternatives for achieving this otherwise desirable objective is unsuitable and unacceptable. Or again, consider the plight of the younger son of an impoverished aristocrat. He finds himself so situated that taking up an appropriate career is somewhere between eminently desirable and absolutely necessary. But each of the specifically available alternatives is infeasible: he is too cowardly for the army, too hydrophobic for the navy, too skeptical for the church, and so on.

The schematic structure of such concretization quandary situations is clear. The circumstance that now arises is that while realizing **A** is desirable in the abstract, it nevertheless remains false that any and every **particular** **A**-realization is in itself something desirable. Those who face such a quandary situation are emplaced in the unhappy position where a certain end, absolutely viewed, looks good—but only as long as one ignores the problematic details of its concrete actualizatiality. There is simply no acceptable way to get there from here.

Desiderata as such are, after all, nothing more than mere abstract wishes—mere indefinite wants: 'Would that the circumstance **A** were realized'. But effective means to their realization require concreteness: some certain **particular** way for that abstract desideratum to be concretely realized. An abstraction may be acceptable to and even desirable for us while nevertheless we shrink from each and every one of the concrete states that would bring it to realization in the actually prevailing circumstances. For it is evident that in adopting an end **we do not** and need not necessarily endorse any one of the particular means available for its realization. (Recall W. W. Jacob's classic short story, 'The Monkey's Paw.') In inauspicious circumstances it can, unfortunately, happen that the cultivation of what is, in and of itself, a perfectly proper desideratum may—in the prevailing circumstances—saddle us with collateral negativities. With such a concretization quandary, there just is no acceptable concretization for that deserved end. Here the apparently best course may well be to leave well enough alone. The princess might end up staying home single with Daddy Ogre.

It is easy to see how concretization quandaries impact upon the workings of democracy in the context of the voting process. For situations frequently arise when policy making reaches a stage where even though a social program or public work is generally acknowledged as something that is abstractly (or generically) desirable and desired, yet nevertheless each and every one of the concrete ways of realizing it is deemed unacceptable. Downsizing the market in illegal drugs, keeping teenage girls out of maternity wards or reducing the exploding public expenditures for medical services, are only a few examples of this. Here on the question of achieving a result **R**-somehow vs. maintaining not-**R**, a decided majority is in favor of **R**. But equally, each and every one of the concrete ways of realizing **R** is opposed by a comparable majority. This sort of situation is something often encountered in the political arena, where we frequently read in the press stories of the following tendency:

> When asked what Congress should do about the federal deficit, two-thirds of the

voters preferred cuts in major spending programs, but this support for spending cuts dissipated whenever it came to specific programs, with two-thirds of the voters opposed to each of the specific ways of achieving these cuts.

Despite an accepted 'Sense of the Congress' resolution, no implementing decision can manage to gain Congressional approval. In such a situation, society confronts a concretization quandary: there simply is no majoritatively acceptable way of reaching a majoritatively accepted goal.

5. A retrospective reflection

The chapter's deliberations have revolved around four significantly problematic issues:

- complexity escalation
- obscurity of consequences and cognitive chaos
- concretization quandaries
- decision gridlock and immobilization

This condition of affairs obviously has substantial and significant implications for the general polity of social decision. In particular, it brings to the fore the question of how a sensible society can proceed in the face of technological progress that impels us into a sphere where the problem-field that confronts us may come to outrun the power of our cognitive capacities for problem resolution.

And this situation seems to obtain on the basis of general principles. For the instruments we forge for the solution of our problems—intellectual and physical—all prove effective only up to a point. And as new problems arise they will require new resources, new methods and devices. But, in the natural evolution of things the creation of ever new and more powerful instruments becomes increasingly difficult. And there is every reason to think that eventually—in the long run of things—the hurdle will be raised to a height that we simply cannot leap. Our standard resource of problem-solving—the use of process-modelling intelligence—may come to prove unavailing. A point may—and potentially will—be reached where the familiar role of modeling and calculation will no longer prove adequate as a problem resolving instrumentality.

Earlier in the present century, the Austrian school of economists argued that the domain of economic phenomena is inherently of so intricate and sophisticated a nature that such theorizing as it is practicable for us to manage really cannot provide an adequate grasp on the phenomena—and certainly not one powerful enough to guide our interventions in establishing effective control. Human phenomena are inherently so complex, volatile, and variegated that the project of capturing them within the confining boundaries of universal laws is unrealizable.

The complexity of the system of social processes at work in the operations of an advanced modern economy is such that there simply is no way for us to calculate the behavior of the system. No model that we devise will be adequate to the details. As they saw it, the very idea of a social science of human behavior is a pipe dream.[7]

We come here to the 'bounded rationality' arising in decision situations when the complexity of a problem-situation substantially exceeds the reasoning powers of the problem-solver. And here, often as not the best strategy is often as not to let 'matters run their course' and use the observation of its processes as a guide for the formation of our policies and programs. Where calculation based on theory is impracticable, the best we can usually do is to observe broad tendencies and let the course of experience be our guide.

A strong case thus obtains for saying that this sort of situation holds not just in economics but far more broadly throughout the social domain. For here too there are, fortunately, other ways of solving problems then by 'figuring it out' through human artifice and calculation. One of these is to leave the solution of the problem to 'the course of events' (either in nature or in a simulation-model of some sort) and then simply sit back and watch what happens. Where the calculations become too complicated for us, such a recourse to the practice of 'watchful waiting,' of examining how the matters work themselves out when left to their own devices, is a variant and sometimes highly useful cognitive resource. In situations of near-impenetrable complexity, our practice in matters of public policy will generally be guided far more effectively by localized experimental trial and observation than by the theorizing resources of intellectual technology.

Notes

1. In such cases enhanced performance is acquired at the cost of elongated training. Technological progress constantly destabilizes the status quo and brings changed processes and procedures in its wake. Obsolescence of devices, procedures, and skills is the price we inevitably pay for enhanced technological sophistication.
2. For a good survey of the issues see Mainzer, 1994.
3. On complexity in relation to social and political issues, see Kohl, 1965.
4. Kant, 1783, sect. 57.
5. Think here of Parkinson's Law as discussed in Parkinson, 1957.
6. For a variety of vivid illustrations see Perrow, 1984.
7. See Popper, 1965; Hayek, 1967, pp. 22-420; Hayek, 1979. On these issues see Rosenberg, 1988.

References

Hayek, F. A. (1967), 'The Theory of Complex Phenomena' in *Studies in Philosophy, Politics and Economics*, Routledge & Kegan Paul: London

Hayek, F. A. (1979), *The Counter-Revolution of Science: Studies on the Abuse of Reasons*, 2nd. edition, The Free Press: Indianapolis, IN.

Kant, I. (1783), *Prolegomena to any Future Metaphysic.*

Kohl, H. R. (1965), *The Age of Complexity*, New American Library: New York.

Mainzer, K. (1994) *Thinking in Complexity: The Complex Dynamics of Matter, Mind, and Mankind*, Springer Verlag: Berlin, etc.

Parkinson, C. N. (1957), *Parkinson's Law*, Houghton Mifflin: Boston.

Perrow, C. (1984), *Normal Accidents Living with High-Risk Technologies*, Basic Books: New York.

Popper, K. R. (1965), *Conjectures and Refutations: The Growth of Scientific Knowledge*, Harper Torchbooks: New York.

Rosenberg, A. (1988), *Philosophy of the Sound Sciences*, Westview Press: New York; 2nd edition, 1995.

3. BEYOND GOOD AND EVIL: NEUTRALITY, TOLERANCE AND INDIVIDUAL MORALITY

Truth and toleration

Jonathan L. Gorman

The spirit of toleration

The theme of the XIXth World Congress of Philosophy held in Moscow in 1993 was 'Mankind at a turning point: philosophical perspectives'. Many there called for a spirit of toleration, and indeed UNESCO provided a set of working papers on the concept.[1] Toleration is a central notion of the liberal tradition. It is internationally recognised as a fundamental value, of a similar status to the corpus of human rights. Yet the concept was little better understood after the World Congress than it was before. It seems plain that toleration must have limits, but it also seems that it cannot have limits. Further analysis readily yields paradoxes, and these familiar points suggest that the problems lie at the foundations of our philosophical understanding. In this essay I propose to contribute to the clarification of these foundations.

Narratives

My own approach to philosophical understanding is as an analytical philosopher, but there are limits to this approach, and some twenty-five years ago I came to believe that those limits displayed themselves most clearly in the philosophy of history. Reflection led me to the view that a full epistemological understanding should include an analysis of historical accounts. Such accounts typically take the form of narrative stories. One of the difficulties involved the preparation of examples, and for an article on objectivity and truth I developed the following two brief passages (A) and (B), each purporting to present a brief outline of the life of William Joyce, known as 'Lord Haw-Haw'.[2] It is an epistemology expressing the understanding stimulated by these passages which will provide insight into the nature of toleration.

(A) Joyce was born in Ireland, according to the application for a British passport made by him in 1933. He became a Fascist, for whom Sir Oswald Mosley, the 'Bleeder', was too moderate. In August 1939, a few days before the outbreak of hostilities, he went to Germany and offered his services to the German ministry of propaganda. He was the Germans's principal English broadcaster (known as 'Lord Haw-Haw' from his manner of speaking). He was executed as a traitor.

(B) Joyce was born in New York. His father was a naturalized American citizen. Joyce never made a formal request for British nationality, though he spent most of his life in England and was regarded as patriotic. In September 1940 he became a naturalized German. Joyce attracted to himself the mythical repute of Lord Haw-Haw. These legends were the manufacture of war-nerves. He was executed as a traitor.

Every sentence in each of these accounts is true. These accounts were constructed avoiding false implications, false conversational implicatures and inappropriate or evaluative rhetoric, and were constructed so that every sentence in them was independently warranted on the basis of the best evidence. Various grounds of epistemological assessment were argued through at length. Such difficulties as may remain were shown to be trivial. It is not the place to present again here the arguments in what came to be a whole book of detail.[3] The main feature of the construction, however, was that these passages were the last of a series of different selections of sentences. Sentences were, in an analytical way, supposed to carry their meaning with them independently of context, so that the cognitive content of each sentence would not vary merely because it was embedded in different contexts. But the series of varying selections of true sentences showed this supposition to be hopelessly implausible. Briefly, the essential point to note is that these two sparingly constructed stories (A) and (B) are incompatible with each other, in that the former is roughly anti-Joyce - it makes the understanding of his execution as a traitor follow in some natural way from what else is said - while the latter is roughly pro-Joyce, and the fact of his execution seems glaringly inappropriate: in the light of the outcome the story is as it stands comparatively unfollowable.

The analytical approach

In his paper 'The method of truth in metaphysics', Donald Davidson expresses in summary form a familiar position of analytical philosophy: that the truth conditions of a sentence be given using only the conceptual resources of that sentence: 'What a theory of truth does for a natural language is reveal structure. In treating each sentence as composed in accountable ways out of a finite number of truth-relevant words, it articulates this structure'.[4] His, and others', task has been to express with clarity the relationships between meaning and truth in the light of this roughly expressed proposal.

What counts as a sentence, for Davidson? In passing he proposes and considers a rule for the word 'true', a rule which begins 'A sentence consisting of a singular term followed by a one-place predicate is true if and only if...'.[5] The rest of the rule is not required. The first half of the rule is enough to exemplify the point that a sentence is typically understood by an analytical philosopher to be short. Analytical philosophers once thought that the vehicle of literal meaning was the word, and now we typically think that it is the sentence; but when we think of sentences we tend to think of them one at a time, and the shorter the better. We know that this approach is not intended to be limited to the kind of sentence mentioned in the rule. Analytical philosophers know that not every meaningful linguistic entity consists of a singular term followed by a one-place predicate. Even grammatically simple sentences are typically more complex than this. But, like Davidson, even when we think we are expressing positions supportive of a philosophical holism, we commonly assume a kind of semantic atomism, in terms of which complex sentences are no more than the sum of their simpler constituent sentences, so that any theoretical understanding of the simple parts will yield a theoretical understanding of the complex whole. It is therefore at the simple level that we typically seek our understanding of meaning and truth. I shall refer to this as the 'analytical approach'.

Stories are longer than simple sentences. It is easy for a grammarian, if not a logician, to distinguish the constituent sentences of a story from each other and also from the story as a whole. Typically a full stop is sufficient to mark the separation. It is regrettable that the full stop has not been, so far as I know, adequately semantically analysed, for I think it important; but I shall leave that aside. While it may be logically standard to treat a story as if it were a conjunction of sentences or even itself one long complex sentence, I shall not speak here as if this were so. I shall generally think of a constituent sentence as limited by a full stop and outside the story context I shall refer to such a sentence as an atomic sentence, although here the word 'atomic' is not used with the exactness a logician would normally give to that. The essence of an atomic sentence is that it is typically short, but I shall say no more about size here either. The distinction between a story and a constituent sentence of the story I take here to be a matter of primitive recognition of meaning.

There are simplistic truth-functional ways in which the analytical approach can be developed. However, Davidson's approach to the meaning of what might be called 'richer' sentences - and he would not regard a sentence, I think, as necessarily ending at the next full stop - is not limited to any mechanically permitted expansion. One of his many theses in the philosophy of truth and interpretation, for example, concerns metaphor, and the thesis is that 'metaphors mean what the words, in their most literal interpretation, mean, and nothing more'.[6] Briefly, his approach depends 'on the distinction between what words mean and what they are used to do. I think', he says, 'metaphor belongs exclusively to the domain of use'.[7] It is clear that we are to understand 'the domain of use' as unhelpful in any serious attempt to make sense of meaning and truth. It is a domain of no relevant cognitive content and of no relevant epistemological or metaphysical interest. Davidson says, 'Literal meaning and literal truth conditions can be assigned to words and sentences apart from particular contexts of use. This is why adverting to them has genuine explanatory power'.[8]

None of this has sufficient genuine explanatory power to make sense of stories. It is plausible to suppose that Davidson would regard every constituent sentence of a story as in principle fully philosophically explicable in terms of his approach, and would regard anything beyond the 'literal' constituent sentences such as the story itself as, like metaphor, best relegated to the domain of 'use'. This analytical approach denies 'meaning as a whole' to stories.

Holistic meaning

I propose to take for granted that which I believe plausible, that stories have a meaning as a whole which is more than, or at least other than, the sum of the meanings of the constituent sentences. You might, if committed to an analytical approach, charitably assume that I am speaking loosely, that my referring to 'meaning' at the level of a whole story is just a manner of speaking. You might think that story-meaning is like metaphor in that it does not involve a distinctive proper or relevant sense of meaning or reference to truth-conditions, and that it is easily defined away in just the way Davidson does with metaphor. Yet the essence of my position is not the bare claim that stories can have meaning as a whole. It is the claim that stories can conflict, as we have seen above with the Joyce examples. Stories have meaning as a whole because they can conflict as a whole. It is important to recall the nature of this conflict.

Consider for a moment atomic sentences. Two particular atomic sentences can conflict. There are two ways in which they can conflict. First, we may assume the conflict to be at the level of the literal in Davidson's sense of this, and in assuming this we would be assuming the sentences to be inconsistent. Second, the sentences might conflict in terms of what he has called the 'domain of use'. Davidson exemplifies the 'domain of use' of sentences by remarking that a sentence might be effective in 'praise and abuse, prayer and promotion, description and prescription'.[9] Such effectiveness is not to the epistemological point according to his understanding of meaning and truth. Using this notion, there is no cognitive contrast to be drawn between one particular atomic sentence and another merely because the first is 'effective' in some context while the second has a conflicting 'effect' in the same context. Similarly, there is nothing of epistemological note in the fact that some particular atomic sentence may have one effect in one context and a conflicting effect in a different context. Nobody would suggest ambiguity or variation in literal meaning or truth here. In summary, atomic sentences which conflict in the domain of use do not, in virtue of that alone, conflict in meaning or truth.

Yet how do stories conflict? One sense in which two stories can conflict is that each contains a sentence which is inconsistent with some sentence in the other story. But this is not of present interest, for the Joyce examples (A) and (B) above show that stories can conflict even when there is no conflict at the level of their constituent sentences. Nor is the story-conflict to be understood in terms of conflicting conceptual schemes. Different stories can have many sentences in common, and it is important to note that the meaning of these sentences does not necessarily vary with their context, although it can do so. Furthermore sentence-inconsistency is always possible in the case of conflicting stories and this in itself requires a shared or at least overlapping conceptual scheme. Yet even when fully consistent at the level of the constituent sentences as the (A) and (B) examples have been argued elsewhere to be, stories can still conflict, and that conflict is not a conflict in the 'domain of use', for those stories are in an important sense about the same thing and conflict about this. This is a holistic conflict in both meaning and truth in a situation where there is no contrast in the meaning or truth of the constituent atomic sentences considered severally, and it is this which forces the conflict of stories to our epistemological attention. There is meaning as a whole because there is conflict as a whole, and the conflict is in virtue of two stories being about the same thing.

Conflict of stories presupposes that they are about the same thing and is therefore not a conflict in the 'domain of use' but a conflict in meaning understood as associated with some kind of truth-condition, a truth-condition analogous to, although not identical with, the truth-conditions we might seek for atomic sentences. In the case of conflicting stories we therefore have alternative conflicting expressions of reality. I use the term 'expressions of reality' here with deliberate vagueness, for I wish to beg no presently irrelevant questions about whether reality is or is not to be understood as independent of the linguistic presentation.

Should we treat conflict between stories as analogous to inconsistency between sentences? If we adopt a classical approach to sentences and apply it to stories, then we will say that there is some conception of inconsistency analogous to but distinct from classical inconsistency in terms of which conflicting stories are inconsistent stories; that there is some conception of truth and falsity analogous to but distinct from classical sentence-truth or sentence-falsity in terms of which inconsistent stories cannot both be true; and we will insist on rejecting stories which are false in this way as failing to be expressions of reality.

Determinacy and indeterminacy

Do we have to adopt a classical approach to sentences? If we do, do we have to adopt an analogous approach to stories? What are the limits of choice here?

Here is Marysia Zalewski presenting postmodernism:

> Postmodernists share one common enemy - the Enlightenment - because of its philosophical assumptions about, for example, the self, knowledge, reality, language and truth. Postmodernists reject the idea that there is a real world out there waiting to be discovered. Knowledge and reality are social constructs and any attempt to discipline the world into a homogeneous intellectual straitjacket is both futile and a reflection of power structures which will continue to define and legitimate what is 'best' and 'right'. Postmodernists rightly deserve the label of 'deconstructionists' since they want to make us think about, and reconsider all we take for granted concerning, the priority of the self and the creation of knowledge, power, truth and reality. Postmodernists revel in denying privilege (for example, to the architect, the philosopher, the author, the composer) and wish to delegitimize and move away from subject-centred enquiry. Rather than searching for coherent epistemologies, postmodernists instead engage in rhetoric and conversation and see themselves occupied with tactical manoeuvrings to disrupt the cosy complacency of confined academia. Contradiction, difference and plurality are accepted and welcomed. Philosophy is a key 'gremlin' in the postmodernist camp specifically in its guise as legitimator and final arbiter of 'truth'. As such, philosophy merely serves to legitimize and maintain the status quo. There is not 'one' truth waiting to be discovered (by philosophers) only vacillating beliefs and opinions.[10]

Here is another expression of postmodern attitude in a philosophically more neutral tone, which comes from Barbara Hernstein Smith: the postmodern attitude is " a general conceptual style or taste, specifically played out here as (a) a conceptualization of the world as continuously changing, irreducibly various, and multiply configurable, (b) a corresponding tendency to find cognitively distasteful, unsatisfying, or counterintuitive any conception of the world as fixed and integral and/or as having objectively determinable properties, and (c) a corresponding disinclination or inability to use terms such as 'reality', 'truth', 'meaning', 'reason', or 'value', as glossed by... objectivist conceptions".[11]

There is little new for philosophers in postmodernism as a philosophical position. In a recent study of R.G. Collingwood, William Dray notes that, "In his Essay on Philosophical Method, Collingwood called upon philosophers 'to avoid the technical vocabulary proper to science', and to choose their words 'according to the rules of literature', the hall-marks of a literary rather than scientific style being expressiveness, flexibility, and dependence upon context (EPM, 207)".[12] Humpty Dumpty thought that words meant what he wanted them to mean, and disagreement about that amounted to the question who was to be master. Quine thought that any statement could be held true come what may, if enough adjustments were made elsewhere in the system, and Rorty followed the pragmatic path out of philosophy altogether. These free spirits contrast with the commendable caginess of the philosopher at the 1995 joint session between the Mind Association and the Aristotelian Society, as reported in the *Independent on Sunday* newspaper: 'Not cagey - it's just I do not wish to say something that is false'.[13] The reporter commented that 'In philosophy, there seems to be a real fear that rash or ill-considered answers might be forever held against one, to the grave: and there seems to be no easy way to make a subsequent retraction'.[14] The reporter's unconsciously postmodern response reminds us of the content of postmodernism as a moral position: that truth makes demands upon us and nothing should make demands upon us. Truth is an unacceptable constraint. For the postmodernist, philosophy is inherently imperialist. Martha Nussbaum, for example, claims the heart of her philosophy as the old question 'how ought we to live?' But there is only properly the question, 'how ought I to live?', and no philosopher other than myself has any business enquiring into it.

In contrast with a postmodern approach, reference to the measure of truth and logic is classically a way of selecting and controlling alternative beliefs, and inconsistency is one of its main targets. 'Selecting', 'controlling', 'target'; I use here military language, to remind you of the postmodern point, that truth offends freedom. Dislike of logic is not always laziness. Debate about postmodernism forces us to recognise that there is a domain of what might be called metaphilosophical politics. We recognise in this domain that the view that reality is determinate arouses controversy. The postmodernist does not believe that reality has objectively determinate properties, and believes that reality is multiply configurable.

Most analytical philosophers are conservative enough to dislike postmodernism. They often ignore it as inherently irrational, as if it obviously involved a self-defeating relativism. Yet many envy at least some of the freedom which postmodernism claims, and I think we can carve a little more freedom from truth without lapsing into chaos. I shall show that there is one fundamental level at which there is no self-defeating relativism.

I am sufficient a follower of Socrates to accept - at least for the sake of the present argument - that reality, to the extent that it is expressed by atomic sentences, is determinate. I therefore try to be classically pure so far as inconsistent sentences are concerned. I prefer to discriminate between true and false sentences and to reject the false ones, and I assume in this paper that we can successfully do that. So, while a paralogician might live happily while knowingly believing inconsistencies or contradictions, I shall ignore this postmodern parapossibility. Yet the problem remains for stories: how far can the analogy between atomic sentences and stories be pushed? Should we be classical or postmodern with regard to story-truth? Is the reality expressed by a story determinate or indeterminate?

We might now wish to think of 'realism', in a sense local at least to this paper, as the claim that reality is determinate and therefore that we have 'no choice' about what we ought to believe. The opposite of 'realism', which I shall call here 'anti-realism', claims, similarly, that reality is not determinate and that therefore we have a 'choice' about what we ought to believe. 'Choice' and 'no-choice' are slippery notions. When we do not know what to believe, we seem to have a choice regardless of our philosophical position. How to make this choice seems not to depend on whether we are 'realists' or 'anti-realists'. We often simply develop the most rational decision procedure we can. That we may think that the best thing to do on occasion is toss a coin does not stop us from being realists, and that the choice is sometimes rationally obvious does not stop us being anti-realists. The difference between 'realism' and 'anti-realism' for this essay lies merely in this: that for the realist it is a priori that there is a decision between conflicting beliefs which ought to be made, while for the anti-realist it is a priori that there is no need to decide at all: we can rationally agree to differ. 'Anti-realism', as I understand it here, permits toleration of alternatives in a way which 'realism' does not. A corollary is that we need not see 'realism' or 'anti-realism', as I have defined them, as global positions, since each may be appropriate for different decision-situations. We may well choose to be 'realist' about what I have called atomic sentences, but choose to be 'anti-realist' about stories, and that is the position I adopt for the purpose of this argument. Given the understanding of 'realism' and 'anti-realism' used here, it would then be a gross error to suppose that the reality expressed by stories was metaphysically less tough than the reality expressed by atomic sentences. There is nothing metaphysical at issue: only the range of choice. Stories and sentences alike express reality.

Given the practical unrevisability of many inherited sentences expressing our beliefs, choices in the area of sentence-truth and sentence-meaning are less apparent than are choices involving stories. With regard to sentence-truth, it is plausible for an analytical philosopher to be a 'realist' in my sense: to believe that postmodern or relativist opponents of truth are not a serious party of opposition in the domain of metaphilosophical politics. It might well be thought that arguments for relativism are at best ladders to be climbed and thrown away. We need truth and our business is to understand it and not get rid of it; scientific predictions are too often right; relativism is self-defeating; skepticism merely sharpens the mind. Metaphysics and epistemology leave everything as it is. And reality is what it is. This is not an empty slogan, although it is a slogan. It is the slogan of the reality-is-determinate party, and this has been the most powerful philosophical party ever since Socrates, so much so that many define philosophy in terms of it. Followers of the Socratic manifesto in this regard happily assume that reality is determinate, and in virtue of that determinacy they seek rational control, or seek to understand existing rational control, of alternative expressions of reality, however 'rational control' is to be understood.

We have inherited practices of rational control for alternative sentences, and it may well be that as philosophers we can justify or believe we can justify such practices. But while many of us may be confident that rational control of alternative sentences is in fact largely available and that philosophical principle does not lag far behind, it really is not so easy in the case of story-meaning and story-truth. While the supposition of determinacy may be both reasonable and widespread for the understanding of sentence-truth, it is not widespread and may not be reasonable in the case of story-truth. By contrast with the case of atomic sentences, we have inherited very few practices of rational control for stories - although there are some - and it may well be that as philosophers we cannot justify what we have inherited, and ought not to attempt the further development of such practices. We can be and indeed typically are 'postmodern' in our attitude to stories. We actually tolerate conflicting stories in ways that we do not actually tolerate inconsistent sentences. 'Postmodernism' at this level does not embody a self-defeating relativism: at the extreme, to say that relativism is true for stories is not to tell a story. Note that it does not follow from any toleration of conflicting stories that just any story can be tolerated. There are criteria which an acceptable story has to meet as a minimum which I shall not elaborate here. What they are is contentious, not least by a postmodernist. I shall say only that the central criterion is the subjective followability of a story.

It is begging the question in favour of a determinate reality to suppose that we must choose between conflicting alternative expressions of reality, regardless of whether those expressions are atomic sentences or stories. It would be begging the question in favour of determinacy to argue as follows: that there is no such thing as proper story-meaning precisely because we should not conceive conflicting stories as alternative expressions of reality, and that we should not conceive conflicting stories as alternative expressions of reality precisely because there may not be a rational choice between stories as alternative expressions of reality. If we do not beg this question in the case of stories, the choice we face becomes a choice between determinacy and indeterminacy, between truth and toleration.

The self as a narrative point of view

I recently came across an unreferenced quotation from John Updike: 'If you are true to yourself you are bound to repeat yourself'. The idea that being true to oneself necessarily involves repetition supposes that, whatever the self is, it is unchanging over time in respect of holding certain beliefs which are regarded as essential to that self. These would not necessarily or indeed typically be beliefs that constitute the self as such, but rather those that are distinctive of one self vis-a-vis other selves. They are matters which express character, perhaps, such that a change of mind, which is permitted with respect to some beliefs, is wrong with respect to these essential beliefs because it involves a loss of integrity, an integrity which unifies one's life in a meaningful way. The kind of self which John Updike's remark involves is a self with a life, and a necessary condition for a life and thus for a self is that it is chronologically ordered. A life has a beginning, a middle and an end. The story of one's life should be a followable and meaningful story without fundamental change of belief or attitude, if one is to be true to oneself. Presupposed by the Updike remark is therefore the view that I have a self of a particular character and I am stuck with it. Reality, so far as my self is concerned, is fixed at some deep level. If we follow Heidegger, we will accept that we are most true to ourselves in the attitude we take towards our death. Reflection on our death forces us to take life seriously, and choose to live it in a manner which our death will round off in a meaningful way. This authentic and meaningful existence characterises what it is to be truly human.[15]

Sartre, by contrast, accepted that if we knew the date of our death we might be able to plan a meaningful wholeness for our lives, but in fact we do not know the date of our death, and unexpected death can rob whatever we do of all meaning. It is chance, thought Sartre, that decides the character of our death and thus chance that decides the meaningfulness of our lives.[16] The meaningfulness of the story of our lives is something judged by others after our death.

Yet a truly free spirit will wish to avoid being characterised by others at all. It is not clear how bound by his or her own character a free spirit might be, but it is clear that he or she ought to wish to avoid being so bound, and would wish a personal autonomy which allowed a continuous change of mind and character. Free spirits do not have to repeat themselves in order to be true to themselves. With the possibility of constant change of mind there is the possibility of constant change of what is said, and the free spirit can happily live with self-contradiction.

When we think of our own selves as ongoing lives we typically consider them as ongoing stories, and talk of the meaning of stories as a whole is thus talk about the meaning of our lives as a whole. There is therefore a reality which is constituted by a story and that is the chronologically ordered reality of our own lives, of our own selves. For each of us it is essentially a reality expressed from and constituted in terms of a point of view, but it is also a contribution to a game in the sense of game-theory, since what we understand our lives to be, in other words what our lives are, depends on our interactions with other people, on interactions with different selves, who describe those interactions from their own different points of view, in terms of different stories. These stories are different stories, and they are conflicting stories, not because individual sentences of those stories can conflict (although of course they can), but because they necessarily involve different selections of sentences, and yet are nevertheless about the same thing, which is our ongoing shared social reality.

We must not think of interpersonal understanding in shared social life, which is the present manifestation of an ongoing historical understanding, as yet another view from nowhere. The ongoing shared social reality through which we all live is a reality constituted by the points of view of all involved. Each story is organised internally, which is another way of saying that each life has an integrity which consists in subjective followability by the person living it, but the story expressing each life conflicts with others because it is not the only story. There is no single story to be told which is 'objective', no determinate reality of the matter independent of the points of view of those involved. Understanding social reality requires understanding the points of view of the others involved, and this requires tolerating their stories because understanding the whole requires it. What we tolerate is another's self-understanding and thus their understanding of the life they share with us. Yet while there might be determinacy about the reality of each constituent sentence of the whole there is no determinate reality for the social story itself. It is nevertheless the one human reality, which is inherently indeterminate. The social world, and I suppose for an analytical philosopher committed to determinacy this can be hell, is other people (cf. Sartre, "l'Enfer c'est les Autres"[17]). Acceptance of otherness is required for its existence. Toleration, not determinate truth, is therefore the essence of the criterion for social reality, and that this is true is the truth of postmodernism.

Let us look at the shared social life from different points of view. First, there is the first person point of view which is perhaps better called the 'autistic' point of view. Here an individual self presents to itself its own life as an ongoing story. It has what it sees as an internal or mental life and has also what it sees as an external or social life which involves interaction with other people. It does not, however, see those others as seriously independent of itself. The characterisation it gives to them, to their actions, and to their ongoing interactions and relationships with it, is a characterisation which is entirely in terms of its own life story. The 'truth' about others, understanding 'truth' here in the story-sense rather than the sentence-sense of that word, is from its point of view a determinate matter relative to its own life story, in which they are essentially and completely included. How determinate its own story is, is a separate issue. It may or may not regard its own life as multiply configurable. I assume that it does not, to avoid irrelevant confusion.

Contrast this autistic point of view with that of the person who fully grasps the nature of social reality. A person who fully grasps the nature of social reality is a person who recognises that it contains other people, other selves, other lives, and therefore grasps that other stories are true of it as a whole. The stories others live through and might express are stories about their full social life including their interrelationships with that person. Yet their stories are different stories from that person's, not because it and they differ in terms of particular beliefs or atomic sentences - although that is irrelevantly possible - but because different selections of sentences are involved. The stories therefore conflict because the selections of sentences conflict, and yet they are about the same thing and therefore differ as expressions of reality. And the reality they differently express is the shared social reality constituted by conflicting stories and thus necessarily an indeterminate reality. To admit the existence of social reality, therefore, is to admit the indeterminacy of social reality, to tolerate the existence of other people and therefore to tolerate conflicting stories as all story-true.

Toleration

The concept of toleration is inherently nothing other than an expression of indeterminacy. It is therefore not surprising that it so readily yields paradoxes. It would not be possible both to accept that the social world exists and not to accept that one is thereby tolerating the existence of other people. Yet toleration is also a primitive moral concept, indeed I think the central primitive moral concept. Even postmodernism is committed to one moral absolute: toleration. It remains the case that there are limits to toleration. These are the limits of a subjectively followable life: the limits of personal integrity. Although it is permissible in postmodern terms for social matters not to be story-followable, that an individual life is story-followable is a pragmatic feature of our existing conceptual scheme, which relies on continuing personal identity as in general unchallengeable. But the justification for this is another story.

Notes

1. Droit, 1993.
2. Gorman, 1974.
3. Gorman, 1982.
4. Davidson, 1977, p. 205.
5. Ibid., p. 205.
6. Davidson, 1978, p. 245.
7. Ibid., p. 247.
8. Ibid., p. 247.
9. Ibid., p. 246.
10. Zalewski, 1991, pp. 31-2.
11. Contingencies of Value, Harvard U.P., 1988, at p. 151, as quoted by Eldridge, 1993, p. 85.
12. Dray, 1995, pp. 27-8.
13. Parker, 1995, p. 4.
14. Ibid., p. 5.
15. These points are made by Law, 1996, p. 2.
16. Ibid., p. 2.
17. Sartre, 1944, sc 5.

References

Davidson, D. (1977), 'The method of truth in metaphysics', in his *Inquiries into Truth and Interpretation,* Clarendon Press: Oxford, 1984, pp. 199-214.

Davidson, D. (1978), 'What metaphors mean', in his *Inquiries into Truth and Interpretation,* Clarendon Press: Oxford, 1984, pp. 245-64.

Dray, W. H., (1995), *History as Re-Enactment: R.G. Collingwood's Idea of History*, Clarendon Press: Oxford.

Droit, R. -P. (ed.), (1993), 'La tolerance aujourd'hui', UNESCO, Division de Philosophie et d'Ethique: Paris.

Eldridge, R. (1993), 'Narratives and moral evaluation', *Journal of Value Inquiry*, 27, pp. 385-90.

Gorman, J. L., (1974), 'Objectivity and truth in history', *Inquiry*, 17, pp. 373-97.

Gorman, J. L., 1(982,) *The Expression of Historical Knowledge*, Edinburgh University Press: Edinburgh and Columbia University Press: New York.

Law, D. R, (1996), 'Heidegger and Sartre on Death', *Philosophy Today*, 21, p. 2.

Parker, I. (1995), 'In a meeting of minds', London, *Independent on Sunday*, pp. 4-5.

Sartre, J. -P., (1944), *Huis Clos,* Gallimard: Paris.

Zalewski, M. (1991), 'The debauching of feminist theory/the penetration of the postmodern', *Politics,* 11, pp. 30-6.

When tolerance is too much to ask

Katri Kaalikoski

One of the main tenets of liberalistic ethics is its emphasis on tolerance. Liberalists hold to the Millian liberal ideal that individuals have the right to do whatever they want, providing that they avoid physically harming another, and providing that they perform their legal contracts and their legal duties as parents or citizens. We are supposed not to interfere with the liberty of action of individuals as long as their action does not cause harm to others. We must let people make their own decisions in order to live the kind of life that they think is best for them. Tolerance derives from respect for general rights to liberty, such as freedom of speech and freedom of religion. We should acknowledge the universality of these rights; they belong to every person, regardless of, for example, ethnic, racial, or sexual differences. The morality of rights is formulated in terms of universal, general principles that are supposed to hold true for all persons, at all times, and all places. The claim for universality requires that our judgement is not directed, for instance, by personal relationships.

I do not propose to argue against the principle of toleration. Tolerance deriving from respect for rights is an essential part of ethics. What I wish to show is that the principles of impartial reason are not always applicable in a moral conflict, and that considerations of justice and rights are sometimes legitimately overridden by considerations of special relationship. In some situations, an individual making a moral decision has to seriously re-evaluate the principle of toleration.

I shall discuss a situation where a conflict between impersonal and personal moral claims generates a conflict between two ethical perspectives. The impersonal perspective presents a claim for toleration that derives from consideration of general rights. However, the general principle of toleration is not applicable in the particular moral situation, because adopting an impersonal viewpoint is not justifiable. Whether we should adopt an impersonal point of view, and whether we should show a tolerant attitude, depends on what morally relevant features are present in each particular situation. A tolerant attitude always needs a moral justification.

Let us think about the following case. Ann Adams, mother of a five-year-old son, is in a difficult situation. Ann is working as a high school teacher, and her son Mike has for three years now been going to a kindergarten called Park.[1] Park specializes in daycare for children with disabilities, and mentally handicapped children make up a third of the children in the kindergarten. Well-educated, proficient staff see to it that every child is treated with equal concern. In Park, the children eat, sleep, and play together in a tolerant atmosphere for which the place is known and highly appreciated, especially among the children's parents. As a liberal educated woman Ann is no exception. She knows that it is very important that children with disabilities are not separated from the healthy. This teaches the healthy children to understand and accept differences between people, and helps the children with disabilities to live as normal a life as possible.

Four-year-old Sam, a newcomer to Park, has difficulties in settling in the kindergarten. Sam has, until now, been in institutional care. Due to slight brain damage from which Sam suffers, his behavior is often unpredictable and aggressive, even violent. One morning Ann's son Mike no longer wants to go to Park. He starts crying and refuses to leave home. He has always been a lively cheerful boy, but suddenly he turns anxious and restless. After many inquiries Mike tells Ann that he is terribly afraid of the new boy, Sam, who has made a habit of attacking him. When Ann takes the matter up in Park, the staff admits that there have been some unfortunate incidents to do with Sam's difficulties in adjusting to the new environment. They promise that these problems will soon be solved. As days go by Mike seems more and more miserable. He does not sleep well at night, does not eat properly, and refuses to tell what is really wrong with him. More than ever before, his moods change quickly from anger to apathetic quietness.

Ann worries about Mike, but the staff does not seem to be particularly concerned about the situation. It almost seems as though the staff at Park have jointly decided to keep quiet about what is really happening in the kindergarten. When Ann tries to ask questions, she is reminded in a pleasant way of Sam's right to be in Park, and the importance of a tolerant attitude. Because Ann has great confidence in the judgement of the staff, she decides to wait until things get better with Mike. But things do not get better, in fact they get worse every day. One afternoon Ann sees bruises and deep scratches on Mike's face and back. This does it. Ann knows that she has to make a difficult decision. She has to make up her mind whether she will do her best to get them to ask Sam to leave Park or not.

Let us suppose for the sake of argument that Ann can be sure that the staff will do nothing about the situation. Let us also suppose that she cannot arrange Mike's daycare in any other way. Therefore, it is left to Ann to decide between two alternatives. The first is that Ann would make an official complaint and demand that Sam be asked to leave Park. The other alternative would be for Ann to decide to leave things as they are. If Ann decides not to do anything to change the situation, her attitude toward Sam's behavior can be said to be tolerant. The question we must confront is whether there are morally justifiable reasons why Ann should be tolerant and, on the other hand, whether there are sufficient reasons why she should not be tolerant in this situation.

Before we begin to answer these questions, we must consider what kind of an attitude tolerance is. There seems to be some confusion about how toleration should be defined. The general problem is that tolerance, as an attitude, is often confused either with approval or with indifference. I think, therefore, that we can best define tolerance by contrasting it with these two other attitudes. Tolerance differs from approval and indifference in two important aspects. First, there is a component of disapproval in a tolerant attitude, and second, tolerance is connected with reasons for action in a way that approval and indifference are not.

Your attitude toward another person's behavior can be described as approving only if you do not think that she is behaving badly. You cannot approve of her behavior if you disapprove of it. Moreover, if you approve of a person's behavior, there is no basic reason why you should wish her behavior to change. If, on the other hand, you have no opinion as to whether her behavior is good or bad, your attitude is best described as indifferent. In this case the question about whether or not you would want her behavior to change does not even arise. What about tolerance then? When can your attitude toward the other person's behavior be said to be tolerant? As I see it, your attitude can be described as tolerant if you more or less disapprove of the other person's behavior, and you would like her behavior to change, but you are nevertheless ready to let her behave in the way she does behave.

The main reason why tolerance often is confused with approval and indifference is that the difference between the three attitudes does not show in action. Take a following example. You feel that premarital sex is morally wrong. You therefore wish that your nephew would not have sex before marriage. Yet you feel it is not for you to decide when he may have sex. Although you disapprove of premarital sex, you are willing to let you nephew do what he wants, and you do not interfere with his decision to have premarital sex. Your attitude toward your nephew's sex-life is tolerant. If, however, you think that premarital sex is a good thing, because it is highly recommendable that people know each other sexually before they get married, your attitude toward your nephew's premarital sex-life is approving. In case you have never even come to think about whether it makes any difference if people have sex before they get married, your attitude is best described as indifferent.

In all three situations you do not interfere with your nephew's sex-life, but the reason for your non-interference is different. If your attitude is indifferent, you cannot even see that there could be a reason for you to interfere with your nephew's behavior. If your attitude is approving, you have no reason to interfere with your nephew's behavior. However, if your attitude is tolerant, you feel you have a reason to interfere with your nephew's behavior, but still you choose not to. The difference between the three attitudes thus does not show in what happens in the world, but we can see that tolerance relates to reasons for action in a way that approval and indifference do not. We also see why disapproval is an aspect of tolerance. The question about whether you should try to do something to change your nephew's behavior only arises if you disapprove of his behavior. Thus you can be said to tolerate your nephew's behavior if you disapprove of it, but choose not to interfere with it. In our example, Ann is convinced that what Sam does to Mike - or rather what the staff lets him do to Mike - is wrong. Ann also believes that she could prevent Sam from doing what he does by making an official complaint. Therefore, Ann will be showing a tolerant attitude if she decides to do nothing about the situation.

It needs to be emphasized that tolerance is an attitude. Attitudes are based on beliefs. Beliefs, of course, can be true or false. You disapprove of premarital sex, because you feel, think, or believe that premarital sex is morally wrong, but it does not follow that premarital sex is morally wrong. Paradoxically, if your belief is false, and premarital sex is not morally wrong, your being tolerant toward your nephew's behavior is morally right. If, however, premarital sex were morally wrong, and your belief therefore true, you should not show a tolerant attitude toward your nephew's behavior. We should not tolerate what is morally wrong.

A tolerant act belongs to the class of actions where a person lets an incident occur which he or she regards as a bad thing. Therefore, he or she must have a good reason for allowing this particular incident to occur. A tolerant attitude must be justified on moral grounds. A traditional way morally to justify a tolerant attitude is to refer to the liberty of action of individuals. This kind of justification has its source in the Kantian view of freedom and the Lockean tradition of natural rights. Kant held a positive view of freedom. Freedom is seen as autonomy or individual self-determination. It is conceived as the rational self-government of the individual agent. People gain moral autonomy when they use reason to determine which moral principles ought to be followed. Thus each person is the source of the moral principles that a person adheres to. The ideal of moral autonomy, on the other hand, forms the foundation for the emphasis on the dignity of the individual person. The doctrine of human dignity manifests itself in the idea of personal liberty, and in the idea of human rights. People are morally allowed and ought to be legally empowered to conduct their lives as they choose, because they are capable of moral autonomy. Moral autonomy thus forms the basis for personal autonomy. The possibility of personal autonomy, in turn, is granted by recognizing a set of rights which protect individuals from others' aggression and other undesirable interference in their lives. Rights ensure for the individual an area of personal liberty.

John Stuart Mill's utilitarianism, in spite of many differences, comes close to the Kantian view because of Mill's abiding concern with personal liberty. Mill shares with Kant an individualistic view of freedom. This view is elaborated in Mill's *On Liberty* (1859), in which he states his famous principle of liberty.

> That principle is, that the sole end for which mankind are warranted, individually or collectively, in interfering with the liberty of action of any of

> their number, is self-protection. That the only purpose for which power can be rightfully exercised over any member of a civilized community, against his will, is to prevent harm to others.[2]

Liberalists generally hold to the Millian ideal that people should be free to envisage and pursue their own plans of life, and no one ought to be authorized to dictate to individuals how they should live their lives, as long as their actions do not cause physical harm - or real psychological harm - to other people. This ideal strongly supports the notion of tolerance. We should not interfere with the lives of other people without sufficient reason.

Mill's principle is, of course, not without problems. The traditional criticism accuses Mill of not giving an explicit account of what should be counted as harm. Should we define harm merely as physical harm, and if we do, what kind of physical harm? If we conclude that harm can be psychological as well as physical, then how do we measure the degree of psychological harm? An incident which one person faces with only a slight feeling of disapproval may in another person cause serious permanent psychological damage. Despite its problems, the harm-principle captures the basic characteristic of morality: the concern for others. Moral considerations, as opposed for example to aesthetic ones, bear on the well-being of others, and the harm done to others. The harm-principle is therefore the best candidate for a basic moral principle that offers a standard for judging the validity of moral beliefs. Premarital sex would be morally wrong, and you should not show a tolerant attitude toward those who practice it, only if premarital sex caused real harm to others.

Ann is about to make a difficult moral decision. She feels there is no way to discover how to make the right decision in this situation. She simply does not know what to do. Before we see what Ann's decision is, let us consider some possible reasons why these kinds of practical moral conflicts arise. In *The Fragmentation of Value* (1979) Thomas Nagel suggests that there are real insolvable moral dilemmas, because different fundamental types of value give rise to basic conflict. I do not entirely agree with Nagel's classification of categories of value, but find it nevertheless worth considering when thinking about Ann's situation. The classification is rather comprehensive in that it calls attention to a variety of different value standards. It helps us to see why, in some situations, there seems to be indisputable support for two or more incompatible courses of action, that is, why there seems to arise a moral dilemma for which a single correct solution cannot be found.

Nagel lists five types of value that bring about practical conflicts.[3] First, there are special obligations to other people and institutions. These are, for example, obligations to one's family, community, or country. These obligations have to be incurred by some special relation to the person or institution in question. Ann has a special obligation towards Mike, because she is Mike's mother. However, and this is something Nagel does not make clear, not all obligations that are generated by special relationships are moral. As a citizen you ought not to break the law, but there may still be situations where you have a moral obligation to break the law, if what the law tells you to do is wrong. As a doctor you may have an obligation to the hospital you work for, but may as well have a moral obligation to ignore your obligation to the hospital if something that happens in the hospital is wrong. If, for example, you have come to know that highly dangerous tests are being made on patients without their consent.

The second category of value that Nagel distinguishes are constraints of action that derive from general rights, such as rights to liberty, or freedom of different kinds. Every individual's right to freedom from assault for instance is quite general, and does not depend on an obligation that others have incurred not to assault. The idea of general rights is naturally a central issue as regards Ann's decision.

The third category is what Nagel calls utility. This, he says, is the consideration that takes into account the effects of one's actions on everyone's welfare 'whether or not the components of that welfare are connected to special obligations or general rights'.[4] Thus utility, according to Nagel, includes all forms of benefit and harm to all people. The general benefits of medical research, for instance, come in this category. Depending on how we look at the matter, Nagel's concept of utility seems either so broad that it is in danger of proving empty, or altogether too narrow. Utility is supposed to include all benefit and harm to other people. But how are we to take into consideration *all* forms of benefit and harm to *all* people? Surely we have to somehow define benefit and harm before we can judge the possible effects of our actions. We have to know, for instance, whether it is economic benefit or the general well-being and good life of individuals that is to be our primary concern.

On the other hand, to define utility as the consideration of the effects of one's actions on everyone's welfare *whether or not* the components of that welfare are connected to special obligations *or* general rights, seems to limit the concept of utility so much as to move it outside the sphere of moral consideration, and to place it only in an economic context. What I mean is that even if it is evident that the consideration of benefit and harm caused by one's actions to all people differs from the consideration that is directed, for instance, by personal relationships, it is not at all evident that the consideration of benefit and harm can be separated from the consideration of general rights. The general benefits of medical research, or education, are *benefits* just because they help individuals realize their own goals in life. It seems to me, therefore, that as long as the principle of utility is to have any moral import, the consideration of benefit and harm must be rooted in the idea of personal liberty and general rights.

The fourth category of value in Nagel's classification is that of perfectionist ends or values. By this he means 'the intrinsic value of certain achievements or creations, apart from their value *to* individuals who experience or use them'.[5] The intrinsic value of scientific discovery and artistic creation are offered as examples. The practice of these activities, Nagel says, has value apart from their worth to individuals who practice them or enjoy their results. This claim is debatable for several reasons. To maintain that some achievement or creation has intrinsic value independent of its value to individuals is a highly controversial metaethical claim, the content of which Nagel does not make explicit here. Scientific discovery, no doubt, has value independent of its value to any particular individual, but with the claim that scientific discovery has value independent of its value to *any* individual one would be committed to obscure metaphysical value objectivism.

For another thing, the notion of intrinsic value does not seem to serve any real purpose here. Nagel speaks about types of value that may conflict when individuals are forced to decide between different courses of action. It is difficult to see how the supposed intrinsic value, independent of thoughts and feelings of individuals, could be among these conflicting values. It is obvious that the value of scientific discovery can enter into individuals' decision processes only if individuals find scientific discovery valuable. Also worth noticing is the fact that Nagel draws together different types of value. Even if, for instance, artistic creation could be thought to have some kind of intrinsic value, it would hardly be moral value. It makes sense to say that artistic creation, or rather the results of artistic creation, have aesthetic value, but to claim that artistic creation has moral value is quite another matter. To attribute moral value to artistic creation echoes the views of the Romantics, who saw artists as somehow morally superior individuals.

The fifth and final value category that Nagel distinguishes is that of commitment to one's own special projects and undertakings. He sees this commitment as a value in addition to whatever reasons one had for starting the projects in the first place. If one, for instance, sets out to climb Everest, the further pursuit of that project, such as daily physical exercise, acquires a value of its own. Nagel says that the value of commitment to one's own special projects and undertakings should not be confused with self-interest, but it is difficult to see what the difference between this kind of commitment and self-interest is supposed to be.

The general difficulty with Nagel's classification is that he draws together many value types of which only a few are moral. Of course, Nagel himself does not argue that all values he distinguishes are moral values. What he says is that where practical conflicts arise they usually have moral components.[6] He seems, therefore, to suggest that even if a practical conflict includes moral components we do not have to treat it as an essentially moral conflict. If this is what Nagel means, I must disagree with him. As I see it, every practical conflict that includes moral components is essentially and primarily a moral conflict.

Nagel claims that practical conflicts do not necessarily have a justifiable solution, although they always have a solution. We have to do something, or decide not to do anything in every situation. This is true, of course. What puzzles me is that Nagel seems to be arguing that values belonging to any of the five categories may have equal *weight* when they enter into a decision that must be made in a problematical situation. In my view, in every conflict situation that includes moral components, moral values must enter into the decision first.

Consideration of moral values must outweigh consideration of other types of value, if the person searching for a solution wants to make not only a decision, but as justifiable a decision as possible.

After these general remarks, let us return to our example and see how Ann deals with her problem. Obviously there are several aspects to the situation which Ann must take into account before she makes her decision. We can divide these different aspects into three general categories according to the classification discussed above. The three basic viewpoints that Ann must consider, then, are those of general rights, utility, and personal obligation. The last of Nagel's value categories I shall comment on later.

What is basically at stake in our example case is a conflict between Mike's rights and Sam's rights. The situation is complicated because both Mike and Sam are children, and particularly complicated because Mike is a mentally handicapped child. We all agree that children have the same fundamental rights as adults. However, children are not, to use Kantian terms, fully capable of rational self-government. They are therefore not fully capable of protecting their rights. This means that adults have to see that the rights of children are respected. Moreover, adults have to take care that the equal rights of children are equally respected. The same applies to people with disabilities. Disabled people have the same basic rights as the healthy, but some disabled people are not fully capable of protecting their rights. Therefore, it is left to healthy people to protect their rights, and to see that their equal rights are respected. In the light of these principles it is obvious that the basic rights of a mentally handicapped child need special protection.

Ann agrees with all of this, but she is not convinced. Even if Sam's rights outweighed Mike's rights in this situation, it would be very difficult for Ann to ignore the harm that is caused to Mike. This is why Ann feels that it is best to consider the situation from the point of view of utility, and look at the consequences of what she decides about everyone's well-being. It is very difficult for Ann to estimate the harm that is caused to Mike if things are left as they are. How much Mike will suffer, and for how long, depends largely on his personal capacity to deal with the frightening situation. It is much easier to foresee the real harm that is caused to Sam if he is asked to leave the kindergarten and is perhaps returned to the institution. Ann is well aware that whatever she decides to do her decision has far-reaching effects on Sam's future well-being.

The harm that will be caused to Sam if Ann decides to demand that he be asked to leave Park thus appears to be greater than the harm that will be caused to Mike if Ann decides to do nothing. Ann knows this, but still she feels that this does not solve the problem. She is Mike's mother. As his mother she has a special obligation to take care that *nothing* that causes serious harm happens to him. This obligation cannot be traced back to general rights. Neither can it, in this situation, be directly founded on considerations of utility or inflicted harm. Nevertheless, Ann feels that her obligation as a mother overrules all other considerations. She cannot know how much Mike will suffer if the situation continues at Park, but she is certain that he will suffer. This fact alone makes Ann finally decide that she will try to get them to ask that Sam be removed from Park. She knows that she is forgetting the claim for tolerance and violating the principle of equal rights, but this does not alter her decision.

Is Ann's decision morally defensible? Are considerations of justice and rights in this case legitimately overridden by considerations of special relationship? It seems so. There are situations where a parent has no moral obligation not to think about his or her own child first, even if the rights and well-being of another child are at stake. I am certainly not arguing that parents have the right to protect their own children's rights and forget about other children's rights whatever the situation. I do not even know exactly in what particular circumstances parents are morally permitted to do this. It would indeed be cold-hearted and unjustified, not to mention silly, to maintain that the boy who happens to pull my little girl's pigtails in the classroom should be deprived of his right to education. It is thus very important to consider carefully in what circumstances the expected harm to a child is severe enough so that parents have sufficient reason to favour their own child.

I have said that in some situations the parents have no moral obligation not to think about their own children first. In other words, there are cases where the parents are morally allowed to do this. Another question is whether the parents are sometimes, not only morally allowed, but also morally obliged to do this. Again I would like to answer in the affirmative. Mothers and fathers sometimes have an obligation to be partial and favour their own children. Contrary to what might be objected, this view is not in conflict with the ideal of maximal protection of rights for all children. Rather, I see it as a basis for recognizing children's rights in the first place. The special obligation-based relationship between a parent and a child constitutes our understanding of what being a child means. And respectively, this understanding is a prerequisite for acknowledging the need for granting specific rights to children.

The reason why Ann chose to protect her own son Mike is simply that he is her son. As I see it, Ann does not need to give further justification for her decision, provided of course that the situation is bad enough from Mike's point of view. Does Ann then make a purely subjective decision? According to Thomas Nagel, the claims of utility are outcome-centered or objective, whereas claims deriving from special obligations and general rights are agent-centered or subjective. Nagel claims that the division between personal and impersonal, or between objective and subjective, is so basic that it 'renders impossible any reductive unification of ethics'.[7] The two perspectives to ethics, subjective and objective, are then fundamentally irreducible to a common basis. Nagel admits that this does not mean that basic practical conflicts have no solution.

> Briefly, I contend that there can be good judgement without total justification, either explicit or implicit. The fact that one cannot say why a certain decision is the correct one, given a particular balance of conflicting reasons, does not

mean that the claim to correctness is meaningless. Provided one has taken the process of practical justification as far as it will go in the course of arriving at the conflict, one may be able to proceed without further justification, but without irrationality either.[8]

Ann makes a decision that she may not be able to totally justify, but her decision is not purely subjective in the sense that Nagel suggests. Ann does not see herself as a person who happens to be a mother, and who therefore has a special right to forget the claim for objectivity in a moral conflict. Rather, before Ann can reach her decision, she is forced to carefully reflect on what it actually means to be a mother. Perhaps we should not, in this situation, see a woman called Ann make a subjective decision, but rather see a mother making a decision as a mother. If Ann not were Mike's mother, she would supposedly decide differently.

For Aristotle, moral deliberation must determine the right thing to do, to the right person, and in the right way. Aristotelian as that may be, I believe that mothers and fathers must make the kind of decisions that their role as parents requires. Every mother and father needs a particular kind of practical wisdom. If we look at Ann's situation in this way, the decision that she makes is not entirely subjective. It is a semi-objective decision in the sense that it is the kind of decision that every mother, as a mother, is morally allowed and sometimes even obliged to make.

At this point I wish to briefly comment on the last of Nagel's categories of value, namely commitment to one's own projects or undertakings. I hope these remarks will clarify my view of what parenthood is, and what it is not. I said before that it is not easy to see the supposed difference between self-interest and the value of carrying on with one's one projects. Nagel says that the importance of carrying on with the projects one has begun, is 'partly a matter of justifying earlier investment of time and energy, and not allowing it to have been in vain', and 'partly a desire to be a sort of person who finishes what he begins'.[9] As I see it, both of these motives are self-interested. What is my pursuit controlled by if not self-interest, if it is important to me to go on practising the piano only because I want to justify the time and energy that practising the piano has already taken, or because I personally want to be the kind of person who does not quit before he can play Mozart. However, the desire to be a good mother or father is not like the desire to learn to play Mozart's piano concerto no. 17 in G. At least it should not be.

The decision to have a child, as well as the decision not to have a child, may of course originally be motivated by self-interest. However, as soon as one has a child, the reason why one finds it important and valuable to carry on with the project of parenthood is not based on self-interest. No doubt there are parents who use children merely as means of fulfilling their own interests. We are all familiar with the story of the child who has to play Mozart's piano concertos because her mother, despite great effort, was never much of a pianist. It is unfortunately easy to think about parents who regard their children merely as extensions of their own existence, but this is not what parenthood is really about. A parent is not motivated by self-interest. A parent is motivated by the interests of the child as an individual. We do not take care of our children because we want to justify the time and energy we have already sacrificed on them. Neither do we take care of them because we do not want to be taken as persons who give up. We take care of our children because it is something we just have to do. There is no explanation, no reason, why we should take care of our sons and daughters other than the simple fact that they are our children.

Parenthood is not, in my view, to be understood as a personal project which we want to carry on with, because we once found it worth committing ourselves to. The motive for a father's desire to fulfil his role as a father is not, or at least should not be, that he *likes to be* a father. The simple fact that he *is* a father should be enough to motivate him. Parenthood is not to be seen as a kind of noble vocation. This is why I would rather speak about parents' obligations than describe parenthood as a personal commitment based on devotion. This is also why I have not, thus far, said a word about maternal or paternal love. Fortunately, we often love our children. However, our duties as mothers and fathers do not derive from love. This is, of course, not to deny the obvious fact that we cannot be really good mothers and fathers if we do not love our children. In any case, we cannot say that a mother has an obligation to love her children, even though we must sincerely hope, for her sake as well as for the children's, that she does love them.

One more comment I wish to make before going back to my main argument. I believe it is very important to recognize that even being an excellent mother or father is not something angelically virtuous. We do our duty as parents just like we do any other duty. Being or trying to be a good mother or father is not something we should be praised for. The duty to try to be as good a father as possible follows necessarily from the fact that one is a father.

I said at the beginning that I take the principle of tolerance and respect for equal rights to be an essential part of ethics. Yet the example I have discussed has led me to defend a view according to which even the claim for equal rights, in some situations, is not enough to justify the value of toleration. This is indeed my view, but I want to stress that it only applies to particular situations which concern the special relationship between a parent and a child. Whether there are other special relationships, for instance between adult relatives, which could morally justify violating the claim for equal rights, is a difficult question which I cannot deal with now. I argue only that a parent in some situations is permitted to violate the principle of toleration as well as that of respect for equal rights, and that this violation is also morally defensible. This means, also, that a morally adequate judgement need not be fully reversible, that is it need not be universalisable in the strict sense.

Ann's difficult situation is good evidence of the fact that a tolerant attitude is sometimes too much to ask, even if we acknowledge the value of the principle of toleration as such. The example also shows that toleration is not something we should unconditionally regard as a good thing. The liberal discussion concerning the value of toleration sometimes loses sight of the fact that it is toleration that has to be morally justified, not intolerance. A tolerant attitude is a good attitude only if it has a moral justification. If I let an incident occur which I regard as a bad thing, I must be able to justify my attitude on moral grounds.

Tolerance as a virtue becomes suspect in our example. The reason why this happens is not that there is something wrong with tolerance in itself. It happens because we have to find a moral justification for tolerance. The main issue, therefore, is not that Ann cannot morally justify her intolerant attitude in the situation in question. Indeed she cannot justify it, at least not in terms of impartial and objective moral principles. The essential question to ask is whether Ann could morally justify a tolerant attitude. As far as I can see the answer is no. Ann Adams, as Mike Adams' mother, could never give such a justification.

Notes

1. My example case takes place in Finland where children usually remain in public daycare until the age of seven.
2. Mill, 1962, p. 135.
3. Nagel, 1979, p. 174-7.
4. Ibid., p. 175.
5. Ibid., p. 176.
6. Ibid., p. 174.
7. Ibid., p. 180.
8. Ibid., p. 180.
9. Ibid., p. 176.

References

Mill, J. S. (1962), *Utilitarianism and On liberty*, edited by Mary Warnock, Fontana Library: London.

Nagel, T. (1979), 'The Fragmentation of Value' in Christopher W. Gowans (ed.), *Moral Dilemmas*, Oxford University Press: New York, 1987.

Taking friendship seriously

Shyli Karin-Frank

A. Introduction

Western daily life has been embedded with tragic stories of choices made between loyalties to personal relationships and commitments to the state, the party, or the moral code. Tragedy arises out of the sense of betraying our most important values, even if betrayal is unavoidable, one way or another, as it is in situations of dilemmas. The question I put to discussion is: how much do we really value our friendships and what should we do when we must choose between personal loyalties and moral obligations? I find this question interesting only on liberal grounds, where it is assumed that pluralism of conceptions of the good life is compatible with the idea that for each moral problem - in terms of rules, principles, or obligations - there is one right solution, as the best or better in the situation.

Friendship has always been morally appreciated, though it is particularistic and partial. On the one hand, the particularistic characteristic of friendship appears to be closely connected with egoism and thus, to exclude friendship from the main stream of morality, where good, value, and right are usually understood as universal and hence connected with altruism. On the other hand, the familiar features of friendship and good friendship, in particular, seem to express everything morality has preached for. Thus, friendship is perhaps a paradigm of morally bridging between egoism and altruism, the never ending attempt of moral theories. Yet, when friendship conflicts with moral obligations, both our personal commitments and our moral convictions seem shaky.

In the following I will suggest that we can take friendship seriously, in the sense that we are sometimes permitted to prefer friendship over general principles and rules of impartial morality. This implies that even if friendship is not constituted in special rights or duties (as I will argue), it is nevertheless a moral good that can be morally weigh against moral obligations from both partial and impartial points of view. Assuming the unity and self identity of the moral agent, it should be possible for us to grasp our experience as morally integrated. Thus, conflicts between friendship and impartial obligations can be resolved in the same manner we resolve conflicts of values or obligations, that is, as the best possible in the situation.

B. Are there special rights or duties of friendship?

What is friendship? As Don Passel argues[1], there is no general, necessary form of friendship but rather, a wide range of particular relations, the historic trait of which allows only for a usual form. Good friendship is the subject of our discussion. In Aristotle's terms, it is a virtue friendship, which can include instrumental friendship, that is, utility and pleasure friendship. Good friendship is commonly perceived of as a developing intimate relationship, which consists of mutuality of affection, attraction, respect, trust, sharing of experiences and activities, care and concern. These are established in a selective, discriminating manner.

Friendships depend upon the unique individualities of people and their contingent biographies and shared experiences. We are attracted to and care for our friend as the very particular friend that he or she is. This means that one's unique personality is essential no less than one's character traits or virtues, and that friends are not easily replaceable.[2] It also means that each friendship has its own form, partly determined by the explicit or tacit agreements posited through time by friends.[3]

Thus, the particularistic nature of friendship becomes a primary feature. Friendship cannot be regulated by universal principles or rules, nor can it be prescribed in terms of moral rights or obligations. Of course, this does not mean that friendship does not involve responsibilities and commitments. On the contrary, daily life seem to support the idea that responsibilities and commitments are central in good friendships. The question is whether or not such responsibilities and commitments include special rights and duties, which are created within concrete friendships and, at the same time, retain a moral quality. In other words, such rights or duties are significant of these personal relations, in the sense that they cannot be transferred to other relations, being inadequate to external contexts, and yet, they are established on moral grounds. Answering this is crucial to understanding the nature of conflict between friendship and moral obligations: what exactly is the moral content of friendship that allows or disallows it to override moral obligations?

If we could argue from special rights or duties of friendship we could somewhat guarantee the moral status of personal relationships. Thus, persons involved in such non political relations could somewhat protect these relations and their personal implications when they are 'threatened' or belittled by moral or political demands: it would not be necessary to betray friendship simply because morality analytically overrides personal relationships and interests.

It has been argued by Blustein, Meyer, Annis, and others[4] that since friendship is essentially a voluntary relationship, it creates special rights or duties which go beyond the ordinary grounds of morality. Such rights or duties are owed by a specific agent to a specific individual and did not exist in a general form prior to the relationship. Under this conception, Annis argues that there is a differential ethical pull based on special relations and that thus, duties of friendship are commonly regarded not as mere instances of general duties which we owe to anyone in certain circumstances, as suggested by Don Passell.[5] Annis gives the example of the right to be treated openly, which in addition to sincerity, involves exposure of one's personality and personal history as well as the sharing of them with another.

This idea presupposes that insistence on rights does not necessarily lead to antagonism and egoism, which contradict friendship. On the contrary, friendship is regarded an adequate context for exercising rights, for it implies and stresses autonomous individuality and its moral worth in both friends. Such a position claims to leave room for other aspects of friendship, which go beyond rights, with the belief that spontaneity of friendship is not destroyed by the assumption of rights.[6]

Since we are dealing with good, but real, non ideal friendship, it appears mistaken to think that any discussion about rights or duties is incompatible with the spirit of friendship or undermines it, or that trust, sharing, and support simply flow from a total harmony[7]. People may enjoy friendship more without duties or rights, but that, in itself, does not mean that friendship is inconsistent with the latter.

Language and common experience allegedly support the notion of special rights or duties of friendship, for we expect our friends to be loyal, supportive, and caring. Also, we are surprised and feel betrayed if they do not fulfil these expectations, unlike the case with strangers, when they threat us unjustly.

Controversy has arisen regarding the ontology of rights and duties of friendship: 1) Assuming (as Annis does) a general pattern of friendship, that is a special relationship which gives rise to special responsibilities, friendship is considered in terms of institution constitutive in rules. Thus, rights and duties are established historically through the fact of friendship. This position attempts to bridge the gap between social and personal relations, through the description of friendship as a close-knit community. The assumption is that 'true friendships share enough characteristic features with genuine communities - mutuality, a complex intermingling of self interest, and some disposition to promote the association itself'.[8]

Since a theory of rights does not exhaust the moral relations of individuals, this position can be located within a wider moral context, so that the exercise of rights between friends can be guided by communal values (such as mutual trust and respect for privacy) or by a theory of virtues that helps the individual to decide when and how to exercise rights in different contexts.

But the very idea of friendship as a minimal community implies that friendship is qualitatively similar to other types of social relationships and institutions, thereby drying out the significant characteristics of friendship and the unique problems which are created through conflicts between personal and moral loyalties. However, even if there are duties of friendship at all, then identifying their source in the fact of friendship is mistaken, as demonstrated by the counter example given by Pasell[9]: suppose I have two friends who need my help and I choose to help the one who has been caring and supportive rather than the one who has been interesting and pleasant, yet, egoistic. My choice will be approved as compatible with the duties of friendship. The reason is that if a duty is institutional, then it is always the other institutional relationship, not friendship, which creates the duty (promise, for example). If the duty is not institutional, it is possible to imagine a parallel situation, where there is no such duty. Therefore, the fact of friendship cannot be the source of duties, and regarding friendship as an institution governed by rules appears incoherent.

2) This gives rise to another conception regarding the duties of friendship: Passell suggests that friendship is a voluntary, not an institutional relationship, thus, not all friendships involve rights or duties. If there are duties of friendship, then they are grounded in general moral obligations as well as in the particular relationships between two friends, which depend on their characters, biographies, agreements, and other contingent conditions.[10] Existing rights and duties are enlarged and strengthened by intimate relations, as imperfect duties, such as helping people generally, become perfect duties through friendship.[11]

This position, too, is mistaken, to my opinion: if there is a duty to help the caring friend in the above example, then it is not established on the fact of friendship, nor on concrete relations or characters which constitute the particular friendship. Rather, such a duty is based on the fact that the friend has helped me in the past, and on the moral obligations of beneficence and reciprocity. Accordingly, if a total stranger helped me in the past, that fact can induce a duty to help that stranger.

If, moreover, duties of friendship are dependent on the friend's needs and on our ability to help, and not on when and how much the friend has helped us in the past,[12] then there is no reason for preferring to help the caring person over the egoist or the total stranger. Furthermore, the very concepts of right and duty may not be adequate to friendship: special rights and duties of friendship have no identifiable source, nor do they include the political traits of rights and duties, namely, claim and protection. The latter are essential to the concepts of right and duty[13], thus, rights and duties seem to be redundant in the context of personal relationships. It has been argued that, after all, what can be achieved by rights is clearly not what is offered by friendship[14], and perhaps friendship can be established as a moral relationship without an appeal to rights and duties.

If indeed there is only a usual pattern of friendship, which is essentially particularistic, then no type of friendship, and not merely good friendship, consists of special duties. It appears mistaken to distinguish, as Passell does, between the fact of friendship and the concrete features of friendship. Friendship or good friendship **is** the relationship constituted in caring, support, and loyalty. This is the meaning of (good) friendship, and the language of rights and duties does not add to the understanding of this relationship, even if it were consistent with it. Duties are inadequate to friendship, in the same manner as duties are inadequate to the laws of physics.

Unlike the case of moral judgments, which are distinguished from the actions they consider, because they are an additional construction on facts, in friendship support and caring are constituents of the relationship. The providing of care and support by friends is neither a 'nice' thing to do nor their duty, but rather, the establishment of the usual pattern of friendship. In other words, friendship with no help and support is not (good) friendship at all.

C. Partiality as the core of commitments of friendship

It cannot be denied that all moral obligations or rights, such as the obligation to tell the truth or the right to life, are applicable to friendship, since friends too are persons subjected to morality. Friendships do not and cannot exist outside social and daily life, thus, rights and obligations are part of friendships as well and affect particular relationships. Unlike strangers, friends do not tend to avoid their obligation to protect their friend's rights, and the actual need to claim and protect such rights does seem to undermine friendship, especially if that need arises too often. This is so even if most friendships are not perfect, so that claiming moral or political rights is sometimes the lesser evil, for it may be better to enjoy respect by claiming it than suffer the loss of respect or friendship.[15]

The question is whether the difference between friends and strangers, with respect to the exercise of rights and duties, is merely a matter of motivation or also a matter of moral preference. The language of commitments and expectations suggests the subjective character of friendship, as distinguished from the universal nature of moral obligations. Such responsibilities and commitments merely take on the form of obligations, alongside sincere motivation and intention, but without the universal conditions which tie persons by obligations. The analogy between the commitment of friendship and moral obligations is based on the tacit pledge made voluntarily by two people. Unlike the case of promise, for example, where two persons are tied together by a moral institution, the pledge of friends is not universal or institutional, but rather emotional and personal. In friendship, the two persons let one another know that they are reliable and trustworthy, and they do rely on and trust each other.[16]

The moral good of friendship, then, does not lie in the exercise of rights or duties, but in the notion of the good life. Assuming Aristotle's position, friendship is a virtue or implies a virtue and it is necessary for human life and happiness. Friendship based on partiality is the most natural form of altruism, since it is constituted, among other things, on respect to the other as an end. Also, through partiality toward friends and loved ones we are able to exercise some virtues which go beyond obligations. In terms of moral education, the ability to treat strangers morally is developed and conditioned by our partial preference toward our friends and loved ones. Furthermore, according to psychological and social research, the development of an autonomous personality requires, among other conditions, personal and intimate relationships. As established in the discussion of privacy, love, friendship, and family life are considered to be human goods and basic human needs.[17]

And more significantly, following Hartman, it is through friendship and personal love that we gain access to the value of the particular individual. In friendship, the person is valued for being that person alone and not as an exemplification of a type; value resides in that person, being a particular instance as distinct from others. It is through friendship that the individual is regarded as having a special, non comparable value, that neither utilitarian nor Kantian morality can capture.[18]

From the utilitarian point of view, friendship, which is based on partiality, promotes happiness and the general good, and particularly self respect and self worth, which are primary values for rational beings. However, as it is with respect to other issues, to which we attempt to apply the principle of utility, it does not follow that an absolute favoring of friends maximizes total utility. It could be the rule that we are to support friends when it maximizes utility but help others when that has the greatest impact on moral overall utility. Defending absolute favoritism on grounds of practical difficulties involved in utility calculations is degrading for both friendship and Utilitarianism.

Lawrence Blum[19] argues that it is impossible to formulate a rule, according to which friendship always promotes the general good better than any other praxis, for it is always possible to imagine another praxis which does this better. Also, we should not attempt to establish impartial justification of partiality, in the form of a general rule that permits or requires a partial action toward anyone who belongs to a certain category, such as friends, family, and loved ones, and with whom we may have special relationships, similar in a relevant way. According to Rescher[20], this will be misleading, because the meaning of partiality refers **only to friends** and not to **everyone who is a friend**. We should therefore abandon the efforts to make room for partiality within the utilitarian or Kantian contexts.

D. Are there two separate moralities?

It has been suggested by Toulmin and others[21] that there are two distinguishable domains of activity. One is grounded in rules and regards impartially strangers and loved ones, while the other is grounded in discretion and remains outside the requirements of institutional justice, but within the context of intimate relations.

Intimate relations raise moral issues that can only reasonably be settled on an ongoing basis and with a sensitivity to context and individuality that precludes routinization of response. Here, we are permitted to prefer on the basis of partiality, even if there are no relevant moral reasons for such preferences. Accordingly, moral wisdom consists of knowing when to switch from one frame of reference to the other: if I am distributing social goods, according to this position, then I should treat friends and strangers alike. Whereas if I am distributing personal goods, then personal favoritism is permitted. This is possible if impartiality is no longer regarded as the sole core of morality. After all, partiality is not equivalent to morality, but is merely the way in which principles are to be justified.

However, it seems to me that all that has been achieved by distinguishing between two domains of morality is that traditional readings of Utilitarianism and Kantianism are shown to permit partiality, **if and when it is restricted to the proper context**. What is being justified is merely the temporal and limited suspension of impartial morality within the intimate context only. Our problem though is to decide if and when partiality can override impartiality in daily conflicts between personal and social requirements, which threaten to tear apart our convictions.

Making room for partial morality means, so far, merely that friendship and other 'private' values can exist alongside public, impartial morality. The existence of private values and their particularistic nature imply subjectivity, with the result that first, universalizability is not required for friendship to be meaningful and valid for the individual, and second, the subjecting of friendship to universal rules is impossible. The immediate implication is that acting upon friendship is unpredictable in the sense of impartial morality, although expectations can be formed. In the same sense that friendship takes the form of universalizability it also takes the form of the preconditions of predictability, that is, accuracy, continuity, stability, and constancy.

It may appear as if friendship is disconnected from public, impartial morality. The reason is that from the point of view of the impartial sphere of morality, private values like friendship, which guide private behaviors and relations, are neutrally valid. Neutrality is a matter of procedure, a political ideal which is the reaction to the pluralism and variety of private values and conceptions of the good life. The question is, on what grounds can we subject our actions to the private value of friendship? If impartial, public morality appears to be indifferent to private values, the result might be that friendship has no moral framework. In other words, the existence of values by themselves does not establish a morality. The absence of predictability, principles, and rules from the sphere of friendship threatens to prevent the possibility of establishing a private morality, adequate to friendship and other private values.

Nevertheless, this does not mean that friendship is irrational, that it can express only emotions and feelings instead of concepts and judgments, and that it is not subject to moral judgments of some kind. Since friendship is recognized as indispensable for good human life, is there a substitute for universalizable morality, so that acting on grounds of friendship does not remain a mere whim?

'Practical wisdom'[22] seems to be appropriate for friendship and other private values. The term itself suggests that practical wisdom consists of free, unspecified, non discoursive 'rules'. These rules resemble the judgments of connoisseurs of wines and food, who act on the basis of their accumulated internalized experience. Although no theory is assumed here, nevertheless, judgments made on wine or friendship are not necessarily arbitrary.

Does this mean that friendship can exist only sporadically, outside impartial morality and through the individual's experience and practical wisdom? Not necessarily: it is through the right to privacy, which belongs to impartial, public morality, that friendship is tightly connected with impartial morality. Privacy involves a requirement of self determination regarding participation in social interactions, exposure, and transfer of information. Accordingly, certain behaviors, relations, and domains of life are immune against public intrusion. The reason is that they are believed to express or symbolize the individual's identity. Friendship cannot be based on impartial morality, yet, being supported by the right to privacy, it can be regarded as connected with the main branch of impartial morality.

E. The conflict between partial friendship and impartial morality

It may appear then that partial and particular relationships can never be preferred over the universal and impartial demands of morality, and that we are morally doomed to betray our friends whenever we recognize a moral principle which is applicable to the situation and the exercise of which competes with our understanding of the preservation of a friendship. This, however, seems to be contrary to the common belief that if you neglect a friend in need while helping a stranger or performing a social duty, then your moral convictions are, at best, confused. Can we support this common intuition in a justifiable manner?

Suppose I made promises to several people and later I discover that I can keep only one. Can I justifiably favor my friend? Can I justifiably help my friend at the price of neglecting a general cause or of failing to help a suffering stranger?

Personal relations seem to require us to treat those who are specially related to us better than we need to, absent such a link. According to Cottingham[23], the partiality which we all do in fact have toward our loved ones is permitted and essential, for it links between ethics and the good for human beings. Denying such a preference of partiality over impartiality is denying love, which is necessary for good human life, and an acceptable morality cannot posit standards which harm the love between individuals. 'Human intimacy is a primary source of value and self realization for most of us, and the special nature of intimacy is partly expressed in the favoritism we show our intimates'.[24]

Although what we do for our friends is unique to our attitude toward them and arises out of the particular relations, so that it cannot be transferred to strangers (as argued by Lawrence Blum), it does not follow that there is no competition between friends and strangers. Favoritism of friends is real, for friends and strangers do compete for our limited time, energy, and motivation.

The conflict between friendship and moral obligations is not due to conceptual contradiction, but due to contingent circumstances. Since friendship has an 'ontology' independent of universal morality, conflicts between friendship and moral obligations are genuine, in the sense that our choices cannot be made simply on the basis of a given scale of values or obligations. If morality offers more than understanding of the constituents of our choices, if it also means some guidance of our actions, then conflicts ought to be resolved morally, that is, a justified preference of one option over the other must be possible.

If a stronger defense of favoritism is possible, then we should be able to argue that universal obligations can be overridden not merely in the context of personal relationships, but also within the social context. This, however, requires that we assume moral heterogeneity: this means that we recognize the multiple origins of morality and the insufficiency of universal principles to take care of all moral aspects of human life. Alongside utility calculations and deontology, partiality is a source of morality. Partiality can be regarded as moral if it is not necessary that only unconditional motivation can create moral values, that is, if we abandon Kantian grounds.

Assuming moral heterogeneity, justification of restricted preference of friendship over moral obligations seems to be possible for both Utilitarianism and Deontology. Utilitarian considerations are fanatic in that they require one to do always what will result in the greatest good overall, yet, perhaps they have a strong claim to override the partiality principle only if the greater good overall is of a specific sort. Deontological considerations are always urgent, positing a restricting frame for our actions. Yet, a non Kantian deontology can present grades of severeness, which introduces some flexibility to impartial morality, and a possible compatibility with a preference for particularistic values.[25]

In the search for resolution of such conflicts it may appear, again, that we are doomed to failure: the reason this time is that partiality and impartiality are created on separate levels, which are qualitatively different, and thus are incommensurable. Yet, incommensurability does not necessarily mean that conflicts are irresolvable. According to current discussions of moral dilemmas[26], moral obligations too can be seen as incommensurable, and still, conflicts are resolvable even when they take the form of dilemmas. When two moral obligations are morally incommensurable, the priority of one option over the other can be established on the basis of additional moral considerations, as the best possible in the situation. The significance of conflicts between moral obligations to our issue is that their resolution implies that all obligations, including primary or ultimate obligations (such as the obligations not to harm life, inflict suffering, or interfere with another's autonomy), are capable of being overridden.

This does not entail moral relativism nor the conclusion that conflicts cannot be morally resolved. Had relativism been entailed, I would have necessarily given up the assumption underlying our discussion: that for every moral problem there can be only one right solution, being the best or better in the situation. However, obligations are capable of being overridden by other obligations, and in different conflicts each obligation can gain a different status, relative to the others. This is possible neither due to the nature of obligations themselves nor due to holding to different moral systems or cultures or social ideologies - as it is with traditional relativism. Rather, it is possible due to and through the inclusion of obligations in larger bodies of moral considerations. Some of these considerations are applicable only to certain conflicts and not to others, which affects the status of obligations in each conflict. To argue that obligations are capable of being overridden is consistent with holding to one framework, which in this case is liberalism. Liberalism may be confused and incomplete, yet, it does hold fiercely to several ultimate obligations[27], as well as to the right to privacy and to the value of friendship.

If obligations are capable of being overridden, in a way that does not involve relativism, we should now proceed to discuss the possibility of resolving conflicts between friendship and moral obligations. We should notice though that there is a difference between the possibility of resolving conflicts of obligations and the possibility of resolving conflicts between friendship and moral obligations: the nature of considerations that play a role in resolution of conflicts of obligations is universal, impartial, because these considerations are rules, principles, standards, policies, distinctions, cognitive tests, etc. This is what makes the variety of considerations homogenous in an important moral sense. Such homogeneity is analytically absent in conflicts between partial friendship and impartial moral obligations, so it might appear that the hope for resolving these conflicts analogous to resolving conflicts of obligations is futile.

If conflicts between friendship and moral obligations are resolvable, then it should be not merely from the point of view of impartial morality, according to which obligations can be overridden only by stronger obligations or by an accumulation of other constraining considerations, which are shown to be relevant and sufficient. The resolution of such conflicts should be made also from the point of view of partiality.

Is an integration of impartial and partial perspectives possible? Liberalism can indeed be seen as the art of separation, as opposed to the idea of society as an organic whole. It permits each individual to lead his or her life in separate spheres, namely, the public and the private. Yet, liberalism also assumes the unity and self identity of the moral agent, which makes it possible to demand moral responsibility and integrity. If liberal separation between the different domains of life does not mean schizophrenia, then it must be possible for the individual to grasp his or her experience on both levels as being more than sporadic occurrences. Personal experience should also be understood and judged as morally integrated. Accordingly, in conflict situations, friendship is not necessarily overridden by impartial morality simply because it is particularistic and not universalistic. Alongside utilitarian and deontological considerations, partiality is a source of morality.

Personal integrity and loyalty to one's commitments are not implied by Utilitarianism or Kantianism, because the moral value of actions or consequences is independent of the particularity of the moral agent. Thus, moral integrity seems to be an additional requirement, to take responsibility over and preserve our integrity. As already observed, there is nothing immoral or egoistic about taking care of your integrity, for it is always connected with taking care of others.[28]

The requirement of moral integration, on the one hand, and the absence of a moral test common to both partial and impartial moralities, on the other hand, suggest that instead of looking for (universal) **justification** of our preferences in conflicts of friendship and moral obligations, we should look for the conditions for **permitting** the preference of friendship over impartial obligations.

Permition or license is morally weaker than justification, and thus, assuming the distinction between moral rules and moral ideals, our question can be formulated in terms of moral tolerability of the preference of friendship over moral obligations. Traditionally, it has been argued that if no harm is inflicted on another person, then our privacy is established in the sense of immunity against public intrusion. Under such conditions, our preference of friendship over other obligations could be permitted. But the traditional approach to limiting tolerance on the basis of harm to others is unsatisfactory, partly because the identification of harm has been highly controversial[29] and especially since it gives the wrong impression that harm can never be morally or legally protected. This ignores the whole context of political dissent - demonstrations, strikes, civil disobedience - which is considered justifiable despite the agreement that harm is possibly involved in it.

It seems to me that instead of looking for uncontroversial identification of harm caused by loyalty to friendship, we should consider the possibility of tolerance of alleged or real harm caused by the preference of friendship as compared with alleged or real harm caused by the preference of impartial moral obligations. The element of endurance implicit in tolerance suggests that tolerance is also adequate to actions and relations which might involve harm, in the form of violation of rights and legitimate interests. Thus, in terms of tolerability of preferences, even if the choice of friends over strangers does involve harm, this in itself is not sufficient for demanding that we neglect our friends. Optional harms can be compared with respect to their reversibility or irreversibility, their proportionality, whether they can be compensated, etc.[30]

For example, integrity of personality presupposes loyalty to and continuous reconsideration of principles and commitments. The latter are constituents of personal identity. Not every breach of loyalty violates one's integrity. That will happen, according to Blustein, if one betrays one's identity conferring commitment.[31] Yet, it seems to me that not every betrayal in an identity conferring commitment is necessarily morally wrong, because preserving our personal identity and moral integrity is not the sole or ultimate good. Other moral obligations can override friendship, as it is, for example, when the danger of death is involved. Or it may be discovered that we have had cognitively mistaken conceptions or morally wrong commitments and loyalties, in the sense that, for example, we were mislead by our friend.

Thus, the possibility of morally preferring friendship over impartial obligations has been established, and yet, the moral decision between favoritism toward our friends and impartial obligations cannot be made a priori. Such decisions can be taken only in connection with concrete conflicts, based on whole bodies of moral considerations, which constitute our priorities, as the best possible in the situation.

Notes

This article is partly based on an earlier version, Karin-Frank 1996b.

1. Passell, 1991, pp. 161-5.
2. Ross, (orig. 1923) 1960, pp. 230-1.
3. Blustein, 1991, p. 188.
4. Ibid., pp. 227-30; Meyer, 1992, pp. 481-3; Annis, 1987, p. 352.
5. Ibid., p. 353.
6. Meyer, 1992, p. 483.
7. Ibid., p. 467.
8. Ibid., p. 470.
9. Passell, 1991, pp. 162-3.
10. Ibid., pp. 164-5.
11. Goodin according to Blustein, 1991, p. 227.
12. Dixon, 1995, p. 78.
13. Contrary to Blustein's position, Blustein, 1991, pp. 229-30.
14. Sandel, 1982, pp. 30-2.
15. Meyer, 1992, p. 480.
16. Contrary to my position, see Annis, 1987, p. 355; and Blustein, 1991, pp. 228-9. Both argue that a tacit pledge creates duties, ignoring the significant differences between promise and friendship.
17. Kappelhoff, 1988, p. 496; Langin, 1987, pp. 1443-60; Ferre, 1988, p. 600.
18. Blustein, 1991, pp. 203, 216.
19. Blum, 1982, pp. 58-9.
20. Blustein, 1991, p. 226.
21. Ibid., pp. 218-23.
22. Hampshire, 1983, pp. 101-25.

23. Blustein, 1991, pp. 222-3.
24. Ibid., p. 224.
25. Larmore, 1987, pp. 142-3.
26. For example, see Gowans, 1987.
27. I have elaborated on the issue in Karin-Frank, 1996a.
28. Blustein, 1991, p. 236.
29. See for example: Menduz, 1985, pp. 102-3; Horton, 1985, p. 114; Edwards, 1985, pp. 77-81; Jones, 1985, pp. 138-56.
30. As I have elaborated on in Karin-Frank (forthcoming).
31. Blustein, 1991, p. 232.

References

Annis, D. B. (1987), 'The Meaning, Value, and Duties of Friendship', *American Philosophical Quarterly*, vol. 24, 4.

Blum, L. (1982), *Friendship, Altruism, and Morality*, Routledge & Kegan Paul: London.

Blustein, J. (1991), *Care and Commitment*, Oxford University Press: New York.

Dixon, N. (1995), 'The Friendship Model of Filial Obligations', *The Journal of Applied Philosophy*, vol. 12, 1.

Edowards, D. (1985), 'Toleration and the English Blasphemy Law', in Horton J. & Mendus S. (eds), *Aspects of Toleration*, Methuen: London.

Ferree, C. W. (1988), 'Bowers v. Hardwick: The Supreme Court Closes the Door on the Right to Privacy and Opens the Door to the Bedroom', *Denver University Law Review*, vol. 64, 3.

Gowans, C. W. (1987), *Moral Dilemmas*, Oxford University Press: New York.

Hampshire, S. (1983), *Morality and Conflict*, Basil Blackwell: London.

Horton, J. (1985), 'Toleration, Morality, and Harm', in Horton J. & Mendus S. (eds), *Aspects of Toleration*, Methuen: London.

Kappelhoff, M. J. (1988), 'Bowers v. Hardwick: is there A Right to Privacy?', *The American University Law Review*, 37.

Karin-Frank, S. (1996 a), 'Conflict Resolution: On Values and Other Constraining Moral Considerations', in Hudson Y. (ed.), *Rending and Renewing the Social Order*, The Edwin Mellen Press: Canada.

Karin-Frank, S. (1996 b), 'When Friendship Conflicts with Moral Obligations', in Hudson Y. (ed.), *Rending and Renewing the Social Order*, The Edwin Mellen Press: Canada.

Jones, P. (1985), 'Toleration, Harm, and Moral Effect', in Horton J. & Mendus S. (eds), *Aspects of Toleration*, Methuen: London.

Karin-Frank, S. (forthcoming), 'Is Tolerance Indispensable for Liberalism?', VIBS.

Langin, D. J. (1987), 'The Right to Privacy and the Question of Intimate Relations', *Iowa Law Review*, 72.

Larmore, C. E. (1987), *Patterns of Moral Complexity*, Cambridge University Press: Cambridge.
Mendus, S. (1985), 'Harm, Offence, and Censorship', in Horton J. & Mendus S. (eds), *Aspects of Toleration*, Methuen: London.
Meyer, M. J. (1992), 'Rights Between Friends', *The Journal of Philosophy*.
Passell, D. (1991), 'Duties to Friends', *The Journal of Value Inquiry*, 25.
Ross, W. D. (1960), *Aristotle*, orig. 1923, Methuen: London.
Sandel, M. J. (1982), *Liberalism and the Limits of Justice*, Cambridge University Press: New York.

Reflections on the value of freedom[1]

John T. Sanders

Even as immense popular demonstrations were mounted in behalf of less dictatorship and more freedom, from Shanghai to Soweto to Santiago, from Rangoon to Timisoara to Port-au-Prince, the cautionary warnings about too much freedom continued to be sounded from left and right alike. Even as a 'Goddess of Democracy' was momentarily set up within the expanse of Tiananmen Square, attracting the attention of the world, even as walls fell in Berlin, even as previously intransigent Albania first felt the movement of a gestating hope for freedom within, many commenters were wary: freedom, we were told, is a mixed blessing. Columnists from a variety of political perspectives warned that all is not rosy in the free world, and that those in the not-so-free world who aspire to freedom are taking a big gamble.[2]

Academics offered warnings of their own.[3] In the United States, which prides itself on being for 200 years in the vanguard of the cause of human freedom, the society has been engaged seemingly forever in what seems to be a relatively popular 'war on drugs', part of whose rationale is that too much individual freedom is bad for people.[4]

The issue over how much freedom society can take while still maintaining its social and political health is not a new one. While one can't help but be suspicious that at least *some* of the cautionary tone is the result of vested interest among those who stand to lose power or status in a world that is less authoritarian, less centrally controlled, this cannot be the whole story. The question 'How much freedom is best?' has been recurrent in the history of the debate, and answers to the question have run the full range from 'no freedom at all' to 'complete, unconstrained freedom'.

Thomas Hobbes was certainly among those who set the tone for subsequent debate. His 'State of Nature', contrived to serve the theoretical goal of illuminating the rationale for government within society – indeed, it ended up providing an apparent rationale for a rather *repressive* government – was supposed to portray human society as it would be if there were no institutional restraint of freedom whatsoever. It was supposed to be a situation in which people were *completely* free, *un*restrained by government or morality. In the state of nature, all were at liberty to do whatever they could to protect themselves and further their own ends, with no right or wrong about it.

In such a situation, though, one would be rather severely limited by what was *possible*. One would be at liberty to do whatever one *could* do, but what one could do would be rather pathetically constricted. Life, Hobbes thought, would be solitary, poor, nasty, brutish and all that.

Such a life doesn't sound very free at all to many people, and the confusion over whether the Hobbesian state of nature is best described as one of *complete* freedom, or of virtually *no* freedom (or both, or neither, or a mixture), has exercised many a mind since the publication of *Leviathan*. Rousseau, for example, distinguished between 'natural' liberty (which people have lots of in the state of nature, but give up when they enter civil society) and 'civil' liberty (which people have none of in the state of nature, but *get* by joining society).[5]

Whether this particular distinction solves the problem or not, it has long been almost universally believed that freedom (in some sense) must be *restrained* if freedom (in some possibly different sense) is to be possible, or worth seeking, or whatever. The following reflects well the traditional liberal version of the idea:

> Complete freedom for all means little effective freedom for anyone... Obviously, then, freedom must be restrained if it is to be effective. What we should aim at is a maximum amount of freedom that is compatible with similar freedom for other people... So the extent of legal authority should be kept to the *minimum* that is needed for the protection of liberty.[6]

Such an argument, however, along with many common counter-arguments, presupposes that freedom or liberty (in *some* sense) is a goal worth seeking. Indeed, the traditional liberal argument supposes that, as far as government is concerned, anyway, freedom is just about the *only* goal worth seeking (or legitimately to be sought), since the character and extent of government is itself to be fully determined by the requirements of freedom.

What if freedom is just not that important, though? A thorough rethinking of the traditional liberal line of argument would be required if it could be shown that that argument has overvalued freedom and neglected other important considerations, or if questions were raised about whether freedom is valuable at all. Is freedom an unquestionable good? Does it (or should it) always have priority over other values that could be sought? Or does the degree to which freedom is a good thing depend upon other factors – perhaps cultural or social factors – which vary from time to time and from place to place?

In what follows, I shall examine the claim that the underlying importance given to freedom within a society's scheme of values varies with historical circumstance and social context (I shall sometimes call this the 'relativist claim'). The point of the examination will be to attempt to determine the manner in which, and the extent to which, this claim really endangers the liberal argument. It will be seen that several apparent challenges may be dismissed, since for one reason or another they do not really threaten traditional liberalism.

When these apparent (but non-threatening) challenges are pared away from the relativist claim, it will be seen that the remaining threat is on the one hand weaker, and on the other hand more dubious, than might have been supposed at first. This rather formal work will then set the stage for a proffered definition of the sort of 'freedom' that is at stake in this discussion, and for my own attempt to offer answers to the questions about the value of freedom that I have raised.

The descriptive claim

Some versions of the claim that the value of freedom varies from time to time and from place to place need not concern the liberal at all. It is, by now, standard practice to draw a distinction between purely *descriptive* versions of the claim, on the one hand, and other versions which have at least implicit normative force.[7] The most straight-forward descriptive version of the claim would be something like 'Many cultures, present and past, do not place great value upon freedom'. Such a claim may, clearly, be accepted by the liberal as a sad fact about human history which, he hopes, can be remedied in the future. This descriptive version of the claim does not imply anything at all about the appropriateness or legitimacy of struggling against certain cultures and value systems which may (in the eyes of the liberal) perversely undervalue freedom. All of this, of course, is well known and widely acknowledged.

It nevertheless remains the case that, among those who question the claim that freedom is valuable (as opposed to the question concerning whether freedom is valued in this or that culture), support for their arguments is frequently drawn from data about what in fact is valued (or has been valued) here and there. Sometimes the evidence marshalled in such arguments is drawn from data about one contemporary society or another, sometimes the data is historical or archaeological. But since a normative claim (namely, that freedom is not really 'valuable') continues to be based at least partially on evidence of this kind (for example, evidence that not all cultures value freedom), it will pay to focus at least a bit of initial attention on the descriptive claim.[8] The point will be to focus attention upon just how little weight it can bear in arguments about the value of freedom.

Far from unequivocally supporting the claim that freedom is *not* valuable, evidence that freedom is not universally valued may lie at the heart of a liberal activist's conviction that freedom must be fought for. Indeed, to the extent that some cultures do not place much value on freedom, it is important for those who do value freedom to know this. Such facts provide a basis for strategy in courses of action that the liberal deems important. The liberal in question (i.e., the freedom-valuer) might be a member of one of the cultures in question, a politician within its institutional framework, an outsider who is traveling within or otherwise dealing with a culture that is foreign to him, a representative of an outside government, etc. The liberal purposes or projects involved may range from simply living life unmolested (or as little molested as possible) to plans as ambitious as undermining or overthrowing the entire cultural or governmental system. In all these cases, it will be important that the liberal know that the culture in question does not value freedom, and it will be important to know just how this is manifested in practice. The liberal, therefore, certainly need not deny that 'many cultures, present and past, do not place great value upon freedom'. This is often the battle cry to action for freedom fighters.

For freedom lovers, the important thing about the fact that it is the *culture* which does not value freedom (wherever this is the case) is that it is then the *culture* that one may have to struggle against, make changes in, etc. If it is the culture that places a relatively low value upon freedom, then it is *not* merely some particular villain or group of villains (or *class* of villains) that the freedom fighter must combat.

The upshot of all this, though, is that the mere *descriptive* claim to the effect that many cultures place little or no value upon freedom is not one that those who *do* value freedom need deny. They might, in fact, agree emphatically, and point out that this is precisely why action needs to be taken.[9]

Considerations such as these are interesting, though, in part because they display one of the more important features of the debate about the value of freedom: there is frequently a crucial difference between what a 'culture' may be said to hold as a value, and what an individual member of that culture values.

In fact, all the logically possible combinations of valuations are routinely instantiated in the real world. In addition to freedom lovers who live in cultures that place little value upon freedom, there are people in the same cultures who have no objections at all to their culture's value scheme. And in cultures that place great value upon freedom there are, similarly, both supporters of and detractors from the prevailing value system.

This confuses matters somewhat, given the continuing conflict about the extent to which people are shaped by their cultures. The following, though, seems relatively uncontroversial: however it comes about, sometimes people yearn to be free of the normal roles and values defined by the culture they live in.[10] It is possible that such yearning is itself a cultural product, but this is neither here nor there. People sometimes yearn to be free, struggle to be free – people *value* freedom, in short, sometimes very highly. This seems to be true of some people in every culture known.

The question is, what *is* it that they yearn for, that they value? Is it good that they value this, whatever it may be? Is it bad? Is the answer totally dependent upon what *that culture* says about it (i.e., the very culture being struggled against)? Or is there something non-arbitrary that can be said about the value of freedom that is independent of what that particular culture says? Most generally, is there a fully culture-free way to address the question of the value of freedom?

Such questions as these indicate the importance of the distinction between the value system of a culture and the value systems (or just the values) of its members.[11] Even if it were the case that human behavior was fully determined by culture – or perhaps by genes and culture – an explanation would still be required of the difference between those people in a culture whose behavior conforms to the explicit cultural norms and those whose behavior does not. Even if culture were omnipotent, in other words, we would still be puzzled by 'The paradox and mystery of culture... [which] lies in the fact that through culture man is able to transcend the limits of any given cultural system and to envisage and construct cultural creations with cross-cultural validity'.[12]

The normative claim: some formal considerations

As important as the distinction between the value system of a culture and the values of its members is, one way of making that distinction may be put aside for present purposes. It might be held that certain things can be valuable for a culture quite apart from the value that they may have for people *in* that culture. Since cultures are not simply identical with the set of persons who 'belong' to them – ways of thought, traditions, and other aspects of culture may be said to lead 'lives of their own' – it may be that cultures require things for their survival that might not be in the best interests of the people that comprise them. Making assessments of such interests is a notoriously complicated affair, but here is the kind of argument that I hope can be dismissed: perhaps in order to maintain its integrity *as* a culture, a culture must discourage too much freedom. For if freedom were tolerated, the *people* would flourish but the *culture* would change; it would no longer be the same culture. To the extent that cultures can be said to live and die, this one would die. Thus freedom may be a source of harm to the culture, even though it serves the interests of its members.

We are here distinguishing between freedom as being of value to a culture *qua* culture, and freedom as being of value to the people *in* the culture.[13] It might be held, for example, that not only did Nazi Germany fail to place great value on freedom (the descriptive claim discussed earlier), but that it would have lost its cultural identity (so to speak) if it had tried to incorporate such a value.

This is an example of the kind of issue that I shall *not* concern myself with in what follows. It is not irrelevant, however. A great many of the complaints against liberal intrusion into other 'value systems' seem to come down to claims that *cultures* have rights that must be observed – not only rights against do-gooder 'outside' liberals, but rights against their own members, in whose behalf such outsiders take action. I dismiss this kind of case not because it is uninteresting or unimportant, but because it seems to presuppose that freedom is an important value. It is the freedom of cultures or national groups that is important, according to such arguments, and not the freedom of individuals, but this is no less an appeal to freedom as a value for all that.[14] While it is an important question, therefore, it cannot be part of an argument against the high value of freedom, and must be treated separately elsewhere.[15]

We saw earlier that the purely descriptive claim – that many cultures do not in fact value freedom – is not an argument against the liberal. We have just now dismissed the argument that the 'freedom of a culture' should be valued more highly than the freedom of its members, on the grounds that such an argument is not germane to present purposes. We have trimmed the issue to the extent that it now looks like this: the fact that many cultures have not valued (or might not value) freedom highly is a potential danger to traditional liberalism only to the extent that this low valuation was (or would be) wise, or right, or proper, or advantageous to the members of that culture. Our issue is, in other words, a value issue. As has been observed frequently, it cannot be settled by anthropological or sociological fact alone, nor can it be settled by appealing to the rights of cultures to be left alone, since that smuggles in a version of the very value judgment that is being scrutinized.

Thus, as anticipated, we can dispose of the 'descriptive' claim. What can be said, though, for the claim that it might in some circumstances be wisest or best to give freedom a low value on a wider scale of values? In this area, too, there are a few lines of argument which do not really threaten the traditional liberal position. Indeed, it is possible to deal with *some* such lines of argument in a relatively formal vein, without first getting clear on precisely what 'freedom' is. It is possible, for these arguments, to draw conclusions either purely formally, or based on only the vaguest characterization of 'freedom'.

For example, it may be that the best strategy, under some circumstances, for achieving greater freedom in the long run, may be to downplay it now. If this were ever the case, the liberal may himself embrace the conclusion that it is wise to stress other values, since this finally leads to greater freedom. Freedom is highly valued even while it is, for the short run, not stressed.

A somewhat more complicated line of argument is this: some cultures place little or no value upon freedom. Neither the culture itself nor anyone in the culture bears responsibility or deserves blame for this; even though people in the culture might be better off if freedom were valued highly, it is no-one's *fault* that it is not in fact so valued. Thus anyone who wishes to change things in this society, in the direction of increasing freedom, must do so without hurting people who do not deserve to be hurt. In particular, due consideration must be given to the values that people *in fact have* in that society, so that people are not hurt by the efforts of freedom fighters.

This is clearly a more difficult and more controversial line of argument. What is important to note here is that it is an issue that can arise *among* liberals. Traditional liberals are not enjoined by their commitment to liberty to pursue the cause of freedom without regard to other considerations. In particular, they need not value freedom *so* highly as to conclude that freedom *now* is worth every conceivable cost, nor that all other values are irrelevant in considering the proper path to freedom and the proper pace with which to proceed along that path. The traditional liberal is able to embrace consistently the view that freedom must be sought cautiously and with due regard to other values. Indeed, in addition to being only right and proper, this is probably the *wisest* strategy, if freedom is to last.[16]

What is left, once these non-threats are pared away from the view under scrutiny, seems to be this: traditional liberalism is threatened by the view that freedom is not valued as highly in different places at different times, only to the extent that the lower valuations 1) can be shown to be best or wisest for the members of the cultures in question, *and* 2) can be shown to be best or wisest for reasons *other* than strategic ones in the quest for freedom.

There is still an ambiguity in the first of these two conditions. Clearing it up can narrow the scope of the threat to liberalism still further. The first condition *might* be interpreted to include cases where it is in the interests of *certain* members of the culture to limit the freedom of certain *other* members of the culture. It is, of course, quite easy to imagine situations in which this would be the case, but unless we are prepared to consider the possibility that liberalism is wrong because it is too even-handed, then this line of argument is a non-starter. It can be dismissed on ethical grounds.

This allows us to refine the conditions above to the following: the relativist claim – that the underlying importance given to freedom within a society's scheme of values varies with historical circumstance and social context – is *threatening* to traditional liberalism only if *both*

1. it can be shown that it is *best* or *wisest*, in some such circumstances or contexts, that the members of a culture place a relatively low value on their *own* freedom; *and*
2. the reason for this is *not* simply that such a valuation will best serve the long-term quest for freedom.

Seen in this light, the argument from historical or social relativism is quite a bit weaker than might have been supposed. Most importantly, it becomes clear that the threat is *not* that liberal values conflict with some anthropological or sociological fact, but that there may be values not adequately considered by the liberal, at least under some circumstances.[17]

In addition, though, there are reasons to think that the challenge is more dubious than might have been thought. Once it is seen that the fact of value variability poses no threat, by itself, to the liberal, what remains is somewhat puzzling.

In particular, there is something rather troubling about (1), above. It seems to suggest that people, under some conditions, ought to choose to place a relatively low value on freedom. Apart from questions about whether people can really choose their fundamental values in this way (objections which may not be fatal), one must be concerned about the apparent general presumption that if conditions warrant a given valuation of freedom, people should act to bring that valuation about, in themselves and (perhaps) within their culture. For what if, after switching (appropriately) to a *lower* valuation of freedom, the culture is (later) faced with a change in conditions, such that freedom *should* be valued more highly? How are people to bring it about that freedom is re-evaluated under these new conditions, if neither they nor their culture (by that time) value freedom? Won't they be debilitated in their capacity to implement the right valuational response to the new conditions, living as they do in a society which places little value on freedom, and thus on such action as may be necessary for the reconstruction of the value system?

This may not be a fatal objection either (it is a *practical* argument, after all, and such arguments are hard to assess against normative claims about what *should* be the case), so it needs to be discussed more fully. Perhaps the society in question could arrange for some mechanical educational procedure (for example) which would itself be responsive to changing circumstance, and would encourage people to place the right degree of value upon things at the right times. Surely one must be suspicious about the practicality of such schemes, but perhaps something of this kind could be made plausible.[18]

There are, though, lots of questions about freedom that are more interesting and more promising. Prisoners' Dilemma problems are prominent among them, and such problems deserve vastly more space for their consideration than is available here. Given the present purpose, it should suffice to note that when the liberal argument is stated in the form of *allowing* – even *demanding* – whatever the degree of restraint that promotes the maximum freedom for all, then the Prisoners' Dilemma appears not so much to threaten liberalism as such as it does the most restraint-free versions of it. The same is true, in general, for all 'public goods' problems (of which the Prisoners' Dilemma may be considered one formalized kind). Thus such problems need not be of concern here.[19]

There are, finally, different ways of understanding the challenge to liberalism posed by the view under scrutiny. Perhaps this view should not be formulated exclusively in terms of what it is *wise* for a person or culture to value under these or those conditions, but also (or perhaps only) in terms of what it is kind or right for outsiders to encourage.

Perhaps, under some conditions, it is unkind of us to encourage others to place a higher value on freedom than they do. Even if this sort of paternalism would be acceptable in principle in some cases, the opportunities for wielding arguments of this kind in a self-serving way may be so great as to discredit the argument-type everywhere and always. This may be thought by some to be too extreme, and more attention really ought to be given to variations on this theme. For example, one might contend that it is not just a matter of paternalism – not just a matter of being unkind – but a question of its being *wrong* in some cases to encourage people to place a high value on freedom. Consider, for example, hypotheticals like 'If valuing freedom were to lead to some great evil, then it would be wrong to encourage such a valuation'. To the extent that the antecedents are implausible, such hypotheticals are not too pressing. But since such hypotheticals may be of great theoretical interest, they merit close examination.

Such an examination of these and other questions will have to wait for another occasion, however. For the purposes set out for this section, it is enough to have made clearer the precise character of the 'relativist' challenge to liberalism. We have seen that the bare fact of variations, from culture to culture, in the degree to which freedom is valued, poses no threat to traditional liberalism. Among possible arguments to the effect that freedom *should* be valued less in some circumstances, we have seen that several may be set aside. Arguments that involve deference to the freedom of cultures *qua* cultures, arguments that refer to strategic moves for maximizing long-run freedom, arguments that urge proceeding cautiously and considerately in the pursuit of freedom, and arguments that appeal to reasons that some may have for restraining others, all may be dismissed; they may be dismissed, in fact, on relatively formal grounds. It remains to be seen what comes of the relativist argument once we get clearer on what it is that people or cultures value when they value 'freedom'.

The normative claim

To this point in the discussion, the matter of the value of freedom has been treated rather formally: I have argued that the idea that freedom is valuable escapes many traps that have been or might be set for it. But perhaps this is, strictly speaking, because the idea of freedom is an especially slippery one. To be a bit more blunt, perhaps the idea of freedom escapes these traps because it is ambiguous or vacuous: perhaps it is the idea of many things, now this, now that, that is valued under the name 'freedom'. Or perhaps it is the idea of nothing, and is valued only in contrast with evils that may *appear* to be its alternatives.

As I hope to show, the idea of freedom is not in quite such bad shape as all that, although it must be admitted that it is a vague (and sometimes confused) notion.

What many people would say, I think, if asked what it is that they value under the name 'freedom', is that it is an absence of constraint. But this may be held to be like believing in Santa Claus. Can there ever really *be* a total absence of constraint?

Perhaps not. But *valuing* things that do not exist is not quite as futile as *believing in* things that do not exist. That people *value* a lack of constraint might very well be a smart thing for them to do – it might offer them a goal to aim at, and thus be of 'heuristic' value – even if it were the case that no-one ever is or can be really free of control or constraint.

It might be thought that, when confronted with arguments against the possibility of total absence of constraint, a freedom lover would lose the 'heuristic value' of valuing freedom. But surely this does not follow at all. And even if some modification in one's beliefs were called for in light of the kind of arguments offered by B.F. Skinner and others, Skinner's *own* position on the matter is not entirely unattractive: freedom might very well be defined as the 'absence of *aversive* control', and might then still function in the same way it always has among freedom lovers and in the 'literature of liberty'.

Nonetheless, one might hope for something a bit richer than the Skinnerian formula. People who value freedom certainly don't *conceive* of themselves, at least, as being merely opposed to unpleasantness. Space ought to be made for something like the liberal's desire to promote the fullest possible opportunity for people to act in accordance with their own projects and goals. This need not conflict even with Skinner's view, according to which those very projects and goals are largely (if not entirely) the results of contingencies of reinforcement.

To formulate such a definition of freedom, it will help to ask ourselves what a *conflict* about the value of freedom might come to.

Does some culture (for example, the Alphabetian culture) value freedom highly? What would it mean to answer such a question in the affirmative?

Without any further specification of context, it seems likely that we would expect that such a culture would be one in which fewer matters, rather than more, were mandated by authority. We would see that *perhaps* what was meant was some such 'freedom of the culture itself' as the one discussed above, and that thus what was valued highly was only that the culture (or society) not be constrained from going its own way. But such an interpretation of the claim, were it really the intended one, would surprise us. If we were told that Alphabetian culture placed high value on freedom, we would anticipate, I think, that Alphabetians would find themselves in a society that encouraged them, to whatever *extent* freedom was valued, to pursue their own goals in their own way, rather than naming goals for them that they would then be expected to pursue.

This is all a matter of degree, of course. The assertion 'The Alphabetian culture values freedom highly' is vague, and does not tell us how *much* freedom is valued in comparison with other things.

What would it mean to say that a different culture – say, the Bellagregian culture – does *not* place much value on freedom? Well, it would seem to mean that the culture does not place much positive value on the individual pursuit of individual goals. Perhaps the culture as a whole appears to have clear ideas (to the extent that a culture as a whole can *have* ideas) on what *is* valuable; perhaps, for example, Bellagregians generally place considerable value on education defined in terms of number of years of study (or on numbers of resulting publications), or on standard of living, or on happiness defined in some way that does not tacitly refer back to freedom (e.g., happiness as net hours engaged in some activity or other, or as net wealth, etc.). Whatever the story may be here, if it were true that the Bellagregians, as a culture, did not value freedom particularly highly, there would be no positive encouragement of non-directed pursuit of goals not mandated by authority (or otherwise by the society), even as this might serve some other independent end. For to value such comparatively free activity, even if only because of what it produces, is to attribute (at least) instrumental value to freedom. The culture that does not value freedom highly is one that not only does not think that it is valuable in itself, but also does not think it is valuable by virtue of anything it produces.

Here is how it could be: the Bellagregians value (let's say) maximizing the per capita pizza consumption within the society. We must not, for the moment, ask *why* they value this. It may appear to the Bellagregians (in general, anyway; we mustn't forbid the Bellagregians their occasional curmudgeonly freedom lovers and pizza haters) that allowing freedom within the society does not serve this overarching end. Indeed, according to the Bellagregians, it might appear that encouragement of individuals to pursue their own goals, using means they choose themselves, would make impoverishment (in terms of per capita pizza consumption) inevitable.

Thus there are at least two components to the picture, and they are important to note separately: a culture that places little or no value on freedom is likely to be one that places high value on something *else*,[20] and it is likely to be one which finds freedom to be useless (or even counter-productive) as an instrument in obtaining that something else.

This picture of what it means to place a low valuation on freedom helps to see the flip side: cultures that place a high value on freedom (that is, the matter of individuals being allowed and encouraged to choose their own goals and pursue them in their own way) may do so because such freedom is itself high on the list of things that are of intrinsic value, or they may do so because they take freedom to be instrumentally valuable in the pursuit of whatever *is* high on that list. We have imagined that the Bellagregian culture does neither of these things.

But the Alphabetian culture, right next door to the Bellagregians, values freedom highly. When asked why, let us imagine that different Alphabetians would say different things: some would argue that freedom itself is intrinsically valuable; some would demur from this claim, but would contend that freedom's value is mostly instrumental; others would claim that the reason that freedom is *so* valuable is because it is *both* of intrinsic value and of instrumental value in the obtaining of other intrinsic values.[21]

We must now ask ourselves if representatives of these two cultures, were they to argue about this difference of opinion, would be arguing over anything of substance. Or would they be simply bashing their conflicting value systems together, accompanied by suitably loud noises and oaths? What would it mean (apart from cheer-leading) to say that either the Bellagregians or the Alphabetians were *right* (as against the other)?

If all we were talking about was the predominant 'tastes' of two cultures (as in whether either, both, or neither of these societies encompass the wide-spread practice of eating bugs), it would be proper to conclude that there really is nothing to argue about, beyond the facts concerning whether each culture did in fact value what we say it does. Such facts have a bit of vagueness about them (what *is* it, after all, for an entire culture to value something?), but that's a different kind of problem. If we accept the idea that a culture can value anything at all, then questions about *what* is valued become questions about generality of practice, not rightness or wrongness of what is valued.

Let us take the conflicting views concerning the intrinsic value of freedom first, and then move on to conflict over freedom's instrumental value, to see whether there may be more at stake than mere matters of taste.

On the question concerning whether freedom has high intrinsic value (among other values), some of the Alphabetians say it does and the Bellagregians say it doesn't. What is meant here? Is it just that the first society *likes* freedom, while the second society does not?

Far from being equivalent, the one claim does not even necessarily follow from the other. It seems possible for everyone in a culture – every individual – to *like* (say) the experience of being inebriated or drugged, especially when the experience is a mild one. Alcohol and other drugs commonly available in contemporary Western society are not the best examples, it seems to me, because it is easy to imagine many people who would simply not *like* these things.

Imagine instead that sodium pentathol were widely available in some safe, mild form. Hmm... those who have never had the experience of waking up after having been anesthetized with sodium pentathol will not be able to follow this very well.

So imagine that it is an easy matter to directly stimulate the brain's pleasure center, and imagine that the technology for doing this (whether electrical, chemical, or other) is readily available and cheap. It is a matter of definition that stimulation of the pleasure center is pleasant, so I take it that it is similarly a matter of definition that everyone must like such stimulation. But there is good reason to think that direct stimulation of the pleasure center would be quite addictive (whatever 'addictive' really means[22]) and, therefore, debilitating in the same way that *any* addiction – or obsession – is debilitating. It places obstacles in the way of accomplishing anything *else*: a society which made the technology in question readily available, it might be felt, would be one in which too many people would give over their entire lives to pounding away at the little pleasure-zapper buttons next to their beds.

Be that as it may, it is evident that people might very well *like* having the pleasure center stimulated directly, but (far from 'placing a high value' on such stimulation) find it debasing, debilitating, destructive of things genuinely valuable, etc. Thus it does not *follow* from the fact that something is *liked* that it is highly valued, at least in connection with the 'values of a culture'.

There are ambiguities galore in this mess: individual values versus social values, things found pleasant versus things held to have 'moral' value, etc. Let us try to avoid these issues if we can. The main thing to pull out of the discussion concerning 'liking' and 'valuing' is that one must be *cautious* in moving from the claim that a culture (or a person) *likes* something to the claim that the culture (or person) *values* that thing. There may be some sense in which such inferences may go through, but the situation is rich in ambiguity. One must also be careful about going the other way. That something is *valued* does not imply (without caution) that something is *liked*. Take hard work, for example.

To say that freedom is valued highly by the Alphabetians, but not by the Bellagregians, is to say something that is not simply equivalent to saying that it is *liked* by the one society, but not by the other. Whether liked or not, freedom is deemed *important* by Alphabetian culture. It is *not* deemed important among Bellagregians (as a general rule). It may even be that (as some would say of pleasure center stimulators) freedom is thought by the Bellagregians to be *dangerous* or *debilitating* in some way.

What, then, would it mean to say that there is a *truth* of the matter? We have gone beyond the *descriptive* claim that Alphabetian culture values freedom (which is true just in case Alphabetian culture really does value freedom), and are trying to appraise a potential argument between an Alphabetian and Bellagregian. What hangs in the balance when such arguments are engaged in?

As regards the claim that freedom is *intrinsically* valuable, it would appear that all that can be meant is that its value is 'basic'; i.e., to be taken as some kind of fixed point. This doesn't go much beyond repeating that the value is 'intrinsic'. Why would anyone make such a claim about *anything*?

In the matter of cultural values, to say that something is intrinsically valuable may be to indicate that its value is implicit in the very notion of culture. Thus a list of some culture's 'intrinsic' valuations offers one *perspective* on that culture's conception of society, of culture itself.[23] In particular, to say that freedom is intrinsically valuable may be just to indicate that individual well-being, defined not so much in terms of the achievement of certain general ends, but rather in terms of relative absence of social constraints on choice of means and ends, is partially *constitutive* of the notion of society or culture. Thus to talk about 'intrinsic' value is to talk about fundamental political and social issues, not just likes and dislikes. To *argue* about intrinsic cultural values is to argue about political and social philosophy. It is to open discussion concerning the *point* of society, or (for those who, like me, are a bit uncomfortable about saying that natural things like societies and cultures are aptly described as having 'points' or 'purposes') concerning the proper conception of the *relation between* society and individual.

Thus the Alphabetian culture, if it places a high *intrinsic* value on freedom, very likely imagines that society and culture can and should contribute to the well-being of individuals, not solely (or even at all) through the provision of particular products and services, but rather through attempting to make space for individual action and choice.

And those Alphabetians who argue in behalf of the intrinsic value of freedom argue for the superiority of a particular conception of the relation between individual and society. To be right about the question of intrinsic value is to be right about a philosophical question. And, it seems, this philosophical question, no less than the question about freedom itself, involves value questions.

Thus we may not escape value issues if we focus only on the 'intrinsic' valuations of contrasting cultures. Progress among Alphabetian and Bellagregian interlocutors who focus attention in this way is possible only if broadening the discussion to questions about the proper relation between individual and society, about what constitutes human well-being, etc., offers greater opportunities for finding common ground. While this is possible – and while this possibility makes clear that considerably more is at stake than matters of taste – it is not at all inevitable. It may very well be that the difference between Alphabetians and Bellagregians over intrinsic value pervades their entire (respective) political and social philosophies. While it is not common for living philosophies (ones that are at work in real people's belief systems) to be as consistent as all that, it is not impossible. Thus it *may* be that nothing will be achieved in the debate between our two cultural representatives (beyond clarification of background belief) if all they pursue is the question of the intrinsic value of freedom.

The opportunities for progress in the discussion are richer, as it happens, if we turn to the question of freedom as *instrumentally* valuable. For here the questions are not all philosophical and systematic. Some of the questions that get generated in a discussion of the instrumental value of freedom appear, from most natural perspectives, to be empirical ones. Nevertheless, this does not mean that they are simple. For judgments concerning the truth of one or another empirical claim are, after all – like all judgments – eminently fallible.

It is perfectly possible that someone might be dedicated to the proposition that freedom has *no* 'intrinsic' value, but that freedom is nevertheless very valuable. It is possible, in other words, for people to have a conception of society and culture, and of the relation of society to individuals, that does *not* understand the main (or *a* main) 'point' of society to be the enhancement of individual well-being (defined for societies that place high intrinsic value on freedom in the terms set out above[24]), but to nevertheless think that freedom to choose and freedom to act are extraordinarily important.

Let us return to the Bellagregians. They do not think that there is anything all that special about freedom. They *do* think there is something special about *pizza*. An Alphabetian might contend that *if* pizza is truly valued by Bellagregians, one ought to expect that encouraging freedom (i.e., individual choice of ends and means) would be most likely to yield what is valued. The argument might well be a market argument: if people really value pizza over other things, then freedom of action and freedom of exchange will tend to yield a situation in which pizza is maximally available.[25] Freedom, the Alphabetian will argue, is thus instrumentally valuable, even on the Bellagregian scheme of intrinsic value. The claim, then, must be that there is something wrong with the Bellagregian value scheme, if it does not even accord *instrumental* value to freedom. And this claim is *empirical*, in that it rests on the contention that pizza can be more widely available if people are allowed and encouraged to be free.[26]

What it would mean, then, for an Alphabetian to be *right* in claiming that freedom is valuable is *not* just a matter of rightly describing himself as *liking* freedom (for valuing something is not equivalent to liking it); neither is it *merely* a matter of correctly ascribing to himself the belief that freedom is important. Even considering only the claim that freedom is *intrinsically* valuable, it is plain that more is at stake. If the Alphabetian is making such a claim, he is right if the overall conception of society and its relation to the individual that is reflected in the claim about freedom is the best one. This is a philosophical question, and it does not escape judgments about values.

But if the Alphabetian is making not (only) a claim about intrinsic value, but rather (or in addition) a claim about instrumental value, then the argument is (in part) an empirical one. It is about what in fact one social arrangement or another will lead to. The contention that freedom is valuable will be correct if it in fact yields maximization of other things that are valuable, and if it does so without producing so many bad consequences as to outweigh the good. The *constraints* (if any) that must be placed on freedom in order to ensure that the good outweighs the bad are sure to be vital parts of the discussion.

The empirical question thus raised will have to be addressed anew for every list of values. There are lots of *conceivable* lists that could be contrived that will easily rule out freedom as a value. It remains to be seen whether any carefully considered list that anyone *really* proposes as being valuable can fail to include freedom. And such lists, of course, are the important ones.

Conclusion

We are now in a better position to attempt to answer the questions about the value of freedom that we have raised.

What *is* it that people yearn for – that they *value* – when they struggle for freedom? On the present analysis, they long for greater autonomy, for greater opportunity to choose their own goals, and to pursue them in their own way.

This claim is not inconsistent with the observation that many or all of 'their own goals' and 'their own ways' have been picked up from the environment within which they have lived their lives. Surely this is true. But only genetically identical biological siblings have identical physical constitutions as they first confront their environments, and no two organisms ever have had or ever will have identical environments. Insofar as environmental conditions are relevant to whatever gets picked up by an organism as a goal or as a means toward a goal, these conditions are unique to each organism. Thus scruples against referring to an organism's goals and strategies as its own are inappropriate. The goals and strategies that it has picked up from its environment simply *are* its own goals and strategies. They are likely to be different – sometimes subtly, sometimes dramatically – from the goals and strategies of other organisms, even among organisms of the same species, the same culture, or the same family.

A consequence of this is that *political* freedom, understood in this way, is not necessarily related to the sort of 'metaphysical' freedom ('freedom of the will') that would be incompatible with environmental shaping of desire and action.[27]

Can people actually *be* free? Or can people only (at best) *think* that they are? Does thinking so make it true? Or is *believing* that you are free quite different from actually *being* free?

Societies surely vary in terms of the degree to which individual autonomy is supported and encouraged. It is hard to understand, of course, what *total* freedom would be like. The goals and strategies that people pick up from their environments are functions, in part, of idiosyncratic variables; but they are equally dependent upon constraints found within the environment. In a sense, then, goals and strategies in the absence of environmental constraint make no sense at all.

Given this understanding of freedom – of the pursuit of personal goals in personally chosen ways – there need be no demand that all environmental constraints be removed. As the critics of the 'literature of liberty' have observed, it is hard to make sense of such a demand; it seems to be an impossibility. But no such demand was ever made in that literature. Instead, what was demanded was encouragement and support for – or at least an end to the suppression of – the pursuit of individually chosen goals in individually chosen ways.

That such things are in fact supported and encouraged within a society is not simply a function of what people believe. People can be sold a bill of goods on this issue, and it is not implausible to contend that they often are. Governments frequently *claim* to support individual liberty. The proof, though, is in what such governments do when citizens – especially curmudgeons who criticize the government – attempt to exercise such freedom.

Whether people are free or not is, thus, not simply a question of whether they think they are. They might be free, in the relevant sense, while not believing that they are; or they might believe that they are free, while in fact they are not. Much depends on what is actually allowed, encouraged, prohibited, and prosecuted in the society, and this is *not* simply a matter of declaration and belief. Indeed, sometimes the truth of the matter is difficult to discern even for those who are best informed.

Is there a fully culture-free way to address the question of the *value* of freedom? The answer has two parts, one dealing with claims about the 'intrinsic' value of freedom, the other with claims about freedom's 'instrumental' value.

As far as claims about intrinsic value is concerned, we have seen that they hang to a considerable extent on philosophical views about the proper relation between society and individual, about the very 'point' of society. The *intrinsic* value of freedom, then, will vary from culture to culture just in case the 'point' or rationale of society so varies.

But claims about the instrumental value of freedom are clearly more empirical, depending as they do upon questions concerning what is and is not likely as the consequence of particular social strategies. Market arguments, in particular, tend to stress the importance, in the achievement of almost *any* particular social product, of taking advantage of the special perceptions of individuals regarding opportunities, available resources, and personal abilities. For central administrators to try to achieve social goals by telling individuals what to do and how to do it is to choose desperately ineffective means, according to such arguments. If individuals are left to their own devices, with incentives that are personally motivating, they will achieve considerably more than if they are centrally directed, given the necessary ignorance of central administrators concerning the details of local and personal conditions. The argument continues: *the larger and the more complex the society, the more important this fact.* And, to return to our present question, this fact (if it is one) is culture-free. It is a putative fact about decision-making in human groups.[28]

Is freedom an unquestionable good? This is a difficult question, surprisingly enough. It is surprising that one might even *consider* the possibility that *any* good is 'unquestionably' good. But if *anything* stands a chance of being a candidate for such a status, it would seem that freedom does.

Surely it is not the case that questions about the value of freedom are foolish. Neither are considered arguments to the effect that freedom can be dangerous. Indeed, it *can* be dangerous, and it may often be wise to contrive ways of limiting one's *own* freedom, upon occasion. It might be that, since I want to consume fewer pistachios, I would be well advised to keep them out of my house. While it is true that I still can choose not to eat them when they are sitting there on the table before me, open-shelled and inviting, it is just too damned hard. Better for me to avoid having to make such choices. This line of argument is not *foolish*, I repeat. It requires careful consideration wherever it is deployed, as it is (for example) in the argument in behalf of keeping psycho-active and other drugs illegal.[29]

What *may* be foolish are questions about whether freedom is ever really valuable at all. Even if the arguments about the intrinsic value of freedom are rejected, surely it is the case that, for many purposes, freedom is (not just valued but) objectively valuable from an instrumental point of view. The achievement of (at least) some social ends requires that people be allowed and encouraged to pursue their own goals in their own ways. Whether the social ends that thus require freedom are themselves the rule or the exception across societies is a matter of debate.

Thus, while the *prima facie* value of freedom is unquestionable, how freedom is to be placed in a hierarchy of values is not obvious. What may come as a surprise to some, though, is the extent to which this is an empirical question.

Does the degree to which freedom is a good thing depend upon cultural or social factors which vary from time to time and from place to place? Well, yes and no.

The degree to which freedom is *intrinsically* valuable depends, in large part, upon which way of characterizing the relation between individual and society is best.

This is a philosophical issue, and like many such issues, it is quite difficult to tell whether it might best be resolved differently in different social circumstances. One can at least say that the intrinsic value of freedom would vary with social and historical circumstances only to the extent that the appropriate answer to the philosophical questions so vary.

It's a bit easier to be clear on the question whether the *instrumental* value of freedom varies from time to time or from place to place. *If* there are no valuable things that freedom helps people to gain, or *if* freedom produces enough bad things as to outweigh whatever good it produces, then it would be apt and wise to place a low valuation on freedom. Whether this is ever the case needs to be examined situation by situation.

What is even clearer, though, is that whether it is a good thing or a bad thing that people yearn for freedom – that they long to be able to pursue their own goals in their own ways – the answer is not merely a function of what the culture they live in may say about such things. Those who express the views that we take to be representative of a culture may, like anyone else, be *mistaken* in their analysis of the right or best relationship between individual and society (however this be interpreted), and they may be mistaken in their judgments concerning what will and what will not happen if people are encouraged to be free.

Finally, how much freedom is best? Should it always have priority over other values that could be sought? What can be said for the claim that it might in some circumstances be wisest or best to give freedom a relatively low value, on a wider scale of value?

Freedom always has some *prima facie* instrumental value with respect to some ends. But if there are circumstances within which freedom does not contribute to the achieving of the most important social goals, or in which freedom actually obstructs the achieving of important social goals, then, in those circumstances, it might be wise to assign a low value to freedom. In those circumstances, freedom should not be sought.

The big question, of course, is whether such circumstances ever really exist. It might seem more plausible that the failure to promote and encourage at least a minimal degree of individual freedom, given the importance of freedom to the achieving of *anything* that real cultures value, would mean the inevitable *death* of society.[30] If freedom is an intrinsic good, or if freedom can be shown to contribute *broadly* to the achievement of things valued in any culture at all, then it could be concluded that it is *never* wise to underestimate the value of freedom.

Notes

1. This paper was discussed at the meetings of the American Section of the International Association for Philosophy of Law and Social Philosophy, University of Utah, Salt Lake City, October 1990. Earlier versions of

portions of the paper were read and discussed at the meetings of the Northern New England Philosophical Association, Keene, New Hampshire, October 1990, at the meetings of the Creighton Club (the New York State Philosophical Association), Skaneateles, New York, October 1988, and at a symposium on 'The Objective and the Subjective' held at the Rochester Institute of Technology in November of 1986. Parts have been published in the *Proceedings of the Creighton Club*, and other parts are to appear under the title 'Freedom's Value' in Robert Moffat, Cornelius Murphy and Noel Reynolds (eds), *Reconciling Liberalism and Community* (New York: New York University Press, 1996). I owe thanks to James I. Campbell, William Clohesy, Randall R. Curren, Timothy Engström, Dane Gordon, Patrick Grim, Richard Lunt, John Morreall, David B. Suits and Victoria Varga for their criticisms and encouragements of various drafts.

2. See, for example, Cal Thomas's syndicated column for 4 January 1990, 'U.S. Churches, Not 'Playboy', Should Be Targeting E. Europe' (Rochester *Democratic and Chronicle*, p. 10A). Thomas wrote 'If Eastern Europe thought communism was a difficult yoke to bear, wait until it gets a sample of Western-style hedonism'. See also Tom Wicker's column on 8 January 1990 ('Freedom's Not Perfect, It's What You Make Of It', *Democrat and Chronicle*, p. 6A). Wicker warned Central and Eastern Europeans about murder, random violence, catastrophic illness, homelessness, crumbling infrastructure, and overwhelming problems of waste disposal. For a general discussion of all these warnings, see Virginia Postrel, 'The Banality of Freedom?', *Reason*, March 1990.

3. Such warnings played a large role in the wash of 'communitarian' literature within American social and political philosophy during the late 1980s and early 1990s. Michael Sandel (*Liberalism and the Limits of Justice,* Cambridge: Cambridge University Press, 1982), 'The Political Theory of the Procedural Republic', in Allan C. Hutchinson & Patrich Monahan, eds, *The Rule of Law: Ideal or Ideology* (Toronto: Carswell, 1987), 'Moral Argument and Liberal Toleration: Abortion and Homosexuality', *California Law Review,* 1989, pp. 533-8 and Alasdair MacIntyre *After Virtue* (Notre Dame: University of Notre Dame Press, 1984), *Whose Justice? Which Rationality?* (Notre Dame: University of Notre Dame Press, 1988) were at the center of controversy. There was considerable debate among Soviet dissidents, for a number of years before the fall of the Soviet Union, about the dangers of freedom. Alexander Solzhenitsyn represented the 'right wing' in this debate, and Roy Medvedev represented the 'left'. Thinkers at both ends of the spectrum were worried about freedom, but for different reasons. For discussion of these contrasting views, see Harvey Fireside, 'Dissident Visions of the USSR: Medvedev, Sakharov & Solzhenitsyn', *Polity*, Winter 1989. For typical western

concerns among academics about increasing freedom in Central and Eastern Europe, see John J. Mearsheimer, 'Back to the Future: Instability in Europe After the Cold War', *International Security*, vol. 15 (Summer, 1990), pp. 5-56, and 'Why We Will Soon Miss the Cold War', *Atlantic*, August 1990, pp. 35-50. In the latter article, Mearsheimer noted that 'Last year [1989] was repeatedly compared to 1789, the year the French Revolution began, as the Year of Freedom, and so it was. Forgotten in the general exaltation was that the hope-filled events of 1789 signalled the start of an era of war and conquest'. For a classic statement of the negative aspects of freedom, see Erich Fromm, *Escape From Freedom* (New York: Avon Books, 1969).

4. See William J. Bennett's 'A Response to Milton Friedman' in *The Wall Street Journal*, 19 September 1989. The letter that Bennett was responding to is Friedman's 'An Open Letter to Bill Bennett', *The Wall Street Journal*, 7 September 1989.

5. Rousseau himself, quite wisely (and contrary to some readings of his work), appeared to prefer the 'natural' variety of liberty, and may have regarded 'civil' liberty as a delusion. See especially William T. Bluhm, 'Freedom in *The Social Contract;* Rousseau's 'Legitimate Chains'', *Polity* XVI (1984). Bluhm uses a reading of Rousseau's *Reveries of the Solitary Walker* to reconcile tensions between such texts as *Emile* and *On the Social Contract.* Although it has nothing to do with Rousseau, in particular, see also in connection with this issue John T. Sanders, 'Political Authority,' in *The Monist*, vol. 66, no. 4 (October 1983), pp. 545-56. And see George Orwell, *1984* (New York: The New American Library, 1961) on using words like 'freedom' and 'liberty' to denote slavery. For an important contribution to the debate about what freedom consists in, see David Miller, 'Constraints on Freedom', *Ethics* 94 (1983).

6. This is D.D. Raphael's characterization of the 'old-style Liberal' argument. See his 'Liberty and Authority', in A. Phillips Griffiths (ed.), *Of Liberty: Royal Institute of Philosophy Lecture Series: 15, Supplement to Philosophy 1983* (Cambridge: Cambridge University Press, 1983), pp. 4-5. It is clear that Raphael does not himself agree with this version of the argument.

7. That a distinction may be made between descriptive and normative relativist claims does not imply that the former are 'scientific' rather than philosophical. See especially Wayne Wasserman, 'What Is a Fundamental Ethical Disagreement?', *Analysis* 45 (1985). Wasserman argues that the doctrine that the values of individuals (or cultures) in fact conflict in a 'fundamental' way – a doctrine which seems itself to be fundamental to descriptive ethical relativism – is hard to make sense of, since it is hard to know what counts as a 'fundamental' ethical agreement or disagreement. See also Richard Brandt, *Ethical Theory: The Problems of Normative and*

Critical Ethics (Englewood Cliffs, N.J.: Prentice-Hall, 1959); Paul W. Taylor, *The Principles of Ethics: An Introduction* (Belmont, CA: Wadsworth, 1975); and Patrick Grim, *Ethical Relativism in the Context of the Social Sciences* (unpublished Ph.D. dissertation, Boston University, 1976).

8. It is true that, for some relativists, the sense in which the argument is in any way normative is elusive. For these relativists, the only reason there would be to say that freedom is not 'valuable' (rather than simply not *valued*) would be because the term 'valuable' just has no *meaning* beyond 'valued'. In my own view, this simply defies common English usage for no good reason. Be that as it may, though, it is an unusual relativist indeed who would endorse the argument that freedom is valuable *simpliciter* (without specification of this society or that). Why should anyone be reluctant about this, if 'valuable' and 'valued' are equivalent? After all, even if what is valued varies from culture to culture or from person to person, that freedom is valued *anywhere* would license the simple claim that freedom is valued (period).

9. The problems created for social scientists by such confrontations in values, as they try to decide how best to do their work, are well-known and much discussed. See, for example, Roger Goodman, 'Is There an 'I' in Anthropology? Thoughts on Starting Fieldwork in Japan', *JASO* XV (1984). For an extremely interesting account of an effort to *undermine* a group by studying it, see Stanley R. Barrett, 'Racism, Ethics and the Subversive Nature of Anthropological Inquiry', *Philosophy of the Social Sciences,* 14 (1984).

10. It is interesting to contemplate the possibility that the manifestation of this phenomenon in cultures that value freedom highly may be the placing of a *low* personal value on freedom. Such contemplation begins to hint at certain confusions that plague both defenses of and attacks on freedom. See the next note for more on this, and see the substantive discussion of freedom, below, for an effort to define 'freedom' in such a way as to capture what is yearned for by all of those who wish to be 'free' of the normal roles and values defined by the culture they live in, whatever those roles and values may be.

11. Many people who appreciate the importance of such a distinction would nevertheless argue that individual values still depend upon some cultural values or other. David Bidney, for example, contends that 'to the extent that the adherents of a culture conform to, and are satisfied with, their traditional institutions, they feel free and are not aware, for the most part, of any significant restraints. It is only upon consciousness of other cultures and critical comparison with their systems of liberties that dissatisfaction tends to arise and complaints are made of coercion and tyranny' [See 'The Varieties of Human Freedom', in Bidney (ed.), *The*

Concept of Freedom in Anthropology (The Hague: Mouton & Co., 1963), p. 23]. Surely, though, it cannot be that these are the *only* circumstances under which such dissatisfaction may arise. For how could one account, if Bidney were right, for the dissatisfaction of those who know of no culture in which the liberty they seek is to be found? How could new extensions of freedom, previously unknown anywhere, ever be possible? Franz Boas, sometimes referred to as a subjectivist who equates freedom with the feeling of harmony with one's culture, is a bit more careful than Bidney in this regard. He says 'We are free in so far as the limitations of our culture do not oppress us; we are unfree when we become conscious of these limitations and are no longer willing to submit to them' (Liberty Among Primitive People', in Ruth Nanda Anshen, ed., *Freedom: Its Meaning* (New York: Harcourt, Brace & Co., 1940), p. 380). Yet there are clearly problems with this understanding of freedom; in the same essay, Boas writes 'It is... certain that intellectual freedom is not entirely absent even in societies in which rigid dogmatic belief pervades the whole life. Among tribes in which the life-histories of individuals are known in some detail, we find disbelievers who disregard sacred teachings and who come into conflict with their fellow-tribesmen' (p. 379). Aren't these *just* the people who would be *un*free on the other account? But Boas here describes such people as intellectually free. We cannot resolve this dilemma by imagining that this intellectual freedom is somehow not substantial, for Boas continues 'More frequently we find those given to speculation who develop or reform the tribal dogma. It would be difficult to understand the complex ceremonial life and the systematic mythology of many peoples if we did not assume that priests or other thinkers have shaped a heterogeneous mass of ceremonial actions, myths, and religious teachings into a more or less consistent whole. A communal growth of such phenomena without individual initiative is unthinkable' (p. 379). The question is, is the person who initiates changes in the culture because of dissatisfaction, whether mild or severe, a *free* person? You can't have it both ways. Bronislaw Malinowski, thought of by many as an advocate of 'objective' criteria of freedom, is a cultural determinist. For Malinowski, what there are objective criteria for is being able to *do* certain kinds of things, quite independently of what is felt (See Malinowski, *Freedom and Civilization* (New York: Roy Publishers, 1944), especially pp. 59-62 and 30-40). David Miller's discussion of 'socialist' freedom (in 'Constraints on Freedom', *op. cit.*) resembles Malinowski's view in some ways. For Ruth Benedict, the feeling of freedom once again becomes central, although she tries to identify objective criteria for the having of this feeling (Benedict, 'Primitive Freedom', reprinted from Margaret Mead, *An Anthropologist at Work: Writings of Ruth Benedict* (Boston: Houghton Mifflin Co., 1959), pp. 386-98). The question here is, though, can people *be* free? Or can people only (at best) *think* that they are? Does thinking so make it true? Or is it irrelevant? B.F. Skinner, from whom one might hope at least to get clear answers to questions of this kind, is not exactly lucid. Sometimes 'freedom' seems to mean (for Skinner) 'the absence of aversive control', which surely obtains occasionally in the lives of some people [see Skinner, *Beyond Freedom and Dignity* (Toronto: Bantam Books, 1971), especially pp. 27-30]. Indeed, Skinner proposes that we build a society that is as free of aversive control as possible (thus, one would think, the most 'free'). But in other places, of course, Skinner takes himself to be denying that people are ever free. Surely he does not mean to deny that people ever find themselves in situations that lack aversive control. This confusion has led to a worse press for Skinner's work than is warranted, it seems to me.

12. Bidney, *The Concept of Freedom in Anthropology*, p. 6. As should be clear from the spirit of this paper, I would not put the matter like this myself; but it is important to document the centrality of this issue even among people who are a great deal more impressed by the effects of 'culture' than I.

13. Further difficulties emerge in sorting out the implications of the distinction between things that might have value (to or for someone or something, or with respect to someone or something) and things that might have values (i.e., might be someone or something with respect to which things might have value). For a discussion of some of these difficulties as they arise for certain especially interesting ethical questions, see John T. Sanders, 'Why the Numbers Should Sometimes Count', *Philosophy & Public Affairs* (Winter 1988), pp. 3-14.

14. Certain uses of the contention that liberty is not of central importance at certain times and laces may thus *require* an underlying principle of liberty if they are to have *normative* force (as in 'leave those cultures alone and don't force freedom on them').

15. It might be thought that the claim in question – that the 'freedom of a culture' ought to be considered as a grounds for denying freedom to people *in* that culture (or for preventing outside intrusion) – may *not* be so easily avoided, since it seems squarely to oppose liberal views of what particular cultures should be like. For example, if a liberal had argued in 1977 that it was morally right that the Khmer Rouge should be overthrown because of the cruelty it practiced against huge numbers of Cambodians, others who support the claim in question might have dismissed such an argument as self-serving Western cultural imperialism, or (in the event) as self-serving Soviet-sponsored Vietnamese imperialism. Thus it might be thought that the argument, quite apart from whether it is good or bad, is surely directed against the liberal and must be confronted. I must confess that this line of reasoning troubles me. But I think that the contention in the text – that

such an apparently antiliberal argument presupposes freedom as a value – is correct. I think that the argument, in fact, presupposes liberalism. Again, it is a liberalism among cultures rather than among individuals, but it is still liberalism. It is a version of liberalism whose influence accounts for some of the indecision among people who think of themselves as liberals about (for example) whether the Vietnamese should have been praised for invading Cambodia, about what position to take on Khmer Rouge participation in future Cambodian governments, about what is to be done to help people in other countries who are oppressed by their governments, etc. But it is a problem generated from *within* liberalism. Thus, I hope, it can be dismissed for present purposes.

16. One must distinguish among classes of cases, therefore. Wherever it is considerations about the best way to achieve a stable freedom that lead to the conclusion that one must accommodate other values, there is not even a conflict between the idea that freedom should be valued *highest* and the idea that such accommodation is called for. In other cases, though, the liberal may need to accept the notion that there are other values than freedom that merit equal (or near-equal) attention. For further discussion of this kind of consideration, see John T. Sanders, 'The State of Statelessness,' in John T. Sanders and Jan Narveson, *For and Against the State: New Philosophical Readings* (Lanham, Maryland: Rowman and Littlefield, 1996), pp. 255-88.

17. Alternatively, the liberal might be charged with ignoring the following putative epistemological fact: freedom will be valued only in those cultures which embrace certain values – and certain factual and logical beliefs – which comprise together *webs* of belief of certain kinds. The liberal, of course, may doubt that there exists any such web (at least among webs that real people work with) that excludes in principle the positive value of freedom, but the proof is to be found in the pudding. The liberal does best to ask for examples of such webs, possible and real, that exclude freedom as a value. In the event that such a web of belief and value is produced, it still remains to be seen whether there are any plausible standards that might be available to evaluate webs against one another. If such epistemological facts be truly factual, in other words, they need not be ignored by the liberal. Such facts would be no more damaging in principle than are sociological and anthropological facts.

18. For discussion of the notion that there can be control over one's values, even though it may not be apt to say that they are *chosen*, see Charles Taylor, 'Responsibility For Self', in Amelie Rorty, ed., *The Identities of Persons* (Berkeley: University of California Press, 1976), pp. 281-99.

19. For discussion of the relation between many-person Prisoners' Dilemmas and various public goods problems, see Philip Pettit, 'Free Riding and Foul Dealing', *The Journal of Philosophy*, 83 (1986), and Raimo

Tuomela, 'Free Riding and the Prisoner's Dilemma', *The Journal of Philosophy*, 85 (1988). The problems posed by 'public goods' for what might be regarded as an extremely unrestrained version of traditional liberalism are discussed in John T. Sanders, *The Ethical Argument Against Government* (Washington: University Press of America, 1980), especially Chapter 6. Finally, for current discussion of some of the most important implications of Prisoners' Dilemma and related theoretical games within political philosophy, see Peter Danielson, 'The Rights of Chickens: Rational Foundations for Libertarianism?'; Jan Narveson, 'The Anarchist's Case'; John T. Sanders, 'The State of Statelessness'; Anthony de Jasay, 'Self-Contradictory Contractarianism'; and Howard H. Harriott, 'Games, Anarchy, and the Nonnecessity of the State'; all in Sanders and Narveson, *For and Against the State: New Philosophical Readings*.

20. Or is this *not* so likely? It is possible, I think, to imagine a culture that did not value freedom, where this is not because of contrast between freedom and some perceived higher value. But the possibility of imagining this seems to be fairly limited. One can imagine, for example, a listless culture that doesn't value much of *anything*; thus it doesn't value freedom. It's just bored and lifeless. Or one can imagine a culture that hasn't really thought about freedom at all. Where this means the individual pursuit of individually chosen goals, it is fairly difficult to imagine this. But perhaps when we imagine a sort of Jaynesian pre-conscious society we imagine such a thing (see Julian Jaynes, *The Origin of Consciousness in the Breakdown of the Bicameral Mind* (Boston: Houghton-Mifflin, 1982)). I confess that my imagination is pressed to the limit of its capacity in trying to imagine people who have not even *thought* about the positive or negative value of individuals doing what they think important, just *because* they think it important. Much easier to imagine is the situation envisioned in the text: people *have* thought about freedom (so understood), and have come to the conclusion that freedom either is not as important as some other value, or (more strongly) that freedom actually obstructs the achievement of some important goals.

21. Some of the differences mentioned here as among the Alphabetians are paralleled in differences between 'natural rights' and 'utilitarian' arguments in what Skinner has called the 'literature of freedom'.

22. For an interestingly novel perspective on the notion of 'addiction', see especially the works of Thomas Szasz. Good sources are *The Manufacture of Madness* (New York: Harper & Row, 1977), *The Myth of Mental Illness* (New York: Harper & Row, 1984), and *Ceremonial Chemistry: The Ritual Persecution of Drugs, Addicts, and Pushers* (Holmes Beach, FL: Learning Publications, 1987).

23. In the case of an *individual's* list of 'intrinsic' values, what is reflected may very well be that individual's conception of a good human life.

24. In terms, that is, not of the achievement of certain general ends, but rather in terms of relative absence of social constraints on choice of means and ends.

25. That this is supposed to be a *tendency* or *liklihood* is an important feature of such arguments. No guarantees are available in this area, but estimates of probable trends or tendencies may be capable of some empirical support. These are, again, fairly tricky empirical questions, and this accounts for the fact that arguments such as these, empirical though they are, remain controversial. For some indication that even some 'rights' that are often held to be deeply fundamental or 'natural' to persons are best explained or defended on what might appear to be empirical grounds, see John T. Sanders, 'Justice and the Initial Acquisition of Property', *The Harvard Journal of Law and Public Policy*, vol. 10, no. 2 (Spring 1987), pp. 367-99.

26. We needn't venture as far as Alphabetia or Bellagregia, of course, to find such a situation. There is some reason to think that Chinese, Cuban, former Soviet, and Central or Eastern European societies have *always* numbered among their 'intrinsic' values such things as individual well-being, health, the general fulfillment of human potential, control of the machinery of society by the people, etc. These societies, though, have not always valued freedom (at least: not on the definition of 'freedom' offered here). The dilemma for them in the 1990s has been how to overcome the debilitating effects of undervaluing freedom even as *instrumentally* valuable. For a more technical argument along the same lines concerning the original arguments of Karl Marx, see *The Ethical Argument Against Government,* Chapter Nine.

27. Critics and proponents of liberalism are therefore alike mistaken if they understand liberalism to require belief in 'metaphysical' freedom from all social and environmental shaping forces. For an example of such a mistake, see Michael Bacharach's identification of 'the doctrine that economic welfare is the product of autonomous individual choices *in vacuo*' as the 'myth of liberalism' (in the last paragraph of 'Commodities, Language, and Desire', *The Journal of Philosophy,* vol. 87, No. 7, July 1990, pp. 346-68).

28. See, for example, F.A. Hayek, *Individualism and Economic Order* (Chicago: University of Chicago Press, 1948), and *The Constitution of Liberty* (Chicago: University of Chicago Press, 1960).

29. Different issues arise, of course, in the case where I am trying to limit my *own* choices and when I attempt to limit the choices of others. If I argue that drugs should be illegal so that *I* am not tempted, the argument is considerably less suspect than when I argue that drugs should be illegal so that *others* are not tempted. If self-defense can plausibly be introduced into the latter argument, it may be made a bit stronger. And if I can make it

plausible that people are so debilitated by drugs that they are no longer truly able to make free choices, then, again, the argument gains in strength. But if the sole rationale for keeping drugs illegal was the contention that, on drugs, other people would not want to contribute to my (or to society's) welfare anymore (ignoring, for the moment, the question as to whether this claim is plausible or not), then the argument would be an argument for slavery, and would share the plausibility of all such arguments.

30. Randall Curren, in his comments on an earlier, shorter version of this paper ('The Value of Freedom', published in the proceedings of the 129th Semiannual Meeting of the Creighton Club, Fall 1988), suggests even that '... there is a certain amount of freedom without which there would be, in a sense, nothing left of us. We would have no opportunity to constitute ourselves as persons, to give ourselves an identity. This much freedom, which I'm tempted to call 'constitutive freedom', we could never have reason to give up'.

References

Anshen, R. N. (ed.), (1940), *Freedom: Its Meaning*, Harcourt, Brace & Co: New York.

Bacharach, M. (1960), 'Commodities, Language, and Desire', *The Journal of Philosophy,* vol. 87, No. 7, July, pp. 346-68.

Barrett, S. R. (1984), 'Racism, Ethics and the Subversive Nature of Anthropological Inquiry', *Philosophy of the Social Sciences.*

Bennett, W. (1989), 'A Response to Milton Friedman' in *The Wall Street Journal,* 19 September.

Bennett, W. (1989), 'A Response to Friedman's An Open Letter to Bill Bennett', *The Wall Street Journal,* 7 September.

Bidney (ed.), (1963), *The Concept of Freedom in Anthropology,* Mouton & Co: The Hague.

Bluhm, W. (1984) 'Freedom in *The Social Contract;* Rousseau's Legitimate Chains', *Polity* XVI.

Brandt, R. (1959), *Ethical Theory: The Problems of Normative and Critical Ethics,* Prentice-Hall: Englewood Cliffs, N.J.

Cal, T. (1990), 'U.S. Churches, Not Playboy, Should Be Targeting E. Europe', *Rochester Democratic and Chronicle,* July 4, p. 10A.

Curren, R. (1988),'Value of Freedom', proceedings of the 129th Semiannual Meeting of the Creighton Club, Fall.

Fireside, H. (1989),'Dissident Visions of the USSR: Medvedev, Sakharov & Solzhenitsyn', *Polity,* Winter.

Fromm, E. (1969), *Escape From Freedom,* Avon Books: New York.

Goodman, R. (1984), 'Is There an 'I' in Anthropology? Thoughts on Starting Fieldwork in Japan', *JASO* XV.
Grim, P. (1976), *Ethical Relativism in the Context of the Social Sciences,* unpublished Ph.D. dissertation, Boston University.
Hayek, F.A. (1960), *Individualism and Economic Order,* University of Chicago Press: Chicago.
Hayek, F.A. (1960), *The Constitution of Liberty,* University of Chicago Press: Chicago.
Jaynes, J. (1982), *The Origin of Consciousness in the Breakdown of the Bicameral Mind,* Houghton-Mifflin: Boston.
MacIntyre, A. (1984), *After Virtue*, University of Notre Dame Press: Notre Dame.
MacIntyre, A. (1988), *Whose Justice? Which Rationality?* University of Notre Dame Press: Notre Dame.
Malinowski (1944), *Freedom and Civilization,* Roy Publishers: New York.
Mead, M. (1959), *An Anthropologist at Work: Writings of Ruth Benedict,* Houghton Mifflin: Boston.
Mearsheimer, J. (1990), 'Back to the Future: Instability in Europe After the Cold War', *International Security,* vol. 15, Summer, pp. 5-56.
Mearsheimer, J. (1990), 'Why We Will Soon Miss the Cold War', *Atlantic,* August, pp. 35-50.
Miller, D. (1983), 'Constraints on Freedom', *Ethics* 94.
Orwell, G. (1961), *Animal Farm,* The New American Library: New York.
Pettit, P. (1986), 'Free Riding and Foul Dealing', *The Journal of Philosophy,* 83.
Postrel, V. (1990), 'The Banality of Freedom?', *Reason,* March.
Raphael, D.D. (1983), 'Liberty and Authority', in A. Phillips Griffiths (ed.), *Of Liberty: Royal Institute of Philosophy Lecture Series: 15, Supplement to Philosophy 1983,* Cambridge University Press: Cambridge.
Sandel, M. (1982), *Liberalism and the Limits of Justice,* Cambridge University Press: Cambridge.
Sandel, M. (1987), 'The Political Theory of the Procedural Republic', in Allan Hutchinson, C. & Monahan, P. (eds), *The Rule of Law: Ideal or Ideology,* Carswell: Toronto.
Sandel, M. (1989), 'Moral Argument and Liberal Toleration: Abortion and Homosexuality', *California Law Review,* pp. 533-38.
Sanders, J. T. (1980), *The Ethical Argument Against Government,* University Press of America: Washington.
Sanders, J. T. (1983), 'Political Authority' *The Monist*, vol. 66, no. 4, October, pp. 545-56.
Sanders, J. T. (1987), 'Justice and the Initial Acquisition of Property,' *The Harvard Journal of Law and Public Policy,* vol. 10, no. 2, Spring, pp. 367-99.
Sanders, J. T. (1988), 'Why the Numbers Should Sometimes Count,' *Philosophy & Public Affairs,* Winter, pp. 3-14.

Sanders, J. T. and Narveson J. (eds), (1996), *For and Against the State: New Philosophical Readings*, Rowman and Littlefield: Lanham, Maryland.
Skinner (1971), *Beyond Freedom and Dignity*, Bantam Books: Toronto.
Szasz, T. (1977), *The Manufacture of Madness*, Harper & Row: New York.
Szasz, T. (1984), *The Myth of Mental Illness*, Harper & Row: New York.
Szasz, T. (1987), *Ceremonial Chemistry: The Ritual Persecution of Drugs, Addicts, and Pushers*, Learning Publications: Holmes Beach, FL.
Taylor, C. (1976), 'Responsibility For Self', in Rorty A., (ed.), *The Identities of Persons*, University of California Press: Berkeley.
Taylor, P. W (1975), *The Principles of Ethics: An Introduction*, Wadsworth Belmont, CA.
Tuomela, R. (1988), 'Free Riding and the Prisoner's Dilemma', *The Journal of Philosophy*, 85.
Wasserman, W. (1985), 'What Is a Fundamental Ethical Disagreement?', *Analysis* 45.
Wicker, T. (1990), 'Freedom's Not Perfect, It's What You Make Of It', *Democrat and Chronicle*, January 8, p. 6A.

In the prison of freedom: human action and its praxiological explanation

Wojciech W. Gasparski

> There is no room within a system of praxeology for meliorism and optimistic fatalism. Man is free in the sense that he must daily choose anew between policies that lead to success and those that lead to disaster, social disintegration, and barbarism.
> - Ludwig von Mises, Human Action

1. The act of - what?: conception?, the emergence of zygote?, the act of being born?... (select, my dear reader, whatever you believe is proper, and this will be your very first value experienced as an act of your freedom) - sentenced me for life like a decisive judge. Before it happened one jury considered me not guilty while the other attached to me the shame of the original sin. Since then I have been put into the prison of free will or simply *freedom*.

Who was the decisive judge? God?, parents?, nature? (select whatever you believe is proper, and this will be your second first value experienced as an act of your freedom).

Sentenced for life but not necessarily within walls (sometimes it happened that one being born in a real prison because of one's mother misbehavior is not imprisoned). Your, his, her, mine prisons are of virtual character: your mind is a helmet and your hand is a glove and your future is the cyberspace out of which you are not allowed to escape. The penalty consists of acting under duress to navigate in the space: *Navigare necesse est, vivere non est necesse* (Plutarch). So as some of the sentenced sooner or later escape from the prison. Escape for sure.

2. Is there any way to help one who lives in this nicest of the worlds (and this is yet another value taken for granted)? Maybe *being informed* makes it easier (this is the value not only of Adam and Eve but of all scholars who believe in it intensively)? So let us explain the situation from a very peculiar (because although the *Oxford English Dictionary* caries the extensive definition of the term only a few are familiar with it) perspective. The nickname of the perspective is praxeology (or praxiology).

As a praxeological term, freedom refers to the sphere within which an acting individual is in a position to choose between alternative modes of action. A man is free in so far as he is permitted to choose ends and the means to be used for the attainment of those ends. A man's freedom is most rigidly restricted by the laws of nature as well by the laws of praxeology. He cannot attain ends which are incompatible with one another. If he chooses to indulge in gratifications that produce definite effects upon the functioning of his body or his mind, he must put up with these consequences. It would be inexpedient to say that man is not free because he cannot enjoy the pleasures of indulgence in certain drugs without being affected by their inevitable results, commonly considered as highly undesirable. While this is admitted by and large by all reasonable people, there is no such unanimity with regard to the appreciation of the laws of praxeology.[1]

The degree of being accustomed to our actions is so high that we consider ourselves as equipped naturally with relevant knowledge (*tacit*, using Polanyi's scholarly notion). We act like native speakers who believed they know everything about they own tongue hating any lessons on their languages, grammar lessons predominantly. Praxeology in relation to human deeds is just such a grammar of action (according to Kotarbiński, a Polish philosopher) or logic of means-ends relationships (according to Mises, an Austrian scholar) or technology general (according to Espinas, a French sociologist) comprehending tools (techniques) to overcome practical situations (Gasparski) man faces in his world (Meloe, a Norwegian philosopher).

All of the praxiology students mentioned above, as well as their followers, share almost the same definition of an action, They accept consciousness, purposefulness and voluntarilyness as characteristic futures of *human behavior* that transform it into *human action*. Among the three characteristics voluntarily is a prerequisite for setting any purpose. It is why there is no one except me whose purpose I am to achieve.

The purpose is always mine not yours. Even if *you* ask me to write this paper the purpose 'to write it' (authotelic) or/and to have it written (heterotelic), after I accepted the invitation, will be mine not yours. It is because I am free to choose. Even if your invitation would be coercive I am free to experience coercion or not. My action is an *ultimate given* says Mises, for nothing but action - external or internal, behavioral or abstain - is the way I am able to manifest consciously and voluntarily towards something I would like to achieve being guided by *my* values, knowledge and beliefs. It is they that create iron (from irony rather than a metal) bars of the cell I am locked in (the paradoxy is that you shouldn't be free and locked) for life.

My purpose P may be great and abstract - as heavens - metaphysical or from the outer world, utopian or real, and in order to achieve it I try to structure everything I am doing in a sequence the final stage of it will hopefully be the P. On the other hand my purpose p may be small, as small as a cup of morning coffee - without connecting it to any further metaphysics. In both cases, as in many others in between of the two extremes, if I am acting to achieve them they are my purposes, and I am free to act and forced to act toward them at the same time. Free, because it is *me* who wants to achieve them, forced because they are *my* purposes, i.e. the most desired states in the slots of the action.

Being not free to act, e.g. being hampered, I am limited in my freedom to some mental actions. I may only think about this or that depending on my purpose in the given situation. I may prey asking God I believe into for help, I may consider a plan how to overcome the situation, or simply meditate. But as long as I am free to choose among different mental activities I experience freedom. Although freedom in this case is bounded like rationality in the Herbert A. Simon's concept of *bounded rationality* it is still freedom.

It is convenient to draw the boundary of the system so that all limits on ability to carry out actions are outside the skin, while all limits on ability to calculate correct actions are inside the skin. Then only the latter limits (which define 'bounded rationality') need be viewed as causes for departure from rationality. [...]

The concept of bounded rationality provides a starting point for economic theory that deals with the areas of neglect without negating those findings of classical theory that have a good basis in empirical evidence. While neoclassical theory derives from a very small but powerful set of empirical assumptions about behavior (the assumptions of maximization of subjective expected utility), theories deriving from bounded rationality require more extensive empirical assumptions, hence call for wider observations of actual human decision-making behavior.[2]

Only being not conscious I am totally out of a prison of freedom. Many would be happy to escape out of this prison exhausted of so many decisions they are forced to make while free. They experience the prison of freedom as more severe than Alcatraz. This is why liberalism is for heroes rather that for ordinary mortals.

3. Freedom is tough because its companion is responsibility. The more freedom one experience the more responsible he or she should be. Enjoying absence of duties is not freedom it is laziness or pathological state of irresponsibility. It leads in many cases to crisis. The famous *liberum veto*, a Polish noblemen (*szlachta*) who rightly and effectively disagreed with what other fellow nobleman wanted to promote in the late medieval times, was of the similar character.

The republic of the nobles could not effectively cope with... problems, especially as a constitutional crisis began to paralyze the functioning of the state. Under the pretense of safeguarding the rights of the 'nation,' the magnates were in fact running the country and catering to their own vested interests. The notorious *liberum veto* - the unanimity rule in the diet - together with elections of kings *viritim* (by all *szlachta*) append the way to all kinds of abuses. The magnates and the foreign powers, using corruption and intimidation, exploited the Polish constitutional system. Prussia and Russia especially were determined to prevent any meaningful reform. While most European powers had adopted absolutism, Poland had been moving in the opposite direction. At a time when other monarchs were creating bureaucracies, effective systems of taxation, and large armies, the kings of Poland had no bureaucracy, an inadequate budget, and a small army. In 1780 the revenues of Poland were allegedly forty times smaller than those of France and ten times smaller than those of Russia. The 'noble nation', which had won impressive personal liberties and political rights for itself and had been in the forefront of constitutionals in Europe, had finally used its position to disrupt the state and to undermine its power and economic stability.[3]

'The simple truth (writes Mises) is that individuals can be free to choose between what they consider as right or wrong only where they are economically independent of the government.'[4] The same valid for social organizations of different types composed of the individuals, nations included.

The difference between an animal and a human being is the first reacts to the impulse while the former acts '... purposively aims at ends chosen. This is what we have in mind in stating that man is a moral person, responsible for his conduct'.[5]

Human beings do not float in eternal regions. Everything that a man does must necessarily in some way or other affect the economic or material sphere and requires his power to interfere with this sphere. In order to subsist, he must toil and have the opportunity to deal with some material tangible goods.

The confusion manifests itself in the popular idea that what is going on in the market refers merely to the economic side of human life action. But in fact the prices of the market reflect not only 'material concerns' - like getting food, shelter, and other amenities - but also those concerns which are commonly called spiritual or higher or nobler. The observance or nonobservance of religious commandments - to abstain from certain activities altogether or on specific days, to assist those in need, to build and to maintain houses of worship, and many others - is one of the factors that determine the supply of, and the demand for, various consumers' goods and thereby prices and the conduct of business. The freedom that the market economy grants to the individual is not merely 'economic' as distinguished from some other kind of freedom. It implies the freedom to determine also all those issues which are considered as moral, spiritual, and intellectual.[6]

4. Why is liberalism so difficult to be experienced? It is for it forces you to rely on yourself. It is nobody else but you who has to make a decision whether to do something in expense of a different thing. There is no human action without spending resources (neither physical nor social *perpetua mobile* exist). Sometimes you have to spend money you have not enough to be able to buy flowers to your beloved wife or a toy for your kid. Sometimes as a politician or a manager you have to privatize an inefficient plant and fire hundreds of workers who were the fuel of Solidarity movement you were also a member of years ago.

In many, perhaps too many, cases when you are serving as a soldier who defends his mother (or father) land, you are forced to wound or kill your country's enemies. Sometimes you are sent by your country to be a part of UN forces defending other than your country territories or enhancing other missions in different corners of the world.

In this and a great deal of other situations you would prefer to have the job done, not for you, but by somebody else. But if you are in a position to find a proxy (like those who are for capital punishment executed by a hired hangman) have you not thought that it might be you whom such an offer may be made? For it may be the proxy you consider as relevant who thinks your way seeing in you the one he or she would like to hire and act in the name of him, his boss, nation or humankind.

[...] In order to preserve the state of affairs in which there is protection of the individual against the unlimited tyranny of stronger and smarter fellows, an institution is needed that curbs all antisocial elements. Peace - the absence of perpetual fighting by everyone against everyone - can be attained only by the establishment of a system in which the power to resort to violent action is monopolized by a social apparatus of compulsion and coercion and the application of this power in any individual case is regulated by a set of rules - the man-made laws as distinguished both from the laws of nature and those of praxeology. The essential implement of a social system is the operation of such an apparatus commonly called government. [...] If the government does more than protect people against violent or fraudulent aggression on the part of antisocial individuals, it reduces the sphere of the individual's freedom an act beyond the degree to which it is restricted by praxeological law. Thus we may define freedom as that state of affairs in which the individual's discretion to choose is not constrained by governmental violence beyond the margin within which the praxieological law restricts it anyway.

This is what is meant if one defines freedom as the condition of an individual within the frame of the market economy. He is free in the sense that the laws and the government do not force him to renounce his autonomy and self-determination to a greater extent than the inevitable praxeological law does. What he foregoes is only the animal freedom of living without any regard to the existence of other specimens of his species. What the social apparatus of compulsion and coercion achieves is that individuals whom malice, shortsightedness or mental inferiority prevent from realizing that by indulging in acts that are destroying society they are hurting themselves and all other human beings are compelled to avoid such acts.[7]

It is because '... although we cannot hope to define or analyse freedom to act in terms of concepts that fully identify the causal conditions of intentional action, there is no obstacle to the view that freedom to act is a causal power of the agent'.[8]

Notes

1. von Mises, 1966, pp. 279-80.
2. Simon, 1992, pp. 25-42.

3. Wandycz, 1974, p. 7.
4. von Mises, 1996, p. 319.
5. Ibid., p. 315.
6. Ibid., p. 319.
7. von Mises, 1966, pp. 280-1.
8. Davidson, 1980, p. 81.

References

Davidson, D. (1980), *Essays on Actions & Events*, Clarendon Press: Oxford

von Mises, L. (1996), 'The Economic Foundations of Freedom', *The Freeman*, May, first published in 1960.

von Mises, L. (1966), *Human Action: A Treatise on Economics*, Contemporary Books, Inc: Chicago.

Simon, H. A. (1992), 'Methodological Foundations of Economics' in J.L. Auspitz, W.W.Gasparski et al, (eds), *Praxiologies and the Philosophy of Economics*, Transaction Publisher: New Brunswick and London.

Wandycz, P.S. (1974) *The Lands of Partitioned Poland, 1795-1918*, University of Washington Pres: Seattle and London.

Evil: a shining in blackness

Martin A. Bertman

I.

In Milton's *Paradise Lost*, Satan is called the 'prince of contradiction'. This Lucifer shines in blackness. As the primary preternatural evil being, he maximizes evil by his treason against God. Milton's contemporary, Thomas Hobbes, said that treason is outside all civil laws by breaking them all at once by opposing their authoritative basis. Hobbes' sovereign is an 'artificial god' and rebellion against him is ontologically possible; the rebel is merely outside the state, in a 'condition of nature'. Differently, Satan's rebellion is an ontological discombobulation, for, as Satan himself realizes, he is an instrument of the omnipotent sustainer of all existences. Milton has it that the Satanic instrument leads Adam on the long road from a childish intimacy with the creator to a maturer relationship with God. Doing evil and knowing that it is the instrument of a greater good seems to keep a tension between (moral) despair and salvationary hope for Satan (or Judas Iscariot). Within a range of variant qualities, such a pattern reoccurs, where evil is an instrument of an ultimate good, even in such an atheist and secular thinker as the Hegelian, Karl Marx.

A leading idea in this pattern is that the contradiction is a condition which depends on time. It is only in time that a warring disorder can occur and have a dénouement. When the temporal order is seen from a non-temporal perspective, as by Kierkegaard's Christian who binds the temporal with the eternal, it loses it's instrumental possibility. Leibniz, whose logical theodicy demands an order that is non-contradictory, and eternally valid, results in viewing this as 'the best of all possible worlds'. Here logic demands the instrumental condition, just as Hegel provides an historical 'body', instrumentalizing logic with a harmony of subjective and objective conditions through cultural-political ideas; later, Marx, making economics the 'base' of a cultural-political 'superstructure', sees the contradictions of 'pre-history', that is, of human time before and at present, as necessary to fulfill human-nature in an ultimately non-contradictory, harmonious social and political world.

Consider a literary presentation of the Marxist view. André Malraux's *La Condition Humaine* has Chen, a Chinese communist, become an assassin for his cause. Chen finds to his horror that he enjoys, even craves, being an assassin and he realizes, like Milton's Satan, that he is in contradiction to the world that is to be created through the intent of his actions. Chen's self-despair over his moral sickness is somewhat unburdened in the hope that he will help create a world through his evil, even though its health, ironically, has no place for him. He obviously stands in contradiction to himself, and indeed, Chen is to be taken as a similitude for everyman in the temporal disorder of pre-history.

Even granting this Marxian redemption through time, there are some grave matters that destroy one's ease. First, there is the injustice and cruelty of what Hegel calls the 'butcher block of history'. The difficulty is the unredeemed cruelty and injustice to particular human beings before the utopian dénouement. Second, even in the best of all possible secular worlds, men still face death. Notwithstanding the harmony of everything else, even forgetting the 'butcher block of history', this is seemingly an ontological limitation of existence in time, and a source of anguish.

In French intellectual life of a generation ago, when communist sympathy was strong, an awareness of what is unredeemed in the Marxist model provided motives for opposition to it. The religious existentialism of a Gabriel Marcel opposed it through the traditional putative remedy of hope in the salvationary goodness of God, and he added Kierkegaardian flavor to this hope by cradling it in existential themes. Moreover, there were two other secular responses to evil: one is that human beings, without salvationary hope in God, create and define their own goods and evils by their choices and attitudes; here justice is not a matter of time but of psychology. Sartre's play 'No Exit' suggests this by considering hell the 'inauthenticity' of the three protagonists in the 'bad faith' of their relations to one another. This secular, psychological approach to values, if it defangs the sting of injustice, nevertheless, still leaves the burden of accident or natural catastrophe, e.g., the Lisbon earthquake that inspired Voltaire's *Candide* against Leibniz cum Dr. Pangloss. Sartre's view doesn't unburden contingent suffering or, especially, death.

This discomfiture elicited another secular proposal: it has a literary location in the absurdist amoralism of Albert Camus' 'Caligula'. The Roman Emperor of that play does the arbitrary because nothing can regulate absurdity. Absurdity is beyond logic: contradiction assumes the non-contradictory, but absurdity occupies everything: it has no logical or cultural antipode. Camus' Caligula kills those who do what is ordinarily called justice, and grants what are ordinarily called benefits to murderers, or not. In an absurd vision only the whim rules. But nature and fortune seem often to be just as arbitrary, and death is made meaningless or valueless if life is considered meaningless. Here events are neither instrumental nor in any way valuable. This is quite a different understanding of absurdity than that of the Christian Church Father Tertullian, who uses it as a notion to revet traditional hope in salvation. Considering a naturalistic perspective, that of Greek philosophers, especially the Epicureans and the Stoics, Tertullian seems to consider unsatisfactory their grin-and-bare-it answers to injustice and death. Death, as considered by these philosophers, is a matter of absurdity cum sickness, rather than meaningless, to which Tertullian says 'Christ is the panacea'. For a salvationary hope for both ultimate justice and immortality, the deepest desires of the heart, Tertullian offers '*credo ut absurdam*', 'I believe because it is absurd'.

Tertullian's 'leap of faith' also offers Christian optimism for redemption of man and world, against the tragic vision of Homeric paganism. Homer, usually considered the greatest tragic poet by the pagan Greeks, had Achilles, in the *Iliad*, choose a short heroic life, rather than an obscure long life; but in the *Odyssey*, when he is interviewed by Odysseus in Hades, he is a dim, bat-like creature who says 'I'd rather be a servant to a poor man on Earth than Achilles in Hades'. In the tragic perspective, even the noblest, most heroic life comes to a mere faint something, if indeed anything at all, and this casts a pallor over our prideful, rather illusory doings.

The hubritic illusions of tragedy do not imply that there is no good and evil. On the contrary, tragedy is based on a view of competing goods which are inexorably intertwined, each and each with a particular evil. Achilles' choice reflects this; however, further, its grand heroism opens to tragedy's pessimism about the inevitable outcome of the natural order and, consequently, optimistic programs and posturings – though they too are part of the human condition – are substantially illusions.

Philosophy, for Tertullian, did not offer more than tragedy; the answer for both was fundamentally courage in acceptance of the natural order. Camus' Caligula's absurdism, an amoral position, however, is beyond illusions in its refusal to give value to anything. This is seen when one is clear-minded, though being clear-minded is no less absurd than not being so. There can be an intellectual turn here in that it is the Buddhists, (as well as Spinoza and Nietzsche, in their qualified ways), for whom being clear-minded means being beyond good and evil in the usual moral sense but who, just so, find evil in illusion because of a lack of clarity. For the introductory sorting out of positions, the important thing to note is that illusion and absurdity must be somehow limited even if merely by a single factor in order for good and evil to count.

II.

So far my comments are merely preliminary to considering a position which I call that of the Marquis de Sade. I have read little of Sade and I have been brought to the following considerations through Timo Airaksinen's interesting book *The*

Philosophy of the Marquis de Sade. From Airaksinen, I have understood Sade to be subtle and perhaps misleading, if not contradictory in his views. Consequently, what I here call Sadean is historically incautious but useful for considering the position of a Sade who defines himself as an evil being. Indeed, I take Sade to hold that one is free by completely dedicating oneself to doing evil. The context of Sade's proposal involves his atheism. Yet, since I use the name Sade for my proponent of evil, and because I do seem to appropriate some characteristics of the historical Sade, I want to quote Airaksinen to punctuate a caution about the unhistorical figure I put forth:

> Sade's pet strategy is to resort to a baroque richness of expressive forms and ultimately to inconsistency. At the same time he both hates and adores the injustice in the social world around him. He denies the laws of ethics but vows friendship and love for his liberated heroes. Moreover, he promotes contradictions and yet wants to tell us a story about them. For him, human life is full of inconsistencies in a peculiarly practical sense. But such a creation of a life-world belongs already to Sade's style and aesthetics. (p. 94)

My Sade is inconsistent in his evil because he is essentially evil. Inconsistency is the work of this essence, as I shall discuss through a consideration of his anti-virtues, whether or not the historical Sade used inconsistency in that way. When I say essential, I do not mean the word to be taken in a technical philosophical sense, as when one says Plato or Husserl is an essentialist. It is used like Jean Genet speaking of himself as essentially a thief, that is, Sade organizes his life in terms of evil. And when I say that Sade is an atheist, I not only consider him to deny a monotheistic God, or any divinity, but also a natural justice after death, e.g., like the one Plato describes in the myth of Ur, that is, reincarnation as a rational device of cosmic justice. I do this even though it may be argued that the existence of an omnipotent good God, or even a rational moral nature, makes evil more potent and poignant in opposition, just as Milton's Satan seems more evil than any of the mortal, wicked characters of the historical Sade's novels and plays.

The essential Sade, then, has a consummate disposition to do evil. Now a disposition is not a whim, like the famous example of a whim to drink a bucket of paint. A disposition has an internal or subjective factor and an external or objective factor. Internally, it is a continuous desire to act for a certain purpose. This is similar to Gilbert Ryle's understanding of dispositions: it is exercised whenever an opportunity presents itself. Externally, it guides choices to create opportunities for it to act. I call Sade's desire to do evil, however, a consummate disposition – to use Dewey's phrase for God appropriation in *A Common Faith*, 'the end of all one's ends' – because it orients Sade's life to seek the opportunities to exercise evil. Thereby, it is the strongest of his dispositions and it can be called a ruling principle. 'Ruling principle' captures rather forcibly the intellectual aspect involved in planning evil, since 'disposition' connotes something more habitual or responsive than the very active understanding I have of Sade's essential evil. Sade enlists all the forces of his emotional and intellectual life for the sake of evil. Further, it is appropriate to use the phrase 'ruling principle' because it proposes to organize and provoke a complex of anti-virtues. Consider: when one, especially in an Aristotelian context, speaks of a good man one implies the good man has a complex of virtues like justice, courage, temperance, etc. and, just so, there must seemingly be in Sade a complex of anti-virtues, each exercised on the right occasion for an evil purpose. Yet the question arises, whether Sade can enlist courage, a virtue, in order to exercise evil. The answer is that rashness and cowardice must be among his essential vices or anti-virtues, though occasionally he will act courageously for the sake of doing evil, just as a person will occasionally fast for the sake of his health.

When applying the Aristotelian view of virtues to Sade's anti-virtues, there are sometimes no difficulties, while at other times there are great difficulties, as suggested by giving two anti-virtues or vices for the above virtue of courage. Let us explore this. It is instructive about the nature of evil.

Aristotle applies the schema he calls the golden mean to virtues as an explanatory characterization. Each virtue is a mean between two vices, one of excess and the other of deficiency of the particular quality of the virtue, so that charity is the virtue of unobliged giving, and its vice, that of giving too much, is called profligacy, and its deficient vice, of giving too little, is called miserliness. Further, each virtue is constrained by circumstance; consequently, to have the virtue of giving or charity, is to give the right amount, to the right person, for the right purpose, at the right time, and in the right manner. Any minor inaptitude taints the virtue, any major breakdown destroys it. This is a functional system of the biological sort since it involves the range consideration of a knack for getting the circumstantial matters right. To do that involves much social skill and knowledge so that a person's habituated talent to exercise a virtue had to develop over a long period of time, where circumstance is prodded and reformed, and therefore, there must be an accurate understanding of the changing environment and relevant factors for exercising the virtue.

Any functional consideration has the Aristotelian practical organon for acting to achieve a purpose, whether that purpose is a specific good or a specific evil. Nature's temporal finger – and this includes human constructions and relations which, for some reasons, it is sometimes useful to contrast as the artificial with nature[1] – points circumstantially to a *this* rather than to a *that*, a *here* rather than a *there*, a *now* rather than a *then*, a *this person*, a *this manner*, a *this amount* for the sake of the particular result. Sade, by ignorance or lack of skill, may not achieve the full measure of evil in a particular category of acting. So, in raping someone, he may not have chosen the right person, say a virgin on her wedding day, rather than an old whore, or the right manner when she is fully aware of the evil done to her, rather than when she is drugged, etc. Of course, imaginative ingenuity – the aesthetic factor – can unendingly provide circumstantial particulars to enhance the quality of the (evil) purpose of the action. In fact, it is important to note, the infinite imagination is a non-classical, romantic factor that drives Sade's striving for evil beyond even functional bounds, as I shall discuss.

But I have chosen rape rather than some anti-virtue, like cowardice, in the functional treatment, that is, I used a category of action rather than, as Aristotle, a category of human character. I have done this because of the difficulties an Aristotelian schema poses for Sadean vices or anti-virtues. The first difficulty is that one cannot speak of excess and deficiency of the anti-virtue, as one does of a virtue. Cowardice is the deficient vice of courage, but even if one allows courage to be the deficiency of cowardice, there seems to be no excess of it. The deficiency moves through courage to its opposite vice, rashness. The essentially evil or vicious person never finds a rest in the virtue by moving from excess to deficiency. Having both vices, he is essentially unstable. So an excess of cowardice seems to be more cowardice; logically, it moves to an asymptote of pathological immobility, of being too cowardly to act at all. This indeed seems to be the case with the excess of anti-virtues taken from Aristotle's list of vices of deficiency: cowardice, miserliness, intemperance. Consequently, such vices seem to reside, but not as a mean, between virtue and the immobility of action.

The situation of the anti-virtues is one that moves between immobility and explosive destruction. Put mechanically, either the machine stops or it obliterates itself. Indeed, whereas the opposite of virtue is two vices, one of excess and the other of deficiency, the opposite of any vice is its partner vice of excess or deficiency. It is a destructive partnership. In the Sadean, who has both, it creates a maddening instability. Without the virtue's middleground, Sade captures the contradictory tendencies of the vices of deficiency and of excess, which move from explosion to the implosion of immobility.

This is helpful in understanding the sense of contrariness in the essentially evil person. Sade moves from rashness to cowardliness, his instability is built into his evil character. Sade's character must embrace both rashness and cowardice to be a fully vicious being. His instability, his contrariness, is built into his character. This swing between the vices of excess and deficiency brings him to the edge of both self-destruction and immobility. Yet he can act courageously for the sake of an evil end just because his disposition is not attached to habit. Rather it is the evil end that is consummate and, this gives him the appearance of a very intelligent being and also of great control and individuality. His intelligence is not of a rational sort since it is motivated by a fundamental conflict which I shall explain later as that of victimizer-victim; his is an intelligence working with a ceaseless imagination to increase pain by ever more refinement of the possibility of evil. Whereas Aristotle views virtue as an appropriate reaction to circumstance, and considers the need for the proper circumstance to exist for the exercise of virtue, Sade is bent to imagine circumstances which ever refine and increase evil. Because of this, since the greatest evils are done against those who are conscious of evil, Sade must be an acute psychologist.

Yet, as a psychologist, how does he understand his victim? For Aristotle, to undo a vicious *hexis* (inclination, habit, disposition) one so to speak bends the tree in its opposing direction. This is rather difficult to do by oneself since the virtuous person is seen by the viciously deficient person as being excessive and vice-versa, so the miser sees the charitable person as a profligate and the profligate sees the charitable person as a miser. But, since Sade embraces both poles of vice how does he look upon the virtue? It seems he knows only evil and cannot recognize the good for he surely does not have an understanding that he is right or virtuous, which is the psychological illusion of the man who is vicious by either excess or deficiency of the virtue but, unlike Sade, not by both. Consequently, it seems that Sade surely knows the pain he causes but not the reality of virtue. It follows that he considers his victims to thereby only have a façade of virtue, which may well involve a self-deceptive belief that the victim thinks himself truly virtuous. The best victim is the most innocent, the so called most virtuous, who is brought to realize that in fact, his innocence is an illusion and that he, like his victimizer, is essentially evil. Thereby, Sade discloses or identifies the victim as essentially himself. The psychoanalyst, Theodore Reik, in his book *Masochism*, views the sadist as masochist and vice-versa. Genet seems to have the same insight in his autobiographical, *The Thief*. Here we have a self-love and a self-hate that identifies victimizer and victim.

I have implicitly given the second major difficulty for applying Aristotle's ethical schema to Sade. For Aristotle, virtue is healthy functioning for the sort of thing that a human being is by nature, and vice is an unhealthy or improper functioning. Indeed, Aristotle understands this in a rational cosmos, that is, where nature or the sum total of existing beings is ordered by a rational principle that guarantees an eternal stable order within a range of rationally recenterable variations. Thereby, virtue is rational action in the fullest ontological sense of our existence. Aristotle, however, does have a way of speaking about rising above our humanity or of falling below it. Perhaps ironically, thinking it *hubris*, Aristotle says Plato's ethics are more fit for gods than men: no doubt, he would consider Socrates statement in Plato's *Crito* as such a rising above humanity, viz., 'nothing can harm a good man except self-inflicted corruption'. As to falling below humanity, Aristotle has a more richly developed discussion. A person can fall to the lower ontological order of the beast; here virtue and vice no longer apply. This is the realm of perversion. I think it can also be called the realm of cannibalism.

Sade embraces the perverse; however, one must explore how an essentially evil being, who doesn't believe in a rationally ordered cosmos, considers perversion. The word 'perversion' means a going against the truth, yet does Sade believe in a truth to go against? Certainly he does not believe in a rationally controlled ontological order. If Sade saw the world as ontologically graded, he would likely see his motivation for evil as sick as it is inhuman, instead he sees doing evil as conjoined to freedom. Sade, then, is not an absurdist but, put broadly, he rather shares with the Buddha, Spinoza and Nietzsche, the turn to put a supreme value, which he calls freedom, in clear-minded understanding of reality. This has an ontology, which takes a stand in time against time. Evil is to be done for its own sake, as some moralists say that good is to be done for its own sake. What evil for its own sake means is a victimizer-victim relation that has the attribute of destroying time, *per impossible*, the victimizer, by creating artificial or theatrical time: making oneself the victimizer.

Let us push further, can one say that Sade is free because evil is in harmony with nature? Or is it that in some fundamental way Sade's *soi-disant* freedom is rooted in opposition to nature by an aspect of man that is in some way outside of nature? I think these two questions do not lead to different realities but are rather perspectively instigated by the human ability to bracket itself from its natural basis, to consider oneself an autonomous will. I shall return to this point. If one speaks of nature in an anthropomorphic manner, it is often cruel and unjust. Indeed, if death is made the *summum malum*, we have nature, as the legend of Saturn eating his children. To be in harmony with this, (though the word 'harmony' has too many pleasant and classical associations to bear the burden of this likeness), is to create just for the sake of a cannibalistic destruction. Perhaps, this is the reason for Sade – the historical Sade now – liking the theater and living life as theater. Harmony with nature, then, is not taken from the Aristotelian viewpoint of rationally fixed and related orders of existence, but from the Saturnian principle of creation and destruction. Man's freedom can therefore be seen perspectively as either within or without nature. Within, he is a victim of the Saturnian principle and emulates it; without, he has a particular faculty, imagination, that infinitely works tricks with this emulation. Sade's imagination is both fostered by nature and works in a dialectic tension with nature, very much like the determinist Hobbes' use of contrasting 'condition of nature' with 'civil society'. For Hobbes, nature brings us to civil society, (through a natural principle of prudence), and ideally the civil laws – human conventions – are in concert with natural laws because they foster the end of nature, and yet, in a factual particularity, (though not in theory, which obliges the citizen practically), the civil law – the mortal sovereign's will – is perspectively autonomous and often actually in opposition to nature. So also Sade's imagination is grounded in nature but, even more dramatically, rather like Milton's Satan, it fights against nature by having himself, a victim of nature, assume a false perspective of existing as a destroyer himself. This is false not because Sade does not have victims, for he must have victims, and real ones. It is false in that such a creator's freedom on the part of Sade, the victim, is an illusion of power or a forgetfulness of nature's power to ultimately make him its Saturnian victim. As Vergil says, 'to fight nature is like throwing hay in the wind, it blows back in one's face'. The freedom that Sade offers is merely the illusory moment before this inevitably happens. This reminds of Sartre's ontology of choice. Freedom, however, in Sade, is the act not of choice but of imagination, before the victimizer is a victim or, as Sartre puts it, once again 'stuck in the glue' of the world. The essential Sade is in the evil possibilities of the imagination; moreover, the very contradiction of the imagination is actualized in the victimizer-victim relation.

It is from this elevation of the imagination as the Saturnian instrument for Sade's freedom, as shabby as it is when viewed from the vantage of its ultimate impotence, that anti-virtues are of less importance, though their structure allows us to consider the contradictoriness of a Sade, in opposing victim-reality with a false victimizer-reality, and it opens us to view the reputation for intelligence and controlled domination – even individualism – of the Satanic personality. Much more can be said of this, but I shall proceed. If one makes a fuss over death and moral limitations, then Aristotle's rational system is without a heart. For the atheist Sade, the romantic or sentimental modern man of the eighteenth century, of the French Revolution, the lonely individual is to be cannibalized by nature. There is a rage, as Dylan Thomas puts it, of not going quietly into death's dark night. Death is viewed as tangential to any rational structures that can be constructed – e.g., the civil laws – to hold some modest good in the cage of the world, before inevitable destruction. Hobbes, among others, offers a rational schema with the intent to preserve our days and maximize benefits but, against this, Sade's Saturnian principle leads the solitary individual to rage rather than to be satisfied by temporary amelioration. Sade's great evil arises because the victim becomes the victimizer only because he himself is inescapably a victim. His moment of freedom as victimizer is a pathetic illusion that ironically is the moment where Sade finds freedom by binding together the illusion and the clear-sighted understanding that it is an illusion. This is theater.

The totalization of evil for Sade is in this action of the victimizer-victim. It is not in Auschwitz, nor in any quantification of brutality; such horrors can and are done for other illusions. Sade's 'nasty, brutish, and solitary individual', using Hobbes' phrase for the natural condition, savors his condition just as he rages against it. Evil has such a contradiction, as it binds the suicidal and the murderous together. It is suicidal in its viciousness, and murderous – by the instrument of an infinitely perverse imagination – in its emulation of Saturnian nature.

III.

If one accepts the premises of a godless world, where death is an ineluctable enrager of human sensibility, one may be tempted by Sade. And yet, even in a godless universe – that is, in a world without a salvationary God, and without an afterlife – must one succumb to Sade's rage, to his cannibalism? I think not. That the world exists rather than not; that each of us exists rather than not, is a counterpoise to the putative facticity of non-existence, of death, that is, of leaving existence. If the heart's desire is continual life, not to die, the heart's desire for life is fulfilled in living just now. The implications of this work against both absurdism and Sade's victimizer-victim psychology. It is the ontologically undeniable assertion of one's existence that is the first step to wisdom. This first 'step' reminds me of the saying of Rabbi Nachman of Bratslav, 'virtue begins with the feet.' For the religious person this brings to mind the psalm: 'Even as I walk in the valley of the shadow of death, I will fear no evil, because you, God, are with me.' But leaving aside both God and Aristotle's, or any such philosophical, belief in a rational cosmos, human beings, in simplicity, understand the concepts of better and worse, if not those of Good and Evil. If persons took 'steps' to increase the fullness of their lives, even in indisputable ways, i.e., better physical and mental health and closer friendships, this would lead to virtue. These quotidian concerns do not jostle the great philosophical conundrums, although at some level they give rise to them. Yet they start one toward virtue, and thereby, to an increase of life. Amelioration is not trivial, it is essential to life; and life is just what one wants, if one fears death: the murderous, suicidal cannibalistic fear that eats away at us.

Note

1. For example, fasting is against our nature in general but, from the perspective of our nature's strong desire to preserve us, it is particularly part of our nature to fast for the sake of recovering health. So Hobbes has it, that it is against our nature to be constrained by civil society. He calls civil society or the state artificial; yet it is in our nature to preserve ourselves and civil society is the only remedy, since it is a possibility of our capacities, in this sense it can be also called natural.

Reference

Airaksinen, T. (1995), *The Philosophy of the Marquis de Sade,* Routledge: London.

Choosing coercion and subordination: a preliminary moral study of academic life

Jay L. Garfield

Introduction

In his pioneering study of coercion, exploitation and social power relations, *Ethics of Coercion and Authority: A Philosophical Study of Social Life* (Airaksinen 1988) Professor Timo Airaksinen develops a compelling theory of coercion. Among the more surprising results of that analysis is his demonstration that coercion has an inherently paradoxical structure. He points out that it is in general the case that the realisation of a coercive threat is against the interests of the coercer, and moreover, that this fact is always known both the coercer and to the victim. (pp. 56-61). In this essay I do not take issue with the general analysis Airaksinen offers of these phenomena. I want, however, to call attention to what appears to be a class of anomalous cases of coercion, and to ask about the special moral problems these anomalous cases engender. In the end, I suspect that given the nature of civil society, these anomalous cases are far more common than one might suspect if one focusses, as does Airaksinen, on such obvious cases as protection rackets and muggers.

The central case that concerns me is one that is perhaps so close to most of Airaksinen's readers and colleagues, and to the readers of this volume, that it escapes notice. It is the situation in which most of us lead the majority of our professional lives – the academy. That situation is one characterised by unequal power relations, particularly, though not exclusively, the relation between teachers and students. Those power relations issue in – and in fact are specifically constituted in order to engender – standing coercive relations and innumerable coercive acts. And indeed, as Airaksinen predicts that they must be, they are made possible by a complex background of coercive institutions instantiating a complex hierarchy of coercive relations.

What strikes me as both especially interesting about these cases, and as especially morally poignant, is that in these cases, unlike those that figure as central in Airaksinen's analysis, the victims enter willingly into the coercion. Moreover, they do so with their eyes open, in full cognisance of the coercive character of the relationship, and in fact tacitly – and often explicitly – with the express desire to be coerced. Moreover, there is nothing especially perverse or irrational in this course of action. Subjecting oneself to such coercion is for many persons, at particular times on their lives, exactly the rational thing to do. Airaksinen does not explain or predict this possibility.

Moreover, I shall argue, there is a further peculiar – at least peculiar when seen from the vantagepoint of Airaksinen's analysis – feature of this circumstances: Whereas, as Airaksinen correctly points out, in the cases he considers there is always a net cost to the coercer in realising a coercive threat, in the typical case of teacher-student coercion there is no such net cost. In fact there is often a net benefit in realising the threat, reflecting and reinforcing other anomalous features of these situations.

All of this requires a special kind of moral analysis. For as academics in relation to our students, we are in a very different set of circumstances than are muggers in relation to their victims. Our institution is properly regarded as legitimate, and our coercion is actively sought. Just as Airaksinen inquires into the conditions of the *possibility* of coercion by muggers and mafiosi, and into the conditions of the rationality of their realising their threats, I would like to inquire into the conditions of the *legitimacy* of academic coercion and into the conditions of the rationality of students' choosing to be the victims of such relatively unconstrained coercers as university lecturers and professors.

1. Airaksinen's analysis of coercive situations

Airaksinen takes as paradigms of coercion such situations as that of a mugger demanding money from a victim, of a mafioso running a protection racket, a policeman making an arrest, or a superior officer compelling obedience from a subordinate. In each of these cases, the coercer, in order to gain compliance from the victim threatens greater disutility to the victim if the victim does not comply with the coercer's demand (pp. 53-4).

Leaving aside cases of uncoerceable victims (those who assign enormous disutility to compliance with coercion either in general or in the particular cases in question) a successful coercer manages to arrange a plausible threat of sufficient disutility and which will be assigned a sufficiently high subjective probability by the victim that the victim maximises his/her expected utility by performing the action demanded. The mugging victim judges that he is better off handing over the wallet than risking being shot; the tavern-owner judges that the protection money is less than the cost of repairing the damage he can expect if he fails to pay; the fleeing robber judges that she will suffer less if she surrenders than if she resists arrest; the soldier prefers to face enemy fire than a court martial for desertion (pp. 56-9).

Now among the most interesting features of coercion revealed by Airaksinen is that successful coercion in general requires coercive institutions. This is because absent such institutions a surprising paradox arises – at least in many central cases. It is in general costly for a coercer to realise his/her coercive threat. The mugger, if she shoots the resisting victim, will be vigorously pursued by the police as a murderer, rather than be ignored as a minor street criminal, and if caught, will be subject to severe penalties. Her expected disutility thus rises if she realises the coercive threat. The mafioso has to pay vandals to wreck the bar, and runs similar risks. The policewoman must expend additional effort and risk serious injury or death if she pursues the fleeing suspect. The officer risks mutiny.

Any rational victim can figure this out. It follows that if the victim resists, the game moves to a point where the rational thing for the coercer, as an expected utility maximiser, to do is to let the victim go without realising the threat. Since the victim knows this, s/he knows that if s/he resists, and if the coercer is rational, she loses nothing. So the rational course of action for the coerced victim appears to be refusal, and for the coercer to walk away. Coercion then should never work.

Airaksinen's solution to this problem is simple but of the first importance for understanding the ubiquitous role of coercion in our social life. He points out that successful coercion is backed up by coercive institutions that raise the expectation of the realisation of the coercive threat. The mugger must either himself regularly make good on his threats or be a member of a (perceived) cohort of muggers each of whom regularly does so. While each individual realisation of a threat may in isolation be counter-utilitarian, the fact that some are realised enables the success of the coercive practice. The protection racketeer must occasionally make an example of a recalcitrant victim. While if that particular case is taken in isolation it may appear irrational, that example can be used to raise the subjective probability of the threat being realised in enough future victims to render the action rational. The policewoman and the army officer each have powerful institutional apparatus on their respective sides which will back up any coercive act. Coercion hence ceases to be paradoxical if there is enough institutional or practical background to provide the right kind of context for an individual act of coercion. But the fact remains that in each of these cases there is at least a local cost in realising the threat, and this is something the victim can from time to time use to even the game. Coercive games, as Airaksinen characterises them, hence have built into them a kind of check on the power of the coercive agent (pp. 93, ff).

2. Why one would never choose to be coerced

It is clear that as Airaksinen characterises coercion, one would never rationally choose to be coerced. Intuitively, to do so is to relinquish some of one's freedom, and to allow in particular, another to choose one's ends and actions for one. This hardly seems like a prudent course of action.

But we can make the point more precisely from within the informal game-theoretic framework Airaksinen mobilises: When one is coerced, the expected utilities of one's alternatives are manipulated so as to reduce the expected utility of a course of action one might have chosen before, and to do so by providing another course of action as the only alternative, which course of action has less expected utility than the initial course of action did prior to the coercive intervention. The mugger by threatening to shoot me reduces the expected utility of my walking down the street, and allows as an alternative doing so without my wallet; the mafioso reduces the expected utility of business as usual, and provides as the only alternative less net profit than I enjoyed before. And so on.

So we see that coercion always issues in our being confronted with choices each of which is less favourable than a choice we had before the coercive intervention. Coercion is hence on this model always a harm to the victim, and hence ought never be rationally chosen. This is hardly surprising, particularly given the range of coercive situations Airaksinen chooses as paradigmatic.

3. Why academic situations are coercive

As teachers we are coercers with respect to our students. We can and do require them to engage in acts in which they would otherwise not engage – reading textbooks, attending impossibly dull lectures, preparing for unpleasant examinations, foregoing enjoyable visits to pubs, etc. We accomplish this by threatening to fail them in classes, or simply by threatening to give them lower grades, more unfavourable evaluations, or less useful letters of recommendation than they would otherwise received. (Of course, there are also positive incentives – but these, in context, fall under the category Airaksinen correctly calls 'coercive offers'(pp. 76-81). That is, they have the effect, despite having the superficial structure of offering a good, of altering the utility function of the victim in exactly the way that coercive threats do.

Students, of course, are acutely aware of the coercive character of academic life. While many – perhaps even most – students would voluntarily read and study much of what we assign; while a few might voluntarily attend our lectures (let's not pretend that we are *that* entertaining!); while fewer might write research papers as a leisure activity, surely *none* would sit examinations without some coercive pressure.

Many of us are aware of this as well (though I suspect that we allow this to slide from our consciousness too often, as is frequently the case with truths we would rather not acknowledge regarding our own position in power relations). We assign penalties for late work; we schedule tests and papers to ensure that students complete work, etc. Some of our number, unfortunately, even abuse this coercive power. More of this below.

To this quick analysis it might be objected that while academic relations appear coercive when viewed in isolation, when seen in a much larger context they are not so coercive. After all, it might be noted, students (typically) choose to attend universities. They are free not to do so. And they are free to leave the university at any time. This is different from the circumstances in which we find ourselves when staring down the barrel of a mugger's gun, or when the restauranteur sits down with the protection salesman, etc.

But this comforting reply is too swift. It ignores the special role that the university as an institution has assumed in our contemporary cultures; the nature of the aspirations of our (typical) students and the role of those aspirations in their conceptions of their lives, as well as certain structural features of the paradigm cases.

Let us take these points in order. First, given the special role the university fulfills as a provider of credentials and as an assessor of abilities, and the consequences of these credentials and assessments for employment prospects and hence for the quality of one's life, it is no more accurate to say that – for many citizens – the pursuit of an education is optional than it is to say that for the restaurant owner staying in business and making a profit is optional. Second, once one takes seriously the centrality of one's core projects for one's self-respect and happiness, any threat to the necessary conditions of realising those projects is a serious threat indeed. The consequences with which we academic coercers can threaten our student victims strike deeply at these projects, and hence – even if we regard the pursuit of higher education as in some sense optional – are severe consequences indeed, at least on a par with those involved in the protection racket case.

Finally, note that even in the paradigm cases this same response could be made: Any of the victims could simply abandon their hopes of realising the projects they pursued antecedent to the onset of coercion and accept a reduced life. In that sense, each has a very real choice. But we see that that sense of choice is hollow, and in no way cuts against the harm represented by a plausible coercive threat. So it is in the academic case: While our students could indeed respond to our coercive threats by abandoning their principal projects, that is cold comfort for one who wishes to see academic life as less coercive than Airaksinen's paradigm cases. We must take seriously, I conclude, the coercive nature of our relationship with our students, and come to terms with its moral dimensions on those terms.

4. Respects in which academic relations are special

While in the foregoing discussion I have stressed those respects in which academic life is continuous with other cases of coercion, it is time to concede that there are in fact respects in which it differs from the paradigm cases we have considered. One important respect is this: Whereas in the four paradigm cases there is a real cost in the realisation of a coercive threat that must be balanced in each case against the global benefits it might entail to the coercer, in the academic case there is generally no cost to the coercer in realising the coercive threat. We can typically lower assessments, fail students, write deprecatory letters of recommendation with absolutely no risk of reprisal and at absolutely no marginal cost to ourselves. Of course there may be the odd appeal, but for the most part, our threats – unlike those of the mugger, the mafioso, the police officer and the military officer – are cost-free. Moreover, there may even be benefits to us in realising these threats – enhancements to our reputations, and the ability to make good on coercive threats in the future, for instance.

Part of the reason for this is the powerful (in the relevant, not the absolute sense) institution that backs up our coercive threats. We can count on the support of colleagues, departments, deans, etc against potential appeals, and students know this. But part of the reason for this is the nature of this peculiar coercive relationship itself: Because of our peculiar expertise, and because the differential in (at least presumed) expertise is constitutive of our teacher-student relation, we have a license to coerce and our victims lack not only sanctioned recourse, but any recourse whatsoever. For this reason, our power is in a peculiar sense more absolute than that of the mugger and his colleagues, in virtue of the absence of any check in the form of costs attaching to threat-realisation.

Moreover, and perhaps most interestingly, this is a coercive situation that is chosen freely by the victim. This fact is, of course, in tension with the claims made in the foregoing section regarding the virtually mandatory character of university education for many of our students. But those claims notwithstanding, there are certain important respects in which there is more choice in this situation than in those others, at least in some respects.

First, even though for many of our students higher education is a necessity, the particular institution, department, or instructor to whom any student subordinates him/herself is a matter of free choice. Secondly, and of equal importance, while other life-options may be substantially less attractive than those made possible by higher education, they are not totally disastrous in the way that death, maming and complete loss of livelihood or freedom are. I stressed above that there is a powerful structural isomorphism between this coercive situation and the paradigm cases. But here it is equally important to stress the difference in degree of the costs to the victim of accepting the realisation of a coercive threat. While in the academic case the victim may forfeit a good life, in the paradigm cases, the victim may forfeit everything, even life itself. This difference in degree is as important as the sameness of structure.

This then poses a set of problems that will occupy the remainder of this essay: What makes it rational for victims to choose not only to be coerced, but to enter into coercive relationships in which the coercer can realise his/her threats with no cost – coercive situations in which the victim cannot even appeal to the irrationality of the realisation of the coercive threat as a way of winning the game constituted by the coercive encounter? This question forces another: Inasmuch as these coercive situations are regarded not only by the coercers and the institutions in which they participate as legitimate, but also are so regarded by the victims, in what does that legitimacy consist? Finally, given this peculiar set of power relations, what special moral demands do these situations place upon the coercers in order to secure legitimation?

5. Why academic coercion is rationally chosen by our subordinates

Why does a student rationally choose to be coerced by a teacher? This is not a difficult question to answer. But it is important to bear the answer in mind given the other questions we will face. A student chooses to be coerced because there are a set of readily identifiable benefits to be gained from participation in this coercive situation. This makes this coercive situation very different from those Airaksinen considers. We don't choose to be coerced by the police, by muggers, or even by superior military officers or mafiosi. And we don't because these coercive situations have no positive payoff for us, except, occasionally, accidental payoff (we may win a medal, or get a reward).

There are both external and internal goods to which a student may expect to gain access: Externally, a student may, as a consequence of enduring our coercive influence, receive grades, certificates, degrees, and the access to other goods such as jobs or status that these enable. Internally, s/he may learn things that they wouldn't otherwise. This is a psychological point. A student often recognises that s/he can better achieve his/her goals by allowing another coercive power over him/her. S/he may correctly believe that left to his/her own devices, for instance, s/he would spend more time in the pub than in the library, despite best intentions to the contrary. By allowing a teacher the power to reward achievement or to punish lethargy, s/he creates for him/herself the additional incentive necessary successfully to motivate the behaviour s/he sees as in his/her best interest, but which s/he would be unable to perform without extra incentive. To put it simply, then, allowing coercion is a cure for akrasia.

I call attention to this feature of the moral psychology of voluntary coercion in the academic context, because – though it is easy to overlook as we naturally fasten on the more explicit and salient external reasons for entering into such relationships – it is the deepest and most interesting reason for entering into these relationships, and this for several reasons: First, it is a motivation which transcends the formal or official academic context. It binds athletes to coaches, devotees to gurus, musicians to their masters, etc, even in the absence of any external coercive structure that would either punish failure to attain personal goals or reward their attainment. Moreover, even in the context of such a superstructure – as in actual academic circumstances – the most important reasons students have for their studies are internal reasons. This is perhaps especially true of students of humanities disciplines, where obvious external expected utility matrices hardly justify the expenditure of energy and resources students must make in their studies, but is also true of students of other disciplines, including the more lucrative ones, such as medicine or law.

Finally, and most centrally for present purposes, because of the role the teacher is given by the student, as a remedial source of moral strength the teacher-student relationship is characterised by a kind of intimacy not present in the kinds of coercive situations Airaksinen takes as paradigmatic. Teachers are invited into the psychic world of their students not to the same degree as physicians, priests or psychotherapists, but in much the same way – as figures in the moral psychology of actions pursuant to our students' most important personal projects. This peculiar position – one which neither teachers nor students often explicitly consider – generates moral demands of its own, just as do the more explicitly recognised positions of physician, therapist or confessor.

6. Conditions of legitimacy

As Airaksinen points out, some, but not all, coercion is legitimate (pp 171, ff). Coercion, in general, is legitimate to the degree that it is exercised by an authority whose right to coerce is established (the police as opposed to the mafia) and who is coercing in the manner and for the reasons generally accepted as legitimate (arresting criminals vs protecting departmental corruption). That is, one must first provide an independent justification of a coercive institution (no small matter) and then demonstrate that a particular instance of coercion is in fact a proper function of such an institution.

The general and fascination problem of political philosophy this raises – what are the legitimate coercive institutions, and in what does their legitimacy consist – receives interesting treatment in Airaksinen's volume. He argues for three individually interesting theses, which stand to one another in a curious tension (though not in contradiction): (1) Instances of coercion are justified only if the coercive institutions that enable them are. (2) Coercive institutions are justified only if the kinds of coercion they enable are morally acceptable. (3) There is no moral archimedean point from which either the global justificatory project or the local one can be conducted. (pp. 192-6)

Now, I am inclined to agree with Airaksinen about this. Nonetheless, of course, this is the central topic of a wide range of literature on authority, particularly, though not exclusively, that of the social contract tradition. A thorough treatment of this problem would require not a brief essay but rather a massive tome. I therefore must leave most of the most interesting problems aside. For heuristic purposes, let us say this much: This suggests that in thinking about the justification of coercion we are often engaged in seeking what Rawls has aptly called 'reflective equilibrium', balancing intuitions regarding particular practices against those regarding general institutions. As Aïraksinen points out in his discussion of such hard cases as that of the prison guard in a democratic society, this is, in practical life, no easy matter.

Moreover, though, it suggests that in assessing the moral dimensions of local situations, we must take the global context as fixed and as morally acceptable if we are to make any progress, *unless* our goal is wholesale social criticism. That is not my project here. I will – as must Airaksinen's prison guard – take for granted the broad legitimacy both of the principal political institutions that provide the context for the educational system in which we operate, and of that educational system, insofar as it provides the context in which we as teachers operate. We can then ask the more specific and more tractable question, 'Given the justice of our coercive roles, what specific kinds of coercion are justified, and what kinds not?', and more subtly, 'Against what kinds of abuse of our coercive roles must we be especially vigilant?'.

I emphasise the last question because one of the important insights emerging from Airaksinen's close attention to the realities of coercion in the non-ideal circumstances of ordinary, actual social and political life is that the moral status of particular acts and even of particular roles is often quite ambiguous, and what passes for justification is often rationalisation. Considerations of moral psychology are as important, or often more important than the application of general moral principles, and the challenges that morality presents are often intensely personal and particular, rather than abstract and clinical as Kant or Mill would have it.

7. Special obligations of academics

This essay is a not a manual of professional ethics. I will hence skip over the obvious points that would be common, *mutatis mutandis*, to a discussion of legal or business ethics, points concerning graft, dishonesty, gross extortion, misrepresentation, betrayal of confidence, fidelity to the client and to our explicit duties, etc. While these may be interesting, and while they do reflect the coercive structure of academic life, they fail to mark out what is peculiar to that structure. I want to emphasise the obligations that arise specifically out of the fact that our charges are coerced by us voluntarily and through a psychologically intimate relationship, with the legitimate expectation of internal rewards, but with the awareness of the threat of significant external and internal harms, harms that can be dispensed by us cost-free.

When the structure of our life is described in this way it becomes clear that for the academic life as we know it to succeed, a great deal of *trust* is required. Why is this so? First, because of the unusual power structure *vis a vis* coercive threats. We, unlike mafiosi, can realise our threats cost-free (indeed, to be not cynical but realistic, we can describe this realisation threats as having positive payoff – for we get the terroristic consequences sought by the mafioso with no real risk). If students had any reason to believe that this power were likely to be abused, it would be irrational to submit to its exercise.

Second, because of the intimacy we have noted that characterises the academic relationship, we have the power to affect – positively or negatively – the values, aspirations, self-image and emotional lives of our students. This kind of power is not given lightly, and is only given where trust of a very special kind can be presumed. This kind of trust is hard to describe precisely. It is multidimensional, and includes the conviction that we will act competently, honestly and compassionately. Failure on any of these dimensions amounts not so much to breach of contract as to betrayal. And again, in bestowing this trust, students must be aware that betrayal is largely cost-free to us.

Moreover, the very intimacy of the relationship and the centrality of academic life to the lives of (most of) our students as well as to our own creates dangerous ambiguities that arise directly from the coercive structure of the relationship. Because of the explosive admixture of coercive power and intimacy voluntariness becomes hard to assess. That is, decisions that we ordinarily make with no question regarding the freedom of our actions, or of those with whom we are in interaction cannot be made with the same confidence in academic contexts.

Two kinds of examples will suffice to make this case: In a noncoercive interaction with a neighbour, I might feel quite free to ask for the loan of a ladder to repair my roof. In making such a request, I know that my neighbour is free to refuse, and I know that he knows that. We also know that there are no significant repercussions either from accession to or from refusal of this request. If, on the other hand, I make such a request of a student, the situation is much different. No matter how much I attempt to bracket the student-teacher relationship this request will have perceived implications for the nature of a relationship important to my student. Refusal of the request may be thought to have repercussions for that relationship as well as possible repercussions for my future assessment of that student, recommendations, etc. Note that it does not matter to the situation whether these perceptions are correct. No matter how scrupulous I am in my dealings, those possibilities are always there, and are there in virtue of the relationship that connects us. The request is hence by its very nature coercive.

A second kind of case is perhaps more problematic. In the ordinary course of life, romantic attachments often develop between consenting adults. In most cases, these represent voluntary commitments between free and equal parties. While such liaisons are always fraught with the complexity that makes for good (and bad) literature and ordinary human agony, they are not by themselves morally problematic. In the academic arena, however, they can be deeply problematic simply in virtue of the intimacy and coercive character of that domain. On the one hand, for all kinds of reasons, but in part because of the closeness of the teacher-student relationship itself, the kinds of triggers for such liaisons are frequent. On the other, however, in the background lies an uneven power relationship and the extraordinary coercive power of the teacher over the student. No matter how much either party or even both parties would like to believe that this fact can be bracketed, it remains a fact that makes the freedom that is a condition of the legitimacy of such relationships impossible. Any such liaison, therefore, despite the views of its participants, is inherently a relationship between unequals, one of whom – perhaps both subtly and unintentionally, though perhaps more consciously and overtly – coerces the other.

When I emphasised the fact that trust lies at the basis of the academic relationship, and that this trust is of a different order than that involved in usual business transactions, it is situations like these two that I had in mind. The student must enter the relationship trusting that situations like this will not arise, and that the teacher will ensure that this is the case. Once the relationship is establised, the student's motivational structure may change. Either through seductive coercion or through coercive seduction the student may come to welcome extra-academic entanglements. But such desires are coloured by a false consciousness, and the student trusts at the outset that should such false consciousness arise the teacher as the superior in the relationship will refrain from exploiting it.

Annette Baier, in a series of essays in (Baier 1994) has explored the centrality of the phenomenon of trust. She notes ('Trust and Antitrust,' p. 105) that trust 'is letting other persons... take care of something the truster cares about...' In our case, we care for a great deal when our students trust us – for their academic well-being, futures, and often their self-images and aspirations. Baier notes that trust often – indeed typically – reflects power inequities, and represents the morally positive side of such inequities: Where there is justified trust, power inequity operates for mutual advantage, as opposed to exploitation. (pp. 106-109) She emphasises that trust can operate in both directions in such cases: Parents can trust employees with their children, for instance, just as children can trust their parents. Similarly, we trust our students to act in good faith just as they trust us to act in their interests. (Ibid., and pp. 120-9) In each case, however, trust figures as the central moral fact in such relationships. Breach of such trust by the more powerful party is a betrayal of what justifies an unequal power relationship, and transforms mere coercion into exploitation; breach of trust by the subordinate is merely disappointment of expectation.

Interestingly, when Baier turns to the role of trust in unequal power relations in the academy ('Trust and its Vulnerabilities') the cases she considers involve relations between university administrators and teaching staff (pp. 137-8) or between department heads and junior faculty members. (pp. 143-5) She correctly emphasises that in such cases the power inequities built into academic institutions demand trust on the part of the subordinate party in those holding superior power. Trust is required, and is required to be justified for these inherently coercive relationships to be non-exploitative and legitimate. Breach of that trust – and not mere coercion – implicates exploitation. I only urge that the more dramatic power inequities and those requiring more justified trust are those in which we, whatever our academic rank, are superordinates.

Only if such trust is in place is it rational for the student to enter such a dangerous arena. Only if it is rational for both parties to enter into it is the relationship itself morally acceptable. And only if we as academics deserve and keep faith with such trust is it reasonable for students to extend it. It hence follows from the structure of academia itself, centrally including its academic structure, both that it is rational for students to voluntarily submit even to such unconstrained coercion, and that teachers have very special obligations to unusually fastidious conduct in order for it to be rational for them to do so.

8. Generality and particularity of coercion and legitimacy

How special is this circumstance? This is an important question to ask, because in answering it we note a dimension to the coercive character of social life that eludes Airaksinen's otherwise astute analysis. For that analysis suggests that coercion is a necessary evil to which it is generally unwise or irrational to submit, and which is legitimised only in virtue of the unfortunate need of governments to use force to maintain order and public safety. Here I have presented a case – that closest to home for many of us – in which it is rational and wise for persons to choose to be coerced, and in which coercive threats are in fact easier to realise than those Airaksinen considers. Such a case demonstrates both that coercion is justified in part by trust, and that coercers in such cases have special obligations to their 'victims'. The moral psychology of coercion in such cases is hence different from that Airaksinen scouts, and more hopeful. Coercion in such cases is not a necessary evil, but a delicate but valuable bond between those involved in a collective enterprise for mutual good.

Interestingly, when we take this kind of coercive situation as paradigmatic, instead of the mugger/mafioso situation, we see that many ordinary coercive situations in social life fit this mould. Doctor-patient relationships are like this, of course. So, too are parent-child relationships. Moreover, so are those between legitimately elected or appointed political or administrative figures and those they govern or whose offices they direct. Details vary: To different degrees are the realisation of coercive threats cost-free. In some cases not at all, but in many such cases, to a very great degree. But in each case, we can see, if we look carefully, that it is often rational for the subordinates in these relationships to choose to be coerced. But in each case that rationality is founded on trust, and in each case special obligations devolve upon the coercers.

This is not in any way to reject or to minimise the importance of Airaksinen's analysis. Rather it is to suggest that while his analysis is accurate over a wide range of cases, it misses an equally wide range of cases central to our social life. And while even in these cases, central features of this analysis are present, there are significant features he overlooks. These features, when attended to, call our attention not only to the ubiquity of coercion, but also to its more positive face. Finally, however, our attention must be drawn to the centrality of trust and worthiness of trust in legitimising these ubiquitous relationships that are so central to our social structures and individual development and to the high standards of conduct to which those who coerce are to be held.

References

Airaksinen, T. (1988), *Ethics of Coercion and Authority: A Philosophical Study of Social Life*. University of Pittsburgh Press: Pittsburgh.

Baier, A. (1994), *Moral Prejudices: Essays on Ethics*. Harvard University Press: Cambridge.